RESEARCH HANDBOOK OF INNOVATION FOR A CIRCULAR ECONOMY

T0327650

Research Handbook of Innovation for a Circular Economy

Edited by

Siri Jakobsen

Nord University Business School, Norway

Thomas Lauvås

Nord University Business School, Norway

Francesco Quatraro

University of Torino, Italy

Einar Rasmussen

Nord University Business School, Norway

Marianne Steinmo

Nord University Business School, Norway

EE **Edward Elgar**
PUBLISHING

Cheltenham, UK • Northampton, MA, USA

Published by
Edward Elgar Publishing Limited
The Lypiatts
15 Lansdown Road
Cheltenham
Glos GL50 2JA
UK

Edward Elgar Publishing, Inc.
William Pratt House
9 Dewey Court
Northampton
Massachusetts 01060
USA

Paperback edition 2023

A catalogue record for this book
is available from the British Library

Library of Congress Control Number: 2021947951

This book is available electronically in the **Elgar**online
Business subject collection
http://dx.doi.org/10.4337/9781800373099

ISBN 978 1 80037 308 2 (cased)
ISBN 978 1 80037 309 9 (eBook)
ISBN 978 1 0353 2033 2 (paperback)

Printed and bound by CPI Group (UK) Ltd, Croydon, CR0 4YY

Contents

List of contributors   viii
Preface   xii

PART I   INTRODUCTION TO INNOVATION FOR A CIRCULAR ECONOMY

1   Introduction to the *Research Handbook of Innovation for a Circular Economy*   2
      Siri Jakobsen, Thomas Lauvås, Francesco Quatraro, Einar Rasmussen and
      Marianne Steinmo

2   Research propels the circular industrial economy from the material to
      the immaterial 'world'   12
      Walter R. Stahel

PART II   FIRM-LEVEL ENABLERS FOR CIRCULAR ECONOMY INNOVATION

3   Sustainability innovations in the manufacturing industry: a comparison
      of circular and climate innovation initiatives   25
      Fanny Hermundsdottir, Ann Elida Eide and Arild Aspelund

4   Value retention in the Norwegian and Swedish outdoor industry   36
      Are Severin Ingulfsvann

5   Toward a sustainable paradigm: circular economy solutions in the
      fashion industry   47
      Won-Yong Oh, Young Kyun Chang, Jung Hwan Park and Sanghee Han

6   From vision to commercialization of a circular economy innovation:
      a longitudinal study of overcoming challenges throughout the full
      innovation process   59
      Jenni Kaipainen and Leena Aarikka-Stenroos

7   Organizing for a circular economy: internal activism and organizational
      boundaries in SMEs   72
      Chia-Hao Ho, David Monciardini and Edvard Glücksman

PART III   COLLABORATIVE INNOVATION FOR THE CIRCULAR ECONOMY

8   Open innovation and the adoption of environmental process
      innovations: information source and proximity to partner types   85
      Robert A. W. Kok, Ward Ooms and Paul E. M. Ligthart

9   A reverse logistics framework for circular supply chains   98
      Stine Sonen Tveit, Ottar Bakås and Maria Kollberg Thomassen

10   Exploring shared value creation in circular food systems: the case of
        a Norwegian food bank   110
        *Heidi C. Dreyer, Luitzen De Boer, Marte Lønvik Bjørnsund and Anna Pauline
        Heggli*

11   How waste becomes value: the new ecology of surplus heat exchange in
        Norwegian industry   122
        Jens Petter Johansen and Jens Røyrvik

12   The circular water economy and the 'seven C's'   133
        Greg O'Shea, Seppo Luoto, Sanne Bor, Henri Hakala and Iben Bolund Nielsen

13   Drivers and barriers for industrial symbiosis: the case of Mo Industrial Park   144
        Siri Jakobsen and Marianne Steinmo

PART IV   TYPES OF CIRCULAR ECONOMY INNOVATIONS

14   Simultaneous adoption of circular innovations: a challenge for rapid
        growth of the circular economy   160
        Arild Aspelund, Martin Fredrik Olsen and Ottar Michelsen

15   Business model innovation for a circular economy: adapting to create value   174
        Maria Figueroa-Armijos

16   Exploring the entrepreneurial landscape and systemic barriers of
        circular business models   183
        Even Bjørnstad and Jorunn Grande

17   How innovations catalyse the circular economy: building a map of
        circular economy innovation types from a multiple-case study   195
        Anil Engez, Valtteri Ranta and Leena Aarikka-Stenroos

18   Salmon farming firms moving towards resource circularity: a typology
        of resource loop innovations   210
        Karin Wigger, Thomas Lauvås, Siri Jakobsen and Marianne Steinmo

PART V   TECHNOLOGY AND DIGITALIZATION FOR A CIRCULAR
          ECONOMY

19   Experimenting with new business model strategies for the circular economy   222
        *Nancy Bocken, Christiaan Kraaijenhagen, Jan Konietzko, Brian Baldassarre,
        Phil Brown and Cheyenne Schuit*

20   How digital technologies boost value potential creation and value
        realization in CE: insights from a multiple case study across industries   236
        Sami Rustholkarhu, Valtteri Ranta and Leena Aarikka-Stenroos

21   The circular economy impacts of digital academic spin-offs   251
        Phuc Hong Huynh and Einar Rasmussen

22 Towards measuring innovation for circular economy using patent data 265
Dolores Modic, Alan Johnson and Miha Vučkovič

23 The geography of circular economy technologies in Europe:
evolutionary patterns and technological convergence 277
Fabrizio Fusillo, Francesco Quatraro and Cristina Santhià

PART VI INFRASTRUCTURE ENABLING A CIRCULAR ECONOMY

24 Fund model innovations for circular economy investing 295
Puck D. Hegeman

25 The circular economy, openness, and dispersed access to research results 307
Haakon Thue Lie, Knut Jørgen Egelie, Christoph Grimpe and Roger Sørheim

26 Opportunity domains for new entrants in the circular economy:
a keyword-in-context analysis of Norwegian R&D tax incentive projects 316
Roberto Rivas Hermann, Are Jensen and Peter Gianiodis

27 Circular public procurement: innovation tool for municipalities? 328
Elena Dybtsyna, Dolores Modic, Kristina Nikolajeva and Raymond Sørgård Hansen

Index 339

Contributors

Leena Aarikka-Stenroos	Unit of Industrial Engineering and Management, Tampere University, Finland
Arild Aspelund	Department for Industrial Economics and Technology Management, Norwegian University of Science and Technology, Norway
Ottar Bakås	SINTEF Digital, Norway
Brian Baldassarre	Industrial Design Engineering, Delft University of Technology, Delft, the Netherlands
Even Bjørnstad	Enova SF, Norway
Marte Lønvik Bjørnsund	Matsentralen i Trøndelag, Norway
Nancy Bocken	Maastricht Sustainability Institute, School of Business and Economics, Maastricht University, the Netherlands
Sanne Bor	LUT University and Hanken School of Economics, Finland
Phil Brown	Industrial Design Engineering, Delft University of Technology, the Netherlands and Circularise, The Hague, the Netherlands
Young Kyun Chang	Sogang University, Sogang Business School, Korea
Luitzen De Boer	Department for Industrial Economics and Technology Management, Norwegian University of Science and Technology, Norway
Heidi C. Dreyer	Department for Industrial Economics and Technology Management, Norwegian University of Science and Technology, Norway
Elena Dybtsyna	Nord University Business School, Norway
Knut Jørgen Egelie	Norwegian University of Science and Technology (NTNU) and NTNU TTO AS, Norway
Ann Elida Eide	Department for Industrial Economics and Technology Management Norwegian University of Science and Technology, Norway
Anil Engez	Unit of Industrial Engineering and Management, Tampere University, Finland
Maria Figueroa-Armijos	EDHEC Business School, France
Fabrizio Fusillo	Department of Economics and Statistics Cognetti de Martiis and BRICK, Collegio Carlo Alberto, Italy

Peter Gianiodis	Palumbo-Donahue School of Business, Duquesne University, Pittsburgh, PA, United States
Edvard Glücksman	University of Exeter, United Kingdom
Jorunn Grande	Nord University Business School, Norway
Christoph Grimpe	Copenhagen Business School (CBS), Denmark
Henri Hakala	LUT University, School of Business and Management, Finland
Sanghee Han	Sogang University, Sogang Business School, Korea
Raymond Sørgård Hansen	Nord University Business School, Norway
Puck D. Hegeman	Norwegian University of Science and Technology, Norway
Anna Pauline Heggli	Department for Industrial Economics and Technology Management, Norwegian University of Science and Technology, Norway
Roberto Rivas Hermann	Nord University Business School, Norway
Fanny Hermundsdottir	Department for Industrial Economics and Technology Management, Norwegian University of Science and Technology, Norway
Chia-Hao Ho	University of Exeter, Business School, United Kingdom
Phuc Hong Huynh (Pru)	Nord University Business School, Norway
Are Severin Ingulfsvann	Nord University Business School, Norway
Siri Jakobsen	Nord University Business School, Norway
Are Jensen	Nordland Research Institute, Norway
Jens Petter Johansen	Norwegian University of Science and Technology, Department of Sociology and Political Science & NTNU Social Research, Norway
Alan Johnson	Nord University Business School, Norway
Jenni Kaipainen	Unit of Industrial Engineering and Management, Tampere University, Finland
Robert A. W. Kok	Institute for Management Research, Radboud University, the Netherlands
Jan Konietzko	Maastricht Sustainability Institute, School of Business and Economics, Maastricht University, the Netherlands
Christiaan Kraaijenhagen	Innoboost, Utrecht, the Netherlands
Thomas Lauvås	Nord University Business School, Norway
Haakon Thue Lie	Norwegian University of Science and Technology and Dehns, Norway
Paul E. M. Ligthart	Institute for Management Research, Radboud University, the Netherlands

Seppo Luoto	LUT University, School of Business and Management, Finland
Ottar Michelsen	Department for Industrial Economics and Technology Management, Norwegian University of Science and Technology, Norway
Dolores Modic	Nord University Business School, Norway
David Monciardini	University of Exeter, Business School, United Kingdom
Iben Bolund Nielsen	LUT University, School of Business and Management, Finland
Kristina Nikolajeva	Nord University Business School, Norway
Won-Yong Oh	Lee Business School, University of Nevada, Las Vegas, United States
Martin Fredrik Olsen	Department for Industrial Economics and Technology Management, Norwegian University of Science and Technology, Norway
Ward Ooms	Faculty of Management, Open University of the Netherlands, the Netherlands
Greg O'Shea	LUT University, School of Business and Management, Finland
Jung Hwan Park	Fox School of Business, Temple University, PA, United States
Francesco Quatraro	Department of Economics and Statistics Cognetti de Martiis and BRICK, Collegio Carlo Alberto, Italy
Valtteri Ranta	Vincit, Finland
Einar Rasmussen	Nord University Business School, Norway
Jens Røyrvik	NTNU Social Research, Norway
Sami Rusthollkarhu	Unit of Industrial Engineering and Management, Tampere University, Finland
Cristina Santhià	Department of Economics and Statistics Cognetti de Martiis and BRICK, Collegio Carlo Alberto, Italy
Cheyenne Schuit	Innoboost, Utrecht, the Netherlands
Roger Sørheim	Norwegian University of Science and Technology (NTNU), Norway
Walter R. Stahel	Faculty of Engineering and Physical Sciences, University of Surrey, UK and Product-Life Institute, Geneva. Switzerland
Marianne Steinmo	Nord University Business School, Norway
Maria Kollberg Thomassen	SINTEF Digital, Norway
Stine Sonen Tveit	SINTEF Digital, Norway

Miha Vučkovič	Logika, d.o.o., Slovenia
Karin Wigger	Nord University Business School, Norway

Preface

The concept of a circular economy – using resources and materials as long as possible and eliminating waste – is as old as mankind itself. Reusing, repairing and rebuilding have until recently been a natural part of society that arose out of necessity. While resource scarcity prevailed for thousands of years, the industrial revolution turned this pattern into mounting consumption and waste. However, our depletion of natural resources and piles of waste have now turned us to again consider circular principles out of necessity. Making the transition to a circular economy offers a solution to these challenges and has caught the attention of policymakers, organizations and individuals. Although many actors and researchers have realized that a systemic turn to a circular economy is necessary, we have limited knowledge on how this could be accomplished, especially at the individual and organizational level.

The field of innovation studies, which focuses on how products, processes and services may be implemented in the market, provides a fruitful foundation for how the circular economy may go from being a promising concept, to an integrated part of all economic activity. Accordingly, this research handbook is the first comprehensive effort to consider the relations between circular economy and innovation, offering various empirical, literature-based, and conceptual studies that focus on how different actors and factors at different levels may facilitate the transition to a circular economy.

The circular economy is both exciting and challenging to study because it comprehends actions from a range of actors, from the system level to the organizational level, and down to the individual level. Further, these levels are connected to, and embedded in one another, and efforts at all levels are necessary to reach a circular economy.

The above considerations brought alive a new aspiration at Nord University Business School, where four Norwegian innovation scholars teamed up with an Italian economist to gather researchers from around the world interested in understanding and further exploring the relations of circular economy and innovation, and to create a research handbook that offers original contributions to, and sets future directions for, the study of innovation for a circular economy.

In spring 2020, we issued an open call for researchers to submit their ideas and ongoing projects to us for possible publication in this research handbook. During the following months, almost 50 proposals were evaluated, and the submitted full chapters went through a blind peer review. The editors also aided the author(s) in aligning their research with the theme of the book. After the first round of blind reviews, we invited contributors to attend a digital workshop in December 2020, to present their works and receive additional feedback. While some chapters have been withdrawn and rejected during the process, we are happy that 27 manuscripts ended up being accepted for publication. These chapters are written by 68 scholars affiliated to institutions in 12 countries – Denmark, Finland, France, Italy, Korea, the Netherlands, Norway, Slovenia, Sweden, Switzerland, United Kingdom, and the United States.

The *Research Handbook of Innovation for a Circular Economy* would not have been published without essential financial and human resources. First, we would like to thank the authors for their interest in publishing their research with us and for their collaboration during the review process. We express our gratitude to the HighEFF research centre and Nord University for providing the funding that made this project possible. We also thank the publisher, Edward Elgar, for expressing their interest in the topic and for the swift and kind assistance provided throughout the publication process.

Although the process of creating this research handbook has come to an end, we hope that the journey continues, and that it becomes an important piece in the field of circular economy and innovation. The book is primarily recommended to those who would like to get acquainted with the topic and different ways of studying it. For example, PhD students may find it a good starting point before submitting their research proposal, but we believe that many other academics, researchers, policymakers and practitioners also can benefit from the variety of chapters included. Finally, to help the reader getting an overview of the content in the book, the chapters are divided into six main groups: Part I introduces the concept of a circular economy; Part II deals with the firm-level enablers for circular economy innovations; Part III discusses the role of collaborative innovation for circular economy; Part IV presents different types of circular economy innovations; Part V focuses on technology and digitalization for a circular economy; and Part VI discusses the infrastructure that enables a circular economy.

PART I

INTRODUCTION TO INNOVATION FOR A CIRCULAR ECONOMY

1. Introduction to the *Research Handbook of Innovation for a Circular Economy*

Siri Jakobsen, Thomas Lauvås, Francesco Quatraro, Einar Rasmussen and Marianne Steinmo

> If it can't be reduced, reused, repaired, rebuilt, refurbished, refinished, resold, recycled, or composted,
> then it should be restricted, redesigned or removed from production.

INTRODUCTION: THE URGENT NEED FOR A CIRCULAR ECONOMY

The above lyric by the American folk singer and social activist Peter Seeger captures the essence of the circular economy (CE). By keeping materials in use, we can reduce the extensive resource extraction and depletion, and the related generation of waste and emissions that are threatening to kill our planet.

At the end of 2020 the weight of human-made objects was estimated to surpass the weight of all plants and animals on the planet (Elhacham et al. 2020). For every person on earth, new materials exceeding his or her bodyweight are produced every week. While the biomass on earth is declining due to deforestation and land-use changes, the amount of human-made objects are expected to double over the next 20 years (Elhacham et al. 2020).

This excessive extraction and use of resources and materials in the current linear economic model is draining the earth's resources and generating waste that pollutes and disturbs natural ecosystems at a rate that is severely damaging the living conditions on our planet. Only 25 per cent of earth's ice-free land can be considered as wilderness, and the population sizes of wildlife (mammals, birds, fish, amphibians and reptiles) have dropped by more than two-thirds since 1970 (Almond et al. 2020). A telling example is the prediction that there will be more plastic waste than fish in the world's oceans by 2050 (Ellen MacArthur Foundation 2017). Humans and livestock now constitute nearly all mammals on earth, only 4 per cent are wild animals and only 30 per cent of birds are wild ones (Bar-On et al. 2018). A growing number of ecosystems are at risk of collapsing, and global warming caused by greenhouse gas emissions is further destabilizing the earth system (Steffen et al. 2015).

It is clear that the constantly growing use of new raw materials and energy has severe consequences and cannot be sustained (Esposito et al. 2018). Paradoxically, most of the materials and resources that are extracted in the current linear 'make-use-dispose' economy quickly end up as waste and emissions, putting a double burden on the living conditions on our planet. Keeping materials and resources in use has the potential of both reducing the extraction of new raw materials and reducing the waste and emissions from discharging used material. Hence, making a transition to a CE that operates with closed material loops may be part of the solution to create a sustainable future (Stahel 2016).

The basic idea of moving from a linear 'make-use-dispose' economic model to a circular one has gained a strong foothold among the public, policy makers, industry leaders and academics (Domenech and Bahn-Walkowiak 2019). Keeping materials and products at their highest utility and value at all times makes sense both from an environmental and a business perspective, and there are many examples of new circular business models that potentially can make the economy more circular (Esposito et al. 2018). Despite this growing interest in the CE, the problems of resource extraction, waste and pollution are growing, and the global economy is currently getting less circular (De Wit et al. 2020).

CIRCULAR ECONOMY AND THE NEED FOR INNOVATION

Research on the CE is growing rapidly and the conceptual thinking behind circular resource flows in the economy is well established (Murray et al. 2017; Geissdoerfer et al. 2017; Sauvé et al. 2016). Much is written about the need for systemic changes to develop value chains that preserve materials and resources at their highest possible utility and value (Manninen et al. 2018), and potential strategies for achieving this. For instance, the extensively used ReSOLVE framework, proposed by the Ellen MacArthur Foundation (2015), defines six business actions for increasing the circularity of the economy: Regenerate, Share, Optimise, Loop, Virtualise, and Exchange (see Table 1.1).

The concept of circular business models has also gained popularity as a way to implement circularity at organizational level (Geissdoerfer et al. 2020; Henry et al. 2020). Circular business models can be defined as "business models that are cycling, extending, intensifying, and/or dematerialising material and energy loops to reduce the resource inputs into and the waste and emission leakage out of an organizational system. This comprises recycling measures (cycling), use phase extensions (extending), a more intense use phase (intensifying), and the substitution of products by service and software solutions (dematerialising)" (Geissdoerfer et al. 2020).

Table 1.1   *The ReSOLVE framework*

ReSOLVE business actions	Description
Regenerate	Shift to renewable energy and materials; reclaim, retain, and regenerate health of ecosystems; and return recovered biological resources to the biosphere
Share	Keep product loop speed low and maximise utilisation of products by sharing them among users (peer-to-peer sharing of privately owned products or public sharing of a pool of products), reusing them throughout their technical lifetime (second-hand), and prolonging their life through maintenance, repair, and design for durability
Optimise	Increase performance/efficiency of a product; remove waste in production and the supply chain (from sourcing and logistics to production, use, and end-of-use collection); leverage big data, automation, remote sensing, and steering
Loop	Keep components and materials in closed loops and prioritise inner loops. For finite materials, this means remanufacturing products or components and as a last resort recycling materials
Virtualise	Deliver utility virtually – books or music, online shopping, fleets of autonomous vehicles, and virtual offices
Exchange	Replace old materials with advanced non-renewable materials; apply new technologies (e.g., 3D printing and electric engines); choose new products and services (e.g. multi-modal transport)

Source: Adapted from Ellen MacArthur Foundation (2015).

Hence, the technical and operational aspects of the CE are relatively well described, and many studies offer practical approaches, providing tools and methods for modelling circular processes (Merli et al. 2018). Indeed, the literature review by Merli et al. (2018) shows that CE research predominantly considers cleaner production practices, while "little consideration is assigned to the design of new products and services, sharing and performance economy and dematerialization practices" (p. 717). Hence, there is a lack of knowledge about the institutional and societal transformations needed to implement circular practices (Moreau et al. 2017), particularly those requiring radical changes at societal and institutional level (Merli et al. 2018).

Indeed, making the transition to a more CE is very demanding because it requires substantial rethinking of the functioning of socio-economic systems. Hence, there is increasing consensus that full implementation of a CE requires a paradigm shift, involving new approaches to regulation and institutions, cultural and behavioural changes, and organizational, process and product innovation (Prieto-Sandoval et al. 2018). Moving from linear to circular resource flows influences and reshapes the design, production, distribution, consumption, and handling of products and materials in all sectors. In essence, the transition to a more CE requires innovation across all levels and actors in the society, i.e., firms, industries, individuals and institutions.

Innovation broadly refers to the process of generating new ideas or new combinations that are put into commercial practice in the form of new products, services or processes. Hence, there is an urgent need for a more comprehensive understanding of how such CE innovations can be achieved. This aligns well with the field of innovation studies, defined by Fagerberg et al. (2012, p. 1132) as "the scholarly study of how innovation takes place and what the important explanatory factors and economic and social consequences are". Despite the important role of innovation for implementing a more CE, the term CE is relatively absent from the innovation literature. We searched the Scopus database early 2021 for the term 'circular economy' in some of the leading innovation journals and found a very limited number of hits (i.e., three in *Research Policy*, none in *Technovation*, none in *Journal of Product Innovation Management*, and none in *Industrial and Corporate Change*).

Hence, we believe there is an untapped potential in applying insights from the innovation literature to provide more specific implications for how to implement the transition from a linear to a CE. Similarly, the CE transition is an excellent context to study innovation processes and their outcomes. Overall, innovation is not only crucial for designing and implementing CE practices, but also an outcome facilitated by the increasing public and private initiatives to promote CE practices. This provides innovative firms with new business opportunities and favours the renewal of the existing ones.

CHARACTERISTICS OF INNOVATIONS FOR A CIRCULAR ECONOMY

The close interplay between the CE transition and innovation discussed above calls for a closer look at the innovation literature. In particular, the environmental benefits associated with the implementation of the CE model make innovations in this domain fall in the realm of what is known in the literature as eco-innovation, i.e., "the production, assimilation or exploitation of a product, production process, service or management or business methods that is novel to the firm [or organization] and which results, throughout its life cycle, in a reduction of environmental risk, pollution and other negative impacts of resources use (including energy use) compared to relevant alternatives" (Kemp and Pearson 2007, p. 7).

Accordingly, the tools and concepts developed in the field of economics of knowledge and innovation can be extended and further specified to analyse CE-oriented innovation. First of all, the Schumpeterian framework would suggest distinguishing between product, process and organisational innovation. Other relevant dimensions are the opening of new markets and the switch to new raw materials or providers (Schumpeter 1934).

Similarly, another important argument concerns the Schumpeterian definition of any kind of innovation as a combination of elements that have never been combined before. This intuition has paved the way to an approach to analysing the production of new knowledge, which is known as the recombinant-knowledge approach (Weitzmann 1998; Fleming and Sorenson 2001). Empirical and theoretical studies in this stream of literature propose that new knowledge emerges out of a recombinant process in which economic agents explore the technological landscape and try new combinations of existing pieces of knowledge to produce novelty (Saviotti 2007; Krafft et al. 2011). Cognitive aspects are crucial in this respect, with relatedness amongst technological domains an important factor affecting the likelihood of success of recombinant dynamics (Nightingale 1998).

The extension of this stream of literature to the analysis of the production of green knowledge has revealed that in the green domain the production of new knowledge on average rests on the combination of inputs pertaining to loosely related technological domains, i.e., on knowledge components that had never been combined together before, or that had been connected in a very limited number of cases. Green technologies are therefore considered as the outcome of pure recombinant creation efforts, rather than reuse. To put it differently, the introduction of new green technologies is strictly dependent on the capacity to command recombinant novelty (Zeppini and van den Bergh 2011).

Basic explanations of this evidence are grounded in the high degree of complexity of green knowledge (Barbieri et al. 2020), and in the observation that often the greening of economic activities requires hybridization of new green technologies with extant non-green ones. The same argument applies to the subset of CE-related technologies, which very often are developed out of combination of different and seemingly unrelated domains. A typical example is the production and utilization of bio-based materials, like bioplastics, which leads to the hybridization of value chains that had been unconnected before.

The emphasis on the importance of recombinant novelty and technological discontinuities has some important implications for the governance of CE-related knowledge production and its commercial exploitation. Increasing complexity of green technologies and the relevance of recombinant creation dynamics call for the establishment of collaborative dynamics to gain access to fragmented and dispersed knowledge. A large body of evidence has been put forward in this respect by extant literature (De Marchi 2012). The concept of open eco-innovation is increasingly used to stress that access to external sources of knowledge might be crucial for compensating the lack or insufficient development of the necessary capabilities to deal with the combination of knowledge components dispersed in the knowledge space (Ghisetti et al. 2015). Collective invention dynamics are expected to be even more important in the domain of CE-related innovation, in which interactions amongst a variety of different institutional actors are crucial to ensure the successful development of innovative solutions. Accordingly, the open CE-innovation is strictly intertwined with the discourse on the composition of CE-innovation ecosystems.

An institutional dimension that has been largely discussed by the eco-innovation literature concerns public intervention and regulation. These aspects are expected to play a crucial role in the CE transition. According to Rennings (2000), eco-innovation is subject to the well-known 'double externality' problem, according to which green knowledge is affected not only by the traditional source of externalities related to the public good characteristics of knowledge, but also by an additional source related to the reduction of environmental degradation. Accordingly, markets will fail in allocating the socially desirable amount of resources to the generation of green knowledge. For this reason, policy intervention is required to restore optimal levels of investments. Public policies can be designed according to the regulatory push-pull framework (Rennings, 2000). In this framework, a variety of policy measures can be leveraged, on the one hand to restore the economic incentives to invest in eco-innovations, and on the other hand to advance the frontier of knowledge in this domain to cope with new needs and challenges (Crespi et al. 2015). Besides these aspects, green public procurement represents an important tool to foster the transition to a CE, both in view of the possibility to adopt circular solutions in the public administration, and as a way to orient the direction of research efforts.

OUTLINE OF THE CONTRIBUTIONS IN THE HANDBOOK

Given our objective of this handbook to explore the connections between innovation and the CE, we have invited a broad set of contributions. The chapters of the handbook are grouped into six parts that relate to different aspects of innovation for a CE. In the following paragraphs we summarize the parts of the handbook and how the chapters are related to key processes of managing CE innovations.

Part I provides an *Introduction to innovation for a circular economy*. Following the current chapter, Chapter 2 by Stahel offers a thought-provoking discussion on the types of innovation required to make progress in the transition to a CE. As one of the pioneers of the CE concept, Stahel reflects on the need for radical innovation not only in the natural and material world, but even more important in the immaterial world. Stahel advocates for a refocus of CE research, and points at several promising avenues for developing circular sciences that would help us achieve a truly circular and sustainable economy.

Part II contains five chapters related to *Firm-level enablers for circular economy innovation*, and captures different CE strategies at the firm level and how these potentially enable the transition to a CE. In Chapter 3, Hermundsdottir et al. examine key differences in the sustainability strategies of manufacturing firms and their approach to address the environmental challenges of overuse of planetary resources and greenhouse gas emissions. Overall, they find that firms dealing with sustainability challenges devise effective strategies, which they expect will contribute to solving their industry's environmental challenges and provide firm-level competitiveness. Chapter 4 by Ingulfsvann further explores how five outdoor brands in Norway and Sweden are creating initiatives for retention and eco-innovation, which represent steps towards circular value chains. In Chapter 5, Oh et al. explore circular solutions in the fashion industry by focusing on how different forms of business activism and conceptions of organizational boundaries can shape firms' motives for embracing CE principles. They also discuss various enablers and barriers of CE, finding that CE improves environmental and social sustainability and creates opportunities for new profitable businesses in the fashion industry.

By adapting a case study of a radical innovation process for a renewable fuel technology, Chapter 6 by Kaipainen and Aarikka-Stenroos examines firm innovation strategies and processes for successful CE innovation. They map challenges and overcoming actions throughout the 25-year innovation process providing insights on how firms can successfully realize sustainable CE innovating processes. Adopting a multiple-case design of 12 SMEs in Cornwall, Chapter 7 by Ho et al. examines different forms of internal activism that trigger organizational change towards a CE and its relationship to four conceptions of CE business organizational boundaries (efficiency, power, competence, and identity). Their findings extend knowledge on organizational boundaries and highlights different organizational logics and distinct forms of CE internal activism.

Part III, *Collaborative innovation for the circular economy* captures the role of inter-firm collaboration and open innovation for CE, shared-value creation for parties involved, as well as circular supply chains and industrial symbiosis in regional circular ecosystems. Using data from the European Manufacturing Survey of Dutch manufacturing firms, Chapter 8 by Kok et al. investigates the relationship between firms' use of open innovation practices and the adoption of environmental process innovations. Their results show that firms who use more open innovation practices, more external information sources, or cooperate with international science-based partners also adopt more environmental process innovations. Chapter 9 by Tveit et al. investigates critical strategic aspects for achieving improved circular performance in the furniture supply chain, proposing a strategic framework for reverse logistics. Adapting a literature review on reverse logistics and an in-depth empirical case study of a furniture manufacturer, the chapter presents critical aspects of operations and business models that can enable or inhibit circularity as a value-creating system.

Further, in Chapter 10 Dreyer et al. explore what and how value is created by organizations in a Norwegian food bank and evaluate the impact of such banks on the sustaining circularity of the food system. Their results suggest that by implementing CE principles, food banks provide a fruitful basis for creating shared value and using economic gains to address environmental and social problems. Drawing on studies of 14 surplus heat exchanges in Norway, Johansen and Røyrvik in Chapter 11 show how valuation processes vary across localities, illustrating three different modes of valuating surplus heat: market commodity, a common good, or a gift between a company and the community. O'Shea et al. conducted a study on a regional CE ecosystem centred in the recycling of wastewater in Finland presented in Chapter 12. Based on 45 user-stakeholder interviews from ten different types of organisations within the ecosystem, their key findings highlight the importance of conscious, collaborative stakeholder support and ecosystem coordination for creating strong sustainable entrepreneurial ecosystems. Jakobsen and Steinmo in Chapter 13 identify drivers and barriers for industrial symbiosis between firms in an industrial park over the course of a decade, finding that developing a circular industry is a long-term process that requires open innovation efforts where academic institutions are essential in mobilizing firms towards circularity. Barriers for developing symbiosis in the park mainly relates to lack of access to risk capital to invest in research-based circular solutions. Finally, by adapting a game theory approach on a case from the fish farming industry, Chapter 14 by Aspelund et al. illustrates the challenges of simultaneous adoption of circular innovations, and discusses governmental interference to spur the adoption of circular practices. They show that the adoption of circular innovations requires coordinated and simultaneous adoption from multiple actors to succeed. As one actor's decision to adopt relies on other actors' actions, circular innovations and closing material loops rarely happen unless they are orchestrated.

Part IV, *Types of circular economy innovations* contains chapters that discuss CE innovations and provide examples from different industries and based on different business models. As current business model frameworks are hardly adjustable to the dynamic process of achieving a CE, Chapter 15 by Figueroa-Armijos proposes an emergent guiding framework, whose building blocks can be interchanged and adapted as progress is made. The framework is intended as a cumulative empirical tool for everyday use in the classroom and in practice to establish a CE foundational logic behind anchor purpose and value proposition. Bjørnstad and Grande in Chapter 16 also key into the debate of CE business models by examining opportunities and barriers for an entrepreneur's ability and incentives to innovate and develop circular and sustainable business models. They suggest that there exist both physical and systemic issues that pose fundamental challenges to the transition to a CE and identify key issues that society must address in the transition to a sustainable CE.

Further, based on an explorative multiple-case analysis strategy and mapping of 27 innovative CE offerings by various companies, Chapter 17 by Engez et al. uncovers several types of CE innovations – the sustainability issues they target, and pursued benefits. They develop a detailed categorization of CE innovation types: novel recycled materials (product innovations), sustainable production processes (process innovations), services for lengthening product lifecycles (service innovations), and business models for reusing and sharing products (business model innovations), that can guide managers in (re-)designing value propositions and business models in line with sustainable development goals. Chapter 18, by Wigger et al., offers a typology matrix consisting of seven types of resource loop innovations through an abductive study of innovation projects developed by Norwegian salmon farming firms. They propose that firms develop resource loop innovations of inbound, inhouse, and outbound resources, which minimize the use of unproductive resources of inbound and outbound resources and expand the range of inhouse resources. Through these resource loop innovations negative externalities are minimized and underutilized resources reused, which leads to increased resource circularity and a more sustainable industry.

Part V contains chapters related to *Technology and digitalization for a circular economy*. Based on action research conducted with over 40 organizations, Chapter 19 by Bocken et al. investigates experimentation practices companies adopt in the transition to a circular business model. As such, they provide an overview of business experimentation practices, possible tools, approaches and lessons learned; showing that significant planning and experimentation are needed to understand how to develop new business models that are not only 'circular', but also desirable for people, technically feasible, and financially viable. Chapter 20 by Rusthollkarhu et al. proposes four roles of digital technologies in CE customer value creation. The roles contribute to the CE literature by explaining how digital technologies enable companies and customers to create value based on CE principles. In practice, the roles help companies to understand the use of digital technologies in planning and executing CE business and help guiding innovation at the managerial level. Further, Chapter 21 by Huynh and Rasmussen explores the role of academic spin-offs and new ventures commercializing technologies by mapping the population of academic spin-offs established in Norway from 1999 to 2012, and identifies several digital innovations with potential CE impacts. The firms commercialized digital product and process innovations that were based on digital infrastructure technologies, which helped increase resource efficiency and optimize production performances. The authors also highlight that digital academic spin-offs play a role as technology suppliers and contribute to the CE by 'narrowing the loop' and reducing the consumption of resources and energy, as well as reducing waste emissions.

Chapter 22 by Modic et al. addresses methodological concerns about measuring and analysing data about technical innovations for a CE through patent data, and suggests a three phase 'budget' Y*-tag method to improve current indicators. In doing so, the authors outline procedures to combine 'Recycle' and other 'R' keyword searches of patent documents with validation of data from other sources, e.g., citations, inventor names, affiliations, locations and content. They also stress valid measurement for CE related innovation, if it is to be analysed with complementary data (e.g., research publications) with appropriate international comparisons to monitor the diffusion and impact of CE. The last chapter in this part, Chapter 23 by Fusillo et al. maps the development of CE technologies in European regions from 1980 to 2015 and identifies a core of CE technologies by using the official list of technological classes (CPC) and patent data from the OECD RegPat database. Their findings suggest that the CE knowledge space is a rapidly developing and dynamic technological field and that regional CE innovative efforts are quite heterogeneous, whereby regions tend to specialize in the generation of different kinds of CE technologies.

Finally, Part VI, *Infrastructure enabling a circular economy* is related to external factors and actors at both the business and system level that facilitate innovation activities for a CE. The contributions capture the role of venture capital and private equity funds, contractual agreements for research partnership, and public policies and procurement practices for innovation for a CE. Chapter 24 by Hegeman examines how venture capital and private equity funds innovate to invest in the CE market and the barriers they encounter. Using three pioneering fund managers as cases, Hegeman shows the need and ability for wide-ranging innovation to the fund model to overcome the issues created by the CE market's inefficiency, thinness, and unproven nature. Further, as many initiatives aimed at achieving CE are based on collaborations between industry and universities, in Chapter 25 Thue Lie et al. demonstrate a novel method for analysing the contractual agreements of research partnerships to investigate whether and to what extent the outcomes of research partnerships will be accessible. Hermann et al., in Chapter 26, further examine the alignment between top-down public policies to promote CE innovations and the interests of a range of stakeholders, including new ventures. Analysing 4,072 project applications to SkatteFUNN (a Norwegian tax deduction scheme aimed at supporting research and development), their findings indicate that the CE concept is much more complex than the few general principles highlighted in the literature. Finally, in Chapter 27 Dybtsyna et al. investigate the status of circular public procurement practices, showing that even in the case of a circularity conscious municipality, the environmental impact of public procurement still plays too insignificant a role for it to make a difference in the process of awarding contracts and steering the actors involved towards more circularity. They further highlight that circular public procurement practices need more specifically designed tender specifications and more susceptibility towards innovative procurement processes.

CONCLUDING REMARKS

Given the urgent need for a CE described initially in this chapter, the contributions of the handbook provide both hope and despair. Many of the chapters provide excellent examples of how CE principles are designed and implemented to make resource flows more circular. In combination the chapters clearly illustrate that conceptual thinking and experimentation with practical implementation of CE innovations take place at a growing rate and have become explicitly supported by actors across both the private and public sector. This offers hope that there exists an interest and capacity to develop circular solutions. However, the pace of this development is slow. Common to most of these examples are that the circular innovation only applies to a small part of a process, makes resource flows only marginally more circular and applies to only a few firms that are forerunners in the transition to a CE. Hence, these potentially novel innovations for a CE need to be implemented at a broad scale across firms, value chains, and industries in order to make a significant impact in terms of lower resource extraction, waste and pollution.

Another, but related, observation is that many of the examples of CE innovations presented in this handbook are relatively incremental, focusing on improving existing processes to reduce resource inputs or recycle to eliminate waste. These efforts are important, but the largest potential for achieving a full transition to a CE lies in making more radical changes. For instance, eliminating the need for products instead of lowering their resource inputs and designing for extended use instead of recycling holds a much larger potential for achieving a CE. However, such radical innovations typically require deeper changes across industry structures, consumer behaviour, and government regulations. Hence, the transition to a CE depends on innovation involving collaboration across sectors and industries, involving all actors in society.

These two observations call for a stronger role for innovation scholars in the CE transition. First, by addressing the need for innovations that optimize resource flows and make sure that CE principles are broadly adopted by all actors in the economy. Here, many of the chapters in this handbook offer inspiring examples for further development and implementation by other firms, industries, and public actors. Second, the need for more radical solutions to realize a CE calls for more coordinated and radical innovation efforts. This pushes the boundaries of innovation research which needs to better understand innovations involving collaborative efforts among a broad range of actors, involving entirely new business models, commercializing technologies and scientific discoveries, and focus on other goals than profitability.

REFERENCES

Almond, R. E. A., Grooten, M., & Peterson, T. (2020). *Living Planet Report 2020: Bending the Curve of Biodiversity Loss*. Gland: WWF.

Barbieri, N., Marzucchi, A., & Rizzo, U. (2020). Knowledge sources and impacts on subsequent inventions: Do green technologies differ from non-green ones? *Research Policy*, 49(2), 103901.

Bar-On, Y. M., Phillips, R., & Milo, R. (2018). The biomass distribution on Earth. *Proceedings of the National Academy of Sciences*, 115(25), 6506–6511.

Crespi, F., Ghisetti, C., & Quatraro, F. (2015). Environmental and innovation policies for the evolution of green technologies: A survey and a test. *Eurasian Business Review*, 5(2), 343–370.

De Marchi, V. (2012). Environmental innovation and R&D cooperation: Empirical evidence from Spanish manufacturing firms. *Research Policy*, 41(3), 614–623.

De Wit, M., Hoogzaad, J., & Von Daniels, C. (2020). *The Circularity Gap Report 2020*. Amsterdam: Ruparo.

Domenech, T., & Bahn-Walkowiak, B. (2019). Transition towards a resource efficient circular economy in Europe: Policy lessons from the EU and the member states. *Ecological Economics*, 155, 7–19.

Elhacham, E., Ben-Uri, L., Grozovski, J., Bar-On, Y. M., & Milo, R. (2020). Global human-made mass exceeds all living biomass. *Nature*, 588, 442–444.

Ellen MacArthur Foundation [EMA] (2015). *Growth Within: A Circular Economy Vision for a Competitive Europe*. https://www.ellenmacarthurfoundation.org/assets/downloads/publications/EllenMacArthurFoundation_Growth-Within_July15.pdf.

Ellen MacArthur Foundation [EMA] (2017). *The New Plastics Economy: Rethinking the Future of Plastics and Catalysing Action*. http://www.ellenmacarthurfoundation.org/publications/the-new-plastics-economy-rethinking-the-future-of-plastics-catalysing-action.

Esposito, M., Tse, T., & Soufani, K. (2018). Introducing a circular economy: New thinking with new managerial and policy implications. *California Management Review*, 60(3), 5–19.

Fagerberg, J., Fosaas, M., & Sapprasert, K. (2012). Innovation: Exploring the knowledge base. *Research Policy*, 41(7), 1132–1153.

Fleming, L., & Sorenson, O. (2001). Technology as a complex adaptive system: Evidence from patent data. *Research Policy*, 30(7), 1019–1039.

Geissdoerfer, M., Pieroni, M. P., Pigosso, D. C., & Soufani, K. (2020). Circular business models: A review. *Journal of Cleaner Production*, 227, 123741.

Geissdoerfer, M., Savaget, P., Bocken, N. M., & Hultink, E. J. (2017). The circular economy: A new sustainability paradigm? *Journal of Cleaner Production*, 143, 757–768.

Ghisetti, C., Marzucchi, A., & Montresor, S. (2015). The open eco-innovation mode: An empirical investigation of eleven European countries. *Research Policy*, 44(5), 1080–1093.

Henry, M., Bauwens, T., Hekkert, M., & Kirchherr, J. (2020). A typology of circular start-ups: An analysis of 128 circular business models. *Journal of Cleaner Production*, 245, 118528.

Kemp, R., & Pearson, P. (2007). *Final Report MEI Project about Measuring Eco-Innovation*. Maastricht: UM Merit.

Krafft, J., Quatraro, F., & Saviotti, P. P. (2011). The knowledge-base evolution in biotechnology: A social network analysis. *Economics of Innovation and New Technology*, 20(5), 445–475.

Manninen, K., Koskela, S., Antikainen, R., Bocken, N., Dahlbo, H., & Aminoff, A. (2018). Do circular economy business models capture intended environmental value propositions? *Journal of Cleaner Production*, 171, 413–422.

Merli, R., Preziosi, M., & Acampora, A. (2018). How do scholars approach the circular economy? A systematic literature review. *Journal of Cleaner Production*, 178, 703–722.

Moreau, V., Sahakian, M., Van Griethuysen, P., & Vuille, F. (2017). Coming full circle: Why social and institutional dimensions matter for the circular economy. *Journal of Industrial Ecology*, 21(3), 497–506.

Murray, A., Skene, K., & Haynes, K. (2017). The circular economy: An interdisciplinary exploration of the concept and application in a global context. *Journal of Business Ethics*, 140(3), 369–380.

Nightingale, P. (1998). A cognitive model of innovation. *Research Policy*, 27(7), 689–709.

Prieto-Sandoval, V., Jaca, C., & Ormazabal, M. (2018). Towards a consensus on the circular economy. *Journal of Cleaner Production*, 179, 605–615.

Rennings, K. (2000). Redefining innovation: Eco-innovation research and the contribution from ecological economics. *Ecological Economics*, 32(2), 319–332.

Sauvé, S., Bernard, S., & Sloan, P. (2016). Environmental sciences, sustainable development and circular economy: Alternative concepts for trans-disciplinary research. *Environmental Development*, 17, 48–56.

Saviotti, P. P. (2007). On the dynamics of generation and utilisation of knowledge: The local character of knowledge. *Structural Change and Economic Dynamics*, 18(4), 387–408.

Schumpeter J. (1934). *The Theory of Economic Development*. Cambridge, MA: Harvard University Press.

Stahel, W. R. (2016). The circular economy. *Nature*, 531(7595), 435–438.

Steffen, W., Richardson, K., Rockström, J., Cornell, S. E., Fetzer, I., Bennett, E. M., … & Sörlin, S. (2015). Planetary boundaries: Guiding human development on a changing planet. *Science*, 347(6223), 1259855.

Weitzman, M. L. (1998). Recombinant growth. *The Quarterly Journal of Economics*, 113(2), 331–360.

Zeppini, P., & van den Bergh, J. C. (2011). Competing recombinant technologies for environmental innovation: Extending Arthur's model of lock-in. *Industry and Innovation*, 18(3), 317–334.

2. Research propels the circular industrial economy from the material to the immaterial 'world'

Walter R. Stahel

INTRODUCTION TO THE CIRCULAR INDUSTRIAL ECONOMY

The circular economy concept is related to the sustainability concept formulated at the 1972 Conference in Stockholm and in the 2015 SDGs (Sustainable Development Goals) of the United Nations. For clarity, this chapter distinguishes between Nature, the world of anthropogenic mass and the immaterial world (see Figure 2.1).

Bio-cycles are the realm of Nature, which is circular by evolution – witness the water, CO_2 and soil cycles – and where waste becomes food for others as long as mankind respects Nature's absorption and regeneration capacities. Humankind has long exploited natural materials and returned spent materials to Nature. When in the early Anthropocene[1] scientists learnt to create synthetic materials with superior properties, society overlooked the fact that these synthetics materials are incompatible with Nature's circularity and imply a producer liability in the immaterial world. The immaterial world encompasses producer liability, policy frameworks as well as the embodied resources present in all anthropogenic objects.

Holistic research is needed in all three worlds: to maintain existing natural capital, to clean up the legacy wastes of the Anthropocene, and to merge the powers of the material and immaterial world in order to find innovative sustainable solutions.

Society needs a new creativity in caring for existing natural, human and manufactured capital, with the objective of maintaining for the longest time their existing value, utility and quality in order to stop anthropogenic climate change, create local jobs and protect the global environment.

The circular industrial economy is about economics, innovation, performance and competitiveness (Stahel 2019b). Its activities to extend the service-life of objects are local, more labour-intensive, produce fewer CO_2 emissions and use less energy than manufacturing activities (Stahel and Reday 1981). The shift from the present linear throughput economy to a mature, near zero-waste and zero-carbon circular economy becomes feasible if society succeeds in exploiting the full research potential of the three worlds.

MERGING THE OPPORTUNITIES OF THE THREE WORLDS

Today, as Elhacham et al. (2020, p. 442) note:

> Humanity has become a dominant force in shaping the face of Earth. An emerging question is how the overall material output of human activities compares to the overall natural biomass. Here we quantify the human-made mass, referred to as 'anthropogenic mass', and compare it to the overall

living biomass on Earth, which currently equals approximately 1.1 teratonnes. We find that Earth is exactly at the crossover point; in the year 2020 (± 6), the anthropogenic mass, which has recently doubled roughly every 20 years, will surpass all global living biomass. On average, for each person on the globe, anthropogenic mass equal to more than his or her bodyweight is produced every week. This quantification of the human enterprise gives a mass-based quantitative and symbolic characterization of the human-induced epoch of the Anthropocene.

In its own interest, society has to protect Nature from being overwhelmed by the anthropogenic mass of human activities. The immaterial world contains the tool box to do so (Figure 2.1).

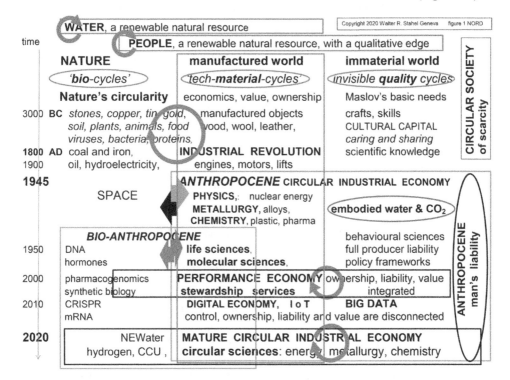

Figure 2.1　　*The evolution of the concept of a circular industrial economy through the three worlds*

The Bio-Cycles

Bio-cycles are the realm of Nature, which is circular by evolution; waste becomes food for others as long as mankind respects Nature's limitations.

Natural capital includes rocks and minerals, fauna, flora and biodiversity, but also water and people, two renewable resources which are unique and cannot be replaced by manufactured objects: without water there is no life; without people there is no society or economy.

Some bio-cycles can profit from human intervention, such as in regenerative agriculture and regenerative medicine. But innovations like gene editing, biosimilars, architectured molecules and pharmacogenomics in the Bio-Anthropocene may jeopardize Nature's dominance of the bio-cycles and create ethical issues for the immaterial world.

The Anthropogenic Material Cycles

These constitute the realm of industrial entrepreneurs. Since the Stone Age, scarcity favoured the reuse and repair of objects through do-it-yourself and local craftsmen, today referred to as the era of 'R'.[2] As long as people used natural materials – stone, leather, wood and wool – the main problem of the material cycles was resource availability and lack of control by the individual owner-users of objects. A survey of the US building stock (Srivastava et al. 2020) showed that an improved energy efficiency of buildings can reduce related carbon emissions by 50 per cent, but requires highly specialized knowledge in operation and maintenance (O&M), which today is largely missing. Owner-user motivation combined with education and training programmes in these skills determines the service-life of objects.

From 1945 onwards, the synthetic materials of the Anthropocene[3] replaced natural resources: plastics and pharmaceuticals in chemistry; alloys in metallurgy; nuclear physics in energy. Together with mass production processes, these innovations led to societies of abundance and created the legacy wastes of the Anthropocene, ultimately resulting in a research need to recover atoms and molecules for reuse – the era of 'D'. Research is needed to de-link synthetic molecules, deconstruct infrastructure and buildings and deal with abandoned objects in oceans and space; challenging tasks for scientists globally.

Research into the Invisible Quality Cycles of the Immaterial World

This is the realm of people and institutions. Knowledge, science, crafts and skills are part of the cultural capital and the immaterial world.

Adapted socio-political framework conditions, including legislation and taxation[4] (Stahel 2013), ethics, trust and value, ownership, stewardship and liability would provide huge incentives for companies to shift to a circular industrial economy. While many policy options are national, concepts like Full Producer Liability could find global acceptance.

Governmental liability is an emerging issue to protect nature and people. More than 1,300 climate-related lawsuits have been filed worldwide by NGOs since 1990. The most successful so far has been the Urgenda Climate Case, where the Dutch Supreme Court in 2019 upheld previous decisions that the Dutch government has obligations to urgently and significantly reduce emissions in line with its human rights obligations.[5]

The resources volumes embodied in anthropogenic mass need to be determined, namely the CO_2 emitted and the energy and water consumed up to the point of sale in mining, manufacturing, transport, production and distribution. Research into Life Cycle Inventory Analysis (LCIA)[6] and Resource Quantity Surveying[7] could initiate government actions to stop climate change by preserving embodied CO_2 thus accelerating the shift to a circular industrial economy.

HOLISTIC APPROACHES

Legislation can be a game-changer: The Minamata Convention on Mercury, an international treaty designed to protect human health and the environment from anthropogenic emissions and releases of mercury and mercury compounds, should radically change corporate strategies. The year 2020 was a milestone for the Convention as parties are now required to cease the manufacture, import and export of many mercury-containing products listed in the Convention.[8]

The Performance Economy

Selling performance and objects as a service merges the material and immaterial worlds, as fleet managers retain ownership and liability of objects and materials and internalize all costs of risks and waste over the full product-life. This provides strong financial incentives to prevent losses and waste and to maximize profits by minimizing costs through efficiency, sufficiency and systems solutions. Fleet managers impose appropriate design to produce objects of high quality, standardized components and a cascading use of objects to minimize life-cycle costs.[9]

Developing innovative smart materials for rent opens opportunities for many material companies. For example:

> The UK's Cookson Group developed a composite powder that can be pressed into any form and, when magnetised, becomes an extremely powerful permanent magnet. The two characteristics, easy shaping and magnetisation on demand, make it an ideal material for use as a rotor in small electric motors. After use, this smart material can easily be demagnetised by grinding it back into a powder and then remixed for its next use. To benefit from the successive life-cycles of its smart materials, the manufacturer has to retain ownership by, for example, leasing the material to component manufacturers with a return guarantee. In this case, the strategy of selling performance in the Performance Economy must be imposed on all levels from material to final product to guarantee a return of the smart material to its manufacturer at the end of the final product's life. (Stahel 2010, p. 32)

Selling goods as a service depends on a caring stewardship attitude by users: *No sharing without caring!* Research into behavioural sciences could help redefining the roles of supply and demand of nation-states, producers, owners and users in changing from ownership to usership (Stahel 2016a; Dumont 2008).

Retaining ownership of objects, materials and embodied resources creates corporate and national resilience and resource security at low cost: the goods of today become the resources of tomorrow available locally today at yesteryear's commodity prices.

For individuals, owning goods makes economic sense if they increase in value over time; owning real estate often makes sense, owning a smart phone or washing machine does not. By renting objects, people gain flexibility in use, and know in advance the cost of, and only pay for, using products. Aficionadas of fashion and constant change can fully live their fancies without causing excess waste, for instance by renting every weekend a different fashionable sports car, costume or handbag.

Public procurement agents buying the cheapest use service instead of buying the cheapest objects fuel innovation in the performance economy. Space X and Blue Origin are two companies that were started in response to a change in NASA's procurement preferences from buying and operating equipment to buying space transport services. Thus including the use phase in the economic optimization means including the Factor Time and opens up new business opportunities, such as long-life goods, multifunctional goods, service strategies and systems solutions. For example:

- Objects sold as a service for *exclusive use* are rental apartments, tools and vehicles for rent, but also public toilets, ISO shipping containers, leased equipment and packaging.
- Goods or systems sold as a service for *shared use* are all forms of public transport (buses, trains, aircraft), public swimming pools, concert halls and laundromats.
- Chemical leasing, also called rent a molecule, enables attributing losses of chemicals into the environment to the guilty lessor, lessee or distributor – a requirement of Toxic Release Inventories.

Opportunities for optimizing product use are of no interest to manufacturing industries selling materials or objects aiming to achieve maximal economy of scale in production. Dow Chemical, through its subsidiary Safe-Chem, was a pioneer of leasing solvents, but for a long time prioritized the sale of solvents, until UNIDO promoted chemical leasing strategies in African countries in order to minimize the health hazards from reusing empty chemicals containers for water or food storage, and to reduce the uncontrolled release of chemicals into the environment.

Junction Issues

Research on 'junction issues' enables to identify research priorities for multiple scientific domains. Few junction studies have been undertaken so far, possibly because they necessitate cooperation between researchers from several scientific disciplines (European Commission 2015).

The digital economy is a junction between the material and immaterial worlds. The Internet of Things, Artificial Intelligence, big data and data analytics could be enablers of the circular industrial economy. However, as many digital technologies are moving sand, little systematic guidance exists on how they can be best used to capture the full potential of circular strategies to improve resource efficiency and productivity in the use of objects as well as protecting the natural capital and the interests of citizens.

DARING AND CIRCULAR SCIENCES

The vision of a circular industrial economy free of new legacy 'waste' demands daring to radically innovate into novel systems, components and materials. Cooperation between scientific disciplines and cultures will be crucial to exploit this innovation potential; many of the following examples fit into different scientific disciplines.

Radical Innovation in the Era of 'R'

The research challenge here is to develop methods and technologies to extend the service-life of manufactured objects through **Reuse, Refill, Repair, Reprogramme** and **Remanufacture.**

As 'R' activities consume only a fraction of the energy needed to manufacture, distribute and market new objects, they greatly reduce global CO_2 emissions. Witness these examples:

- Brooklyn Bridge in New York City, commissioned in 1883, is to become more accessible and safer for pedestrians and cyclists through a redesign by some of the best-known urban planners. The competition 'Reimaging Brooklyn Bridge' was launched by New York City Council and the Van Alen Institute to stimulate a debate about New York City's infrastructure.[10]
- Airlines routinely transform passenger jets into cargo jets to extend their service-life, saving the embodied CO_2 and 80 per cent of the cost of a new cargo plane. Railways remanufacture periodically their high-speed trains to state of the art technology, saving the embodied CO_2 and 88 per cent of the cost of buying new trains.
- Transmission electron microscopes (TEM) are standard kits for imaging atomic-scale objects such as viruses and nanoparticles staying still for at least a few seconds. A 25-year-old TEM has been retrofitted by June Lau and her colleagues to make films of events lasting just trillionths of a second. The researchers designed a mechanism that generates pulses of electrons and upgraded a 25-year-old TEM to capture an event that took only 30 trillionths of a second. The upgraded instrument can still be used normally as well. The upgrade will allow other laboratories with existing electron microscopes to study ultrafast, atomic-scale events. June Lau works at the US National Institute of Standards and Technology in Gaithersburg, Maryland, USA.[11]

Radical Innovation in the Era of 'D'

The research challenge here is to develop processes and technologies to recover atoms and molecules of high value and purity from the legacy wastes of the Anthropocene through technologies and methods such as **D**e-polymerize, **D**e-alloy, **D**e-laminate, **D**e-vulcanize, **D**e-coat objects and **D**econstruct high-rise buildings and major infrastructure. Many of today's recycling technologies do not maximize material value (Material Economics 2018) but minimize waste costs.

Collecting used goods and sorting these into components and clean material fractions is a precondition. Where materials are mixed (automobile shredders), dispersed (rubber wear from tyres, micro-plastics in sun creams) or objects are deliberately released into the environment (drink containers, balloons), other solutions such as biodegradable materials may be feasible.

Examples of this innovation trend to recover atoms and molecules are:

- Dr Biao Cai from the University of Birmingham's School of Metallurgy and Materials has invented a technology to improve the purity of recycled aluminium by removing iron, a detrimental element making aluminium brittle and limiting its use in premium applications such as aircraft. Biao's simple, inexpensive technique uses magnets and a temperature gradient to remove iron contamination.[12]
- Wastefront AS combines new and existing technologies in a tyre recycling plant to convert locally sourced used tyres into liquid hydrocarbons and carbon black to be reutilized as alternative fuel and in rubber manufacturing.[13]
- Researchers from the University of Surrey are working on a novel technique of engineered microbial communities to digest two types of plastic polymers, PET and polyurethane, and

transform them into molecules that can be used to develop a more environmentally friendly material, Bio-PU, used as construction and insulation material. This makes industrial-scale biological recycling possible.

- A mutant bacterial enzyme that breaks down plastic bottles in hours has been created by scientists. The enzyme, discovered in a compost heap, reduces bottles to chemical building blocks that are then used to make high-quality new bottles. Existing recycling technologies produce plastic materials only good enough for clothing and carpets.[14]
- Researchers have engineered an enzyme that effectively breaks down PET into its constituent monomers (Tournier et al. 2020). This could allow for more complete recycling of bottles and clothes.
- Enespa in Saxony has developed a thermolysis process that produces paraffin oil and gas from mixed plastic waste. The paraffin oil can be used as raw material for the production of new plastic granules, and the gas to operate the plant.[15]

Innovation in Circular Sciences: Energy, Chemistry, Metallurgy

In a mature circular industrial economy, innovations in circular sciences are a global challenge for scientists, R&D and academia. A biology–chemistry–energy nexus demands multidisciplinary approaches that differ from the silo structure of many academic institutions.

Circular energy includes green hydrogen, ammonium, iron powder and geothermal but also such concepts as integrated energy management systems, energy service companies and plus-energy districts. Green hydrogen, probably the most versatile circular energy, can be produced in different ways:

- Research on the topic of plastic-to-hydrogen has shown how the structure of the essential molecular complex responsible for the first step in the secretory pathway, called the 'Sec61 translocon', changes when it is inhibited. A first plastic-to-hydrogen facility in the UK using pioneering DMG (Distributed Modular Generation) technology was developed by Powerhouse Energy Group plc.[16]
- Photocatalytic water splitting can be done with a quantum efficiency of almost unity (Takata et al. 2020).
- Steam reformation of bio-methane can split methane molecules (CH_4) into carbon dioxide (CO_2) and hydrogen (H_2), or turn bio-methane into hydrogen and graphite.

Circular chemistry includes recyclable polymers, Carbon Capture and Utilization (CCU), commercial strategies such as rent-a-molecule and NEWater:

- Polydiketoenamines (PDKs) are a new type of recyclable polymer with low energy and water consumption developed by the Brett Helms Research Group.[17] The source materials are 100 per cent recoverable as pure monomers that can be reused (even in the presence of additives and fibres) for the same polymer. Polydiketoenamines can easily be manufactured, used, recycled and reused without losing value points to new directions in designing sustainable polymers with minimal environmental impact (Christensen et al. 2019).
- CCU, Carbon Capture and Utilization – a carbon-chemistry to replace petro-chemistry – is discussed by University of Michigan, ETH Zürich and other leading players organized in the Global CO_2 Initiative. The CO_2 will be extracted from the ambient air and converted

into the high-purity carbon powder Carbon Black, which can be used as raw material for high-tech applications.

- Non-edible plants are a promising alternative to crude oil in producing chemicals and fuels with high yields. The conversion of biomass, for example the lignocellulose of dead wood into usable end products today is done by enzymes and bacteria in three separate processes. Scientists have developed a lactate platform, which is a spatially separate bioreactor in which several different micro-organisms coexist, each of which carries out one of the three steps of lignocellulose processing (Shahab et al. 2020).
- The delignification of wood can produce a high-strength wood for construction (Empa Quarterly 2019).
- There's a new way to 'eat' carbon dioxide. Researchers have built an artificial version of a chloroplast, the photosynthetic structures inside plant cells. It uses sunlight and a laboratory-designed chemical pathway to turn CO_2 into sugar (Miller et al. 2020). The pathway, called the CETCH cycle, is a complicated network of enzymes that is 20 per cent more energy efficient than the pathway used in natural forms of photosynthesis.
- Molecules as a service are business models for chemicals with a catalytic function or high toxicity, and applications beyond.
- Metal leasing is proposed by scientists (Hagan et al. 2019) as a strategy for mining companies and governments of mining regions. It would give governments and mining companies a smaller short-term income than selling the minerals but guarantee constant long-term revenue and political stability.
- Singapore – an island – has developed a fully circular method to purify wastewater into drinking quality NEWater, albeit at high cost and technology input.[18]

Circular metallurgy includes the reuse of steel beams, re-refining tailings and urban ores, and 'sustainable steel'. Among the leading players are the Iron and Steel Society in the UK, the Royal Institute of Technology in Stockholm and a UK group of researchers.[19] Circular Mining and Metals are developing fast to cope with the rising demand for critical minerals, particularly in the clean energy and high tech industry. Economic and geopolitical factors can limit the scope of primary production and turn the secondary production of raw materials into a growing business opportunity, using technologies to recover atoms from tailings, innovative refining and chemical extraction and purifying.

Even using iron powder as circular fuel for heavy industries is considered:

- Researchers and students of SOLID at TU Eindhoven (TU/e), together with Swinkels Family Brewers and the Metal Power consortium developed the world's first industrial installation to use iron powder as a new circular fuel. This iron fuel is CO_2-free, reusable, safe, compact and easy to transport. By successfully connecting the installation to the brewing process of brewery Bavaria, they have proved that iron fuel can be applied as a sustainable fuel in heat-intensive industries and power plants. The team's ambition is to convert a first coal-fired power plant into a sustainable iron fuel plant by 2030.[20]

Innovation in *systems solutions* demands integrated holistic approaches marrying research, engineering, industry and politics. Witness the following examples:

- A machine-learning approach has spotted powerful new types of antibiotic from a pool of more than 100 million molecules, including one that works against bacterial strains considered untreatable. This is the first time artificial intelligence has identified completely new kinds of antibiotic from scratch, without relying on any previous human assumptions (Stokes et al. 2020).

- In collaboration with colleagues at universities and institutions in the UK, China and the Kingdom of Saudi Arabia, researchers in the Edwards/Xiao group at Oxford's Department of Chemistry have developed a method of converting plastic waste into hydrogen gas which can be used as a clean fuel, and high-value solid carbon, using a new type of catalysis developed by the group, which uses microwaves to activate catalyst particles to effectively 'strip' hydrogen from polymers (Jie et al. 2020). The researchers mixed mechanically-pulverized plastic particles with a microwave-susceptor catalyst of iron oxide and aluminium oxide.

- Tata Steel in the UK produces each year 100 million square metres of building cladding for use as facades and roofs of buildings. Dave Worsley[21] developed coating technologies for metallic and organic systems, which give cladding a guaranteed lifetime of up to 40 years. Coupled with innovation in printed solar cells with laboratory efficiencies of over 28 per cent, and combined with solar thermal collectors for inter-seasonal storage, the potential of this systems solution to absorb the sun's energy is around 1GW peak power per year of Tata's cladding production, with a lifetime of around twice that of current solar panels.

- In 2019 the building materials group LafargeHolcim presented ORIS as the "world's first digital building materials platform" designed to help optimize the planning of road projects through the intelligent use of local resources and materials. ORIS can evaluate road pavement plans from different perspectives, recommend efficient construction and maintenance options and reduce road design and construction costs by up to a third and CO_2 emissions by up to half. At the same time, the durability and useful life of roads can be tripled. ORIS is now to be further developed with IBM Services' expertise in artificial intelligence, machine learning and the Internet of Things.[22]

Innovation in Circular Economics

COVID-19 has shown pitilessly that the dominant linear industrial economy has high vulnerability, little resilience and lacks sustainability. The 2020 lockdowns imposed by governments for sanitary reasons further showed that maximum economy of scale through globalization of production goes hand-in-hand with maximum diseconomy of risk, even a catastrophe risk potential. This contrasts with:

- local production of essential goods, such as food, medicines and medical equipment, and local essential services in health and equipment maintenance, which continued to function even in a complete lockdown;
- stocks of buildings, vehicles and equipment, which remained available even if their production was stopped.

The latter are part of an intelligent decentralized economy, which includes the circular industrial economy: repair and reuse services are best done locally where clients and their objects are situated (era of 'R'); in the circular economy of atoms and molecules (era of 'D'), new regional players acting as re-smelters and fleet managers of molecules will appear; local by definition are the business models of the performance economy.

Decentralized production is already a must for nanotech products that cannot be stored or transported, such as carbon nano-tubes (CNTs) and short-lived tracer elements used in medical examinations. A decentralized production of pharmaceuticals could become the preferred corporate strategy to reduce logistics hazards and facilitate the scaling up to high volume production in case of emergencies, according to the CEO of Roche.

A circular industrial economy requires rethinking economics, including producer ownership and liability (Stahel 2010; Clift and Druckman 2016; Oesterberg and Malmaeus 2018; Orasmaa et al. 2020) and rethinking politics (Stahel 2016b). So far, only the latter has started: "a more modern and circular economy will make us less dependent and boost our resilience.[23] This is the lesson we need to learn from the COVID-19 crisis", stated Ursula von der Leyen, the President of the European Commission, at the European Parliament session on a coordinated response to the coronavirus and its consequences. "The coronavirus crisis will likely redefine our politics, our geopolitics and possibly globalisation itself." COVID-19 has furthermore shown that society needs 'caring' to maintain existing stocks, including human capital, in addition to producing added value. To achieve a truly circular and sustainable economy, society will have to develop circular sciences.

CONCLUSIONS

The junction of circular economy, intelligent decentralization, novel materials and new business models hides a wealth of economic opportunities. The key to unlock these is research into circular materials, use-focused corporate strategies and innovative policymaking.

The circular economy is about maintaining the value and utility of a number of stocks – natural, cultural, human, and manufactured capitals – for the longest time in several distinct domains:

1. Bio-cycles are the realm of Nature, which is circular by evolution. Water and people are key renewable resources for a sustainable future.
2. Material cycles of natural and anthropogenic origin are the realm of entrepreneurs, of crafts and industry; decisions are strongly influenced by framework conditions and the owner-users of objects.
3. Invisible quality cycles of the immaterial world are the realm of policymakers and game changers to a sustainable future and a competitive economy.
4. Circular sciences are a global domain of daring and among the key drivers of a mature circular industrial economy. Innovation to broaden and speed up the applications of a circular economy is the realm of scientists, research institutions and academia.

NOTES

1. To define a new geological epoch, a signal must be found that occurs globally and will be incorporated into deposits in the future geological record. The 35 scientists of the Working Group of the Anthropocene (WGA) decided at the beginning of 2020 that the Anthropocene started with the nuclear bomb in Hiroshima on 6 August 1945. The radioactive elements from nuclear bomb tests, which were blown into the stratosphere before settling down to earth, provided this 'golden spike' signal. See https://www.theguardian.com/environment/2016/aug/29/declare-anthropocene-epoch -experts-urge-geological-congress-human-impact-earth.

2.   The terms "the era of 'R'" and "the era of 'D'", created and defined in Stahel (2019a), are today widely accepted.
3.   See note 1.
4.   Sustainable taxation, including taxing non-renewable resources instead of taxing labour (Stahel 2013).
5.   See https://www.urgenda.nl/en/themas/climate-case/.
6.   The LCIA, Life Cycle Inventory Analysis from cradle to the point of sale, complements LCA from cradle to grave.
7.   The Royal Institute of Chartered Surveyors in the UK estimates that 35 per cent of the lifecycle carbon from a typical office development is emitted before the building is opened; for residential premises the figure is 51 per cent. With rising energy efficiency of buildings, the weight of the embodied resources rises exponentially.
8.   See http://www.mercuryconvention.org.
9.   Xerox very early imposed its commonality principle of the same components across its equipment range. Airbus used from the start a standardized flight deck for all its aircraft, saving airlines O&M costs in parts management, crew training, and stand-by crews.
10. See https://www.vanalen.org/projects/reimagining-brooklyn-bridge/.
11. See https://www.nature.com/articles/d41586-020-00644-x.
12. See https://www.circularonline.co.uk/news/aluminium-recycling-technology-boosted-by-crystallisation -research/.
13. See https://www.circularonline.co.uk/news/scandinavian-waste-tyre-recycling-start-up-to-open-plant -at-port-of-sunderland/.
14. See https://www.theguardian.com/environment/2020/apr/08/scientists-create-mutant-enzyme-that -recycles-plastic-bottles-in-hours.
15. See https://www.enespa.eu/.
16. See https://www.circularonline.co.uk/news/20m-plastic-to-hydrogen-plant-moves-forward/.
17. See https://foundry.lbl.gov/helmsgroup.
18. Singapore's NEWater initiative: https://en.wikipedia.org/wiki/NEWater.
19. See https://www.sustainsteel.ac.uk.
20. See https://ironfuel.nl/technology/.
21. Professor Dave Worsley from Swansea University was awarded the Bessemer Gold Medal for 2020 by IOM3 and presented the Sir Henry Bessemer Lecture on 21 October 2020.
22. See http://e3.marco.ch/publish/lafargeholcim/1184_3104/04082020-LafargeHolcim_IBM_Oris_D _final.pdf.
23. For the author, this is both satisfaction and regret: in 1976, he had submitted his report, which first analysed and defined a circular industrial economy, to the then Commission of the European Communities in Brussels.

REFERENCES

Christensen, P. R., Scheuermann, A. M., Loeffler, K. E., & Helms, B. A. (2019). Closed-loop recycling of plastics enabled by dynamic covalent diketoenamine bonds. *Nature Chemistry*, 11(5), 442–448.
Clift, R., & Druckman, A. (eds.) (2016). *Taking Stock of Industrial Ecology*. Berlin: Springer.
Dumont, F. (2008). *A History of Personality Psychology*. New York: Cambridge University Press.
Elhacham, E., Ben-Uri, L., Grozovski, J., Bar-On, Y., & Milo, R. (2020). Global human-made mass exceeds all living biomass. *Nature*, 588, 442–444.
Empa Quarterly (2019). Issue no. 66, October. https://www.empa.ch/documents/56164/11638132/Empa _Quarterly66_EN_Web.pdf/4bbcba41-b37e-44d0-9339-c13b364f8e91.
European Commission (2015). *The Junction of Health, Environment and Bioeconomy: Foresight and Implications for European Research & Innovation Policies*. Brussels: DG for Research and Innovation, Foresight Programme. https://ec.europa.eu/research/foresight.

Hagan, A. J., Tost, M., Inderwildi, O. R., Hitch, M., & Moser, P. (2019). The license to mine: Making resource wealth work for those who need it most. *Resources Policy.* https://doi.org/10.1016/j .resourpol.2019.101418.

Jie, X., Li, W., Slocombe, D., et al. (2020). Microwave-initiated catalytic deconstruction of plastic waste into hydrogen and high-value carbons. *Nature Catalysis*, 3, 902–912.

Material Economics (2018). *Ett värdebeständigt svenskt materialsystem* [Retaining Value in the Swedish Materials System]. https://materialeconomics.com/new-publications/ett-vardebestandigt-svenskt -materialsystem.

Miller, T. E., Beneyton, T., Schwander, T., et al. (2020). Light-powered CO_2 fixation in a chloroplast mimic with natural and synthetic parts. *Science*, 368(6491), 649–654.

Oesterberg, R., & Malmaeus, M. (eds.) (2018). *Ekonomi för Antropocen* [An Economy for the Anthropocene]. Stockholm: Carlsson Bokförlag.

Orasmaa, A., Lourita, L., & Liimatainen, H. (2020). Rethinking ownership: Producer ownership models in a circular economy. *Sitra Studies*, 176. https://media.sitra.fi/2020/12/02164106/rethinking -ownership.pdf.

Shahab, R. L., Brethauer, S., Davey, M. P., et al. (2020). A heterogeneous microbial consortium producing short chain fatty acids from lignocellulose. *Science*, 369(6507).

Srivastava, R., Awojobi, M., & Amann, J. (2020). *Training the Workforce for High-Performance Buildings: Enhancing Skills for Operations and Maintenance.* Washington, DC: American Council for an Energy-Efficient Economy.

Stahel, W. R. (2010). *The Performance Economy*, 2nd edition. Basingstoke: Palgrave Macmillan.

Stahel, W. R. (2013). Policy for material efficiency: Sustainable taxation as a departure from the throw-away society. *Philosophical Transactions of the Royal Society A*, 371, 20110567. https://royalsociety publishing.org/doi/10.1098/rsta.2011.0567.

Stahel, W. R. (2016a). Comment: A new relationship with our goods and materials would save resources and energy and create local jobs. *Nature*, 531, 435–438.

Stahel, W. R. (2016b). From sustainability talk to policy walk: Stepping up EU action on climate, biodiversity and circular economy. *EUropainfo*, 3/16, European Environmental Bureau, Vienna, 23–24.

Stahel, W. R. (2019a). *The Circular Economy: A User's Guide*. Abingdon: Routledge [*Sirkulær Økonomi – En handbook*. Trondheim: SINTEF, 2019].

Stahel, W. R. (2019b). Innovation in the circular and the performance economy. In F. Boons & A. McMeekin (eds.), *Handbook of Sustainable Innovation*. Cheltenham, UK and Northampton, MA, USA: Edward Elgar Publishing, 38–58.

Stahel, W. R., & Reday, G. (1981). *Jobs for Tomorrow: The Potential for Substituting Manpower for Energy*. New York: Vantage Press [Published text of a 1976 report to the Commission of the European Communities, Brussels, on the potential for substituting manpower for energy by the authors then working at The Battelle Research Centre in Geneva].

Stokes, J. M., Yang. K., Swanson, K., et al. (2020). A deep learning approach to antibiotic discovery. *Cell*, 180(4). https://doi.org/10.1016/j.cell.2020.01.021.

Takata, T., Jiang, J., Sakata, Y., et al. (2020). Photocatalytic water splitting with a quantum efficiency of almost unity. *Nature*, 581, 411–414.

Tournier, V., Topham, C. M., Gilles, A., et al. (2020). An engineered PET depolymerase to break down and recycle plastic bottles. *Nature*, 580, 216–219.

PART II

FIRM-LEVEL ENABLERS FOR CIRCULAR ECONOMY INNOVATION

3. Sustainability innovations in the manufacturing industry: a comparison of circular and climate innovation initiatives

Fanny Hermundsdottir, Ann Elida Eide and Arild Aspelund

INTRODUCTION

Humanity at large, and the manufacturing sector in particular, currently face two major environmental challenges. The first relates to overexploitation of planetary resources and materials and is often referred to as the *resource challenge* (UNEP 2011). The resource challenge is defined by extraction of more resources than the planet can regenerate. The second major environmental challenge is related to climate change (IPCC 2020). Currently, climate change occurs because of emissions of greenhouse gases from human activity (Ramli and Munisamy 2015). We refer to this as the *climate challenge*, and like the resource challenge, it is a major hurdle in the process towards global sustainability (UN 2015). For the purpose of this study, we label these two challenges the sustainability challenge.

The manufacturing industry constitutes a significant part of the sustainability challenge (Schrettle et al. 2014). The industry's vast material usage and greenhouse gas emissions contribute to the global sustainability challenge of today (Tang et al. 2018). Hence, to keep their licence to operate, manufacturers need to develop and adopt sustainability innovations that decouple value creation from material usage and greenhouse gas emissions. The problem is that the two types of innovations are different: Resource innovations are primarily related to efficiency and circularity of input factors, whilst climate innovations focus on reducing the externalities of production processes.

This study investigates whether there are systematic differences between firms that try to solve the resource challenge from those that seek to solve the climate challenge, and those who try to pursue both or none. There is a need for more research on what distinguishes firms that proactively implement sustainability into their strategies and innovation processes, from firms that do not (Dyllick and Muff 2016). Our research question is: Are there any differences between firms that, to various degrees, implement different sustainability innovations?

To investigate this question, we create a typology of firms that approach the sustainability challenges differently and compare them on factors related to firm characteristics, strategic sustainability-focus, growth strategies and impact. This knowledge can enhance our understanding of what measures are needed to solve the sustainability challenges. This is important, as academic research according to Montiel and Delgado-Ceballos (2014) "has failed to effectively inform management practice about sustainable development" (p. 132).

THEORETICAL BACKGROUND

Most actors in society agree that businesses need to change their interaction with the natural and social environments in which they operate (García-Sánchez et al. 2020). The United Nations has defined 17 Sustainability Development Goals, which include both social and environmental challenges. For the purpose of this study, we will focus on the two most significant global environmental challenges – *the climate challenge* and *the resource challenge*.

The climate challenge is caused by emissions of greenhouse gasses and leads to global warming. The pressure to deal with the climate challenge is acute, particularly in the manufacturing sector as it is responsible for over one-third of the energy consumption and CO_2 emissions in the world (International Energy Agency 2007). Intuitively, the costs of reducing climate gas emissions seem overwhelming, however the argument can also be flipped – emissions can be viewed as economic waste and inefficient use of resources, which leads to non-value-adding activities in terms of storing of waste and handling of emissions (Porter and van der Linde 1995). Hence, reducing emissions can lead to better ways of utilizing the resources and energy. Reduction of CO_2 emissions can be obtained by cleaning emissions as an end-of-pipe-solution, by using less energy from fossil fuels or by using more energy-efficient production methods (Fujii et al. 2013). Hence, in the following we will label the innovations that seeks to solve the climate challenge *climate innovations*.

The resource challenge is caused by overuse of planetary resources and this challenge is also strongly associated with the manufacturing industry due to increasing use of resources and major waste issues globally (Singh et al. 2017). For example, in the US 93 per cent of the extracted natural resources are not actually integrated into any end product, and 80 per cent of the products are not reused (Sempels and Hoffman 2013). The solution to the resource challenge is argued to be a shift towards a circular economy, which is defined as "an economic system that is based on business models which replace the 'end-of-life' concept with reducing, alternatively reusing, recycling and recovering materials in production/distribution and consumption processes" (Kirchherr et al. 2017, p. 224). We label innovations that will seek to solve the resource challenge and forward the shift to a circular economy *circular innovations*. Examples of circular innovations are measures to reduce waste including redesign of products and packaging, employment of reusable materials, and recovering resources to reuse them in the production of new products (Singh et al. 2017) – in essence circular innovations include keeping materials in the economic loop as long as possible at a highest possible quality.

As manufacturers are meeting pressure from external stakeholders such as the public, consumers, regulators and suppliers they respond by developing and adopting climate and circular innovations (Lin et al. 2019). These innovations can take different forms. For example, product innovations can increase products' life cycle by improving their reuse, recyclability and durability, or by using more environmentally friendly materials (Xie et al. 2019). Managerial innovations include redesigning value-creating or organizational processes or services to be more environmentally friendly (Burki et al. 2018), while process innovations comprise reducing energy or material consumption (Xie et al. 2019). Whatever the form, resource and climate challenges can be said to be focused on distinct parts of the manufacturing process: the first is linked to input factors in the production process, meaning how the input factors are put to use in the final product solution, and the second relates to the use of energy in the production process and outcome in the form of emissions from this process. Hence, the innovations needed to solve these challenges will be different. The question we raise is whether they are also handled differently by the organizations that implement them.

As external pressure has led firms to implement sustainability innovations, the link between the adoption of sustainability innovations and firm competitiveness becomes highly relevant. Many studies show how sustainability innovations can lead to cost reductions by reducing the amount of resources, materials, or energy use in terms of water, soil, electricity, and gas. Cost reductions can also be accomplished by the reuse and recycling of materials and resources (Rezende et al. 2019). Further, sustainability innovations can lead to market differentiation by targeting sustainability-oriented segments or markets, and lead to increased revenues with premium prizing (García-Sánchez et al. 2020; Rezende et al. 2019). By implementing sustainability innovations firms can also experience improved image and reputation (García-Sánchez et al. 2020). Due to high complexity, uncertainty and the long-term focus often associated with sustainable innovations, many firms are reluctant to invest in them (Cai and Li 2018). However, a consensus is emerging in the literature that overall, there are economic benefits for firms in developing and adopting sustainability innovations (Hermundsdottir and Aspelund 2020). However, we know little about differential effects between innovations that target the resource versus climate challenge. Neither do we know whether firms approach these innovations differently.

We do know though that firms often adopt sustainability innovations either proactively or responsively depending on the expected outcome. For example, Wong (2012) shows how sustainable innovations are a reaction to either compliance or regulations (responsive) or a more proactive move where the firm sees opportunities for increased profitability or reduced costs (proactive). Xie et al. (2016) show that climate innovations such as end-of-pipe solutions are often compliance driven whereas clean technologies are adopted with a proactive approach. As a consequence, end-of-pipe-solutions tend to dominate as they are pressured upon industrial actors by strong external stakeholders. Clean technologies are less common as they are more complex and "often associated with barriers such as the need for more coordinated research and development actives and higher fixed costs" (Triebswetter and Wackerbauer 2008, pp. 30–31). Consequently, the economic benefit for firms needs to be very convincing for them to proactively adopt environmental innovations.

Hence, we know from previous research that circular and climate innovations are different in nature, but we know little about whether firms strategically approach these innovations differently, or if they expect different economic outcomes from adopting them. This study seeks to examine these questions by investigating the following hypotheses:

H1: There are differences in managerial and strategic approaches between firms that to various degrees seek to adopt circular and climate innovations.

H2: There are differences in expected economic and strategic outcomes between firms that to various degrees seek to adopt circular and climate innovations.

METHOD

The study adopts a quantitative approach based on survey data from the Norwegian manufacturing industry. A questionnaire with 110 questions related to sustainability and firm performance was sent to all firms with NACE code C Industry (N = 4,299). The questionnaire was targeted to the CEO and was collected in early 2016. We obtained 682 responses, resulting in a 25.9 per cent response rate. To test whether this sample was representative for the whole population, a comparison of the population and the sample on measures including firm size, age and industry code was done. No significant differences were found between the groups, indicating that the sample was representative for the population of Norwegian manufacturers.

Eighty-three per cent of the firms were predominantly focused on products, while 17 per cent were mainly focused on services. Average firm age was 22 years and average firm size was 64 employees. Further, 48.7 per cent of the firms had international sales, 77.5 per cent relied on international imports and 8.8 per cent had international production.

The measures used in the questionnaire were developed from previous studies (most notably Porter and Kramer 2006, 2011; Willard 2012). We use nine constructs. These are: sustainability strategies (extent that sustainability is implemented in business strategy, 10 items), environmental initiatives (extent of environmental sustainability initiatives adopted, 6 items), social initiatives (extent of social sustainability initiatives adopted, 5 items), overview of sustainability challenges (extent of awareness of own industry's sustainability challenges, 2 items), motivation for sustainability (CEO personal motivation, 3 items), impact of initiatives (extent leaders think sustainability strategies will solve the challenges of the industry, 2 items), value creation (extent leaders think sustainability strategy will give the firm increased value creation, 8 items), cost reduction (extent leaders think sustainability strategy will give the firm lower costs, 2 items) and risk reduction (extent leaders think sustainability strategy will give the firm reduced risk, 3 items). In addition, we use single item questions related to growth strategies. All items are measured on a 7-point Likert scale, ranging from 1 (not at all) to 7 (to a great extent). The constructs used in the analysis were validated by factor analysis, with principal component factor extraction method and oblimin rotation. The items with high cross loadings were discharged and all factor loadings were over 0.5 indicating high convergent validity (Cai and Li 2018). The reliability of the constructs was validated using Cronbach's alpha. All alpha-values were over 0.7, indicating good internal consistency (Pallant 2016). Due to space limitations we cannot include variable analyses in the chapter, but they are available from the authors on request.

The hypotheses are investigated by a two-step cluster analysis approach which is appropriate for large datasets (Rundle-Thiele et al. 2015, p. 526). The firms were clustered according to their differences on two variables: one related to the adoption of *circular innovations* and one related to adoption of *climate innovations*. Results from the cluster analysis show that the cluster quality was above 0.5 on the silhouette measure of cohesion and separation, indicating good cluster quality (Wendler and Gröttrup 2016). Clusters were compared using ANOVA and Tukey HSD post-hoc test.

RESULTS

Cluster Analysis

The cluster analysis resulted in four clusters differing on the level of adoption of circular innovations and climate innovations. Cluster 1 (N = 115, 26.6 per cent) has low scores on both (2.37, and 2.17, respectively), and is hence called "Sustainability laggards". Cluster 2 (N = 83,

19.2 per cent) is the smallest cluster and is characterized by high adoption of circular innovations (6.29) and low on climate innovations (3.65). We label them "Circular innovators".
Cluster 3 (N = 120, 27.8 per cent) is high on climate innovations (5.27), but low on circular
(4.28). This is the biggest cluster and is labelled "Climate champions". Finally, cluster 4 (N
= 114, 26.4 per cent) scores high on both (6.35 and 6.48) and is thus labelled "Sustainability
leaders". There are no statistically significant differences between the clusters regarding characteristics such as firm age and size, international sales or production, but the Sustainability
laggards (hereafter called Laggards) are slightly less dependent on imports. The clusters are
plotted in Figure 3.1.

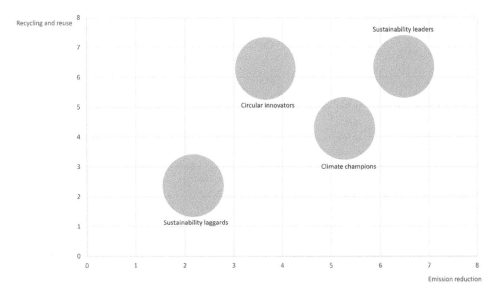

Figure 3.1   *Illustration of clusters*

Comparative Analysis of Clusters

The clusters are compared on sustainability approaches and expected outcomes. The analyses
are structured according to the two hypotheses.

H1: Managerial and strategic approaches to sustainability
Table 3.1 reports the results of the analyses. There are many significant differences between
the clusters on the variables related to H1 – sustainability strategies, implemented environmental and social sustainability initiatives, overview of industry's sustainability challenges and
leader motivation. As expected, the overall pattern is that Cluster 1 (low) and Cluster 4 (high)
are significantly different at each end of the scale. This applies for all analyses. Actually, the
Sustainability leaders score significantly higher than all other clusters on all measures except
on social initiatives (similar to clusters 2 and 3), and overview of challenges (similar to the
Circular innovators). These results suggest that it takes a broad range of environmental and

Table 3.1   Sustainability focus, growth strategies and impact

Construct	Mean values				ANOVA
	Cluster 1: Sustainability laggards	Cluster 2: Circular innovators	Cluster 3: Climate champions	Cluster 4: Sustainability leaders	F-value
Sustainability strategies	2,4153[b,c,d]	3,5906[a,d]	3,6414[a,d]	4,4470[a,b,c]	64,095***
Environmental initiatives	2,8316[b,c,d]	4,6345[a,d]	4,6422[a,d]	5,5617[a,b,c]	147,778***
Social initiatives	5,7769[b,c,d]	6,1616[a]	6,1629[a]	6,3362[a]	9,904***
Overview of sustainability challenges	3,3522[b,c,d]	4,5542[a]	4,3793[a,d]	4,9079[a,c]	29,115***
Motivation for sustainability	3,9330[b,c,d]	4,9625[a,d]	4,9760[a,d]	5,5270[a,b,c]	27,817***
Growth Strategies					
The company seeks growth through/ by…					
… Innovation	4,46[b]	5,20[a]	4,87	4,97	3,081**
… Internationalization	3,12	3	3,37	3,43	0,946
… Cost leadership	2,71[c,d]	3,15	3,26[a]	3,4[a]	3,899**
… Differentiation	4,86	5,22	5,23	5,18	1,587
… Customized products and services	5,12	5,46	5,55	5,54	2,252*
… Sustainability	2,84[b,c,d]	3,96[a]	4,27[a]	4,44[a]	25,229***
Impact of Initiatives	2,8596[b,c,d]	4,3072[a]	4,2899[a,d]	4,7566[a,c]	42,886***
Value Creation	3,7988[b,c,d]	4,4190[a]	4,3626[a]	4,5649[a]	11,861***
Cost Reduction	3,6274[c,d]	3,9688	3,9823[a]	4,2877[a]	7,484***
Risk Reduction	3,9346[b,c,d]	4,7792[a]	4,4722[a]	4,7259[a]	12,925***

Note: *: $p<0.1$, **: $p<0.05$, ***: $p<0.001$.
[a], [b], [c], [d]: denote significant group difference in post-hoc tests (Tukey HSD).

social initiatives, and motivated and strategically focused leaders for manufacturing firms to target to solve both the resource and the climate challenge.

Cluster 2 and Cluster 3 – the Circular innovators and the Climate champions – position themselves in between the other two clusters on all measures. Regarding the managerial and strategic approaches to sustainability, these two clusters are surprisingly similar on our measures. The only measure where there are tendencies for differences are on the overview of the sustainability challenges where the Circular innovators score slightly higher. This might be due to the fact that material streams are easier to quantify than emissions. Hence, H1 is supported, but the findings suggest that the differences are related to the extent the firms try to solve sustainability challenges overall – rather than on the emphasis on either solving the climate or resource challenge.

H2: Expected economic and strategic outcomes

Regarding expected economic and strategic outcomes of sustainability strategies we have ana-lysed growth strategies, impact of initiatives and expected economic rewards in terms of value creation, cost or risk reduction. We see that Circular innovators is the cluster with the highest levels of growth strategies through innovation – significantly higher than the Laggards. Growth strategies through internationalization, differentiation or customization show little differences. However, it is interesting to observe two things. One, cost leadership strategies are more common in all other clusters than the Laggards, and most among Climate champions and Sustainability leaders. One might assume that cost leadership was a strategy that was more common among Laggards that might be reluctant to make investments in sustainability, but here we observe the opposite. Second, unsurprisingly the Laggards are significantly lower than the others on sustainability growth strategies. The other clusters have fairly high scores on this measure, suggesting that sustainability is a relatively common growth strategy among Norwegian manufacturers.

When it comes to the outcomes we also observe a strong belief in the economic impact of the strategies and their ability to solve the challenges of the industry. The Laggards score significantly lower than all the other clusters on impact of initiatives, the Sustainability leaders significantly higher, and clusters 2 and 3 in between. More or less the same patterns emerge for the expected economic rewards in terms of value creation, cost reductions and risk reductions. The Laggards have little belief that sustainability strategies can provide economic benefits for the firm. However, economic benefits are understood to come out of strategic sustainability by Circular innovators, Climate champions and, most of all, Sustainability leaders. Overall, we see a clear pattern that sustainability motivation, expected impact on the industry, and expected economic rewards are systematically correlated with the clusters that do increasingly more for the environment. Regarding the Circular innovators and the Climate champions, they are relatively similar when it comes to expected outcomes, but we also observe that it is the Circular innovators that have the highest expectations of risk reduction of their sustainability strategies.

These results support H2 that there are differences in expected strategic and economic outcomes based on the level of adoption of circular and climate sustainability strategies. However, even though there are notable differences between the Circular innovators and the Climate champions, like H1 the strongest explanatory power is the degree the firms try to solve the sustainability challenges overall.

DISCUSSION

This study defined and created four clusters of manufacturers based on their degree of adoption of circular and climate innovations. The analyses gave us insight into differences in managerial and strategic approach to sustainability and the expected strategic and economic outcome.

The study departed from the question of whether manufacturing firms can solve *both* the resource and climate challenge as these challenges seem to require different innovation types and organizational foci. However, the analyses showed that an integrated sustainability strategy that incorporated both circular and climate innovations, as in the Sustainability leaders cluster, are common. Moreover, strategic focus on either the climate or resource challenge does not demand specific organizational approaches or differentiated expected outcomes. The Sustainability leaders see sustainability as a strategic way of obtaining increased firm performance (Baumgartner and Ebner 2010). In this sense Sustainability leaders are more strategically focused on achieving these strategic benefits than those who focus primarily on either the resource challenge or the climate challenge. We found that the Circular innovators and the Climate champions show fewer tendencies to integrate sustainability in their core business strategy than the Sustainability leaders. Integrated sustainability strategies have also been found in previous research to be essential because they lead to organizational practices that helps the organization to identify profitable business opportunities related to sustainability (Kennedy et al. 2017).

Another interesting feature of the Sustainability leaders that differentiates them from the other clusters is the high levels of CEO motivations for sustainability. This notion is supported by Eide et al. (2020) who also find that top managers' personal motivation influences both firms' ability to implement sustainability strategies, and also their capacity to turn it into increased competitiveness. This positive attitude and leader motivation can also be explained by firms having experienced earlier success with sustainability (Schrettle et al. 2014). Further, managerial concern towards sustainability is found to positively strengthen green innovations' effect on competitiveness, as it positively influences the adoption of green strategies (Tang et al. 2018). Consequently, our results indicate that leader motivation is an important factor for sustainability-oriented behaviour in firms.

The study finds that all the clusters that seek to solve the sustainability challenges – meaning Circular innovators, Climate champions and Sustainability leaders – have positive managerial and strategic approaches towards sustainability, devise efficient strategies and expect them to solve the industry's challenges and provide economic and strategic benefits for the firm. This is in stark contrast to the Laggards.

Laggards stand out by scoring significantly lower than the other clusters on almost all measures. They have low motivation, little overview over environmental challenges, do not devise appropriate strategies, nor believe they can be effective and provide firms with economic or strategic benefits. This is similar to what Baumgartner and Ebner (2010) call an introverted strategy, meaning that firms with low sustainability maturity do not implement any sustainability measures other than those imposed by law and regulation. Legislation has in fact been shown to be one of the most important drivers for sustainability innovations (Hojnik and Ruzzier 2016) and it seems to be especially important if one wants to effect change among the Laggards.

Overall, the analyses show few differences between the Circular innovators and the Climate champions. However, two issues are notable. The Climate champions seem to have higher emphasis on cost reductions than the other clusters. This is an indication of a conservative strategy, where cost efficiency and sustainability processes have the highest focus (Baumgartner and Ebner 2010) and it is also in line with the reasoning of Porter and Van der Linde (1995) who argue that high levels of emissions can be seen as high levels of inefficiency and waste. Hence, lower emissions mean higher resource efficiency and less process waste. Based on this, it may seem like the Climate champions engage in emission reductions because of expectations of lower costs.

The second difference is that Circular innovators are strongly focused on innovation as a growth strategy. One explanation could be that circular innovations are more complex as they require coordinated actions from multiple parties to turn traditionally linear value creating processes and value chains into circular processes and value chains. If we follow this line of reasoning it might also explain why Circular innovators have greater overview over sustainability challenges than the Climate champions – they experience more pressure from institutional, market and social actors (Hojnik and Ruzzier 2016).

Despite these issues, there are more similarities than differences between the Circular innovators and the Climate champions. Broadly, what separates them is their focus on the two distinct aspects of the sustainability challenge. Other than this, we observe that firms that work with different aspects of the sustainability challenge have similar organizational characteristics, strategic and managerial approaches and seek similar economic and strategic outcomes. Hence, this study suggests that firms can use comparable strategic and managerial approaches regardless of which environmental challenge they seek to solve. Rather, as Sustainability leaders have shown in this study, it is the extent of managerial and strategic focus to solving the challenges that will influence firms' ability to successfully create a truly sustainable business, and still remain competitive.

The findings in this study point to the importance of firms moving whole-heartedly into solving the sustainability challenge. We see that firms that implement both circular and climate innovations perform better both in terms of solving challenges, both also in their ability to create competitiveness for themselves. This, in addition to the insight that similar approaches will work for solving the resource and climate challenge, remains the key managerial implication of this study. For policy, we conclude that distinct policies aimed at decreasing the cost of innovation for manufacturers could be beneficial in generating greater advances in environmental impact, especially for the group of Climate champions. For the Circular innovators, the most effective action might be to use regulations to solve the problems associated with the need for coordinated adoption of circular innovations from multiple actors in the value chain simultaneously. However, the effectiveness of policy measures is not investigated in this study and should be given more attention in future research.

CONCLUSION

In this study we aimed to investigate the differences between firms' approach to the sustainability challenge. We created four clusters based on firms' efforts to solve the resource and climate challenge. These clusters were labelled (1) Sustainability laggards – having little focus on either challenge, (2) Circular innovators – with high focus on recycling and circularity, (3) Climate champions – displaying high focus on emission reduction, and (4) Sustainability leaders – showing high focus on both the resource and climate challenges. The study identifies differences between the clusters – predominantly between those who have different levels of engagement towards sustainability in general, and less on whether they focus especially on the resource or climate challenge. We conclude that all three clusters that actively seek to solve environmental sustainability challenges have positive managerial and strategic approaches towards sustainability, devise effective growth strategies, expect to solve the industry's challenges and expect economic and strategic benefits for the firm.

REFERENCES

Baumgartner, R. J., & Ebner, D. (2010). Corporate sustainability strategies: Sustainability profiles and maturity levels. *Sustainable Development*, 18(2), 76–89.

Burki, U., Ersoy, P., & Dahlstrom, R. (2018). Achieving triple bottom line performance in manufacturer-customer supply chains: Evidence from an emerging economy. *Journal of Cleaner Production*, 197, 1307–1316.

Cai, W., & Li, G. (2018). The drivers of eco-innovation and its impact on performance: Evidence from China. *Journal of Cleaner Production*, 176, 110–118.

Dyllick, T., & Muff, K. (2016). Clarifying the meaning of sustainable business: Introducing a typology from business-as-usual to true business sustainability. *Organization & Environment*, 29(2), 156–174.

Eide, A. E., Saether, E. A., & Aspelund, A. (2020). An investigation of leaders' motivation, intellectual leadership, and sustainability strategy in relation to Norwegian manufacturers' performance. *Journal of Cleaner Production*, 254, 120053.

Fujii, H., Iwata, K., Kaneko, S., & Managi, S. (2013). Corporate environmental and economic performance of Japanese manufacturing firms: Empirical study for sustainable development. *Business Strategy and the Environment*, 22(3), 187–201.

García-Sánchez, I. M., Gallego-Álvarez, I., & Zafra-Gómez, J. L. (2020). Do the ecoinnovation and ecodesign strategies generate value added in munificent environments? *Business Strategy and the Environment*, 29(3), 1021–1033.

Hermundsdottir, F., & Aspelund, A. (2020). Sustainability innovations and firm competitiveness: A review. *Journal of Cleaner Production*, 124715.

Hojnik, J., & Ruzzier, M. (2016). What drives eco-innovation? A review of an emerging literature. *Environmental Innovation and Societal Transitions*, 19, 31–41.

International Energy Agency. (2007). *Tracking Industrial Energy Efficiency and CO2 Emissions*. http://citeseerx.ist.psu.edu/viewdoc/download?doi=10.1.1.194.500&rep=rep1&type=pdf.

IPCC (2020). *Climate Change and Land*. Geneva: Intergovernmental Panel on Climate Change.

Kennedy, S., Whiteman, G., & van den Ende, J. (2017). Radical innovation for sustainability: The power of strategy and open innovation. *Long Range Planning*, 50(6), 712–725.

Kirchherr, J., Reike, D., & Hekkert, M. (2017). Conceptualizing the circular economy: An analysis of 114 definitions. *Resources, Conservation and Recycling*, 127, 221–232.

Lin, W. L., Cheah, J. H., Azali, M., Ho, J. A., & Yip, N. (2019). Does firm size matter? Evidence on the impact of the green innovation strategy on corporate financial performance in the automotive sector. *Journal of Cleaner Production*, 229, 974–988.

Montiel, I., & Delgado-Ceballos, J. (2014). Defining and measuring corporate sustainability: Are we there yet? *Organization & Environment*, 27(2), 113–139.

Pallant, J. (2016). *SPSS Survival Manual: A Step by Step Guide to Data Analysis Using SPSS*, 6th edition. Maidenhead: Open University Press.

Porter, M. E., & Kramer, M. R. (2006). The link between competitive advantage and corporate social responsibility. *Harvard Business Review*, 84(12), 78–92.

Porter, M. E. & Kramer, M. R. (2011). Creating shared value. *Harvard Business Review*, 94(1/2), 1–17.

Porter, M. E., & Van der Linde, C. (1995). Toward a new conception of the environment-competitiveness relationship. *Journal of Economic Perspectives*, 9(4), 97–118.

Ramli, N. A., & Munisamy, S. (2015). Eco-efficiency in greenhouse emissions among manufacturing industries: A range adjusted measure. *Economic Modelling*, 47, 219–227.

Rezende, L. D. A., Bansi, A. C., Alves, M. F. R., & Galina, S. V. R. (2019). Take your time: Examining when green innovation affects financial performance in multinationals. *Journal of Cleaner Production*, 233, 993–1003.

Rundle-Thiele, S., Kubacki, K., Tkaczynski, A., & Parkinson, J. (2015). Using two-step cluster analysis to identify homogeneous physical activity groups. *Marketing Intelligence & Planning*, 33(4), 522–537.

Schrettle, S., Hinz, A., Scherrer-Rathje, M., & Friedli, T. (2014). Turning sustainability into action: Explaining firms' sustainability efforts and their impact on firm performance. *International Journal of Production Economics*, 147, 73–84.

Sempels, C., & Hoffmann, J. (2013). *Sustainable Innovation Strategy: Creating Value in a World of Finite Resources*. Basingstoke: Palgrave Macmillan.

Singh, S., Ramakrishna, S., & Gupta, M. K. (2017). Towards zero waste manufacturing: A multidisciplinary review. *Journal of Cleaner Production*, 168, 1230–1243.

Tang, M., Walsh, G., Lerner, D., Fitza, M. A., & Li, Q. (2018). Green innovation, managerial concern and firm performance: An empirical study. *Business Strategy and the Environment*, 27(1), 39–51.

Triebswetter, U., & Wackerbauer, J. (2008). Integrated environmental product innovation and impacts on company competitiveness: A case study of the automotive industry in the region of Munich. *European Environment*, 18(1), 30–44.

UN (2015). *Transforming our World: The 2030 Agenda for Sustainable Development*. https://sdgs.un.org/publications/transforming-our-world-2030-agenda-sustainable-development-17981.

UNEP (2011). Decoupling Natural Resource Use and Environmental Impacts from Economic Growth. https://wedocs.unep.org/bitstream/handle/20.500.11822/9816/Decoupling_FReport_EN.pdf ?sequence=1&isAllowed=y.

Wendler, T., & Gröttrup, S. (2016). *Data Mining with SPSS Modeler: Theory, Exercises and Solutions.* Cham: Springer.

Willard, B. (2012). *The New Sustainability Advantage: Seven Business Case Benefits of a Triple Bottom Line.* Gabriola Island: New Society Publishers.

Wong, S. K. S. (2012). The influence of green product competitiveness on the success of green product innovation. *European Journal of Innovation Management*, 15(4), 468–490.

Xie, X., Huo, J., Qi, G., & Zhu, K. X. (2016). Green process innovation and financial performance in emerging economies: Moderating effects of absorptive capacity and green subsidies. *IEEE Transactions on Engineering Management*, 63(1), 101–112.

Xie, X., Huo, J., & Zou, H. (2019). Green process innovation, green product innovation, and corporate financial performance: A content analysis method. *Journal of Business Research*, 101, 697–706.

4.   Value retention in the Norwegian and Swedish outdoor industry

Are Severin Ingulfsvann

INTRODUCTION

In this chapter, I explore how five different outdoor brands in Norway and Sweden are creating initiatives for retention and on what types of eco-innovation they are basing them. These initiatives represent steps towards circular value chains, and it is important to highlight good practices that can help other firms to move towards circularity.

Prieto-Sandoval et al. (2018, p. 613) defined the circular economy as:

> an economic system that represents a change of paradigm in the way that human society is interrelated with nature and aims to prevent the depletion of resources, close energy and material loops, and facilitate sustainable development through its implementation at the micro (enterprises and consumers), meso (economic agents integrated in symbiosis) and macro (city, regions and government) levels. Attaining this circular model requires cyclical and regenerative innovations in the way society legislates, produces, and consumes.

Following this definition, closing the energy and material loops requires a change in the design and the ways in which products are created and producers and consumers interact to extend products' life. The latter includes a system for recycling when the product is finite. A common word for activities that close the loop is retention, and Reike et al. (2018) identified ten different retention options: refuse, reduce, reuse, repair, refurbish, remanufacture, repurpose, recycle, recover, and remine. These different retention options are therefore relevant to different stages of a product's life cycle. Identifying potential retention options, developing feasible activities, and implementing them require innovation, as stated by Prieto-Sandoval et al. (2018). Prieto-Sandoval et al. (2018) suggested eight categories of eco-innovation: business model innovation, network innovation, organizational structure innovation, process innovation, product innovation, service innovation, market innovation, and customer engagement innovation. These could all be relevant to develop retention options.

One could expect that the main challenge for these innovative activities is related to the technical side. However, according to Kirchherr et al. (2018), who ranked 15 barriers facing businesses and policymakers, the three top barriers to the circular economy for businesses are cultural: consumers' lack of interest, operating in a linear system, and a hesitant company culture. Willingness to cooperate in the value chain is the last cultural barrier, ranked as the sixth most important. Regarding technological barriers, limited circular design was ranked eighth, while too few large-scale demonstration projects, a lack of data on impacts, and the ability to deliver high-quality remanufactured products shared the eleventh place (Kirchherr et al. 2018). This indicates that cultural barriers are more significant than technical ones.

Businesses that have implemented circular initiatives have overcome some of the barriers. Exploring the concrete initiatives that they have implemented is therefore important for two reasons: (1) to highlight practices that other businesses can adopt and implement; and (2) to describe the connection between retention opportunities and eco-innovation to understand how these are linked together. As far as the authors are aware, the link between retention and eco-innovation has not been explored in depth previously, and an enhanced understanding of the interlinkages between these ten retention options and eight types of eco-innovation is important to increase circularity. The chapter contributes to the literature on the circular economy by using empirical information from the brands in the Scandinavian outdoor sector to show how eco-innovative initiatives are combined with retention options to move towards circularity. Ingulfsvann (2020) found that, in two years, the information on solutions for redistribution in this industry had almost doubled, indicating that circularity is important and new possibilities and solutions are being developed and communicated to stakeholders. Even though this indicates that brands are showing an interest in sustainability, it will be interesting to determine whether it results in tangible initiatives that move them towards circularity.

Based on this review, I formulated the following research question: Outdoor brands market many initiatives to show how sustainable they are, but which combinations of retention and eco-innovation create tangible initiatives?

THEORY

The overall point of a circular economy is to change the economy from take, make, and dispose to an economy in which the resources that are already in use are kept in the loop. The goal is to improve sustainability. Retention refers to options for preserving the product, parts of the product, or the resources used in the product.

Reike et al. (2018) identified ten different types of retention. Refuse (R0) means that the consumer chooses not to buy or that the producer refuses to produce a product or refuses to use specific materials. The latter acknowledges that the content of products is important since not all materials and chemicals have the necessary prerequisites for becoming circular. Reduce (R1) means using products for longer, sharing products, or using less material in their production. Resell/reuse (R2) refers to buying or selling used products without changes or repair and using systems created by the producer or seller to resell returned products. Repair (R3) means bringing a product back into functional order. This can be undertaken by the "customers or people in their vicinity, at the customer's location, and through a repair company" (Reike et al. 2018). Repair is closely connected to the practices of refurbishing (R4) and remanufacturing (R5). Refurbishing is a solution for large multicomponent products in which the overall structure is intact and components can be replaced or repaired. Remanufacturing happens when a product is dismantled, inspected, and cleaned and the necessary parts are repaired or replaced. Repurpose (R6) (rethink or redesign) means using discarded products for something new. Recycling (R7) involves reacquiring nearly pure materials from post-consumer products or post-producer waste streams. Unlike R4–R6, these materials can be applied anywhere. Recycling, then, has two sides: producers can use recycled materials and they can establish systems for recycling their products after the end of their use. Recover (R8) means extracting energy from waste, while remining (R9) is the process of mining out materials or retrieving materials from landfills and other types of waste plants (Reike et al. 2018). It is important to note that the retention options are connected and the possibilities for implementation depend on choices made in the design and production process.

The implementation of retention opportunities for a product requires businesses to rethink the products and the interactions with customers (Weetman 2017). Prieto-Sandoval et al. (2018, p. 612) argued that eco-innovation in a circular economy context should benefit "environmental regeneration, improve the capacity of systems to close the material loops and create value for nature and humans". This is closely linked to the retention options since the object of retention is to keep the product in use for longer (R1–R3), open up the possibility for using part of the product in other products (R4–R6), or keep the resources in the loop (R7–R9) instead of discarding them. Prieto-Sandoval et al. (2018) suggested eight kinds of eco-innovation needed to transform the economy. The first is business model innovation (E1), described as relating to how companies create and capture value. The second is network innovation (E2), involving how companies work with others. The third is innovation of the organizational structure (E3) by developing new organizational and management practices to support the environmental strategy. Fourth, process innovation (E4) is linked to the way in which products are made or services are offered. Fifth is product innovation (E5) – related to work to improve the quality and functionality of products. Service innovation (E6), in a CE context, is characterized by creating solutions to decrease ownership, meaning that a product can be used by many, that is, through rental. Market innovation (E7) is created through the brand's values, the positioning of the products, and the use of communication channels. The last type – customer engagement innovation (E8) – concentrates on customers' experiences and meeting their needs and desires (Prieto-Sandoval et al. 2018).

METHOD

The brands examined were selected from among the 44 Norwegian and Swedish full members of the Scandinavian Outdoor Group in 2019. The brands were examined to determine how much information they provided on their web page regarding 16 criteria for circular responsibility (Ingulfsvann 2020). The information that brands give to their customers on their web page is highly relevant because, according to Ormazabal et al. (2016, p. 1049), companies at the top level of environmental management maturity are also reference companies for environmental efforts through communication and marketing. From the 44 brands, those working within apparel or shoes that provided information on at least ten different criteria were selected for further examination. The requirement for at least ten criteria was set because it indicates that brands have a wide focus on their circular activities and they have not narrowed it down to focusing only on information on a single part of the value chain. Five brands remained: Bergans, Haglöfs, Fjällräven, Houdini, and Icebug. Table 4.1 summarizes the characteristics of these brands.

Bergans (2020) is the largest Norwegian brand within the outdoor products sector. It markets its policies actively to inform its customers and to develop new business models (rental and redesign) while trying to adopt a circular economy. Haglöfs (2020) is the largest Swedish brand and argues that it is important that products can be used in many different activities. Fjällräven (2020) is a traditional and well-known Swedish brand that sees it as necessary to reduce its environmental footprint.

Houdini (2020) began early with activities connected to repair, the closed loop, and circularity. It argues that "sustainability is at the heart of everything we do", and views sustainability as good business and essential in the long run. Icebug (2020) believes that, as an outdoor

Table 4.1   *Characteristics of the brands*

Brand	Bergans	Haglöfs	Fjällräven	Houdini	Icebug
Country	Norway	Sweden	Sweden	Sweden	Sweden
Established	1908	1914	1960	1993	2001
Products	Apparel	Apparel	Apparel	Apparel	Shoes
	Backpacks	Backpacks	Backpacks		
	Canoes	Sleeping bags	Tents		
	Sleeping bags				
	Tents				

brand, it has "an extra obligation to take care of nature". It has a strong focus on emissions, claiming to be the first climate-positive outdoor shoe brand.

The three oldest brands, Bergans, Haglöfs, and Fjällräven, have operated in quite a traditional market; they have produced a product, found customers, and tried to improve the product or at least give the impression that the product has changed in some way to convince the customers to buy something new. Then, as time has passed, it has become important to adapt to customers who expect responsibility. The brands with a shorter history, Icebug and Houdini, have integrated environmental responsibility from the beginning and built their position on pushing the industry in an environmental direction.

Within the Scandinavian outdoor sector, these brands are at the forefront; they are the reference companies that, according to Ormazabal et al. (2016), are the most mature. They are therefore suitable for further exploration to find out how tangible their initiatives are.

The data were gathered in July 2020 by accessing the websites of the companies, and all the information on activities and initiatives related to the environment, sustainability, and the circular economy was saved. The information was then considered to be a document that could be analysed through document analysis (Bowen 2009). Document analysis has been described as "a systematic procedure for reviewing or evaluating documents" (Bowen 2009, p. 27), including material from the Internet. This analysis consists of three steps: skimming, reading, and interpretation. The skimming process gave an overview, the material being found under headings like environment, CSR, sustainability, and responsibility. The material was saved and read thoroughly while looking for initiatives that could relate to the ten retention options. The different initiatives and actions that the brands put forward were interpreted and connected to their corresponding retention using a hermeneutical approach. Taylor (1999) pointed out that text must be understood in its context. Initiatives were interpreted as tangible if they added something to ordinary practice towards circularity and could be experienced in practice without comparing the experience with, for example, the life span of other products. The forms of retention were understood as different cycles, and the first step of the interpretation was to understand the type of cycle of which the actual initiative is a part. The next step was to connect the initiative to types of eco-innovation by interpreting the initiative in context to determine how the practice has changed. The threshold for describing a practice as innovative was low. The reason lies in the definition of eco-innovation as benefiting environmental regeneration.

Bowen (2009) put weight on understanding the purpose of documents. The original purpose was to provide potential customers with information and communication, and the technical details of the initiatives are therefore sometimes not especially clear. One problem with relying on information given on web pages is that brands try to seem more interested in practising circular initiatives than they really are. On the other hand, finding out what they focus on shows what the brands believe to be important and possible.

FINDINGS

The findings are structured with the forms of retention as a guideline. Each initiative is briefly described in the respective retention category and connected to one or more types of eco-innovation. All the companies state their values clearly in the way in which they present their work and position their products and brand as environmentally friendly through their web page (E7).

R0 Refuse

Initiatives to refuse were found for Houdini (2020) and Icebug (2020); Houdini has a checklist for its designers, the first question of which is "Does this product deserve existence?" Icebug simply points out that you should not buy the product if you do not need it. This initiative does not demand much, but it helps in positioning the brand and showing its values to its customers. We can therefore classify it as an attempt at a market innovation (E7).

R1 Reduce

Attempts to reduce were found for all the brands. All of them aim to reduce the use of hazardous chemicals, which implies a change in the process (R4).

Houdini (2020) and Bergans (2020) both have pilot programmes for subscription and rental – which can reduce the production volume. Houdini's subscription programme gives customers access to a clothing library for a monthly fee. The subscription programme of Bergans is aimed at outer clothing for growing children. They deliver the clothes to the door when the season and size are changing and then wash, repair, and prepare the clothing for another child. The rental solutions are based on payment per rental. Houdini (2020) offers rental at its brand stores and includes a question in its checklist for designers: "Is it durable enough for our rental programme?" (E5). Bergans (2020) offers rental solutions through its flagship stores and in cooperation with the Norwegian Tourist Association and other actors to bring the offer to other locations. These initiatives, subscription and rental, can be linked to business model innovation (E1) since they create and capture value without selling the product; in addition, they can be linked to service innovation (E6) because they reduce ownership and increase the number of users of a certain product. The rental solution adopted by Bergans also uses network innovation (E2).

Haglöfs (2020) makes second-grade products available at a lower price and reduces the waste from production (E1). Icebug promotes "Use what is produced", keeping models on sale if it has them in storage instead of removing unsold old models from the market. This is mostly a way of displaying its values to its customers (E7).

All five brands specifically argue that their products are made to last. They focus on design and material choices that enable a product to endure for a long time. Even though this is not particularly new, it is important and can be classified as a product innovation since it increases quality and functionality (E5).

R2 Reuse/Resell

Bergans (2020) makes used, repaired, and b-products available in its flagship stores. Houdini (2020) has organized sales of used clothes in its stores, through its web store, and on Instagram. This attracts attention to used clothing from a wider audience. Pieces of business model innovation (E1) are apparent here since organizing the sale of used or repaired clothing is not part of these companies' original business model. However, Houdini also applies market innovation by using the available communication channels (E7).

Fjällräven (2020) and Icebug (2020) encourage customers to resell/reuse garments. Encouraging reselling and making the customer aware of the possibility are positive actions, but it is difficult to argue that they represent more than stating values (E7).

R3 Repair

Fjällräven (2020) has a repair service and gives customers advice on how they can mend products themselves. Houdini (2020) offers to repair products. Haglöfs (2020) designs products to be easy to repair and provides spare parts. Repairing items is not something new, but it has become more and more difficult to find repair shops, and the more technical and advanced products become, the harder it is for customers to undertake repairs themselves. Making products that are repairable relates to quality and functionality, and businesses rely on product innovation (E5). Bergans (2020) offers repair services at its location and through a car travelling to different places. Customers can follow it through Facebook (E7) to find out when it will be in their city. Icebug (2020) offers to repair products and has a solution whereby customers can use their local shoemaker to mend shoes. Icebug supplies the material and reimburses the shoemaker. It cooperates with different shoemakers and creates a network (E2).

R6 Repurpose

Bergans (2020) makes new and unique products from products that have lost their function. Parts from broken products or leftover materials from production are resewn to make new products, and the new products are available in flagship stores. Bergans performed a stunt with a fashion school in which the students were given 250 used garments and redesigned them into "spectacular fashion" to be displayed on Black Friday. Haglöfs (2020) uses leftover materials from production to create unique products. The systematization of leftovers to figure out what they can produce demands a new process (E4). The cooperation between Bergans (2020) and the fashion school relies on both network (E2) and market innovation (E7) by setting the focus on redesigned fashion on Black Friday.

R7 Recycle

All the brands have initiatives for recycling. Bergans (2020) delivers garments that can be resewn or sold to the UFF, an organization that collects, sells, distributes, and recycles textiles. Bergans acknowledges that its missing link is determining how it can reuse recycled garments. Houdini (2020) offers to collect used clothing and uses recycled fibres, only employing biodegradable, renewable, recycled, or recyclable material (BRRR). It advises that natural fibres can be composted, arguing that woollen garments take 6 to 12 months to decompose. In 2016,

Houdini (2020) initiated a test in which it composted wool clothing and used the soil to grow vegetables, which were served at a gourmet restaurant. As a follow-up, it initiated a scheme for "compost for worn out sportswear at the beautiful Rosendals Garden in Stockholm", the object being to show "how natural clothes can transform into healthy soils which becomes nutrients for flowers, fruits and vegetables". Both the restaurant and the garden create an engagement opportunity for customers (E8). Both brands use network innovation (E2), Bergans with the UFF and Houdini with the garden and the restaurant. Both brands also work with process innovation (E4), but Houdini seems to have progressed further in only using BRRR material and showing that it is so clean it can be used for food production. There is obviously a value statement and a marketing gimmick in this (E7), but it requires effort in rethinking products to achieve it (E5).

For Icebug (2020), it is important to find "mono materials", materials in which the fibres are not mixed to prepare them for future recycling. Non-recyclable materials are shifted to recyclable ones using nylon from old fishing nets. It works to find out how biodegradable materials like algae and hemp can replace less recyclable material. This requires both product (E5) and process (E4) innovation. Haglöfs (2020) uses recycled materials in many products, and it is putting effort into increasing the amount. Fjällräven (2020) claims that its products are recyclable due to their simplistic design and the use of only one or two types of materials in each product.

R9 Remine

Houdini (2020) has taken the initiative to "integrate regenerative materials such as waste from land, ocean or air turned into resource". This is a future goal, and it clearly indicates that activities towards sustainability have an important value (E7). Achieving the goal requires process innovation (E4).

Table 4.2 sums up the findings on retention initiatives and shows that reduce, reuse, repair, and recycle are present in all seven brands. Refuse is found in the material from Houdini and Icebug, repurpose in Bergans and Haglöfs, and remine in Houdini. It is important to see the issues in combination. Materials and design are fundamental to sustainable consumption since the choices made in the starting phase will have implications for whether the products are durable enough to be resold, made to be repairable, or recycled.

Table 4.3 summarizes the different types of eco-innovation found in the different brands.

Table 4.4 presents the different eco-innovations found in connection with initiatives for retention.

Table 4.2   *Overview of retention initiatives found in the different brands (R4–5 and R8 not found)*

	Refuse (R0)	Reduce (R1)	Resell/ Reuse (R2)	Repair (R3)	Repurpose (R6)	Recycle (R7)	Remine (R9)
Bergans		X	X	X	X	X	
Haglöfs		X	X	X	X	X	
Fjällräven		X	X	X		X	
Houdini	X	X	X	X		X	X
Icebug	X	X	X	X		X	

Table 4.3   *Eco-innovations found in the different brands*

Brand	Eco-innovation
Bergans	Business model (E1), network (E2), process (E4), product (E5),
Houdini	service (E6), market (E7), customer engagement (E8)
Icebug	Network (E2), process (E4), product (E5), market (E7), customer engagement (E8)
Haglöfs	Business model (E1), process (E4), product (E5), market (E7)
Fjällräven	Process (E4), product (E5), market (E7)

Table 4.4   *Overview of the eco-innovation types connected to the forms of retention*

Retention	Refuse (R0)	Reduce (R1)	Reuse/ Resell (R2)	Repair (R3)	Repurpose (R6)	Recycle (R7)	Remine (R9)
Eco-innovation	E7	E1	E1	E2	E2	E2	E4
		E2	E7	E5	E4	E4	E7
		E4		E7	E7	E5	
		E5				E7	
		E6				E8	
		E7					

DISCUSSION

In the findings, we can see a wide variety of initiatives linked to the types of retention described by Reike et al. (2018) and their links to the different types of eco-innovation described by Prieto-Sandoval et al. (2018). All the brands actively communicate their efforts. Market innovation, the part of stating values, was found in connection to all the retention options in all the brands. Given the barrier of lacking consumer interest (Kirchherr et al. 2018), it is necessary to inform customers about and arouse their interest in all the initiatives. Communicating values and encouraging consumers to take responsibility for the retention of the product are important initiatives. However, the transferal to circularity demands tangible initiatives.

Therefore, tangible initiatives linked to other types of innovation are more important to implement circularity at the micro level, as stated in the definition by Prieto-Sandoval et al. (2018). All the tangible initiatives that we are investigating have product and partly process innovation as underlying preconditions. Since all these initiatives are based on extending the product life, the product must be developed to support this through a combination of durability, repairability, and recyclability.

If we look at the initiatives to reduce, we can see especially that Bergans and Houdini are moving towards circularity by combining their business model and service innovation. These two share a practice, but each of them has its own twist, which the others may be able to include. Bergans makes rental available at more locations through cooperation and network creation. Houdini has developed two different business models for its rental, the library model for clothing and one-time rental. The subscription to winter clothing for children introduced by Bergans is very limited and at a trial stage but represents a good idea since these types of garments are typically used for only a short period. It captures value in a different way, and it turns the product into a service. Houdini could have acted like Bergans and rented garments out through others to increase the potential for customers to choose renting before buying.

Consumers selling their used clothing is not a new idea, but a brand collecting and systematizing the sale of used clothing with its brand is, if not new, quite uncommon. Houdini is a little ahead of Bergans since Houdini also offers used clothing online – even through Instagram. It heightens consumer awareness, but it also demands customers' interest and loyalty. It is doubtful that a low-price brand could adopt the same approach.

There are several initiatives to repair, from non-binding statements – products designed to be repairable, changes in the product to enable repair, and offering advice and spare parts – to concrete repair offerings. Icebug's inclusion of local shoemakers is the most tangible initiative since it makes repairs easy. It is easier to walk to your local shoemaker (if you have one) than to send your shoes away to Icebug. The effect of this network innovation might not be so strong, but giving repair work to local shoemakers can potentially help the shoemakers' business to survive.

Repurposing is not a very systematized activity and seems to be at a trial stage of testing what can be achieved. There is some potential for combining used products and leftovers, but there could be more systematization and there is probably more potential for combining it with pre-recycling activities, like sorting out materials from discarded clothing to increase the resource supply.

Recycling combines network, process, product, market innovation, and customer engagement. Reducing the use of chemicals is not a direct initiative towards circularity, but it can be a precondition for recycling. Houdini and Icebug seem to be the most committed to renewable materials. The cooperation between Bergans and the UFF shows potential for including other partners. Houdini's compost initiative is interesting because it raises awareness and demands changes to design and production processes to meet new standards. Houdini's plan to remine resources is still at a visionary stage. It is not a tangible initiative. Organizational structure innovations were not found in connection to a specific retention option but might be the underlying factor for many of the other innovations.

CONCLUSION AND IMPLICATIONS

The focus on creating circularity in most of these brands indicates that the barrier of a hesitant company culture has been overcome. The tangible initiatives aim to reduce, reuse, repair, and recycle. The brands' focus on these initiatives indicates that they are trying to challenge the linear system and that the use of market innovation is aimed at heightening customers' interest. The most promising initiatives are rental and subscription, collecting and reselling used clothing, and using local shoemakers for repairs. Rental and subscription combine the business model and service innovation primarily to reduce, but, since the brand owns the products, it can apply different retention options at different stages depending on the state of the product. Rental and subscription reduce consumption if more people refrain from buying, the product can be repaired and rented out for longer, and pieces for redesign can be picked before finally recycling the rest of the product. Organizing reuse and resale through the brand can boost customer interest since it makes used product comparable to and available in the same place as new clothing. The use of local shoemakers for repairs is based on network innovation, but it is also necessary for the customer to engage in the process of finding the shoemaker and establishing contact.

When it comes to recycling, raising awareness of the need to implement a plan for the whole life cycle of the product is necessary, and this involves mainly the product and the process as the practical part but also market innovation to inform and network innovation to collect.

Implications for Practice

Establishing solutions for rental or subscription could have potential for other brands or products for which the products are not used daily. Finding potential partners that could enable a widespread solution could improve the potential but would also be more costly. Establishing a return system and reselling used products can be applied by other brands and products. The idea of including local repair shops has the potential to be used by other brands and for other types of product to increase consumers' opportunity to repair products.

Limitations and Future Research

As the five brands studied here are quite expensive, it is doubtful that these practices could be transferable to low-cost brands, but they could be adopted by other premium brands. Future research could concentrate on the revenues from the side models and the use of repair services and assess the viability of these practices.

REFERENCES

Bergans (2020). *Bergans of Norway*. Retrieved 8 July 2020 from https://www.bergans.no.

Bowen, G. A. (2009). Document analysis as a qualitative research method. *Qualitative Research Journal*, 9(2), 27–40.

Fjällräven (2020). *Välkommen til Fjällräven*. Retrieved 8 July 2020 from https://www.fjallraven.com/se/sv-se/om-oss/hallbarhet.

Haglöfs (2020). *Material*. Retrieved 8 July 2020 from https://www.haglofs.com/se/sv-se/sustainability/.

Houdini (2020). *Sustainability*. Retrieved 8 July 2020 from https://www.houdinisportswear.com/en-no/sustainability.

Icebug (2020). *It's about taking responsibility*. Retrieved 8 July 2020 from https://icebug.com/sustainability20.

Ingulfsvann, A. S. (2020). What does the brand tell us? Sustainability and responsibility in a circular perspective. *Journal of Cleaner Production*, 246, 118993.

Kirchherr, J., Piscicell, L., Bour, R., Kostense-Smit, E., Muller, J., Huibrechtse-Truijens, A., & Hekkert, M. (2018). Barriers to the circular economy: Evidence from the European Union (EU). *Ecological Economics*, 150, 264–272.

Ormazabal, M., Prieto-Sandoval, V., Jaca, C., & Santos, J. (2016). An overview of the circular economy among SMEs in the Basque country: A multiple case study. *Journal of Industrial Engineering*, 9(5), 1047–1058.

Prieto-Sandoval, V., Jaca, C., & Ormazabal, M. (2018). Towards a consensus on the circular economy. *Journal of Cleaner Production*, 179, 605–615.

Reike, D., Vermeulen, W. J. V., & Witjes, S. (2018). The circular economy: New or refurbished as CE 3.0? Exploring controversies in the conceptualization of the circular economy though a focus on history and resource value retention options. *Resources, Conservation and Recycling*, 135, 246–264.

Scandinavian Outdoor Group (2019). *Scandinavian Outdoor Group*. Retrieved 20 March 2020 from https://www.scandinavianoutdoorgroup.com.

Taylor, C. (1999). Interpretation and the sciences of man. In C. Taylor (ed.), *Philosophy and the Human Sciences. Philosophical Papers 2*. Cambridge: Cambridge University Press.
Weetman, C. (2017). *A Circular Economy Handbook for Business and Supply Chains*. London: Kogan Page.

5. Toward a sustainable paradigm: circular economy solutions in the fashion industry

Won-Yong Oh, Young Kyun Chang, Jung Hwan Park and Sanghee Han

INTRODUCTION

The fashion industry plays a substantial economic role and is a significant driver of economic growth (Gazzola et al. 2020). However, this industry is often considered one of the most destructive industries to the environment, with high water usage, disposal of a large number of unsold stocks, and pollution from chemical treatment (Hiquet et al. 2018). This problem results from the growing gap between production and utilization of clothing. For example, while clothing production has significantly increased, clothing utilization (i.e., the average number of times clothes are worn before they cease to be utilized) has decreased by 36 per cent globally, and most seriously by 70 per cent in China. Globally customers have been wasting US$460 billion each year by dumping clothes even though they are still fit to wear (Ellen MacArthur Foundation 2017).

As the sales–utilization gap in the fashion industry has become more intensified, there have been increasing concerns about corporate social responsibility (CSR) and sustainability through which the fashion industry has an impact on society and the environment (e.g., Pedersen et al. 2018). As a result, companies in the fashion industry have begun to recognize the importance of a transition towards a circular economy (Fischer and Pascucci 2017; Kirchherr et al. 2017; Prieto-Sandoval et al. 2018), as stakeholders are more aware of the importance of the removal of non-recyclable, non-renewable and non-reusable waste from our ecosystem in a fundamental way. The circular economy is regarded as an important approach in achieving sustainable environmental and economic development (Korhonen et al. 2018).

In this chapter, we discuss the definition of circular economy and review its key dimensions (3Rs), such as reduce, reuse, and recycle. In particular, three innovative business cases – Patagonia, I:CO, and Spiber – are discussed as examples of sustainable companies implementing the key dimensions of circular economy in the fashion industry. We argue that a circular economy perspective will improve the overall environmental and social responsibility of the fashion industry. Furthermore, utilizing circular solutions in the fashion industry provides an opportunity to create new profitable businesses.

THEORETICAL BACKGROUND

Conceptual Framework: Circular Economy

A circular economy involves employing the natural cycles of the earth (i.e., the end of one life is the basis for the beginning of another life). This concept contrasts to the linear model of production (i.e., 'take-make-dispose') in which materials are extracted, products are manu-factured, and consumers use and ultimately discard the produced goods (Pitt and Heinemeyer 2015). As such, the circular economy "requires eco-innovations to close the loop of the prod-ucts lifecycle, get valuable products to others from waste and solve the needs of environmental resilience" (Prieto-Sandoval et al. 2018, p. 605).

Fundamentally, a circular economy differs from a linear economy and necessitates a para-digm shift. Simply put, in a linear economy, raw materials are extracted, produced, used, and then disposed of. However, in a circular economy, the cycle of all these raw materials is closed (i.e., the loop among extraction, production, and post-use is closed) (Bocken et al. 2016). This closed cycle necessitates a broader approach than simply recycling raw materials. Circular economy is based on the "careful alignment and management of resource flows across the value chain by integrating reverse logistics, design innovation, collaborative ecosystem, and business model innovation" (Goyal et al. 2018, p. 730). Specifically, the circular economy is often viewed as "operationalization for businesses to implement the much-debated concept of sustainable development" (Kirchherr et al. 2017, p. 227). As such, what is required is for a company to change how it creates and preserves value, namely, the business model itself.

Fashion Industry

Over the last decades, clothing production has significantly increased; however, the way fashion companies do business has been almost completely in a linear way. This trend is also exacerbated with the increased popularity of 'fast fashion' business models (Ellen MacArthur Foundation 2017). The business model of fast fashion companies, such as H&M, Zara, Top Shop, and Uniqlo is characterized by the frequent introduction of new styles, low prices, and efficient supply chain.

However, while fast fashion is often regarded as one of the most important innovations in the fashion industry (Cachon and Swinney 2011), there has been increasing criticism of the current business model of the fashion industry, since the production, distribution, and con-sumption are extremely wasteful and polluting (Ellen MacArthur Foundation 2017). Indeed, the negative impacts of the fashion industry could be catastrophic, especially with the rapidly growing demand for clothing. Furthermore, as a result, fashion companies face reputational risks and regulatory requirements, given the social context within which consumers' behav-iours evolve according to shifts in societal interest (Hiquet et al. 2018). In other words, con-sumers begin to perceive the conflict between individual interest (i.e., cheap price of fashion products) vs. social interest (i.e., high social environmental and social cost for the society).

3Rs Dimensions of Circular Economy: Reduce, Reuse, and Recycle

As interest in the circular economy grows and the influence of fashion companies on the environment and society increases, scholars (e.g., Goyal et al. 2018; Todeschini et al. 2017) identified key aspects of circular economy, such as 3Rs (reduce, reuse, and recycle). While the concept of circular economy is often operationalized differently (Reike et al. 2018), this chapter follows the most well-adopted framework. Specifically, based on the analysis of 114 circular economy definitions, Kirchherr and colleagues (2017) noted that circular economy is frequently depicted as a combination of reduce, reuse, and recycle activities. Table 5.1 summarizes how each of 3R dimensions suggests alternative models with related examples.

Table 5.1   *3Rs: alternative models and examples*

	Alternative model	Example
Reduce	Reduce-make-dispose model	Producers use animal manure to produce paper
Reuse	Share-reuse-prolong model (Tse et al. 2015)	Airplane parts are reused in a new craft
Recycle	Take-make-recycle model (Goyal et al. 2018)	Fabrics go to textile recyclers and are used as industrial rags

Reduce

The adoption of *reduce* dimension involves the utilization of resources during production and consumption, especially non-renewable and toxic raw materials. Fundamentally, this approach focuses on decreasing the demand for new raw materials, and thereby contributing to sustainability. For example, paper production requires cellulose pulp and fibres from trees. Recently, some companies produce paper from the manure of animals (e.g., elephant, horse, and cow), thereby decreasing the use of trees in paper production (Goyal et al. 2018). In this regard, the *reduce* dimension tries to transform the take-make-dispose model to 'reduce-make-dispose' model, which emphasizes the reduction of raw materials.

Reuse

Reuse refers to "various means for prolonging the practical service life of textile products by transferring them to new owners" (Sandin and Peters 2018, p. 354). The key aspect of the reuse dimension is to extend the functional lifecycle of the product. For example, some airplane parts, including galley carts, overhead bins, and trays, can be reused in a new aircraft. Also, French automaker Renault redesigns certain components, such as gearboxes to improve the reuse ratio (World Economic Forum 2014). This reuse dimension aims to transform the traditional take-make-dispose model to the share-reuse-prolong model (Tse et al. 2015).

Recycle

Recycling is converting materials from after-use products to produce different products. In particular, textile recycling specifically refers to "the reprocessing of pre-or post-consumer textile waste for use in new textile or non-textile products" (Sandin and Peters 2018, p. 354). While recycling is relatively well adopted in the fashion industry, a number of studies (e.g., Roos et al. 2017) argue the great potential of further recycling as fashion products are disposed of before the end of their technical lifecycle.

For example, currently, most recycling in the fashion industry is *downcycling* (i.e., clothing is used to produce low-grade blankets). In contrast to downcycling, *upcycling* is the recycling of materials to produce new goods that have equal or higher quality, value, and utility than the original products (Dissanayake and Sinha 2015). As upcycling involves the creative reuse of textile waste to create better quality products, it also becomes a source of competitive advantage in the fashion industry (Todeschini et al. 2017). This approach allows for the creation of original or unique products from what one may consider to be waste. As such, from a business viewpoint, it is an efficient way of value creation by utilizing leftover materials (Park 2015).

BUSINESS CASE STUDIES

This chapter introduces three business cases to show how creatively 3Rs dimensions have been implemented in each organization. These cases are selected through purposive sampling to ensure that each case provides an in-depth description of business activities based on the circular economy.

Patagonia

Patagonia, a US outdoor clothing company, is well recognized for its with pro-social, pro-environmental activities around the world (O'Rourke and Strand 2017). In terms of the circular economy perspective, they repair, reuse, and recycle their products through a 'Worn Wear' programme. Specifically, Patagonia began to collect used clothes from their customers since 2005 through a 'Common Threads' programme that later changed its name to 'Worn Wear'. Moreover, by cooperating with Japanese textile companies, such as Teijin and Toray, Patagonia broadened the type of clothes materials they can recycle, such as wool, polyester, and nylon (Patagonia, n.d.-a). According to an article issued by Patagonia, 6,797 pounds of its products were recycled in 2018 (Patagonia, n.d.-b).

By further utilizing the concepts of reduce, reuse, and repair (Patagonia, n.d.-a), the company focuses on reducing the negative impact on the environment through reusing old clothes by repairing them. The renamed 'Worn Wear' programme continued to focus on repairing and recycling their old products (Patagonia, n.d.-a). In order to minimize the negative impact on the natural environment, 'Worn Wear' focuses on extending the lifecycle of its products through reducing (i.e., repairing), reusing, and recycling (Patagonia, n.d.-c). According to the Waste and Resources Action Programme (WRAP) (2012), 20 per cent of water-related waste and 30 per cent of carbon footprint can be saved through this programme.

In terms of *reducing*, Patagonia takes a repairing approach that focuses on lowering the demand for new raw materials, and thereby contributing to sustainability (Patagonia, n.d.-c). If people can repair their products on their own, then it will help them spend less money on buying new clothes, which finally reduces garment production along with raw materials and corresponding level of pollution. Patagonia cooperates with IFIXIT, a web-based company that provides manuals for fixing and caring for products, and through the IFIXIT webpage, customers can access out manuals for removing stains and caring for the fabrics of their Patagonia products (Patagonia, n.d.-c).

Patagonia has developed a *reusing* system as well. They resell used clothing with stamps. They collect used products and clean them and mark the date and price of products using a stamp in order to prevent abuse of the return process (Patagonia, n.d.-d). Patagonia keeps encouraging their customers to reuse their products every nine months of the extended life of their clothes through the 'Worn Wear' programme.

In the final stage, if clothing is non-functional or fully worn out, it is *recycled* through three steps: (1) collecting used Patagonia clothes from customers in the world, (2) upcycling products into new Patagonia clothing, (3) if upcycling is not possible, mechanically and chemically disassembled clothes are recycled into materials for industrial purposes (Patagonia, n.d.-d). Specifically, they collect used products and produce upcycled clothes, and sell these handmade recrafted items through their online store. Through these three steps, most Patagonia clothes are recycled in a closed-loop process. As a result, the amount of clothes that are incinerated or dumped in landfills can be minimized.

I:CO

I:CO (originally named I Collect) is not a single entity, but a collector and an international circular solutions provider. The collection of clothes is a critical part of implementing a circular material flow in the industry because materials from customers should be brought back to producers in order to be reused or recycled (Leonas 2017; Carlsson et al. 2015). Currently, an increasing number of clothing companies (e.g., Bestseller, Boomerang, Filippa K, Gina Tricot, H&M, Indiska, KappAhl, and Lindex) have been collaborating with I:CO (Stål and Corvellec 2018). I:CO developed a take-back system and organized the global logistics network in more than 60 countries to achieve their mission. There are approximately 61 million items of clothing and shoes collected, and more than 40 partners (I:CO, n.d.-a). In order to achieve sustainability in this textile waste stream, I:CO provides reverse logistics solutions (i.e., take-back system) and conducts relevant activities, including sorting, reselling, and recycling (Sandvik and Stubbs 2019).

The I:CO take-back system provides retailers and customers with a logistics network that can improve the level of resource utilization in a closed recycling loop by the following procedure (I:CO, n.d.-b). Specifically, the I:CO webpage details three steps. First, participating retail stores are supposed to receive used clothing or shoes from their customers, regardless of brand, and provide incentives to customers for their return. I:CO collects clothing and shoes from their partners and sorts them by hand to categorize them according to the needs of the partners. Second, categorized clothing and shoes are identified based on whether they are wearable or not. Wearable items are stored and sold as secondary goods. Items that cannot be worn are separated into materials for reuse. Third, some materials from unwearable items, such as recovered fibres, can be used within the textile industry for the production of new clothing or shoes. Some materials are reused for products in various industries. For example, fibre is used to make insulation materials in the construction industry.

Thus, I:CO is adopting a *reuse* and *recycling* dimension. I:CO is a second-hand trading platform with a worldwide network that promotes circulation and increases the efficiency of the reuse dimension. Also, I:CO engages in an upcycling practice that operates an innovative logistics system to convert discarded materials into high-quality products. Overall, I:CO makes a unique contribution to the circular economy through the partners' collective efforts.

Spiber

Founded in 2007, Spiber is a Japanese biomaterials company, specializing in synthetic spider silk and other protein-based materials (Spiber 2020). Spiber produces a material that mimics nature called 'Spider's Brewed Protein™' for the fashion industry. According to Spiber (n.d.), Brewed Protein™ is produced through a fermentation process that utilizes sugars and microbes derived from nature, not petrochemicals or animal-derived materials. Spiber believes that protein-based materials will have a positive impact on the sustainability of the world and has collaborated with fashion brands such as The North Face and Yuima Nakazato (Spiber 2020).

Table 5.2   A summary of circular economy cases

Company	Reduce	Reuse	Recycle
Patagonia	Patagonia cooperates with IFIXIT, a web-based company that provides manuals for repairing and caring products for customers. Motivating customers to repair products is a fundamental way to reduce material uses for production.	Patagonia resells used clothing with stamps. To do so, Patagonia collects and cleans used products, and then marks the date and price of products using a stamp in order to prevent abuse of the return process.	Patagonia upcycles old products and sells them through its online store. If upcycling is not possible, mechanically and chemically disassembled clothes are recycled into materials for industrial purposes.
I:CO	I:CO aims to reduce the use of resources by improving the level of resource utilization	I:CO is a collecting agency. It collects clothing and shoes from its partners across brands, and categorizes them based on whether they are wearable or not. Wearable items are sold as secondary goods.	Items that cannot be worn are recycled to be used within the textile industry for the production of new clothing or shoes.
Spiber	Spiber reduces harmful petrochemicals by producing a biodegradable material that mimics nature. Spiber's Brewed Protein™ is produced through a fermentation process that utilizes sugars and microbes derived from nature.	N/A	N/A

Brewed Protein™ is inspired by the silk of spider, which is stretchy and strong. For example, the silk released by the Madagascan bark spider can stretch up to 25 metres, and the silk made by the *C. darwini* spider is known as 'the toughest thread' because it is even stronger than steel (Bourzac 2015). The most important and attractive property of silk is that it is environmentally friendly and biocompatible due to its organic nature. Brewed Protein™ can be processed into a variety of forms, from dedicated fibres such as silk to wool that absorbs heat and moisture well (Spiber, n.d.). There are several ethical and environmental benefits of using it (Spiber, n.d.). First of all, it is bio-based, and thus can be designed to be renewable and does not create microplastics in the ocean. It is also ethical in that it does not require any animal-derived ingredients. It even emits fewer greenhouse gases during production compared to animal fibre.

Spiber is largely adopting a *reduce* dimension. The essence of the dimension is to turn harmful ingredients into 'good' ones that do not harm humans and nature. With the use of toxic ingredients, products are not sustainable and cannot be cycled within the industry. Spiber understands this and works to achieve a circular economy with good materials. Brewed Protein™, a biodegradable and sustainable material, can be used to produce not only fashion items but also a wide variety of products from medical to household goods (Spiber, n.d.). Table 5.2 summarizes the 3Rs dimensions of these case studies.

FACTORS FACILITATING CIRCULAR ECONOMY

Sustainability concerns (e.g., high water usage, disposal of a large number of unsold stocks, and pollution from chemical treatment during production) in the fashion industry fundamentally come from the gap between production and utilization of clothing. Overproduction causes

Table 5.3   *Factors facilitating circular economy dimensions*

	Key factors
Firm	Financial and organizational resources
	Advanced technological solutions
	Managerial awareness and attention
Industry	Availability of best practice (at industry level)
	Industry-level collaborative action
Government	Legal and regulatory requirements
	Governmental supports (i.e., financial support and tax policies)
Consumers	Consumer's responsible consumption behaviour
	Satisfaction level from engaging in sustainable consumption

problems like higher usage of water and petrochemicals as well as severe environmental pollution, whereas underutilization also engenders problems like huge disposal of unsold products through landfilling and incineration. As such, the fashion industry could be more sustainable by closing the gap between production and utilization. From a circular economy standpoint, this goal can be achieved through reducing, reusing, and recycling dimensions (Goyal et al. 2018; Todeschini et al. 2017).

Although establishing the system of circular economy (3Rs) in the fashion industry may be beneficial to all involved stakeholders, it is not always easy to implement. Previous studies (e.g., Kirchherr et al. 2018) have discussed several barriers and enablers such as cultural, market, regulatory, and technological factors. There are some key factors in the fashion industry that may enable or hinder circular systems from being implemented successfully. Key factors facilitating circular economy dimensions are summarized in Table 5.3. It is important to have a multidimensional, dynamic, and integrative approach with multiple actors (De Jesus and Mendonça 2018).

Firm Factors

Individual firms in the fashion industry should be the ones most accountable for sustainability. First, establishing sustainability measures involves substantial costs and investments (Oh et al. 2019). For instance, implementing a recycling plan generally entails investments requiring financial and organizational resources. Thus, financial and organizational resources could serve as an enabler when affordable or a barrier otherwise.

Second, it is cost-efficient for firms to use the technologies that are already in place and also depend on their existing suppliers. As such, some firms may not be able to adopt more advanced technological solutions or disruptive procedures, which can contribute to a circular economy model (Trianni and Cagno 2012). Thus, maintaining technological skills and seeking innovative solutions for sustainable development could serve as an enabler or a barrier when they are lagging behind or absent.

Last, managerial awareness on the importance of sustainability (e.g., Oh et al. 2016) is also a key factor. While the implementation of sustainable approaches requires a substantial investment during the initial stage, in the long run, it can be beneficial for organizations by improving the operational efficiency of their resources, both financially and environmentally. Besides, managers should be aware of the value of creating a good image for consumers as an additional benefit (Ellen MacArthur Foundation 2017). As such, it is a key for the circular system to be successful whether top managers are aware of and pay attention to the benefits of the circular model.

Industry Factors

The success of circular economy for the fashion industry can be achieved through the collective actions of companies within a network of industries. First, the fashion industry needs to make improvements in the production process readily available to all manufacturers varying in capacity. In fact, most textile plants are small to medium enterprises (SMEs) and operate on limited budgets and human resources. Making best practice cases available would allow SMEs to benefit from cost savings and enable them to reduce their own resource usage. As such, allowing SMEs to have opportunities to learn the best practice could be an enabler to make the circular model successful or a barrier otherwise.

Second, the adoption of sustainability measures often requires high upfront costs with a long-term payoff, and thus this is a substantial burden to individual manufacturers. To reduce the burden of each participant, the fashion industry needs to develop industry-level long-term collaborative action (Hiquet and Oh 2019). Specifically, Van Tulder (2012, p. 8) noted that "most of the issues we face today are neither owned nor solved by individual stakeholders anymore. With growing interdependence comes a growing need to search for collaborative approaches." Brands and retailers could collaboratively leverage their scale to invest in sustainable manufacturing to improve resource utilization. Thus, establishing an industry-level collaboration could be an enabler to make a circular model successful.

Governmental Factors

Governmental factors are mainly associated with concerns for legislative strength (*stick*) and governmental supports (*carrot*). The legal and regulatory requirements serve as a powerful signal for all participants regarding what and how much they should be concerned about the circular economy. At the same time, individual producers are often encouraged to adopt sustainable measures by governmental supports, such as financial support and tax policies (Moffat and Auer 2006). However, what makes the circular model most successful depends upon how well these two concerns are integrated and balanced since ineffective policies would pose administrative and financial burdens for businesses to adopt sustainable measures.

Consumer Factors

A lack of consumer interest and awareness is considered one of the major circular economy barriers (Kirchherr et al. 2018). Recently, consumers are increasingly challenging business practices of conventional fashion business models (e.g., through consumer boycott), and often engage in responsible purchase behaviours (Hiquet et al. 2018). As such, it is critical for consumers whether or not they have a positive experience in practising sustainable consumption behaviours (e.g., repairing or reusing their owned clothing by themselves, or purchasing reused/upcycled products). The greater the consumer's positive experience, the higher the company's chances of realizing benefits from it.

DISCUSSION

The fashion industry is forecasted to continue to grow, particularly due to a substantial growth of clothing consumption in the emerging markets – for instance in Asia and Africa – yet faces a huge challenge of sustainability concerns at the same time. According to the Ellen MacArthur Foundation (2017), more than $500 billion is lost because of clothing underutilization and the lack of sustainable textile use (e.g., reduce, reuse, and recycle). This is an important challenge for the fashion industry, which faces not only economic losses but also ecological imbalance and environmental impact.

The fashion industry and consumers have become increasingly aware of the detrimental impact of the current linear system of production (Hiquet et al. 2018). Fashion companies have begun to address environmental challenges with their supply chains through industry-wide endeavours. However, most of these efforts have focused on decreasing the negative impact of the linear model, such as reducing the impact of materials or adopting more efficient production techniques, rather than addressing the root-cause problems of the entire production system, such as low clothing utilization as well as reinforcing the circular system. As such, this chapter aims to inform why the circular system matters to the fashion industry and describe some key enablers and barriers for the system along with three novel business cases to show how circular economy can be realized in this field.

Insights from Business Cases

Our first case is Patagonia. Patagonia is well known for its commitment to society and the environment. Patagonia takes a holistic approach to sustainability by taking full advantage of the 3Rs. Patagonia *reduces* the material use by helping customers be more responsible for their consumption, *reuses* products by reselling the used ones, and *recycles* products for other industrial purposes. For Patagonia, every part of a firm's value chain activity seems to be operated to achieve its sustainability goals.

Second, I:CO is good evidence that collective actions at the industry level can be a crucial catalyst for the circular economy. As a collecting agency, I:CO focuses on the collection of clothes based on the belief that collection is an initial, but critical part of circular material flow in the fashion industry, since clothes from customers can be brought back to producers to be *reused* or *recycled*.

Lastly, Spiber shows why circular models need to be innovative. As alternative sustainable approaches are becoming popular in other fields (e.g., protein-based meats and chicken), Spiber produces raw ingredients for clothing through a fermentation process that utilizes sugars and microbes derived from nature. This innovative process fundamentally *reduces* harmful petrochemicals and pollutions from manufacturing.

In summary, our business cases show how the adoption of 3Rs activities can fundamentally transform business operations away from relying on non-renewable use of resources towards more sustainable production and consumption. Specifically, four lessons are identified from these case studies.

- *Creating value from waste.* This is achieved by alternative ways of creating and capturing value. For example, Patagonia successfully creates both social and economic value from old products.

- *Network innovation*. As shown in the case of I:CO, an international collecting organization, and Patagonia's cooperation with IFIXIT, a circular economy can be realized through working in symbiosis with other companies.
- *Process and product innovation*. Companies need to develop new ways to make their products and improve the quality and functionality of the products, as depicted in the case of Spiber's bio-based production.
- *Material efficiency optimization*. By closing the loops for waste, materials are used with optimized efficiency. As shown in Patagonia's case, clothes can be recycled in a closed-loop process, thus improving material efficiency.

Advice for Stakeholders, Industry, and Policymakers

All stakeholders involved should be aware that the circular economy will improve social responsibility, environmental impact, and eventually sustainability of the fashion industry. Specifically, fashion companies should recognize that utilizing circular solutions also provides a new avenue to create new profitable businesses, and thus serves as an investment opportunity (Oh et al. 2019), rather than additional costs. In order to improve customers' participation in circular economy, fashion companies should make consumers' sustainable efforts easier and more accessible. Policymakers also need to design appropriate legal and regulatory requirements as well as provide incentives to encourage sustainable practices (e.g., McDowall et al. 2017), such as financial support and tax subsidies. In particular, despite a shared conceptual basis and common goals, it should be noted that circular economy policymakers face different industrial structures and governance systems in different countries (McDowall et al. 2017). In sum, all stakeholders' engagement in sustainable practices based on circular economy, which are less dependent on the consumption of energy and materials, leads to restoring and regenerating natural capital by redefining the business models.

REFERENCES

Bocken, N. M., De Pauw, I., Bakker, C., & van der Grinten, B. (2016). Product design and business model strategies for a circular economy. *Journal of Industrial and Production Engineering*, 33(5), 308–320.
Bourzac, K. (2015). Web of intrigue. *Nature*, 519(7544), S4.
Cachon, G. P., & Swinney, R. (2011). The value of fast fashion: Quick response, enhanced design, and strategic consumer behavior. *Management Science*, 57(4), 778–795.
Carlsson, J., Torstensson, H., Pal, R., & Paras, M. K. (2015). *Re: Textile – Planning a Swedish Collection and Sorting Plant for Used Textiles*. Borås: University of Borås.
De Jesus, A., & Mendonça, S. (2018). Lost in transition? Drivers and barriers in the eco-innovation road to the circular economy. *Ecological Economics*, 145, 75–89.
Dissanayake, G., & Sinha, P. (2015). An examination of the product development process for fashion remanufacturing. *Resources, Conservation and Recycling*, 104, 94–102.
Ellen MacArthur Foundation (2017). *A New Textiles Economy: Redesigning Fashion's Future*. https://www.ellenmacarthurfoundation.org/assets/downloads/publications/A-New-Textiles-Economy_Full-Report.pdf.
Fischer, A., & Pascucci, S. (2017). Institutional incentives in circular economy transition: The case of material use in the Dutch textile industry. *Journal of Cleaner Production*, 155, 17–32.

Gazzola, P., Pavione, E., Pezzetti, R., & Grechi, D. (2020). Trends in the fashion industry. The perception of sustainability and circular economy: A gender/generation quantitative approach. *Sustainability*, 12(7), 2809.

Goyal, S., Esposito, M., & Kapoor, A. (2018). Circular economy business models in developing economies: Lessons from India on reduce, recycle, and reuse paradigms. *Thunderbird International Business Review*, 60(5), 729–740.

Hiquet, R., Brunneder, J., & Oh, W. Y. (2018). From myopia to boycott: Consumer acceptance of, and resistance to, fast fashion. In C. Becker-Leifhold & M. Heuer (eds.), *Eco-Friendly and Fair: Fast Fashion and Consumer Behaviour*. London: Routledge, 58–68.

Hiquet, R., & Oh, W. Y. (2019). Ethics issues in outsourcing to emerging markets: Theoretical perspectives and practices. In O. Osuji, F. N. Ngwu, & D. Jamali (eds.), *Corporate Social Responsibility in Developing and Emerging Markets: Institutions, Actors and Sustainable Development*. Cambridge: Cambridge University Press, 336–347.

I:CO (n.d.-a). *Mission*. http://www.ico-spirit.com/en/homepage/mission/.

I:CO (n.d.-b). *Services*. https://www.ico-spirit.com/en/services/.

Kirchherr, J., Piscicelli, L., Bour, R., Kostense-Smit, E., Muller, J., Huibrechtse-Truijens, A., & Hekkert, M. (2018). Barriers to the circular economy: Evidence from the European Union (EU). *Ecological Economics*, 150, 264–272.

Kirchherr, J., Reike, D., & Hekkert, M. (2017). Conceptualizing the circular economy: An analysis of 114 definitions. *Resources, Conservation and Recycling*, 127, 221–232.

Korhonen, J., Nuur, C., Feldmann, A., & Birkie, S. E. (2018). Circular economy as an essentially contested concept. *Journal of Cleaner Production*, 175, 544–552.

Leonas, K. K. (2017). The use of recycled fibers in fashion and home products. In S. S. Muthu (ed.), *Textiles and Clothing Sustainability: Textile Science and Clothing Technology*. Singapore: Springer, 55–77.

McDowall, W., Geng, Y., Huang, B., Barteková, E., Bleischwitz, R., Türkeli, S., Kemp, R., & Doménech, T. (2017). Circular economy policies in China and Europe. *Journal of Industrial Ecology*, 21(3), 651–661.

Moffat, A., & Auer, A. (2006). Corporate environmental innovation (CEI): A government initiative to support corporate sustainability leadership. *Journal of Cleaner Production*, 14, 589–600.

Oh, W. Y., Choi, K. J., Chang, Y. K., & Jeon, M. K. (2019). MNEs' corporate social responsibility: An optimal investment decision model. *European Journal of International Management*, 13(3), 307–327.

Oh, W. Y., Li, Z., & Park, S. (2016). The effects of CEO characteristics and incentives on corporate social responsibility. In R. Manos & I. Drori (eds.), *Corporate Responsibility: Social Actions, Institutions and Governance*. London: Palgrave Macmillan, 162–182.

O'Rourke, D., & Strand, R. (2017). Patagonia: Driving sustainable innovation by embracing tensions. *California Management Review*, 60(1), 102–125.

Park, H. H. (2015). The influence of LOHAS consumption tendency and perceived consumer effectiveness on trust and purchase intention regarding upcycling fashion goods. *International Journal of Human Ecology*, 16(1), 37–47.

Patagonia (n.d.-a). *Closing the Loop: A Report on Patagonia's Common Threads Garment Recycling Program*. https://www.patagonia.com/stories/closing-the-loop-a-report-on-patagonias-common -threads-garment-recycling-program/story-19961.html.

Patagonia (n.d.-b). *Recycling Is Broken. Now What.* https://www.patagonia.com/stories/recycling-is -broken-now-what/story-73479.html.

Patagonia (n.d.-c). *FAQ. Worn Wear.* https://wornwear.patagonia.com/faq.

Patagonia (n.d.-d). *Patagonia Post-Consumer Recycling Strategy & Upcycling Policy.* https://www .patagonia.com/static/on/demandware.static/-/Library-Sites-PatagoniaShared/default/dw2ca0a0c1/ PDF-US/Patagonia-Global-Recycling-Strategy-and-Upcycling-Policy.pdf.

Pedersen, E. R. G., Gwozdz, W., & Hvass, K. K. (2018). Exploring the relationship between business model innovation, corporate sustainability, and organisational values within the fashion industry. *Journal of Business Ethics*, 149(2), 267–284.

Pitt, J., & Heinemeyer, C. (2015). Introducing ideas of a circular economy. In K. Stables & S. Keirl (eds.), *Environment, Ethics and Cultures*. Rotterdam: Sense Publishers, 245–260.

Prieto-Sandoval, V., Jaca, C., & Ormazabal, M. (2018). Towards a consensus on the circular economy. *Journal of Cleaner Production*, 179, 605–615.

Reike, D., Vermeulen, W. J., & Witjes, S. (2018). The circular economy: New or refurbished as CE 3.0? Exploring controversies in the conceptualization of the circular economy through a focus on history and resource value retention options. *Resources, Conservation and Recycling*, 135, 246–264.

Roos, S., Sandin, G., Zamani, B., Peters, G., & Svanström, M. (2017). Will clothing be sustainable? Clarifying sustainable fashion. In S. S. Muthu (ed.), *Textiles and Clothing Sustainability: Textile Science and Clothing Technology*. Singapore: Springer, 1–45.

Sandin, G., & Peters, G. M. (2018). Environmental impact of textile reuse and recycling: A review. *Journal of Cleaner Production*, 184, 353–365.

Sandvik, I. M., & Stubbs, W. (2019). Circular fashion supply chain through textile-to-textile recycling. *Journal of Fashion Marketing and Management*, 23(3), 366–381.

Spiber (2020). *About Us.* https://www.spiber.jp/en/about/.

Spiber (n.d.). *Brewed Protein™.* https://www.spiber.jp/en/brewedprotein/.

Stål, H. I., & Corvellec, H. (2018). A decoupling perspective on circular business model implementation: Illustrations from Swedish apparel. *Journal of Cleaner Production*, 171, 630–643.

Todeschini, B. V., Cortimiglia, M. N., Callegaro-de-Menezes, D., & Ghezzi, A. (2017). Innovative and sustainable business models in the fashion industry: Entrepreneurial drivers, opportunities, and challenges. *Business Horizons*, 60(6), 759–770.

Trianni, A., & Cagno, E. (2012). Dealing with barriers to energy efficiency and SMEs: Some empirical evidences. *Energy*, 37(1), 494–504.

Tse, T., Esposito, M., & Soufani, K. (2015). Why the circular economy matters. *European Business Review*. http://www.europeanbusinessreview.com/?p=8372.

Van Tulder, R. (2012). Foreword: The necessity of multi-stakeholder initiatives. In M. M. Huijstee, *Multi-Stakeholder Initiatives: A Strategic Guide for Civil Society Organizations*. Amsterdam: SOMO, 8–9.

Waste and Resources Action Programme (WRAP) (2012). *Valuing Our Clothes: The Evidence Base.* https://www.wrap.org.uk/sites/files/wrap.

World Economic Forum (WEF) (2014). *Towards the Circular Economy: Accelerating the Scale-Up across Global Supply Chains.* http://www3.weforum.org/docs/WEF_ENV_Towards_CircularEconomy_Report_2014.pdf.

6. From vision to commercialization of a circular economy innovation: a longitudinal study of overcoming challenges throughout the full innovation process[1]

Jenni Kaipainen and Leena Aarikka-Stenroos

INTRODUCTION

Although circular economy (CE) is expected to drive sustainable development (Ghisellini et al. 2016), to date it remains unclear how real-life firms can realize CE's promises (Brown et al. 2021; De Jesus and Mendonça 2018). What we know by far is that minor adjustments are not enough; we crucially need innovation to fuel CE (De Jesus and Mendonça 2018; Jakobsen et al., Chapter 1 in this volume) and sustainable business (Goodman et al. 2017; Seebode et al. 2012). Yet, more research is needed under the particular lens of innovation management (De Jesus and Mendonça 2018) to overcome the challenges of circularity (Geissdoerfer et al. 2017). In this chapter, we address this need by investigating firm-level CE innovation as a longitudinal process requiring support from diverse actors.

With innovation, we emphasize process perspective over outcome, and refer to a novel technology, product or service that involves marketing and/or technological discontinuity, is diffused beyond the innovator firm, and provides economic value (Garcia and Calantone 2002). Firms' innovation strategy focuses on creating this value, allocating resources, and managing trade-offs (Pisano 2015) while innovator firms execute innovation process activities from visioning to commercialization. As both the innovation process and innovation strategy involve continual processes of experimentation, learning, and adaptation (Pisano 2015), a process perspective is essential in innovating. Firms need to rethink their innovation processes particularly when implementing CE (Aarikka-Stenroos et al. 2021), as sustainable innovating goes beyond firms' core activities (Mousavi and Bossink 2017) and challenges them to abandon old practices (Seebode et al. 2012). However, processes of sustainable (Seebode et al. 2012; Wicki and Hansen 2019) and CE innovating (Brown et al. 2021) remain underexplored. Therefore, we consider a processual approach necessary for capturing the challenges and needed actions throughout overarching CE innovating.

Innovating challenges are not limited to the innovator firm, but often relate to managing diverse actors in the encompassing innovation ecosystem (Adner 2006). For CE innovating, expertise needs to be compiled from various actors (Ghisellini et al. 2016), which is why identifying and involving them is critical (Brown et al. 2021). To understand how actor diversity and their engagement (Driessen and Hillebrand 2013) can support the full innovating process, particularly for CE (Brown et al. 2021; De Jesus and Mendonça 2018; Jakobsen et al., Chapter 1 in this volume) and sustainability (Goodman et al. 2017; Wicki and Hansen 2019), more empirical evidence is needed (Aarikka-Stenroos et al. 2014). When innovating for sustainability in complex environments – such as CE ecosystems (Aarikka-Stenroos et al. 2021) – participating actors may co-evolve during the process (Seebode et al. 2012). Investigating such actor dynamics over time calls for processual (Brown et al. 2021) and longitudinal (Phillips and Ritala 2019) research approaches, which remain currently underexplored.

Addressing the gaps and firms' pragmatic need to realize sustainable CE business, this chapter examines from a firm perspective a longitudinal CE innovation strategy and process, occurring from early vision to global commercialization with support from diverse actors. Our research goal is to learn "How can a firm, together with its ecosystem actors, realize sustainable innovating despite the challenges of the CE innovation process?"

To best respond, we take a critical forerunner case that allows a longitudinal investigation of diverse actors and actions in CE innovating. The selected case, Neste Oyj, demonstrates a radical, even disruptive innovation process for renewable energy production, a field considered particularly challenging for CE (Ghisellini et al. 2016). Radical innovation refers to novelties that – from the customer and market perspectives – change behaviours and consumption patterns and require learning on the part of the target market, value chain and customers (Chiesa and Frattini 2011). From the innovator firm perspective, radical innovations are challenging to manage, as they create new business lines, requiring the firm to face unfamiliar product categories and infrastructures (Aarikka-Stenroos et al. 2014). Our case displays these features over an innovating period of 25 years, which required both the markets and the firm to learn and adapt for successful, radical CE innovation.

The chapter is structured as follows. First, we discuss innovation processes in the light of innovation, technology, and business management research. Then, we provide an illustrative analysis of the case study's 25-year CE innovation strategy and process. Last, we discuss the findings, and sum up the contributions for CE and innovation management literature as well as pragmatic implications, and provide avenues for future research.

THEORETICAL BACKGROUND ON INNOVATION PROCESSES AND ACTORS

Diverse conceptualizations and theoretical models illustrate how innovation and innovating occur as a process. Conventionally conceptualized, linear process models, comprise front-end or ideation and visioning, research and technical development and commercialization (including launching, facing markets, and disseminating the innovation) (see, e.g., Chiesa and Frattini 2011). In contrast, more iterative models have also been suggested, which consider commercialization and technical development/R&D as parallel and complementary processes (O'Connor and Rice 2013). Because of this parallel nature, what might initially be considered a good solution can later lead to unintended problems. Hence, the process typically entails regressions and loops. In general, key characteristics of successful innovation processes are innovation and commercialization strategy and its implementation, which explain the iteration mechanism. An innovator firm takes a strategic direction with the potential innovation, refines the activities and decisions described above based on experience and then modifies the innovation strategy and implementation for the next iteration (Lynn et al. 1996).

The process for radical innovation often begins with a vision, which drives both the innovation's technical and commercial development (O'Connor and Veryzer 2001), followed by a techno-market match analysis to define commercializability (Jolly 1997). Finally, the process moves to market learning and commercialization activities, aiming to convert the radical novelty into a commercial success (Siegel et al. 1995). For the innovator firm, radical innovation often requires learning and experimentation about the driving forces impacting innovation success, particularly in specific market contexts (Chiesa and Frattini 2011; Lynn et al. 1996). Moreover, radical innovation can develop completely new operations and value propositions along the industry and its actors (see Möller and Svahn 2009). Consequently, radical innovations have the power to expand firms' strategic frames (O'Connor and Rice 2013).

However, instead of limiting to the innovator firm's boundaries, innovating should also involve stakeholders from the surrounding multi-actor networks and ecosystems. Researchers in the field of ecosystem, network, and stakeholder research have acknowledged that engaging and involving diverse actors from the business, innovation, and knowledge ecosystems is essential for successful innovating (Aarikka-Stenroos et al. 2014). These may include other complementary and competing firms, public organizations, regulators and policymakers, experts, universities, research organizations, user communities, and associations (see Aarikka-Stenroos et al. 2014; Driessen and Hillebrand 2013). Managing the involvement of these actors throughout innovating is important as it is found to partly improve and partly complicate the process. On one hand, stakeholder diversity expands the breadth of available resources and increases learning and creativity (Driessen and Hillebrand 2013). On the other hand, actor diversity increases heterogeneity in knowledge, logics, competences, and power, and thus increases mismatches between actors' goals, understandings, and technologies, leading to risks and conflicts (Aarikka-Stenroos et al. 2017).

METHODOLOGY

Research Design and Case Selection

To best cover the overarching CE innovation process and its challenges, we follow a qualitative research design with an illustrative, extreme, and critical single-case study (Stake 1995, p. 3). Studying a single-case allows deep-diving to the *collaborative process phases and practices within a circular-oriented innovation context* (Brown et al. 2021, p. 6). Adding a longitudinal approach, we unfold the diverse incidents, activities, and stages during the studied process (Van de Ven 1992).

Having accumulated technical competences since 1948, Finnish oil refiner Neste invented a technology (NExBTL) that expands and creates new lifecycles for renewable feedstocks, waste, and residue by transforming them into renewable fuels (Neste Oil 2011). Such biomass-based fuels are considered clean, environment-friendly, and efficient renewable energy resources (Yilmaz and Atmanli 2017), advancing a major CE challenge (Ghisellini et al. 2016) by converting biowaste into energy (Vanhamäki et al. 2020). Calculated in compliance with the EU Renewable Energy Directive, NExBTL-based fuel results in 90 per cent lower greenhouse gas emissions over its lifecycle compared to fossil fuels (Neste Oil 2011).

In contrast to Neste having started with sourcing Russian raw oil and processing it in Finland, Neste nowadays collects and processes more than ten types of renewable feedstocks globally. Ensuring that the feedstocks are certified and the production complies with the EU's sustainability requirements, all NExBTL refineries have acquired third-party audited International Sustainability & Carbon Certification (ISCC) (Neste Oil 2011), governed by an association of over 140 members, including research institutes and NGOs (ISCC website). Having expanded from Northern European fossil fuel markets, Neste-branded renewable fuel is nowadays distributed to business and customer markets in Europe and Northern America. Next to road transportation fuels, the same technology is nowadays being applied to jet fuel production and adapted to research in renewable plastics. With its 25-year NExBTL-based innovation strategy, Neste has transformed from a traditional oil refiner to the world's largest renewable fuel producer, with operations in 14 countries and an approximate 40 per cent share of the world's total renewable diesel production. Such an extreme case satisfies our selection criteria by allowing investigating how a longitudinal, full CE innovation process unfolds over time.

Data Gathering, Analysis and Assuring Quality

To illustrate an in-depth, longitudinal case and creating a retrospective case history over time (Van de Ven 1992), we multisource primary data from seven semi-structured interviews of top managers, two focus groups and 16 annual reports published between 2006 and 2021. We interviewed top managers across departments to fully understand the managerial perspective in change processes (Van de Ven 1992), covering research and technology, new feedstock, marketing, sustainability, public affairs, regulation, communications, and sales departments. The interviews were followed by focus groups, one for the interviewed managers, another for the strategy team. Primary data insights were complemented and validated by diverse secondary data from trade journals, magazine and newspaper articles, firm-related presentations and lectures, news releases, blog posts, and stakeholder websites.

Following an iterative, discovery-allowing research process with abductive logics (Dubois and Gadde 2002), our analysis evolved between rich empirical findings and theory-based innovating activities. Supported by the literature review on innovation processes and actors, we mapped the case firm's innovation process and innovation ecosystem using critical incident technique and Kumu.io ecosystem software. After mapping the events, actions, and actors with year-level detail onto a timeline, we classified them according to the theory-driven key innovation process activities the incident principally contributed to: visioning and ideation, research and development, and acceleration and commercialization (see Figure 6.1), to study the emerging process patterns.

Research quality is improved with various strategies: data and informant triangulation allowed reaching data saturation and developing a critical viewpoint to the case; researcher triangulation enhanced interpreting findings with objectivity; and carefully describing the methods and context improved methodological transparency. We also validated the initial findings in focus groups and interviewee commentary rounds.

FINDINGS

We first provide an overview of the case firm's full innovation process. Then, we elaborate the process activities in more detail, explaining the key challenges, actions and supporting actors throughout the process.

NExBTL technology was invented already in 1996 but not advanced until markets and regulators showed growing interest for sustainability in early 2000s. Reacting quickly to early signals, Neste ramped up NExBTL production in 2005, yet the investment become profitable only in 2011. During the non-linear process with overlapping critical incidents (see Figure 6.1), Neste has overcome many challenges, supported by diverse actors (see Table 6.1). Although the technology has remained fairly unchanged over time, it has launched business model innovation to meet the new, sustainable value proposition (follow for example the vision updates in Figure 6.1), extend supply chain operations globally (follow feedstocks in Figure 6.1), and serve new customers and markets (follow external commercialization activities in Figure 6.1).

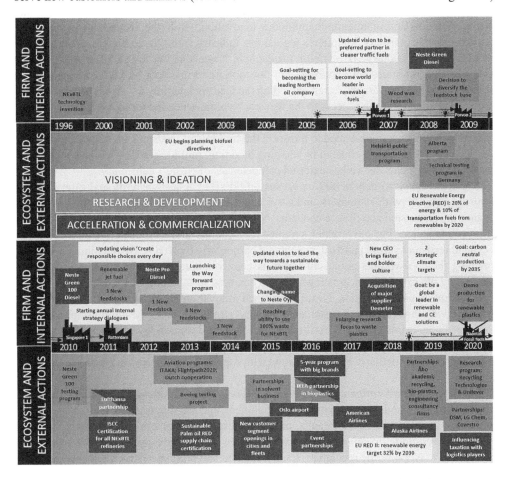

Figure 6.1   *Overview of the full CE innovation process and its critical incidents involving internal and external actions*

In *visioning and ideation*, the key challenges were inventing the technology and gaining internal support for it, while the key ecosystem actors were competitors, public audience, markets, and policymakers. To *invent the technology*, technically skilled individuals were needed and encouraged by the innovation-supporting organizational culture, originating from both experiment-encouraging leadership and Neste's technological pioneer heritage.

Regarding ecosystem actors, experimentation was motivated for maintaining competitive advantage while competitors worked with similar bio-based fuel technologies.

For ensuring *internal support for the CE invention*, sustainability-oriented strategizing and bold visioning was crucial when Neste top management evaluated future potential of the new CE-based business idea. From 2000s onwards, early signals from public, markets, and policymakers gave internal faith towards renewable fuels' future. Later in the innovation process, internal support was sealed through firm-wide strategy dialogues.

In *research and development*, the key challenges were in production scaling, answering the external concerns and maintaining continuous innovation, while the needed key actors were research-oriented partners, suppliers, regulators, industry, non-governmental organizations (NGOs), and a subsidiary. To *scale up production*, Neste was not too small in terms of not having enough resources for exploring, but not too large to neglect NExBTL because of its early marginal revenue stream. Later, extending the feedstock variety to various vegetable oils, waste and residue supported access to the feedstock volumes needed for industrial production. As one example of using residue feedstocks, Neste uses McDonald's cooking oil to produce renewable fuel, which is circulated to transport the cooking oil feedstock to Neste's production site. Scaling up was also facilitated by learning by doing, multidisciplinary competences, and cross-functional teams, as well as external competences of Neste's subsidiary.

To address the *ecosystem actors' concerns* on NExBTL's sustainability and safety, Neste discussed actively with regulators, industry, and NGOs, for which NExBTL was new. To advance the discussion and relieve concerns, Neste built credibility through third-party certifications, technical testing and research-oriented partnerships, and established supplier contracts to expand feedstocks from palm oil, questioned particularly by NGOs. By remaining open and providing their viewpoints on sustainability issues, collaborating actors supported Neste in overcoming the external concerns regarding its business sustainability.

As for *continuous innovation*, Neste maintained innovation-encouraging culture, supported by co-evolving innovation and sustainable business strategies. With the multidisciplinary and cross-functional teams as well as existing competences and technology, advancing sustainable CE accelerates new business openings in renewable jet fuels and plastics. Continuous innovation is supported particularly by collaborating with suppliers, customers, and research-oriented partners.

Challenges in *acceleration and commercialization* relate to hindering regulation, adopting launched products, and ensuring business sustainment, and are supported by regulators, industry players, competitors, NGOs, media, public discussion, customers, and research partners. To address *regulation prohibiting commercialization*, Neste keeps discussing with regulators and industry players. While regulation, standardization and product safety statements were not existing, concerns remained; as an extreme example, some even wondered if animal fat-based fuels could transmit mad cow disease. Credibility-building from the R&D stage assures ecosystem actors of product safety and influences regulation for commercialization. Additionally, competitors help in pressuring regulators along with NGOs, media, and public discussion.

Adoption of new products was facilitated by innovating emotional brand marketing and communications, a radical move for a traditional oil refiner to target new sustainability-valuing customers and public. Meanwhile, facts-based arguments were still needed for demonstrating NExBTL products' safety, technological advantages and credibility compared to fossil fuels. Additionally, feedstock expansion in the R&D stage allowed large customers to choose from different feedstocks, facilitating their adoption.

Finally, Neste *ensured its sustained business* with risky refinery investments, which in turn required securing sufficient feedstock volumes, resulting in not only establishing new supplier networks, but also supplier acquisitions. Lastly, partnering with both customers and research partners sustains long-term business.

Neste's story illustrates the challenges, overcoming actions and diverse actors needed during the CE innovation process activities. Our full findings are presented in Table 6.1 with illustrative quotations.

DISCUSSION AND LESSONS FROM THE CASE

This chapter illustrated through an extreme case how a CE innovation process can occur from an innovator firm perspective, from visioning a CE-based solution to commercializing it globally. We next discuss the lessons learnt from the case.

The concluding actor column (Table 6.1) evidently demonstrates ecosystem actors' importance for innovating activities, supporting prior literature findings (Aarikka-Stenroos et al. 2014; Driessen and Hillebrand 2013). As radical innovation develops new operations and value propositions along encompassing actors (see Möller and Svahn 2009), our findings highlight that both the importance and number of innovation-supporting actors increases along CE innovating process. Yet, even sustainability-valuing actors, particularly NGOs and regulators, can hinder the process if the credibility and value of new CE innovation is not properly communicated to them early on. Therefore, the innovator firm needs to seek for collaborations already in R&D, or even visioning. This is because most key actors in R&D activities accelerate commercializing activities later in the process: for example, suppliers expand renewable feedstocks both for R&D resources and new offerings. Similarly, research partners, NGOs, and strategic customers not only facilitate competence-building for R&D, but also build adoption-facilitating credibility. Then again, NGOs and pioneer customers accelerate the public sustainability demand, pressuring regulators to permit market openings and encouraging diffusion to customers.

The complexity of inherently challenging sustainable innovating (Wicki and Hansen 2019) manifests in the case through parallel-role actors; for example, an actor being both a customer and research partner simultaneously. When parallel roles result from the limited partner candidates in the innovation ecosystem, as we estimate to be the case here, the innovator firm needs to establish strategic partnerships with the limited partner candidates, meanwhile seeking partnerships beyond traditional ecosystem boundaries. Developing innovation ecosystem and CE innovation process seem interlinked; accordingly, accelerating the process through innovation ecosystem development is important since visioning. Despite the complexity and collaborator diversity of CE ecosystems (Aarikka-Stenroos et al. 2021), the case displays that determined ecosystem development is the key for successful CE innovating.

Our critical incident mapping shows how innovating activities overlap (see O'Connor and Rice 2013) meanwhile developing new business model innovation from technology innovation, as these innovation types can be interlinked (see Engez et al., Chapter 17 in this volume). This demonstrates also how sustainable CE requires reconfiguring innovation approaches as a major strategic undertaking (see Seebode et al. 2012), for which both innovation and business strategies need to co-develop. The found overlapping process structure also supports

Table 6.1   Challenges, overcoming actions, and diverse actors needed during CE innovation process activities

	Challenges in CE innovating	How can the firm respond to overcome the challenge?	Which ecosystem actors support overcoming the challenge; how?	Illustrative quotation from the case data
Visioning & Ideation	Inventing the technology innovation	– Innovative individuals with technical skills – Explore-encouraging organizational culture & leadership – R&D sector resourcing – Cherishing technological pioneer heritage	*Competitors* – Signalling interest in biofuels, encouraging to follow the trend and secure competitiveness via technological experiments	Young researchers in late 90s were encouraged to "*look beyond and do their thing.*" – Strategy Team
	Gaining internal support for the CE idea	– Visionary individuals in top management – Courageous and ambitious goal setting aligned with sustainable business strategy – Unifying the vision with internal dialogue, value programmes and branding	*Regulators, potential customers* – Providing early signals of emerging markets and regulation that encourage taking strategic risks with the CE innovation	"*We did not have much else than the vision that the product is good, and markets are developing, but regulation did not properly exist*" – Sustainability and Public Affairs, Senior Vice President

	Challenges in CE innovating	How can the firm respond to overcome the challenge?	Which ecosystem actors support overcoming the challenge; how?	Illustrative quotation from the case data
Research & Development	Scaling the invention to industrial production	– Firm size is suitable for allowing experimentation – Learning by doing – Building multidisciplinary competences – Cross-functional cooperation – Feedstock expansion to ensure sufficient supply	*Subsidiary* – Subsidiary's complementary competences allowed building first refineries without building first a conventional demo plant	*"When opening the world scale refineries, we went forward quite boldly even if there were big question marks in feedstock supply and markets."* – Renewables Platform, Top Manager
	Ecosystem actors questioning the product	– Active participation in ongoing discussions to learn and interact – Feedstock expansion to meet external requirements and worries related to some of the existing feedstocks – Ensuring that own operations and processes meet the requirements for third-party certification	*Third-party auditors, research-oriented partners, technical testing programmes, NGOs, customers, regulators* – Build credibility for innovation and innovator firm's competency through collaborating – Remaining open and active in ongoing discussions with the innovator to allow learning from others who value sustainability	*"The firm cooperates with local NGOs in Southeast Asia and actively supports work in the areas of legislation and certification aimed at preventing the irresponsible production of palm oil."* – Neste Annual Report 2011
	Continuous innovation	– Experiment-encouraging culture and leadership as part of sustainable strategizing – Feedstock expansion for incremental innovation – Multidisciplinary competences & cross-functional teams – Developing tech innovation into business model innovation	*Research partners, customers, suppliers* – Building technical and sustainability-related competences together – Customer cooperation for new solutions with NExBTL technology – Supplying new feedstocks to allow expanding the scope of CE innovation	*"If you want to stand out, you need to do a bit differently from others."* – Marketing, Top Manager

	Challenges in CE innovating	How can the firm respond to overcome the challenge?	Which ecosystem actors support overcoming the challenge; how?	Illustrative quotation from the case data
Acceleration & Commercialization	Regulation prohibits commercialization	– Active participation in industry discussions – Gaining particularly technical credibility through actions taken in research and development activities	*Industry associations, regulators, competitors, NGOs, media, public* – Collaborating with industry associations for awareness of regulative progress and to stay ahead of competition – Increase in the number of competitors can pressure regulators for allowing the products in new markets – NGOs, media, and public discussion increase regulator attention	*"Implementing the directive can be very different in different countries, sometimes purpose-directed, or even protectionist."* – Public Affairs & Feedstock Regulation, Top Manager
	Facilitating the adoption of launched products	– Emotional and sustainable brand marketing for new, sustainable value proposition – Product launches in new geographic areas increase diffusing the innovation – Feedstock expansion to meet customer requirements	*Customers, suppliers, public, media* – Innovation adoption through direct customer transactions – Suppliers provide feedstock variety from which big customers can choose their orders to be produced – Public audience and media share experiences and information that encourages looking for sustainable products such as NExBTL	*"We won't tell people to do anything. We wake them to think and inspire them."* – Marketing, Top Manager
	Ensuring the business sustainment	– Risk-taking in investments – Strategic acquisitions for ensuring supply – Maintaining the strategic sustainability orientation	*Customers, public; research partners, suppliers* – Strategic collaborations with customers, research partners and suppliers to expand existing business and explore new business openings over time – Increasing public interest in sustainability mega trends supports regulative development, customer acquisition, and finding suppliers	*"CE has an important role in our new strategy. Now it is the right time to advance circular solutions, like replacing raw oil with waste plastic in oil products."* – Neste Annual Report 2018

Brown et al.'s (2021) idea of involving actors in a dynamic process, engaging new partners over time for collaborative CE innovating.

CONCLUSIONS AND IMPLICATIONS

Theoretical Contributions

We enrich innovation management and CE literature with understanding of the CE innovating process, showing how firms can overcome challenges with diverse actors to implement and accelerate CE innovation over time. This culminates in two key contributions.

First, by taking the innovation management lens (De Jesus and Mendonça 2018) to study CE innovation, we build new understanding of the innovation process from a new perspective (Aarikka-Stenroos et al. 2014; O'Connor and Veryzer 2001). By taking a longitudinal approach (Phillips and Ritala 2019) to investigate the lacking yet fruitful process perspective (Wicki and Hansen 2019), we provide evidence of the looping and iterative innovation process structure (O'Connor and Rice 2013), which has remained unclear particularly regarding sustainable (Seebode et al. 2012; Wicki and Hansen 2019) and CE-oriented innovating (Brown et al. 2021).

Second, we contribute to innovation management and CE literature with understanding how and when ecosystem actors support innovating activities. Aligned with prior innovation studies (Aarikka-Stenroos et al. 2014; Phillips and Ritala 2019; Seebode et al. 2012), our findings support the view that CE innovation makes no exception among innovations that critically need collaboration over time (Brown et al. 2021), both to provide needed competences and resources for R&D (Driessen and Hillebrand 2013) and to radically switch the value proposition in commercializing (Möller and Svahn 2009). Extending prior CE research, our findings display that CE innovating requires firms to establish strategic partnerships, seek collaboration beyond traditional boundaries (as noted previously with sustainable innovations; e.g., Seebode et al. 2012), and actively engage in public discussion involving encompassing actors, such as NGOs and regulators, early in innovating.

Practical Implications

Table 6.1 supports technology and business managers in identifying the main challenges and choosing what actions to take and when in CE innovating. It also advises who to involve and when to overcome the emerging challenges during CE innovating. Three key managerial implications give pragmatic advice as follows:

1. Strengthen innovative organizational culture with experimentation-encouraging leadership and sufficient resourcing to proactively initiate and accelerate new CE innovation processes.
2. Build multidisciplinary competences, also across firm boundaries, and facilitate their use with cross-functional teams already in early CE innovating to allow new, parallel business opportunities to emerge.
3. Establish strategic partnerships with sustainability-valuing actors and seek collaboration beyond traditional boundaries early on to facilitate both R&D and commercialization activities.

This chapter demonstrates how instead of choosing between them, managers can pursue both sustainability and economic gains through executing CE innovation strategies and processes, meanwhile strategically renewing for sustainability with aligned innovation and business strategies. Moreover, the advantages of successful CE innovation are not limited to benefits from the firm perspective; sustaining future production and consumption with firms' sustainable practices and solutions is societally crucial. Consequently, contributing to ensure success of firms' full CE innovation processes is of great interest for many, including regulators, NGOs, and customers.

Limitations and Future Research

Many firm features, such as size, innovation, or market features (e.g., industry and stakeholder conservatism; Möller and Svahn 2009) can shape CE innovation processes. As actions and actors crucial throughout innovation processes may vary based on firm features, as well as innovation types, further research is needed to complement our findings on a primarily technological CE innovation case with business model innovation features. Further, as the processual view to CE innovating remains new and underexplored (Brown et al. 2021), more examinations are needed on diverse sustainable/CE innovation processes, across industries in ecosystem and market creation settings. Lastly, seeing the power of sustainable/CE innovating to strategically transform the way firms do business, we encourage investigating the impact of sustainable/CE innovating under a strategic management lens.

ACKNOWLEDGEMENTS

The data generation and writing of this chapter were supported by the Strategic Research Council, Academy of Finland, through the research project "Circular Economy Catalysts: From Innovation to Business Ecosystems" (CICAT2025) (grant ID 320194). We also thank Erkki Paasikivi Foundation, Tampere Foundation for Economic Education, and Kansan Sivistysrahasto for supporting Kaipainen's work.

NOTE

REFERENCES

Aarikka-Stenroos, L., Jaakkola, E., Harrison, D., & Mäkitalo-Keinonen, T. (2017). How to manage innovation processes in extensive networks: A longitudinal study. *Industrial Marketing Management*, 67, 88–105.

Aarikka-Stenroos, L., Ritala, P., & Thomas, L. (2021). Circular economy ecosystems: A typology, definitions and implications. In S. Teerikangas, T. Onkila, M. Mäkelä, & K. Koistinen (eds), *Research Handbook of Sustainability Agency*. Cheltenham, UK: Edward Elgar Publishing.

Aarikka-Stenroos, L., Sandberg, B., & Lehtimäki, T. (2014). Networks for the commercialization of innovations: A review of how divergent network actors contribute. *Industrial Marketing Management*, 43(3), 365–381.

Adner, R. (2006). Match your innovation strategy to your innovation ecosystem. *Harvard Business Review*, 84(4), 98–107.

Brown, P., Von Daniels, C., Bocken, N. M. P., & Balkenende, A. R. (2021). A process model for collaboration in circular oriented innovation. *Journal of Cleaner Production*, 286, 125499.

Chiesa, V., & Frattini, F. (2011). Commercializing technological innovation: Learning from failures in high-tech markets. *Journal of Product Innovation Management*, 28(4), 437–454.

De Jesus, A., & Mendonça, S. (2018). Lost in transition? Drivers and barriers in the eco-innovation road to the circular economy. *Ecological Economics*, 145, 75–89.

Driessen, P. H., & Hillebrand, B. (2013). Integrating multiple stakeholder issues in new product development: An exploration. *Journal of Product Innovation Management*, 30(2), 364–379.

Dubois, A., & Gadde, L. E. (2002). Systematic combining: An abductive approach to case research. *Journal of Business Research*, 55(7), 553–560.

Garcia, R., & Calantone, R. (2002). A critical look at technological innovation typology and innovativeness terminology: A literature review. *Journal of Product Innovation Management*, 19(2), 110–132.

Geissdoerfer, M., Savaget, P., Bocken, N. M. P., & Hultink, E. J. (2017). The circular economy: A new sustainability paradigm? *Journal of Cleaner Production*, 143, 757–768.

Ghisellini, P., Cialani, C., & Ulgiati, S. (2016). A review on circular economy: The expected transition to a balanced interplay of environmental and economic systems. *Journal of Cleaner Production*, 114, 11–32.

Goodman, J., Korsunova, A., & Halme, M. (2017). Our collaborative future: Activities and roles of stakeholders in sustainability-oriented innovation. *Business Strategy and the Environment*, 26, 731–753.

Jolly, V. K. (1997). *Commercializing New Technologies*. Boston: Harvard Business School Press.

Lynn, G. S., Morone, J. G., & Paulson, A. S. (1996). Marketing and discontinuous innovation: The probe and learn process. *California Management Review*, 38(3), 8–37.

Möller, K., & Svahn, S. (2009). How to influence the birth of new business fields: Network perspective. *Industrial Marketing Management*, 38(4), 450–458.

Mousavi, S., & Bossink, B. A. G. (2017). Firms' capabilities for sustainable innovation: The case of biofuel for aviation. *Journal of Cleaner Production*, 167, 1263–1275.

Neste Oil (2011). *Annual Report*. https://www.neste.com/sites/default/files/attachments/corporate/investors/agm/review_by_the_board_of_directors_2011.pdf.

O'Connor, G. C., & Rice, M. P. (2013). New market creation for breakthrough innovations: Enabling and constraining mechanisms. *Journal of Product Innovation Management*, 30(2), 209–227.

O'Connor, G. C., & Veryzer, R. W. (2001). The nature of market visioning for technology-based radical innovation. *Journal of Product Innovation Management*, 18(4), 231–246.

Phillips, M. A., & Ritala, P. (2019). A complex adaptive systems agenda for ecosystem research methodology. *Technological Forecasting and Social Change*, 148, 119739.

Pisano, G. (2015). You need an innovation strategy. *Harward Business Review*, 93(6), 44–54.

Seebode, D., Jeanrenaud, S., & Bessant, J. (2012). Managing innovation for sustainability. *R&D Management*, 42(3), 195–206.

Siegel, R. A., Hansén, S.-O., & Pellas, L. H. (1995). Accelerating the commercialisation of technology: Commercialisation through co-operation. *Industrial Management & Data Systems*, 95(1), 18–26.

Stake, R. E. (1995). *The Art of Case Study Research*. Thousand Oaks, CA: Sage Publications.

Van de Ven, A. H. (1992). Suggestions for studying strategy process: A research note. *Strategic Management Journal*, 13(S1), 169–188.

Vanhamäki, S., Virtanen, M., Luste, S., & Manskinen, K. (2020). Transition towards a circular economy at a regional level: A case study on closing biological loops. *Resources, Conservation & Recycling*, 156, 104716.

Wicki, S., & Hansen, E. G. (2019). Green technology innovation: Anatomy of exploration processes from a learning perspective. *Business Strategy and the Environment*, 28(6), 970–988.

Yilmaz, N., & Atmanli, A. (2017). Sustainable alternative fuels in aviation. *Energy*, 140, 1378–1386.

7. Organizing for a circular economy: internal activism and organizational boundaries in SMEs

Chia-Hao Ho, David Monciardini and Edvard Glücksman

INTRODUCTION: THE MICRO-FOUNDATIONS OF CIRCULAR ECONOMY

Circular economy (CE) has been an active field of research for over two decades and has been regarded as an antidote to socio-economic challenges such as resource scarcity and negative environmental impacts, and as driving environmentally responsible business behaviour. According to the Ellen MacArthur Foundation (2015, p. 2), CE is 'an economy that is restorative and regenerative by design'. Its central objective is to challenge the dominance of unsustainable linear economic models through the design of a closed-looped flow of materials to reduce pollution (Geng and Doberstein 2008; Jawahir and Bradley 2016; Winans et al. 2017). Although theoretical aspects are well documented, a key gap in the literature pertains to practical business circular innovations aiming to facilitate and optimize a CE transition. The system theory paradigm that dominates the CE discourse gives little attention to agency within micro-organizational dynamics (Blomsma and Brennan 2017; Kirchherr et al. 2017; Korhonen et al. 2018). CE research remains 'superficial and unorganized' (Korhonen et al. 2018). In particular, we know little about individual struggles and organizational micro-dynamics that foster or discourage the development of circular business models.

We propose to fill this gap by focusing on two intertwined and understudied elements: Firstly, business internal activism which promotes CE principles; and secondly, the redefinition of traditional organizational boundaries. Through the concept of organizational boundaries (Santos and Eisenhardt 2005), our research empirically investigates how these different forms of business activism and conceptions of organizational boundaries can shape firms' motives for embracing CE principles.

The contribution of this work to existing CE literature is threefold. Firstly, it draws attention to CE's micro-foundations by looking at agency, i.e. internal activism, in triggering organizational change towards a CE. Secondly, it builds on the body of knowledge on SME strategies which supports firms to translate their varying motivations into different CE organizational boundary conceptions. Finally, it offers a working business support mechanism for policymakers and practitioners, and provides insight that might guide CE transformation processes, particularly for early-stage ventures and SMEs.

ORGANIZATIONAL BOUNDARIES AND AGENCY IN CIRCULAR BUSINESS

The CE literature often mentions that traditional organizational boundaries need to be redefined or even transcended (Haney et al. 2019) to extend value and material flows to an inter-organizational and even societal level (Boons and Lüdeke-Freund 2013; Laasch 2018). However, existing research has taken a very normative approach – stating how CE organizational boundaries ought to be rather than looking at the reality of emerging examples of CE business organizations. As demonstrated by Pieroni et al. (2019), the majority of methods and tools still adopt traditional organizational boundaries, highlighting that 'future research should explore how to take the inter-organizational or societal boundaries into account' (p. 210). The literature on organizational boundaries can help to fill this gap.

For the scope of our study, boundaries refer to 'the demarcation between the organization and the environment' (Santos and Eisenhardt 2005, p. 491). As such, within organizational boundaries activities operate under a specific logic of identity that shapes how things are done in the organization (Kogut 2000) and how resources possessed by the firm are allocated (Helfat 1997), and this determines the sphere of control of the organization (D'Aveni et al. 2001). From the strategic management and organization theorists' point of view, the dominant logic of the nature of a firm is linked with the transaction cost economy that tends to conceptualize organizational boundaries as relatively stable and static. However, recent research is rapidly progressing to more contextual and dynamic settings such as nascent markets (Santos and Eisenhardt 2009), business ecosystems (Radziwon and Bogers 2018; Velter et al. 2020), identity-driven business (Santos and Eisenhardt 2009), early-stage ventures (Santos and Eisenhardt 2005), and community-based enterprise (Hertel et al. 2019). In particular, we were inspired by the seminal work of Santos and Eisenhardt (2005, 2009) that developed four boundary conceptions (see Table 7.1) and which can help to shed light on the relationship between CE-based organizations, other organizations and the broader environment in which they operate.

Anchored in the concept of bottom-up forces within an organization, we contend that CE organizational boundaries are shaped by the agency of internal activists that use their resources and views to 'induce change' (Walker 2012, p. 582) and shape the application of CE principles and embed it within organizational goals. According to Davis et al. (2008, p. 391), 'Organizations are places where social life happens and, as such, can be the location of strug-

Table 7.1   *Four conceptions of organizational boundaries*

Efficiency	Linked to the transaction cost theory of the firm revolving around make and buy choice. Decision-making based on cost minimization.
Power	Draws attention to collaborative and coordinative strategic relationship that firms establish as control mechanisms over multiple stakeholders.
Competence	Linked to resource-based view and dynamic capacity theory of firms that emphasize the (re)configuration of resources for competitive advantage. Growth is central to decision-making. Product development and process innovation are typical initiatives in the organization.
Identity	Linked to the cognitive view of the firm that manifests through an ongoing defining process of 'who we are'. The central goal is to align the organizational activities with organizational identity. According to this view, 'cognitive boundaries exist at the perimeter of aspects of identity, and these boundaries can vary in permeability' (Kreiner et al. 2006, p. 1322).

gles over broader issues of social justice. [...] Thus the stakes of wider social struggles are often enacted within firms.'

There is an emerging scholarship on the way that activist entrepreneurs induce change. According to Geiger and Gross (2018), market 'misfire' accelerates the adoption and diffusion of innovations or new values that are incubated by incumbents or challengers. In this context, various types of corporate activism (Corvellec and Stål 2019; Skoglund and Böhm, 2020) have been discussed by organizational scholars, insofar as researchers have increasingly tried to reconcile the domains of activism and markets. Specifically, the focus has been on CEO activists (Chatterji and Toffel 2019); social intrapreneurs (Davis and White 2015); institutional entrepreneurs (Battilana et al. 2009); organizational entrepreneurs (Courpasson et al. 2016); grassroots activists (Scully and Segal 2002); and tempered radicals (Meyerson and Tompkins 2007). These individuals usually speak out on a specific social or sustainable issue and are devoted to solving it within their organization.

Drawing on the above different forms of internal activism, we argue that internal activists have more knowledge of their organization and resources, which helps induce change, shaping a CE-focused business identity. They could be regarded as CE field's gatekeepers, aligning the organizational goal with external opportunities, particularly if these internal activists hold a managerial role. From the cognitive management perspective, Helfat and Peteraf (2015) demonstrate the link between managerial cognitive process (i.e. sensing, seizing, and reconfiguring) and enterprise-level capabilities. They stated that top managers could affect strategic change in organizations via their information structure and mental processes. In other words, they will sense CE as an opportunity from the external environment, i.e. their motivation for embracing the CE and mobilizing and deploying organizational resources into a CE-based organizational logic. In association with the notion of the organizational boundary, the organizational goal directs the scope of business and how the boundary is defined. The interplay of internal activism and organizational boundary is typically formed at the early stage of the transition process with a focus on the entrepreneurial and self-defining process. Hence, this research adopts a multiple-case design, focusing on SMEs where the CE initiatives were induced by manager or founder. Then, we investigate how their motivation and mobilization process lead to different types of boundary interfaces in CE activism.

METHODS

Research Context

This study is a spin-off from a larger programme called Tevi (tevi.co.uk), funded by the European Regional Development Fund (ERDF), which aims to support economic and environmental growth in Cornwall and the Isles of Scilly, one of the UK most economically deprived regions. The programme started in 2018 and is set to run until 2022.

So far, Tevi has supported over 250 SMEs to grow whilst at the same time contributing to strategic regional goals around environmental growth and a CE transition. Environmental growth, which broadly aligns with national 'net gain' priorities, is enshrined in a long-term strategy at the county council level. A transition to a more CE is a regional priority, designing waste out of the economy and building resilience across communities with historically low rates of productivity and innovation. Through national and international partnerships, Tevi is also facilitating the transfer of best practice knowledge into Cornwall.

The Tevi programme is delivered by academics and knowledge exchange specialists at the University of Exeter's campus in Penryn, Cornwall, in partnership with Cornwall Wildlife Trust, Cornwall Council and Cornwall Development Company. All registered SMEs receive bespoke one-to-one support, ranging from product development research to land or waste management plans to strategic advice around growth. Tevi also dispenses a capital grant fund for equipment, consultancy or other services that specifically contribute to increasing an SME's contribution to environmental growth or the CE. Over a thousand participants have thus far attended Tevi events and workshops which brought SMEs together to receive a crash course in how to apply CE methods to their product and service development. In this context, our cases were selected from SMEs who were part of Tevi's business network.

Case Selection

The case selection process was purposive. All the authors are directly or indirectly involved in the Tevi project and our study emerged from a reflection on this common experience and daily conversations with local business representatives involved in CE activities. First, we began by selecting out of all the 200+ SMEs involved in the Tevi project. We clustered companies linked to the same ownership and deleted others that are no longer in business. Second, the initial number was further reduced to 82 companies based on their clear commitment to CE principles and nominations from the Tevi team members. Third, through the discussion with Tevi members and substantive information from Tevi archival documents, for the scope of this chapter, we selected a sample of 12 organizations which represent each boundary conception (see Table 7.2).

Table 7.2   *Key information on the relevant cases*

Firm	Size	Industry	CE initiative	Conception
ID1	Micro	Manufacturing	Products made by recycled food waste	
ID2	Micro	Wholesale/Retail	A plastic-free wholefood shop	Identity
ID3	Micro	Manufacturing	Making zero-waste product	
EF1	Micro	Manufacturing	Develop B2B products to reduce the waste	
EF2	Medium	Manufacturing	Production process with 3R* principles	Efficiency
EF3	Medium	Wholesale/Retail	Production process with 3R principles	
PW1	Micro	Manufacturing	Products reconfigured by reused material	
PW2	Small	Mining	Business model with 3R principles	Power
PW3	Micro	Manufacturing	Products made by recycled waste	
CP1	Small	Manufacturing	Products made by recycled plastic waste	
CP2	Micro	Manufacturing	Products made by recycled plastic waste	Competence
CP3	Micro	High Tech	A platform to share surplus material	

Note: *3R = reduce, reuse, recycle.

Data Collection and Data Analysis

Our research project started in May 2019. Data were collected from the following sources: (1) Tevi archival documents (e.g. an open-question-based questionnaire filled out by SMEs, initial interview transcripts, and minutes of meeting and emails); (2) publicly available secondary data (e.g. SME's website); (c) semi-structured interviews.

We conducted 12 semi-structured interviews, three with Tevi team members who co-worked with the local businesses and nine with SMEs (owners, managers or senior employees involved in the Tevi project). The former were asked about their own experience in working with SMEs, in particular, the main drivers of SMEs' involvement in CE initiatives as part of the Tevi project. Tevi interviews were used for 12 cases selection based on four boundary conceptions. The latter comprised preliminary interviews with five companies identified as CE champions and four additional interviews with the owners or managers (ID1, EF3, PW2, and CP3).

As for data analysis, we decided to deploy Santos and Eisenhardt (2005) as our analytical framework (i.e. efficiency-, identity-, power-, and competence-driven). Pedalling back and forth between the raw data, our preliminary research questions and the literature (Denzin and Lincoln 2005) helped us to identify major themes, pertaining to internal activism and organizational boundaries. Through the above sources and processes, we soon realized that their motivation for embracing a CE model was linked to a limited number of recurrent patterns. Thus, we decided to explore more in details and systematically this phenomenon, focusing in particular on the business motives for becoming more circular and their conceptions of the environment in which they operate. After that, an additional four interviews were conducted to validate our preliminary findings. Then we separately analysed the raw data and then discussed together our analyses based on our emerging analytical framework.

FINDINGS AND ANALYSIS

Our findings highlight four distinct conceptions of organizational boundaries that are recurrent in the CE-engaged companies (see Table 7.3). It is worth underlining that we understand the different conceptions as ideal types that can provide insights into the micro-dynamics of business engagement with the transition towards more circular approaches. In a Weberian sense, ideal types are analytical constructs for use as yardsticks for measuring the similarity and difference between concrete phenomena and case studies (Kvist 2007). In reality, the large majority of the companies that we have studied are characterized by a combination of the four conceptions of CE organizational boundaries and business activism, although one conception might be more pronounced than the others.

Efficiency-Driven CE Organizational Boundaries and Business Activism

The first conception is broadly characterized by the opportunity for lowering the cost of products/services by embracing elements of CE business. It emerged that circularity is instrumentally adopted to the extent that it allows the company to 'better run' and 'have lower costs'. For instance, both EF2 and EF3 adopted a CE approach to save time and money by minimizing waste:

> We use a lot of cardboard boxes which we will then collect back. We reuse them whenever we can. And if not, then we've got plastic and cardboard recycling and bins [...] We also collect wasted cooking oil that we sell from our customers, which is obviously an issue that they have to get rid of. We store it and then we have a local guy that comes around once a week and picks everything up that we've collected and reuse it. (EF3)

Table 7.3   Four conceptions of CE organizational boundaries and business activism

	Efficiency	Identity	Power	Competence
CE organizational boundaries	**Conception:** Conventional organizational boundaries based on whether a transaction should be governed by market or organization. **Central goal:** *Cost minimization* by minimizing the resource use and waste resulting from transactions undertaken within and outside the organization.	**Conception:** Organizational boundaries based on shared values and norms used as cognitive frames that reduce ambiguity, facilitate decision-making and enhance internal coherence. **Central goal:** *Address social problems* by aligning organizational activism in the community with organizational identity.	**Conception:** Boundaries are defined by the sphere of influence that facilitates coordination to reduce dependence and uncertainty and exercise power. **Central goal:** *Increased autonomy* by maximizing control over strategic relationships and wielding market power.	**Conception:** Boundaries defined by a unique resource bundle, dynamically determined by matching organizational resources needs with environmental opportunities. **Central goal:** *Maximize value* by coevolving resource configurations with market opportunities.
Motivation for embracing CE	**Instrumental:** Embrace CE based on its 'business case'. CE is seen as a win–win situation that can create financial benefits as well as social and environmental.	**Issue-based:** Use business as a vehicle to spur collective awareness/commitment to tackle specific issues (e.g. plastics).	**Resilience:** CE allows to exert greater influence over supply chain and stakeholders and to enjoy resilience.	**Performance:** Maximizing the remaining value of waste/materials through innovations and optimizations that change the market or consuming behaviour.
Form of CE business internal activism	**Strength:** Incremental **Scope:** organization and supply chain **Forms:** Tempered radicals	**Strength:** Holistic **Scope:** local or community **Forms:** Social entrepreneurs; grassroots activists; community-based enterprise	**Strength:** Institutional **Scope:** Industry, market, or regional **Forms:** institutional entrepreneurs	**Strength:** Innovative **Scope:** Product and market **Forms:** Organizational entrepreneurs; social intrapreneurs.

Besides this, EF2 is interested in improving 'internal monitoring and how to reduce the amount of plastic with food which can be recycled'. EF1 offers another slightly different example in that it provides other businesses solutions to become more efficient. Although EF1 embraces a CE approach, their services are presented as aimed at fostering efficiency rather than circularity per se. All these companies incidentally mention that this is 'also a general right thing to do' (EF3). This suggests that addressing environmental and social issues remains a nice to have add-on to becoming more efficient, not their main driver.

Overall, CE in efficiency-driven firms is perfectly compatible with a business-as-usual approach based on transaction governance. Because their central goal is to maximize revenues and lower costs, business internal activism typically promotes incremental changes using the 'business case' for CE to portray organizational changes as a 'win-win' situation, i.e. 'doing well, by doing good' (Kotler and Lee 2008; Urbinati et al. 2017). For example, EF3 highlights the importance of being cost-effective: 'if somebody developed a type of universal reusable packaging that is not going to break the bank [...] cost-wise, then that would be the game-changer.'

The concept of 'tempered radicals' (Meyerson and Tompkins 2007) applies to this form of business internal activism which comes to terms with the status quo and works towards transformational ends through incremental changes. In doing so, internal activism struggles to balance their personal values and concerns with building careers in companies that are more concerned with profits than social and environmental issues.

Identity-Driven CE Organizational Boundaries and Business Activism

This conception is driven by the opportunity for adopting CE principles and practices to promote social and environmental causes. The main difference with efficiency-driven organizations lies in the relationship with the external environment. While the former did not aim at changing their customers and suppliers' behaviour (transactional relationships), identity-driven firms are committed to transforming the context in which they operate. Thus, identity-driven organizations have much more blurred inter-organizational or societal boundaries as compared to traditional businesses. Because of their holistic approach, they tend to become part of the local community and often their central goal is to deal with localized concerns and issues (Hertel et al. 2019). For instance, ID1 is a micro enterprise that deals with wasted fruits:

> And then you get more of the community involved. It's quite interesting to see that sort of impact: how people are prepared to commit that much to stopping waste [...] and what you'll then become is a reference point for anybody looking for fruits that are going wasted. (ID1)

Other examples we came across include a zero-waste shop (ID2) that 'was born on a 500 mile plastic-free hike' undertaken to raise money for an NGO in which the business founder visited 'islands filled with plastic pollution' and became determined to raise awareness of the issue and 'prove that people can live without producing waste'. The shop has become a 'hub' of like-minded sustainable businesses and individuals in Cornwall: a platform for collective action and commitment. Yet another example is a surfboard producer that uses upcycled or locally sourced wood and no packaging. This organization offers people from all over the world two- to four-week mental health workshops based on the process of making handcrafted surfboards, combining social and environmental CE principles (ID3).

In terms of CE business activism, we cannot find the tensions and conflicts that 'tempered radicals' are purported to face. On the contrary, businesses are vehicles for expressing the values and personal motivations of their founders and employees. Focusing on the question of 'who we are' rather than 'who I am', these individuals share purpose and perceptions of the value of wasted resources that are conventionally treated as worthless, distinguishing themselves from our 'waste culture' (Hawkins and Muecke 2002). We can find echoes of this type of activism in the vast literature on social enterprises (Mair and Marti 2006) and more recently in research on 'community-based enterprises' (Hertel et al. 2019). As noted by ID1, 'the biggest driver is that people hate seeing them [fruit] wasted'. The way ID1 responds to this issue has been to establish a business model where the wasted fruit is supplied by voluntary donation from the community. Overall, these examples suggests that identity-driven entre- preneurs are grassroots activists that have transformed the workplace into a locus of activism (Scully and Segal 2002).

Power-Driven CE Organizational Boundaries and Business Activism

We found that some CE activities were driven by the opportunity for gaining greater resilience and control over their supply chain and strategic partnerships. For instance, PW1, a small furniture making company, contended that its central goal is to 'create a locally and sustain- ably produced alternative to IKEA'. They locally source their wood appealing to individuals seeking to return to a simpler, more sustainable and traditional lifestyle.

The shift away from a linear business model to greater circularity here is framed as an opportunity for 'taking back control' of supply markets that have become increasingly complex and globalized. According to our interviews, this idea of sourcing, producing, and selling local products to local people has become ever more relevant in the current COVID-19 pandemic context. However, this is also attractive, and it has currency in the current political climate that emphasizes localism and renewed economic protectionism. For example, PW2, a local mining company, aims to reclassify and reuse waste and highlights the benefits of local extraction plans for the British economy:

> The government is very interested in capturing some of that value back over in the UK. And I think the government is also very interested to see whether we can produce some of the [anonymized] that the UK is going to need over the next few years from domestic sources. (PW2)

Thus, we found that this power-driven boundary is based on the opportunity of reducing dependency on external forces or exerting greater control over them. Organizational bounda- ries are used defensively but also offensively to improve network positioning and enhance the sphere of influence of the organization. Thus, from the perspective of power-driven organiza- tions, CE also becomes a chance for exercising influence on the market, industry and region in which they operate. For instance, PW3 which produces reusable cups uses the currency and acceptance of CE principles as a source of market power and competitive advantage. Their website emphatically states that 'The Future is Circular' and stresses the power of their CE products that have saved '187 million single-use caps from contaminating our environment' (PW3).

In terms of CE business activism, the power-driven entrepreneurs we have studied are institutional entrepreneurs often located at the periphery of the economic and institutional field and are engaged in recreating and transforming it (Battilana et al. 2009). As noted by PW2:

> It's kind of a disruptive model for the mining industry. Everything is kind of geared towards that bigger goal [...] We're trying to make that link, especially to people in government, if you want to have the clean energy transition in the UK [...] and we are already engaging with other stakeholders in the supply chain about what they think they might want in five or ten years time rather than what they use right now.

These examples demonstrate that they will exercise influence on the existing institutional environment through their ability to coordinate collective change, collaborate with larger corporate players (Veleva and Bodkin 2018), and build a wider and cohesive network.

Competence-Driven CE Organizational Boundaries and Business Activism

The last conception is based on the opportunity for using CE to enable new products and processes. The boundaries of competence-driven organizations are dynamically determined by the match between organizational resources and environmental opportunities. The central goal is to develop high-performance CE product or process innovations that recombine material or/ and human resources to exploit a business opportunity. For example, CP1 is strongly committed to re-innovating their product from recycled plastics and eliminating all single-use plastic packaging to contribute to tackling marine pollution. However, it must make sure that the recycled materials will maintain the high performance of its products. This situation creates an interesting conundrum that requires CE dynamic capabilities and innovation to be addressed. Thus, CP1's inter-organizational or societal boundaries dynamically evolve in response to its resource configuration. CP3 is another example which provides an innovative solution for local businesses' unwanted packaging:

> I think that once we had the idea, all the other justifications for it sort of came out of that [...] we wanted to work out how to connect this business with his packaging to this other business that needed packaging. [...] I feel like I've got something really great to offer. [...] That is going to save you money. It is good for the environment. It will get more people into your premises. (CP3)

Thus, competence-driven businesses differ from the other conceptions because they are built around the opportunity for exploiting a CE business idea for better products and services. At the same time, they have elements of efficiency ('saving money') and identity-driven organizations ('good for the environment'). Another example is CP2 which offers a product innovation based on recycled fishing nets. The product innovation process includes cross-industrial collaborations between high-tech manufacturing and the fish industry which sees it 'as a great way of recycling the old netting and ensuring the recycled material is put to good use' (CP2).

In terms of activism, the main focus of their action is the CE innovation per se rather than solely addressing social problems, saving costs, or increasing resilience. As illustrated by the example of CP3, the business idea and value proposition come first. And then, business activism is gathered on the basis of their skills and the business innovation process. This can be seen in relation with the emergent literature on 'social intrapreneurs', who are change-agents working in for-profit organizations to advance socially oriented innovations that may range from 'not-for-loss' to market penetration (Davis and White 2015). Another stream of research related to this is 'organizational entrepreneurs' (Courpasson et al. 2016). This body of literature highlights how R&D teams can create spaces for creativity and entrepreneurship within an organizational space that challenge established structures, practices and strategies. This suggests that competence-based CE activism may indirectly impact consumer behaviour by linking CE innovations with intrinsic attributes of human behaviour such as values, ethics, or social and psychological factors (Parajuly et al. 2020; Singh and Giacosa 2019).

DISCUSSION, CONTRIBUTION, AND FUTURE RESEARCH

Our findings suggest that the organizational boundaries literature and the work of Santos and Eisenhardt (2005) can help shed light on the relationship between CE organizations and the environment in which they operate. Contrary to idealized approaches to CE, our analysis found various organizational boundary conceptions linked to different motivations and forms of CE business internal activism. Our conceptions range from efficiency-driven incremental approaches aligned with conventional business to identity-driven conceptions that are radically opposed to 'business-as-usual' transactional approaches. There are also power-driven and competence-driven conceptions that extend the current focus of CE debates on sustainability and economic efficiency to consider also control and resource configuration. Our conjecture – that will need further empirical research – is that this wide range of approaches to organizational boundaries is related to distinct forms of business internal activism that can open new avenues for future research.

Our findings have the potential to drive change in business support mechanisms such as the notion of transition broker (Cramer 2020), making them more impactful, contextually sensitive and better aligned with enterprise growth strategies. For example, programmes like Tevi could pinpoint CE indicators within the enterprises they work with by identifying internal activist characteristics and organizational boundary conceptions. Our conceptual framework gives business support practitioners additional tools for delivering bespoke services, co-created around enterprise needs. This work builds on burgeoning research on effective knowledge transfer between experts and practitioners, highlighting opportunities for academic research co-designed with practitioners. We hope that our preliminary and exploratory study could inspire several avenues for future research. First, we suggest further expanding on our typology by considering the synergies between the four conceptions of CE business organizational boundaries that we do not understand as mutually exclusive. For instance, a company could be primarily driven by cost minimization (efficiency) but also aim at achieving greater autonomy (power). Second, we suggest investigating the implication of organizational scale. We found prominence of efficiency-driven businesses in larger enterprises while many identity-driven CE companies are relatively small. We suggest that future scholars expand on this insight to understand how the size of firms influence CE drivers and organizational boundaries, particularly in relation to the challenge of scaling-up (André and Pache 2016). Lastly, most of our CE SMEs have developed a strong relationship with local communities and organizations. A more contextualized approach to CE research could be particularly fruitful. For instance, in line with our exploration of CE internal activism, future research could focus on the role of regional networks of CE activism (e.g. local government and civil society organization) in driving business collective action towards a more circular economic model (Rousseau et al. 2019).

REFERENCES

André, K., & Pache, A.-C. (2016). From caring entrepreneur to caring enterprise: Addressing the ethical challenges of scaling up social enterprises. *Journal of Business Ethics*, 133(4), 659–675.

Battilana, J., Leca, B., & Boxenbaum, E. (2009). How actors change institutions: Towards a theory of institutional entrepreneurship. *Academy of Management Annals*, 3(1), 65–107.

Blomsma, F., & Brennan, G. (2017). The emergence of circular economy: A new framing around prolonging resource productivity. *Journal of Industrial Ecology*, 21(3), 603–614.

Boons, F., & Lüdeke-Freund, F. (2013). Business models for sustainable innovation: State-of-the-art and steps towards a research agenda. *Journal of Cleaner Production*, 45, 9–19.

Chatterji, A. K., & Toffel, M. W. (2019). Assessing the impact of CEO activism. *Organization & Environment*, 32(2), 159–185.

Corvellec, H., & Stål, H. I. (2019). Qualification as corporate activism: How Swedish apparel retailers attach circular fashion qualities to take-back systems. *Scandinavian Journal of Management*, 35(3), 101046.

Courpasson, D., Dany, F., & Martí, I. (2016). Organizational entrepreneurship as active resistance: A struggle against outsourcing. *Entrepreneurship Theory and Practice*, 40(1), 131–160.

Cramer, J. M. (2020). The function of transition brokers in the regional governance of implementing circular economy: A comparative case study of six Dutch regions. *Sustainability*, 12(12), 5015.

D'Aveni, R. A., Gunther, R. E., & Cole, J. (2001). *Strategic Supremacy: How Industry Leaders Create Growth, Wealth, and Power through Spheres of Influence*. New York: Simon & Schuster.

Davis, G. F., Morrill, C., Rao, H., & Soule, S. A. (2008). Introduction: Social movements in organizations and markets. *Administrative Science Quarterly*, 53(3), 389–394.

Davis, G. F., & White, C. J. (2015). The new face of corporate activism. *Stanford Social Innovation Review*, 13(4), 40–45.

Denzin, N. K., and Lincoln, Y. S. (eds.) (2005). *The Sage Handbook of Qualitative Research*. London: Sage Publications.

Ellen MacArthur Foundation (2015). *Towards a Circular Economy: Business Rationale for an Accelerated Transition*.

Geiger, S., & Gross, N. (2018). Market failures and market framings: Can a market be transformed from the inside? *Organization Studies*, 39(10), 1357–1376.

Geng, Y., & Doberstein, B. (2008). Developing the circular economy in China: Challenges and opportunities for achieving 'leapfrog development'. *The International Journal of Sustainable Development & World Ecology*, 15(3), 231–239.

Haney, A., Krestyaninova, O., & Love, C. (2019). *The Circular Economy: Boundaries and Bridges*. Oxford: Saïd Business School.

Hawkins, G., & Muecke, S. (2002). *Culture and Waste: The Creation and Destruction of Value*. Lanham, MD: Rowman & Littlefield Publishers.

Helfat, C. E. (1997). Know-how and asset complementarity and dynamic capability accumulation: The case of R&D. *Strategic Management Journal*, 18(5), 339–360.

Helfat, C. E., & Peteraf, M. A. (2015). Managerial cognitive capabilities and the microfoundations of dynamic capabilities. *Strategic Management Journal*, 36(6), 831–850.

Hertel, C., Bacq, S., & Belz, F.-M. (2019). It takes a village to sustain a village: A social identity perspective on successful community-based enterprise creation. *Academy of Management Discoveries*, 5(4), 438–464.

Jawahir, I., & Bradley, R. (2016). Technological elements of circular economy and the principles of 6R-based closed-loop material flow in sustainable manufacturing. *Procedia Cirp*, 40, 103–108.

Kirchherr, J., Reike, D., & Hekkert, M. (2017). Conceptualizing the circular economy: An analysis of 114 definitions. *Resources, Conservation and Recycling*, 127, 221–232.

Kogut, B. (2000). The network as knowledge: Generative rules and the emergence of structure. *Strategic Management Journal*, 21(3), 405–425.

Korhonen, J., Nuur, C., Feldmann, A., & Birkie, S. E. (2018). Circular economy as an essentially contested concept. *Journal of Cleaner Production*, 175, 544–552.

Kotler, P., & Lee, N. (2008). *Corporate Social Responsibility: Doing the Most Good for Your Company and Your Cause*. Hoboken, NJ: John Wiley & Sons.

Kreiner, G. E., Hollensbe, E. C., & Sheep, M. L. (2006). On the edge of identity: Boundary dynamics at the interface of individual and organizational identities. *Human Relations*, 59(10), 1315–1341.

Kvist, J. (2007). Fuzzy set ideal type analysis. *Journal of Business Research*, 60(5), 474–481.

Laasch, O. (2018). Beyond the purely commercial business model: Organizational value logics and the heterogeneity of sustainability business models. *Long Range Planning*, 51(1), 158–183.

Mair, J., & Marti, I. (2006). Social entrepreneurship research: A source of explanation, prediction, and delight. *Journal of World Business*, 41(1), 36–44.

Meyerson, D., & Tompkins, M. (2007). Tempered radicals as institutional change agents: The case of advancing gender equity at the University of Michigan. *Harvard Women's Law Journal*, 30(2), 303–322.

Parajuly, K., Fitzpatrick, C., Muldoon, O., & Kuehr, R. (2020). Behavioral change for the circular economy: A review with focus on electronic waste management in the EU. *Resources, Conservation and Recycling*, 6, 100035.

Pieroni, M. P., McAloone, T. C., & Pigosso, D. C. (2019). Business model innovation for circular economy and sustainability: A review of approaches. *Journal of Cleaner Production*, 215, 198–216.

Radziwon, A., & Bogers, M. (2018). Managing SMEs' collaboration across organizational boundaries within a regional business ecosystem. In W. Vanhaverbeke, F. Frattini, N. Roijakkers, & M. Usman (eds.), *Researching Open Innovation in SMEs*. Singapore: World Scientific, 213–248.

Rousseau, H. E., Berrone, P., & Gelabert, L. (2019). Localizing sustainable development goals: Nonprofit density and city sustainability. *Academy of Management Discoveries*, 5(4), 487–513.

Santos, F. M., & Eisenhardt, K. M. (2005). Organizational boundaries and theories of organization. *Organization Science*, 16(5), 491–508.

Santos, F. M., & Eisenhardt, K. M. (2009). Constructing markets and shaping boundaries: Entrepreneurial power in nascent fields. *Academy of Management Journal*, 52(4), 643–671.

Scully, M., & Segal, A. (2002). Passion with an umbrella: Grassroots activists in the workplace. In M. Lounsbury & M. Ventresca (eds.), *Social Structure and Organizations Revisited*. Bingley: Emerald Group Publishing, 125–168.

Singh, P., & Giacosa, E. (2019). Cognitive biases of consumers as barriers in transition towards circular economy. *Management Decision*, 57(4), 921–936.

Skoglund, A., & Böhm, S. (2020). Prefigurative partaking: Employees' environmental activism in an energy utility. *Organization Studies*, 41(9), 1257–1283.

Urbinati, A., Chiaroni, D., & Chiesa, V. (2017). Towards a new taxonomy of circular economy business models. *Journal of Cleaner Production*, 168, 487–498.

Veleva, V., & Bodkin, G. (2018). Corporate-entrepreneur collaborations to advance a circular economy. *Journal of Cleaner Production*, 188, 20–37.

Velter, M., Bitzer, V., Bocken, N., & Kemp, R. (2020). Sustainable business model innovation: The role of boundary work for multi-stakeholder alignment. *Journal of Cleaner Production*, 247, 119497.

Walker, E. T. (2012). Social movements, organizations, and fields: A decade of theoretical integration. *Contemporary Sociology*, 41(5), 576–587.

Winans, K., Kendall, A., & Deng, H. (2017). The history and current applications of the circular economy concept. *Renewable and Sustainable Energy Reviews*, 68, 825–833.

PART III

COLLABORATIVE INNOVATION FOR THE CIRCULAR ECONOMY

8. Open innovation and the adoption of environmental process innovations: information source and proximity to partner types

Robert A. W. Kok, Ward Ooms and Paul E. M. Ligthart

INTRODUCTION

The transition towards a circular economy requires firms to rethink their business models (Pieroni et al. 2019) and to reduce the flow and use of materials and energy through the adoption of new environmental processes and product technologies (Blomsma et al. 2019). A reduction in manufacturing firms' energy demand is essential for a circular economy because energy usage and supply lead to negative environmental effects (Gahm et al. 2016). However, energy is a non-substitutable production factor, and limiting the reduction in energy demand depends on the desired production output. Therefore, the improvement of energy efficiency is one of the central aspects of circularity (Blomsma et al. 2019). In this chapter, we focus on environmental process technologies and investigate the conditions under which open innovation practices influence their adoption.

Open innovation – the "purposive inflows and outflows of knowledge to accelerate internal innovation and to expand the markets for the external use of innovation" – is characterized as a boundary-spanning activity (Chesbrough 2006, p. 1). It is associated with the exploitation of intellectual property while using a large variety of knowledge sources for innovation, including customers, rivals, academics, and firms in unrelated industries (West and Gallagher 2006).

Environmental development has remained largely ignored in open innovation research (Hossain 2013). Most studies on open innovation effects focus only on overall firm or product innovation performance. Few researchers have actually investigated the link between open innovation and sustainability (Perl-Vorbach et al. 2014, p. 169). Moreover, the impact of open innovation practices on process innovation has hardly been addressed. Process innovation refers to the new elements introduced into a firm's production or service operation (Utterback and Abernathy 1975) to achieve greater efficiency (Stadler 2011).

The extant open innovation research has left several important issues unaddressed. First, there is reason to expect different effects of open innovation on process innovation compared with product innovation due to the variations in R&D related to partner type (Un and Asakawa 2015), the incompatibility of the exploration and exploitation processes (Benner and Tushman 2002) and differences in the knowledge of partners due to their main activities (Du et al. 2014) and geographical proximity (e.g. Capone and Lazzeretti 2018). Second, environmental process innovation requires unique strategies (Bönte and Dienes 2013), and its adoption relies on input from different specialists (Dewar and Dutton 1986). Choosing the right information sources and partner types for their open innovation activities is relevant for firms because the search for external knowledge can be costly (Mina et al. 2014). Hence, we aim to answer the following research question to examine these moderation effects: *What is the influence of the proximity of partner type and the type of information source on the relationship between open innovation practices and the adoption of environmental process innovations by manufacturing firms?*

The next section presents a literature review and conceptual framework, including our hypotheses. Then we describe the methods of the survey and analyses. The following section reports the empirical findings, and then we conclude the chapter by discussing these findings.

LITERATURE REVIEW AND CONCEPTUAL MODEL

Environmental Innovation and a Circular Economy

Environmental innovation requires more integrated thinking and the connection of a wider range of considerations compared with traditional innovation (Bos-Brouwers 2010). Consistently, we define it as a type of innovation placing "emphasis on a reduction in environmental impact, whether such an effect is intended or not" (OECD 2009, p. 13). Combined with the definition of process innovation, environmental process innovation is defined in our research as the creation of new knowledge and ideas aimed at improving internal production processes and reducing their environmental impacts.

Environmental process innovation is a key strategy for manufacturing firms to achieve circularity because these innovations can help individual firms restore, reduce, avoid the negative environmental impact of their operations (e.g. Blomsma et al. 2019; Potting et al. 2017), and even help to transform entire supply chains, closing the existing loop (e.g. Schenkel et al. 2015). Ultimately, environmental process innovation may help achieve the use of only "the absolute minimum input required to run a [manufacturing] process" (Blomsma et al. 2019, p. 10).

Open Innovation

Open innovation practices
Open innovation practices refer to the processes deciding "when, how, with whom, with what purpose, and in what way [a firm] should cooperate with external partners" (Huizingh 2011, p. 6). Inbound and outbound practices need to be included because they have different effects depending on internal and external conditions (Enkel et al. 2009). These practices are further categorized as technology exploitation practices, including venturing, outward IP licensing, employee involvement, and technology exploration practices, including customer involvement, external networking, external participation, outsourcing R&D, and inward IP licensing (van de Vrande et al. 2009) and are used in our study (see Figure 8.1 for the conceptual model).

Open innovation and environmental process innovations
Environmental process innovation typically requires firms to operate at the technological and knowledge frontier (De Marchi 2012; Jones 2009) and likely requires firms to look for and rely on the knowledge, skills and competences only available beyond firms' own boundaries (De Marchi and Grandinetti 2013). Firms pursuing innovation with environment-related goals tend to seek cooperation with external partners (e.g. De Marchi 2012; De Marchi and Grandinetti

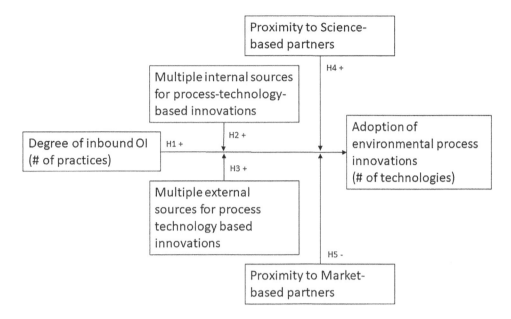

Figure 8.1   Conceptual model

2013), though an 'in-house strategy' may work equally well when using external knowledge through other channels, e.g., in-licensing and the purchasing of scientific services, rather than collaboration (Bönte and Dienes 2013). Both types qualify as open innovation practices. Therefore, we hypothesize the following:

H1: The degree of open innovation is positively related to the adoption of environmental process innovations.

Internal and External Information Sources

Irrespective of partner type, information sources may be internal (R&D, production, customer service and management) or external (customers, suppliers, research institutes and conferences/fairs) to the firm. However, firms are likely to be unsuccessful in absorbing external knowledge when they lack internal R&D (Cohen and Levinthal 1990). Internal knowledge sources help firms assess the value of external knowledge and enable the use of such knowledge in firms' internal processes. Hence, open innovation targeted at the acquisition of new knowledge, both from inside and outside the firm, is likely to help firms adopt environmental process innovations. Therefore, we hypothesize the following:

H2: The degree of internal information sources used for technological process innovation positively moderates the relationship between open innovation and the adoption of environmental process innovations.

H3: The degree of external information sources used for technological process innovation positively moderates the relationship between open innovation and the adoption of environmental process innovations.

Type and Location of Partner

There is good reason to consider engagement with different types of partners, as knowledge differs with the types of partners accessed (Danneels 2002; Faems et al. 2005).

Science-based partners serve primarily as sources of both scientific and technological knowledge (Perkmann et al. 2013), aimed at basic knowledge more than applied knowledge (Gilsing et al. 2011). Collaboration with science-based partners yields a number of advantages for environmental process innovation, as it maintains a broad knowledge base to tap into multiple disciplinary areas all at once (Klomp and Van Leeuwen 2001), aims to find solutions to specific technological problems (Fleming and Sorenson 2004) and excludes competitive forces (Hyll and Pippel 2016).

For collaboration with science-based partners, geographical proximity is advantageous. Knowledge is 'sticky' (Von Hippel 1994) and, therefore, more easily transferred between geographically close partners. Geographical proximity stimulates the development of other non-spatial proximities, which helps partners coordinate their collaboration efforts (Mahdad et al. 2020). Firms working with universities in their vicinity attain innovation outcomes in their R&D projects more easily (Broström 2010). Hence, we hypothesize the following:

H4: Collaboration with science-based partners who are geographically proximate to the focal firm enhances the positive effect of the degree of open innovation on the adoption of environmental process innovation.

Market-based partners such as customers, suppliers or competitors serve primarily as sources of customer or market knowledge (Danneels 2002). In general, market partners are more likely to have a similar knowledge base (Hyll and Pippel 2016), serving the continuity of current product offerings and related processes (Faems et al. 2005). Partners that are too 'proximate' create lock-ins, which inhibit innovation (Boschma 2005; Knoben and Oerlemans 2006) or favour incremental innovation (Jakobsen et al. 2019). Some market-based partners are not very helpful concerning environmental process innovation, where end users are less knowledgeable about operations related to the product on which they focus (Un and Asakawa 2015), and partners have an interest in protecting their knowledge (Lhuillery and Pfister 2009). Nevertheless, empirical evidence shows that collaboration with customers has a positive effect on the adoption of environmental process innovation, but collaboration with suppliers has no effect, although it does lead to cost savings (Grekova et al. 2016).

In terms of collaboration with market-based partners, geographical proximity can also have a positive effect. While collaboration with local firms may be beneficial in some respects in regard to technical advice, it needs to be complemented by firm partnerships at a larger geographical distance to obtain knowledge that is useful for innovation (Rodríguez-Pose and Fitjar 2013). Finally, market-based partners may have motives to discourage innovation unless they are serving different geographical markets (Faems et al. 2005). Consequently, we hypothesize the following:

H5: Collaboration with market-based partners who are geographically proximate to the focal firm attenuates the positive effect of the degree of open innovation on the adoption of environmental process innovation.

METHODS AND ANALYSIS

We use data on Dutch manufacturing firms using the European Manufacturing Survey (EMS) in 2015. The EMS uses a self-reporting questionnaire on modernization trends in manufacturing (ISI-Fraunhofer 2017). Respondents are the CEOs or operations managers of manufacturing firms (codes 10 to 33; NACE rev 2 2008) with 10 or more employees. The survey's focus on the factual measurement of practices in separate sections of the questionnaire reduces the risk of common method bias (Podsakoff et al. 2003).

Sample

The sample of 174 cases is weighted using the national population statistics from CBS (2015), making the reported findings representative with respect to sector (types of products) and firm size (number of employees).

Measures

Dependent variable
The adoption of environmental process innovations is measured as a metric count variable included in six yes/no-items: Control system for shut down of machines in off-peak periods, Control-automation systems for energy-efficient production, Technologies for the recuperation of kinetic and process energy, Switch-off systems not in use, Efficiency improvement of existing machines, and Premature replacement of existing machines. Respondents indicate whether or not the firm has adopted a new technology.

Independent variables
Open innovation is measured as a metric count variable, including the five inbound practices (Customer engagement, External networks, External participation, and Outsourcing of R&D) and three outbound practices (Spin-offs, Outgoing IP, and Employee engagement) suggested by van de Vrande et al. (2009) and using content validity assessments based on De Jong and Marsili (2006). Respondents answered the question 'How often has your organization conducted the following activities since 2012?' with scores of 0, 1 for one time and 2 for more than once, the last two of which were recoded into a 'more than once' category. The variables ranged from 0 to 8, indicating zero to all open innovation activities, respectively.

Moderating variables
The degree of external and internal sources of information used are measured as count variables. By answering the question 'Which of the following information sources are most relevant for the innovation incentives/ideas in your firm in the following fields?', respondents can indicate which internal sources (R&D department, production, customer service, and

management) and external sources (customers/users, suppliers, research institutes/universities, and management/organization consultants) are considered relevant for the innovation of new products, new process technologies, new services, and new organizational concepts. Both variables range from 0 (no sources used) to 4 (all sources relevant).

Proximity to science- and market-based partners is measured using dummies based on the question 'Does your firm cooperate with other firms/organizations in the following fields?', where cooperation is defined as collaboration beyond one-time transactions between firms. Using the answer categories '(1) regional (<50 km), (2) national (<50 km) or (3) international', proximity to science-based partners is measured using the item 'Cooperation in R&D with research institutes' (for example, universities and applied research institutes), and proximity to market-based partners is measured using the item 'Cooperation with customers or suppliers', in line with other works (e.g. Werker and Ooms 2020). The group of firms not engaged in any partnerships is used as the base category.

Control variables

Firm size is used to control for economies of scale. Size makes a difference in regard to innovation (Camisón-Zornoza et al. 2004) and environmental innovation propensity (Hemmelskamp 1999). Firm size is measured by the logarithm of the number of employees given the highly skewed distribution. Industry dummies are used to account for differences across industries (van de Vrande et al. 2009) (see Table 8.1).

RESULTS

Descriptive Statistics and Correlation Coefficients

With a mean of 1.4 (out of a maximum of 6 technologies), Dutch manufacturing firms have adopted only a limited number of environmental technologies (see Table 8.1). The degree of open innovation is moderate, with a mean of 3.5 out of 8. The use of external and internal information sources is below average, with means of 1.3 and 1.2, respectively. In addition, firms cooperate more with market-based than science-based partners, but in both cases, the use of national partners is dominant. The correlation between the adoption of environmental process innovations and open innovation is statistically significant.

Regression Results

Model 1 ($F=10.13$, $p<0.001$) has an R^2 value of 0.269 and shows the control variables with a statistically significant size effect, as expected (see Table 8.2). Only the Food and Textile industry appears to adopt significantly more environmental process innovations than does the Metal industry (base category). In model 2 ($F=6.85$, $p<0.001$), the main variables are added, which results in an R^2 value of 0.350, which is significantly different ($p<0.001$) from that in model 1. Model 3 ($F=4.78$, $p<0.001$) with added interaction variables does not improve the main effects of model 2. The adjusted R^2 value decreases somewhat given the larger number of parameters included in the full model ($R^2=0.342$, $p=0.622$).

We found support for Hypothesis 1, predicting that open innovation is positively related to the adoption of environmental process innovation, in model 2 ($B=0.155$, $p<0.0217$). The more

Table 8.1 Correlation statistics

	%	Mean	Std. dev.	Min.	Max.	1	2	3	4	5	6	7	8	9	10	11	12	13	14	15	16	17
1 Adoption of environmental process innovations		1.370	1.423	0	6	1																
2 Size (number of employees, log)		3.468	1.019	2.303	8.962	0.513	1															
Metal (base)	22.7																					
3 Food	15.2			0	1	0.078	-0.030	1														
4 Textile	13.2			0	1	0.070	-0.063	-0.165	1													
5 Construction	3.6			0	1	0.032	0.086	-0.081	-0.075	1												
6 Chemical	10.2			0	1	0.054	0.040	-0.142	-0.131	-0.065	1											
7 Machinery	23.7			0	1	0.038	0.075	-0.236	-0.217	-0.107	-0.188	1										
8 Electronic	11.4			0	1	-0.061	0.029	-0.152	-0.140	-0.069	-0.121	-0.200	1									
9 Open innovation		3.015	1.618	0	8	0.352	0.376	0.045	-0.044	0.090	0.029	0.048	0.023	1								
10 Internal sources of information		1.283	0.834	0	4	-0.051	0.069	-0.016	-0.018	0.050	0.107	-0.072	0.094	0.191	1							
11 External sources		1.179	0.889	0	4	0.172	-0.042	0.079	-0.136	0.043	-0.042	0.154	-0.112	-0.044	-0.451	1						
12 Regional science-based partners	15.9			0	1	0.131	0.312	-0.055	-0.081	0.060	0.094	-0.017	0.098	0.299	0.043	-0.047	1					
13 National science-based partners	27.5			0	1	0.247	0.270	0.106	-0.074	0.042	0.024	0.012	0.118	0.459	0.128	0.008	0.281	1				
14 International science-based partners	13.2			0	1	0.408	0.400	0.007	-0.052	-0.019	0.132	0.055	0.138	0.366	0.019	0.068	0.386	0.591	1			
15 Regional market-based partners	23.9			0	1	0.119	0.350	-0.075	-0.023	0.037	-0.156	0.101	0.053	0.266	0.105	0.000	0.423	0.251	0.299	1		
16 National market-based partners	43.2			0	1	0.226	0.232	-0.004	0.057	0.006	-0.059	0.150	-0.001	0.390	-0.100	0.092	0.205	0.442	0.349	0.353	1	
17 International market-based partners	31.4			0	1	0.236	0.256	-0.028	-0.027	0.003	0.083	0.023	0.056	0.311	0.128	-0.013	0.137	0.500	0.474	0.299	0.427	1

Note: 100% = N = 174 weighted, coefficients are significant > |0.124|.

Table 8.2   Regression results with environmental process innovation as the dependent variable

	Model 1		Model 2		Model 3	
	B	Std. Error	B	Std. Error	B	Std. Error
Intercept	-1.445***	0.359	-1.654***	0.44	-1.381**	0.514
Size (number of employees, log)	0.718***	0.092	0.605***	0.1	0.549***	0.112
Industry sector						
Metal (base)						
Food	0.636*	0.305	0.37	0.297	0.347	0.302
Textile	0.697*	0.318	0.628*	0.307	0.697*	0.315
Construction	0.235	0.527	0.066	0.503	0.111	0.509
Chemical	0.464	0.348	0.153	0.349	0.248	0.361
Machinery	0.322	0.271	0.063	0.264	0.065	0.272
Electronic	0.026	0.334	-0.121	0.326	-0.029	0.335
Open Innovation (OI)			0.155*	0.067	0.128	0.084
Sources of information						
Internal sources of information			-0.027	0.125	-0.037	0.131
External sources of information			0.287*	0.114	0.288*	0.12
Location of R&D partners						
Regional science-based partners			-0.268	0.287	-0.433	0.338
National science-based partners			-0.21	0.276	-0.29	0.323
International science-based partners			1.007**	0.365	0.816+	0.463
Regional market-based partners			-0.344	0.255	-0.323	0.262
National market-based partners			0.028	0.224	0.064	0.229
International market-based partners			0.107	0.238	0.117	0.249
Interaction OI * Sources of information						
OI * Internal sources					-0.124	0.076
OI * External sources					-0.023	0.071
Interaction OI * Location of R&D partners						
OI * Regional science-based partners					0.156	0.212
OI * National science-based partners					0.23	0.209
OI * International science-based partners					0.09	0.275
OI * Regional market-based partners					0.008	0.166
OI * National market-based partners					-0.184	0.164
OI * International market-based partners					0.029	0.178
Model statistics						
Adjusted R square	.269		0.350		0.342	

	Model 1		Model 2		Model 3	
	B	Std. Error	B	Std. Error	B	Std. Error
F	10.134	df (7,167)	6.850	df (16,158)	4.775	df (24,150)
Sig. model	0.001		0.001		0.001	
Sig. F-change	-10.134***	df (7,167)	3.314***	df (9,158)	0.779**	df (8,150}

Note: N= 174 weighted, B = unstandardized coefficient; significance level: + p< 0.10, * p<0.05, ** p<.01, and *** p<.001: p-value is based on two-sided tests).

open innovation practices a firm uses, the more environmental process innovations it adopts. With the interaction effects of the location of partner type included in the full model, the open innovation effect is only conditional for firms in the base category, i.e., those having no research partners. In this specific case, open innovation is not significant (B=0.128, p<0.129).

There is no support for Hypotheses 2 and 3, predicting that the external and internal sources of information moderate the relationship between open innovation and the adoption of environmental process innovations (see model 3). However, model 3 shows that the conditional effect in which having more external sources of information for firms without open innovation practices positively affects the adoption of environmental process innovations (B=0.288, p<0.0178).

Additionally, there is no support for Hypotheses 4 and 5, predicting that the proximity of the type of partner moderates the relationship between open innovation and the adoption of environmental process innovations (see model 3). However, model 3 shows that having international science-based partners is positively related to the adoption of environmental process innovations (B=0.816, $p_{one-sided}$ <0.0399). This conditional effect of location means that the more distant a science-based partner is, the more likely it is that environmental process innovations will be adopted, even if firms are not engaged in open innovation practices, contrary to our expectations.

DISCUSSION AND CONCLUSIONS

Controlling for organizational size and industry, we conclude that firms conducting more open inbound and outbound innovation practices also adopt more environmental process innovations. Larger Dutch manufacturing firms adopt more environmental process innovations compared to other firms. However, open innovation does not contribute to the adoption of environmental process innovations if firms do not collaborate with any partners.

Irrespective of the use of open innovation practices, the use of more external sources of information and collaboration with international science-based R&D partners benefit the adoption of environmental process innovations. Apparently, both types of activities work as alternatives to open innovation practices. One explanation is that for circular business models to work or for circular production processes and supply chains to operate, an interorganizational perspective is required (e.g. Blomsma et al. 2019; Schenkel et al. 2015). A second explanation is that for environmental innovations in production processes, international science-based partners are needed for the advancement of the basic research conducted (see e.g. De Marchi 2012; Jones 2009), but such partners are not necessarily available at an arm's length to the firms. Not surprisingly, we find no support for the positive effects of proximity for regional or national science-based partners; they may simply not have the appropriate knowledge.

Additionally, no support is found that the adoption of environmental process innovation is (a) related to the use of internal sources of information; (b) related to collaboration with market-based partners, whether regional, national or international; and (c) subject to moderation by types of sources of information and/or the proximity to different types of partners.

Theoretical Implications

This research contributes to the theory on the impact of open innovation practices, paying limited attention to (environmental) process innovation, industrial sector differences, and organizational factors (Chesbrough 2003; Huizingh 2011). Our research shows that having more open innovation practices is important but that the use of more external sources of information and working with international science-based partners is relatively more important for the adoption of environmental process innovations. That is, the latter two activities promote environmental process innovation, even for firms that have no open innovation practices, which is different from the view of Van de Vrande et al. (2009). These findings reaffirm the results of previous studies that point to the relevance of cooperation with external partners (Perl-Vorbach et al. 2014) but contradict the findings by Bönte and Dienes (2013), suggesting that a cooperation or external strategy does not have an effect. Our findings also suggest that having international science-based partners, in contrast to market-based partners, makes a difference, in line with some studies (e.g. Bönte and Dienes 2013; Danneels 2002; Du et al. 2014) but contradicting others (e.g. Un and Asakawa 2015).

Limitations and Future Research

First, while this study provided insights into the adoption of environmental process innovations, future research can investigate the radicalness and adoption timing of environmental process innovations to determine their relationship with open innovation practices. Second, using the Dutch sample of the EMS limits the generalizability outside of this context. Third, theoretically, the success of newly implemented technologies depends on several other factors, including firm-, technology-, and cooperation-specific factors.

Managerial and Policy Implications

This study also has important managerial implications. It suggests that managers need to be careful in choosing partners for their firms' R&D collaborations. Engaging in R&D collaborations with universities and suppliers appears to be helpful for process innovation.

This research encourages firms to practise inbound and outbound open innovation, use more external information sources, or cooperate with international science-based partners because it helps them achieve a greater adoption of environmental process innovations. These practices and collaborations provide access to different knowledge bases. However, we should point out that these practices substitute rather than reinforce each other. Conversely, cooperation with market-based partners – whether regional, national or international – does not appear to stimulate environmental process innovations. Hence, firms should focus on particular external information sources, such as external networks of process equipment suppliers, the outsourcing of

R&D, or external equity participation. Alternatively, firms can develop science-based partnerships either with international universities or with applied research institutes to obtain help. Similarly, governments can stimulate environmental innovations and the circular economy at large by investing in fundamental research at universities and other research institutions.

REFERENCES

Benner, M. J., & Tushman, M. (2002). Process management and technological innovation: A longitudinal study of the photography and paint industries. *Administrative Science Quarterly*, 47, 676–706.

Blomsma, F., Pieroni, M., Kravchenko, M., Pigosso, D. C., Hildenbrand, J., Kristinsdottir, A. R., et al. (2019). Developing a circular strategies framework for manufacturing companies to support circular economy-oriented innovation. *Journal of Cleaner Production*, 241, 118271.

Bönte, W., & Dienes, C. (2013). Environmental innovations and strategies for the development of new production technologies: Empirical evidence from Europe. *Business Strategy and the Environment*, 22(8), 501–516.

Bos-Brouwers, H. E. J. (2010). Corporate sustainability and innovation in SMEs: Evidence of themes and activities in practice. *Business Strategy and the Environment*, 19(7), 417–435.

Boschma, R. A. (2005). Proximity and innovation: A critical assessment. *Regional Studies*, 39(1), 61–74.

Broström, A. (2010). Working with distant researchers: Distance and content in university–industry interaction. *Research Policy*, 39(10), 1311–1320.

Camisón-Zornoza, C., Lapiedra-Alcamí, R., Segarra-Ciprés, M., & Boronat-Navarro, M. (2004). A meta-analysis of innovation and organizational size. *Organization Studies*, 25(3), 331–361.

Capone, F., & Lazzeretti, L. (2018). The different roles of proximity in multiple informal network relationships: Evidence from the cluster of high technology applied to cultural goods in Tuscany. *Industry and Innovation*, 25(9), 897–917.

CBS (2015). Q2 2018. https://opendata.cbs.nl/statline/#/CBS/nl/dataset/81589NED.

Chesbrough, H. (2003). The era of open innovation. *MIT Sloan Management Review*, 44(3), 35–41.

Chesbrough, H. (2006). Open innovation: A new paradigm for understanding industrial innovation. In H. Chesbrough, W. Vanhaverbeke, & J. West (eds.), *Open Innovation: Researching a New Paradigm*. Oxford: Oxford University Press, 1–14.

Cohen, W. M., & Levinthal, D. A. (1990). Absorptive capacity: A new perspective on learning and innovation. *Administrative Science Quarterly*, 35, 128–152.

Danneels, E. (2002). The dynamics of product innovation and firm competences. *Strategic Management Journal*, 23, 1095–1121.

De Jong, J. P., & Marsili, O. (2006). The fruit flies of innovations: A taxonomy of innovative small firms. *Research Policy*, 35(2), 213–229.

De Marchi, V. (2012). Environmental innovation and R&D cooperation: Empirical evidence from Spanish manufacturing firms. *Research Policy*, 41(3), 614–623.

De Marchi, V., & Grandinetti, R. (2013). Knowledge strategies for environmental innovations: The case of Italian manufacturing firms. *Journal of Knowledge Management*, 17(4), 569–582.

Dewar, R. D., & Dutton, J. E. (1986). The adoption of radical and incremental innovations: An empirical analysis. *Management Science*, 32(11), 1422–1433.

Du, J., Leten, B., & Vanhaverbeke, W. (2014). Managing open innovation projects with science-based and market-based partners. *Research Policy*, 43(5), 828–840.

Enkel, E., Gassmann, O., & Chesbrough, H. (2009). Open R&D and open innovation: Exploring the phenomenon. *R&D Management*, 39(4), 311–316.

Faems, D., Van Looy, B., & Debackere, K. (2005). Interorganizational collaboration and innovation: Toward a portfolio approach. *Journal of Product Innovation Management*, 22(3), 238–250.

Fleming, L., & Sorenson, O. (2004). Science as a map in technological search. *Strategic Management Journal*, 25(8–9), 909–928.

Gahm, C., Denz, F., Dirr, M., & Tuma, A. (2016). Energy-efficient scheduling in manufacturing companies: A review and research framework. *European Journal of Operational Research*, 248(3), 744–757.

Gilsing, V., Bekkers, R., Freitas, I. M. B., & Van der Steen, M. (2011). Differences in technology transfer between science-based and development-based industries: Transfer mechanisms and barriers. *Technovation*, 31(12), 638–647.

Grekova, K., Calantone, R., Bremmers, H., Trienekens, J., & Omta, S. (2016). How environmental collaboration with suppliers and customers influences firm performance: Evidence from Dutch food and beverage processors. *Journal of Cleaner Production*, 112, 1861–1871.

Hemmelskamp, J. (1999). The influence of environmental policy on innovative behaviour: An econometric study. Fondazione Eni Enrico Mattei Working Paper No. 18.99. Milan.

Hossain, M. (2013). Open innovation: So far and a way forward. *World Journal of Science, Technology and Sustainable Development*, 10(1), 30–41.

Huizingh, E. K. R. E. (2011). Open innovation: State of the art and future perspectives. *Technovation*, 31(1), 2–9.

Hyll, W., & Pippel, G. (2016). Types of cooperation partners as determinants of innovation failures. *Technology Analysis & Strategic Management*, 28(4), 462–476.

ISI-Fraunhofer (2017). European Manufacturing Survey. http://www.isi.fraunhofer.de/isi-en/i/projekte/fems.php.

Jakobsen, S., Lauvås, T. A., & Steinmo, M. (2019). Collaborative dynamics in environmental R&D alliances. *Journal of Cleaner Production*, 212, 950–959.

Jones, B. F. (2009). The burden of knowledge and the "death of the renaissance man": Is innovation getting harder? *Review of Economic Studies*, 76(1), 283–317.

Klomp, L., & Van Leeuwen, G. (2001). Linking innovation and firm performance: A new approach. *International Journal of the Economics of Business*, 8(3), 343–364.

Knoben, J., & Oerlemans, L. A. (2006). Proximity and inter-organizational collaboration: A literature review. *International Journal of Management Reviews*, 8(2), 71–89.

Lhuillery, S., & Pfister, E. (2009). R&D cooperation and failures in innovation projects: Empirical evidence from French CIS data. *Research Policy*, 38(1), 45–57.

Mahdad, M., Minh, T. T., Bogers, M. L., & Piccaluga, A. (2020). Joint university-industry laboratories through the lens of proximity dimensions: Moving beyond geographical proximity. *International Journal of Innovation Science*, 12(4), 433–456.

Mina, A., Bascavusoglu-Moreau, E., & Hughes, A. (2014). Open service innovation and the firm's search for external knowledge. *Research Policy*, 43(5), 853–866.

OECD (2009). *Eco-Innovation in Industry: Enabling Green Growth*. Paris: Organisation for Economic Co-operation and Development.

Perkmann, M., Tartari, V., McKelvey, M., Autio, E., Broström, A., D'Este, P., et al. (2013). Academic engagement and commercialisation: A review of the literature on university–industry relations. *Research Policy*, 42(2), 423–442.

Perl-Vorbach, E., Rauter, R., & Baumgartner, R. J. (2014). Open innovation in the context of sustainable innovation: Findings based on a literature review. Paper presented at the 9th International Symposium on Sustainable Leadership.

Pieroni, M. P., McAloone, T. C., & Pigosso, D. C. (2019). Business model innovation for circular economy and sustainability: A review of approaches. *Journal of Cleaner Production*, 215, 198–216.

Podsakoff, P. M., MacKenzie, S. B., Lee, J. Y., & Podsakoff, N. P. (2003). Common method biases in behavioral research: A critical review of the literature and recommended remedies. *Journal of Applied Psychology*, 88(5), 879–903.

Potting, J., Hekkert, M., Worrell, E., & Hanemaaijer, A. (2017). *Circular Economy: Measuring Innovation in the Product Chain*. The Hague: PBL Publishers.

Rodríguez-Pose, A., & Fitjar, R. D. (2013). Buzz, archipelago economies and the future of intermediate and peripheral areas in a spiky world. *European Planning Studies*, 21(3), 355–372.

Schenkel, M., Caniëls, M. C., Krikke, H., & van der Laan, E. (2015). Understanding value creation in closed loop supply chains: Past findings and future directions. *Journal of Manufacturing Systems*, 37, 729–745.

Stadler, C. (2011). Process innovation and integration in process-oriented settings: The case of the oil industry. *Journal of Product Innovation Management*, 28(s1), 44–62.

Un, C. A., & Asakawa, K. (2015). Types of R&D collaborations and process innovation: The benefit of collaborating upstream in the knowledge chain. *Journal of Product Innovation Management*, 32(1), 138–153.

Utterback, J. M., & Abernathy, W. J. (1975). A dynamic model of process and product innovation. *Omega*, 3(6), 639–656.

van de Vrande, V., de Jong, J. P. J., Vanhaverbeke, W., & de Rochemont, M. (2009). Open innovation in SMEs: Trends, motives and management challenges. *Technovation*, 29(6–7), 423–437.

Von Hippel, E. (1994). "Sticky information" and the locus of problem solving: Implications for innovation. *Management Science*, 40(4), 429–439.

Werker, C., & Ooms, W. (2020). Substituting face-to-face contacts in academics' collaborations: Modern communication tools, proximity, and brokerage. *Studies in Higher Education*, 45(7), 1431–1447.

West, J., & Gallagher, S. (2006). Challenges of open innovation: The paradox of firm investment in open-source software. *R&D Management*, 36(3), 319–331.

9. A reverse logistics framework for circular supply chains

Stine Sonen Tveit, Ottar Bakås and Maria Kollberg Thomassen

INTRODUCTION

Twenty years ago, most companies were busy fine-tuning linear supply chains from raw material to the end customer. Now, there is a growing interest in obtaining value from products that have reached their end-of-use (Rubio and Jiménez-Parra 2014). Circular economy (CE) offers an alternative model replacing disposal with reuse of materials in production, distribution, and consumption. CE is based on the principles of designing out waste and pollution, keeping products and materials in use, and regenerating natural systems (Ellen MacArthur Foundation 2019).

Reverse logistics (RL) plays a vital role in a circular economy model and has the potential to decrease material usage by manufacturers. A common definition of RL in literature is the process of planning, implementing and controlling backward flows of raw materials, in-process inventory, packaging and finished goods, from a manufacturing, distribution or use point, to a point of recovery or proper disposal (De Brito and Dekker 2004; Rubio et al. 2008). During the last decades, RL has received growing attention, due to a combination of economic, environmental and social factors (Agrawal et al. 2015) and is becoming a key competence in modern supply chains (Morgan et al. 2016).

RL places new requirements for innovation and collaboration across actors in a reverse supply chain, which typically involves more independent actors than traditional forward supply chains (De Angelis et al. 2018). Traditional SCM often describes the chain of value creation in a linear, one-directional fashion, with fewer interfaces and responsibilities. In a circular model, the flow of value is sustained by combining the variety of possible configurations (Masi et al. 2017). Innovation is needed to enable circular business models with novel product flow loops between actors (Geissdoerfer et al. 2018). Therefore, the topic of RL is deemed particularly interesting to enable innovation for a circular economy.

Several industries, such as automotive, electronics and textile have experienced an increase of RL practices in recent years, as companies have embraced the potential for value creation and environmental benefits (Alshamsi and Diabat 2015). While RL has been known for a long time to benefit the environment, the progress has been slow, partly because the activities have rarely been considered as a value-creating system from a business perspective (Guide and Van Wassenhove 2009). Some actors have been forced to take back products, while others have proactively done so (De Brito and Dekker 2004). In general, high recovery rates are needed to obtain financial sustainability. Altekin et al. (2008) found that reuse and recycling rates higher than 58 per cent were required to achieve profitable operations within electronic product groups.

There has been a steady increase in the amount of research on RL issues since the 1990s, indicating a growing interest in the field (see for instance literature reviews by Agrawal et al. 2015; Govindan et al. 2015; Rubio et al. 2008). Even so, more research addressing strategic factors of RL systems are called for (Rubio and Jiménez-Parra 2014). RL practices are still underdeveloped in many industries, and existing models are not easily transferable across sectors (Kumar and Putnam 2008). There is a need to develop a further understanding of the role of RL related to current challenges and future opportunities in different sectors (Govindan et al. 2015).

The furniture industry is identified to have a major improvement potential. This sector contributes yearly with large waste volumes and low product recovery rates. Today, approximately 10 million tons of furniture are discarded every year in the European Union, and the overall recycling rate for furniture is estimated at only 10 per cent (European Commission 2019). The furniture industry has a particular challenge of relatively low residual value of products. France is the only country in Europe that has introduced Extended Producer Responsibility (EPR) for the furniture sector (European Commission 2019). EPR is a policy approach where the producer's responsibility for a product is extended to the post-consumer stage of the lifecycle (OECD 2016).

Circular economy has the potential to contribute to value recovery, economic growth and job creation while saving on resources and environment. Even though there is a potential to exploit major CE benefits in the furniture industry, RL practices are still rarely deployed (Forrest et al. 2017). Therefore, two research questions were designed to study the topic in further detail.

RQ1: What are the key strategic aspects of designing a reverse logistics system?

We identify key strategy aspects of reverse logistics, based upon current research literature. These findings are summarized in a framework for RL, aimed at contributing to a holistic view of critical decision areas when transforming from linear supply chains to circular business models with reverse logistics.

RQ2: What are the major challenges and opportunities related to the strategic aspects for reverse logistics in a furniture supply chain?

Here, we present a case study from a large manufacturer in the furniture industry. We apply the strategic framework to highlight specific challenges for furniture manufacturers. This chapter describes possibilities and challenges in achieving a supply network with reuse of materials.

The structure of the chapter is as follows: First, the methodology of the research is presented. Next, a theoretical framework is presented, with key strategic aspects of reverse logistics. Then, a case study is presented, highlighting challenges and opportunities within the strategic factors. Last, the findings are discussed, comparing theory and practice, and highlighting implications for practice and further research.

METHODOLOGICAL CONSIDERATIONS

This research is based upon a case research strategy, including a literature review and an empirical study of a furniture manufacturer. The study is part of a three-year research and innovation project addressing circularity strategies for furniture.

The literature review aimed to identify strategic aspects of RL by investigating current state-of-the-art in existing research literature. Search engines, such as Web of Science and Google Scholar, combined with snowballing method, were used to identify relevant literature. The review was carried out iteratively and in parallel with the empirical study, allowing a continuous adjustment of scope during the research process. The empirical study involves data of a RL system of a furniture manufacturing company (hereafter referred to as Alpha). Through a strong commitment and major investments in sustainability and design for more than 40 years, Alpha has become a leading supplier of furniture with low environmental impact in the market. The case company Alpha was selected because of its pioneering role in applying sustainability practices in the industry.

Various methods for data collection were used. Data were collected primarily from Alpha, but also from four other companies to provide relevant insight to current practices and potential development of the RL system for furniture. Data collection was carried out between 2018 and 2019, including 17 interviews, four site visits and three workshops in addition to documents, reports and observations. Respondents were selected representing top management, operations and supply chain, research and development, sales and marketing, product management, business development and environmental management. Interviews were semi-structured with a set of guiding topics.

THEORETICAL FRAMEWORK

We have identified seven key strategic aspects of reverse logistics from literature. The key aspects are customers, partnerships and networks, collection, sorting, disassembly, recovery and information and communications technology (ICT). An overview of the key aspects is given in Table 9.1 and further presented below.

Table 9.1   *A reverse logistics framework with key strategic aspects identified in literature*

Key aspect	Elements	References
Customers	Return willingness, knowledge, education and information, financial incentives	De Brito & Dekker 2004; Guide & Van Wassenhove 2009; Shaharudin et al. 2015
Partnerships and networks	Network design, roles and responsibilities, transportation, location of facilities	Dekker et al. 2004; Rubio & Jiménez-Parra 2014; Özceylan & Paksoy 2013
Collection	Quality and volumes, location, involvement of actors	Das & Chowdhury 2012; Krumwiede & Sheu 2002; Sangwan 2017
Sorting	Product volumes and variation, quality, recovery options, sorting skills	Galbreth & Blackburn 2006; Sangwan 2017
Disassembly	Product volumes and variation, design for disassembly, automation	Altekin et al. 2008; Desai & Mital 2003; Özceylan & Paksoy 2013
Recovery	Process considerations, quality assurance, recovery options (reuse, repair, re-manufacture, recycle)	Cannella et al. 2016; Sangwan 2017
Information and communications technology (ICT)	Costs and benefits, automation, supply chain information sharing and collaboration	Kokkinaki et al. 2004; Olorunniwo & Li 2010

Customers

In RL systems, customers are typically identified as key actors (De Brito and Dekker 2004), especially with regards to the return of products after use to ensure reversed product flows. An important element is customers' willingness to return their obsolete products (Shaharudin et al. 2015). Customers need to have enough knowledge and information on how to handle end-of-use or end-of-life products in a sustainable way to avoid final disposal (Guide and Van Wassenhove 2009). Customers may be stimulated to return products by incentives such as offering discounts, charity donations or direct fees in exchange for returned products (De Brito and Dekker 2004).

Partnerships and Networks

A typical challenge in RL is the overall network design, including deciding the number and location of facilities, and establishing material flows between facilities (Rubio and Jiménez-Parra 2014). Reverse networks typically involve several actors with different roles and responsibilities, and multiple decision-makers make choices that determine the efficiency of the process (Dekker et al. 2004). An understanding of the supply chain is important for managing arrival, storing and disposal of recovered modules and products. Decisions regarding network design can be based upon cost considerations related to location, transportation, capacity and storing, remanufacturing facilities and allocation of material flows (Özceylan and Paksoy 2013). Even if RL is assumed to have a positive environmental contribution, there is a risk that environmental benefits are lost if distances between locations are too long. Systems for returnable containers have been developed that may help to reduce the need for transportation.

Collection

Two critical aspects of the collection process are the location of collection centres and collection methods of the involved actors, such as retailers and logistics providers (Sangwan 2017). The collection process is also dependent upon the quality of products and components (Das and Chowdhury 2012). There is often high uncertainty related to product quality and volumes, which makes it difficult to anticipate workload and profit. The need for end-user efforts and challenges with distances between locations typically depend upon whether products are collected from individual users or organizations. Collection can be carried out directly by the manufacturer, through a network of distributors and retailer, or through third-party logistics providers. By procuring assistance from third-party providers, logistics costs can be reduced (Krumwiede and Sheu 2002).

Sorting

Sorting involves deciding which of the used products should be recovered and which should be scrapped (Galbreth and Blackburn 2006). Inspection and sorting include operations that determine product quality, whether a given product is suited for recovery, and involves decision regarding degree of disassembly (Sangwan 2017). All used products need to be tested and sorted according to suited recovery processes. Responsible parties must have sufficient expertise to consider product-specific characteristics to channel them to the right recovery option. Due to high uncertainty in terms of quantity, quality and time needed, it is important to consider the value of sorting related to the availability of recovery options.

Disassembly

Disassembly is a method for separating a product into its constituent parts, sub-assemblies or other groups (Altekin et al. 2008). Product volumes, demand level and product structure are key factors for efficient disassembly (Özceylan and Paksoy 2013). The product development phase is critical in achieving an effective RL system, since product design determines the effectiveness of disassembly (Desai and Mital 2003). Typical guidelines for design for disassembly include repetition of parts, use of common materials and simple product structures (Desai and Mital 2003). Disassembly is often costly, as it relies heavily on manual labour. Automation of disassembly operations is challenging with high product variation in terms of size and composition.

Recovery

The recovery process generates new economic value of returned products. Different recovery options should be considered when products are inspected and sorted. The main types of product recovery are *reuse, repair, refurbishment, re-manufacturing* and *recycling*. Reuse means that products are used for the same purpose more than once. This option is relevant if a product is in a good condition, fulfils its original functions and there is an active secondary market. Repair involves maintenance and minor fixes of a defective product so it can be used with its original function. Refurbishment means restoring used products and bringing them up to date, a way of upgrading used products. Re-manufacturing implies an extensive process of restoring the used products to a common standard. Recycling means that returned products lose their identities, and only the economic value of the raw materials is recovered. Recycling into raw materials may turn into new business opportunities by re-injecting these materials into the beginning of a new product lifecycle (Cannella et al. 2016; Sangwan 2017).

ICT

Information and communications technologies are found to be critical for efficient RL practices. Various technologies are widely applied in product data management, operations support and e-marketplaces (Kokkinaki et al. 2004). Still, there is lack of insights to its use in RL processes and associated costs and savings. Typical challenges are lack of product return systems, difficulties in cost-justification, automation issues due to high degree of exceptions in returns and processes spanning across company boundaries (De Brito and Dekker 2004). ICT for supply chain collaboration is an essential aspect for RL performance. Information sharing can reduce uncertainties by giving access to accurate and timely information on the status, location and condition of products (Olorunniwo and Li 2010).

CASE FINDINGS

This chapter describes opportunities and challenges related to the development of RL practices identified in the case company, the furniture manufacturer Alpha. Findings are presented based upon the framework of key strategic aspects identified in literature.

Customers

Alpha mainly operates within the business-to-business (B2B) segment of office furniture. A main challenge for the case company has been to ensure a stable volume of product returns from their customers. They seek to reduce return barriers for customers by providing clearly available information and guidelines about the return process. Alpha has established a strategic collaboration with a service provider, that buys batches of used furniture in good condition from customers. The buying-back solution constitutes an incentive for return and customers contact the service supplier when they need to upgrade their furniture. Alpha experiences a high variation in the environmental awareness among office furniture customers. The service supplier offers company visits to educate customers on sustainability and how to handle their products at end-of-use/end-of-life.

A major problem is the high labour and service costs for reverse flows of used furniture. Alpha experiences that due to high RL costs, the price difference between new and recovered furniture is still too small to see a major increase in recovered products among their customers.

Partnerships and Networks

Alpha experiences generally low profitability for recovered furniture due to low levels of demand in some markets. It is thus challenging to identify partners and establish a stable set of roles and responsibilities in the reverse supply chain. Alpha has actively explored potential partnership opportunities in developing new RL practices, testing solutions in collaboration with various partners, and adopting an open innovation approach. In one of their international markets with a high demand of recovered products, Alpha has established collaboration with a third-party supplier offering services such as sorting, disassembly, cleaning, re-assembly and storage. The supplier's ambition is to extend the lifespan of returned office furniture up to 20 years by dismantling and rebuilding products according to certified standard procedures. Components are reused according to specifications and waste is minimized.

Even though third-party logistics providers, waste collectors or other specialized RL partners are involved in the reverse supply chain, Alpha is responsible for ensuring that their recovered second life products meet certified standards. It is thus important that actors per-forming the services and remanufacturing have necessary skills to perform the processes in line with Alpha's standards.

To avoid long transportation distances and reduce emissions, Alpha seeks to locate collect-ing points, disassembly centres and plants for recovery processes close to customers. There are several opportunities for filling up trucks in both directions, for example providing services for collection of old furniture when delivering new products or renting services, including collec-tion of used furniture after the rental period. Furthermore, Alpha collaborates with suppliers to reuse containers and loads carriers to optimize truck loads and to protect returned products from being damaged during handling.

Collection

Alpha sells several hundred thousand furniture products each year to customers all over the world. Establishing suitable collection points for returned furniture is critical, whether they engage a third-party logistics provider, collection centres or retailers. However, the long lifespan of their furniture, combined with the high variation in customers' awareness and demand makes the collection process unpredictable. Due to high uncertainty of incoming volumes and quality of products, it is difficult to design an optimal network.

Alpha's third-party service provider operates in a market where customers often are aware of the importance of product recovery. Still, they have difficulties making their circular services economically feasible and have to offer a broad set of services alongside refurbishment of furniture. By establishing both in-house and outsourced service teams in the collection process, Alpha can monitor used products and give feedback to internal operations, that can help to improve product development and manufacturing.

Sorting

A critical aspect of the sorting process is the product competence of the actor performing it. The service suppliers specialized in the field of circular solutions have several sorting processes. Preliminary sorting is based on product brands. Other sorting criteria are transport considerations (recovery centres vs. manufacturing facilities), component quality (level of defects) and separate sorting for recycling. Alpha and their service partner have entered an exclusivity agreement. This has enabled the service partner to obtain specialized knowledge of sorting considerations within each of the brands in Alpha's broad product range.

Determining a categorization mechanism for quality levels of components and products is critical to be able to sort efficiently. Specific classification can easily be measured with picture examples for each model. However, in a long-term perspective a potential route for Alpha is to expand their range of smart furniture with self-monitoring and communication capabilities.

Disassembly

Due to high product variety and manual workstations, the disassembly process of Alpha products is costly and time-consuming. Alpha provides necessary jigs, equipment and competence for the manual disassembly and re-assembly processes of the third-party service provider. Even though automated disassembly lines may facilitate return of products at any dismantling centre and improve efficiency, the financial risk is high due to high uncertainty in the flow of incoming products. Also, Alpha assists the supplier in initial training and support related to how to carry out maintenance of new equipment, as well as supplying necessary components when broken parts are replaced. Each product typically consists of over a hundred components. A reduced number of components may increase efficiency of inspection, sorting and disassembly and reduce risk of damaging components.

There are also opportunities for new product innovations based upon design for disassembly principles combined with monitoring of RL activities. For example, modularity and standard locking mechanisms can enhance the disassembly process and facilitate separation of components. By considering design for disassembly principles and use of recyclable materials in product development, major innovation opportunities may be identified that support increased product recovery.

Alpha experiences several disassembly challenges, such as poor component quality due to high use of recycled materials. Design for disassembly is key for the further development of Alpha's RL strategy. Expanded guidelines for design for disassembly were developed, helping Alpha to improve efficiency in disassembly and make it easier for RL partners to perform the disassembly without special equipment. The guidelines, which encompass components and materials, product structure, disassembly mechanisms and operation, can also be used for developing more financially sustainable RL systems with flexible automation technology.

Recovery

Alpha's office furniture is of high quality and long lifespan. However, due to changing trends in interior design, the appearance of furniture may become outdated. This can be handled through refurbishment and applying new textiles. Partial recovery and reuse of components as well as easy repair practices can contribute to extend lifespans. However, Alpha experiences that their customers are rarely aware of how to maintain and repair their office furniture to prolong and extend the lifespan. Most recovery is carried out at the recovery facility of the third-party service provider. A final screening determines the suitable type of recovery process for each product. The high cost of recovery and lack of spare parts often means that customers choose new furniture over recovered products.

Alpha uses recycled materials from various waste sources in ordinary products and in special product editions. A high share of recycled materials in Alpha's standard product portfolio combined with increased communication can help to increase the environmental awareness among customers and generate new circularity opportunities. However, high uncertainty in regulations and standards is a problem for industrial scalability as well as for developing efficient disassembly and transportation methods. With increasing volumes of returned furniture, Alpha sees opportunities to establish dedicated production lines for used furniture in combination with existing production sites.

ICT

In circular tenders, providing product documentation for meeting circular performance requirements often imposes a major challenge for Alpha. Information on material properties needs to be collected from a wide range of suppliers and partners in the supply chain. As each individual company has its specific supply chain relationships with multiple tiers of suppliers, several issues arise. Alpha experiences that information is rapidly outdated and too detailed, few standards are available, and the process is highly time-consuming.

ICT systems that support sharing information on products and suppliers across companies in the supply chain regarding circular performance will therefore be critical. To achieve further RL systems improvements, Alpha sees major opportunities in further development of the procurement process where suppliers understand barriers and enablers of efficient information sharing, such as data sharing possibilities and tracking of materials and emissions within transportation.

DISCUSSION

This study proposes a framework with a set of key strategic aspects for designing RL systems to improve circularity performance. Many of these aspects are related to relationships with various actors in the supply chain, involving customers, suppliers, and other partners. This is in line with the general understanding in current literature that reverse supply chains typically involve more independent actors than traditional forward supply chains and impose further requirements for collaboration between actors (De Angelis et al. 2018; Guide and Van Wassenhove 2009).

The framework further gathers and describes key aspects based upon the current body of research addressing RL issues that has been growing during the last decades. Since a wide range of industries were included in the literature review, the framework adds to an improved understanding of general key aspects that can be applied in various industry settings, contributing to improved transferability of RL systems across industries that has been called for in previous research (Kumar and Putnam 2008).

By applying the framework in a furniture manufacturing firm, this study provides further empirical insights into major opportunities and challenges of designing RL systems. The empirical findings add to an improved knowledge of the role of RL related to current challenges and future opportunities in different sectors that is called for in previous research (Govindan et al. 2015), by providing further detailed empirical insights into issues that are specific for the furniture industry. While there has been an increase of RL practices in selected industries (Alshamsi and Diabat 2015), increased environmental awareness and new legislations may drive the development of RL practices in other sectors. It can thus be expected that we will see a further growth in empirical studies of RL practices in additional industries.

The aspects identified in the literature were confirmed to have high relevance for the specific case company. The case especially highlights the importance of collaboration with a specialized third-party RL service provider and the potential for achieving environmental benefits by adopting an RL strategy for handling used products. In addition, the case shows that RL systems can be financially challenging due to the high costs related to reverse product flows and services for disassembly and recovery of used products. The findings thus confirm that stable and predictable volumes of ingoing products as well as high volumes are important for developing profitable RL operations (Ene and Öztürk 2014). Major opportunities lie in the development of new policy instruments, such as the EPR scheme for furniture established in France, that may provide incentives for increased volumes and drive the development of improved RL practices.

The length of the products' lifespan also seems to be important for improving predictability of quantity and quality of returned products. In the professional B2B office furniture market, customers rarely buy office furniture only from one manufacturer, but rather several competing manufacturers distributing through same retailers. This implies that there is a high mix of various furniture potentially returned at the same time. To be a relevant RL partner for customers, the collection process should include all brands of office furniture. This complicates the sorting process and volume predictions to recovery centres and manufacturing facilities. Due to lack of specialized skills and equipment for disassembly of used furniture from other manufacturers, the case shows that the manufacturer prioritizes its own products.

Besides the importance of incoming flows of used furniture, the case reveals that the demand for recovered furniture is especially critical. The case company experiences increased circularity requirements in public tenders, and it has a strong focus on design for disassembly in product development to ensure the most efficient manual disassembly processes, which may help to reduce marked prices for second life furniture and lead to increased demand. The case highlights the potential to improve IT support for obtaining environmental data from suppliers. The sourcing process, with supplier evaluation, plays a vital role in this regard.

Regarding circular economy innovation, the study reveals several innovations related to RL in the case company to achieve better CE performance. Organizational and supply chain innovations involve strategic collaboration with RL partners to be able to offer circular services within markets with high demands of circular solutions. Also, the company has realized new product innovations to accomplish higher reuse value of materials and components by design for disassembly and monitoring used products to eliminate usual wear and tear.

CONCLUSION

This research proposes a framework of key strategic aspects for RL and identifies major challenges and opportunities in the supply chain of a furniture manufacturing company. Some previous works exist addressing critical aspects of RL in supply chain settings, for instance De Brito and Dekker (2004), and Rubio and Jiménez-Parra (2014). However, current research provides only limited practical support for companies seeking to explore new business opportunities in a CE context. Also, relevant research on RL addressing issues in furniture supply chains is limited. This study contributes to the research field, by structuring current research in a theoretical framework for RL and adding further details by including empirical insights to challenges and opportunities in designing RL systems in the supply chain of a furniture manufacturer.

The research is expected to have implications for other researchers interested in investigating current RL practices and seeking further understanding of how to develop new solutions. The suggested framework and strategic aspects provide support to future research by highlighting relevant aspects for further investigation. Also, managers in companies that seek to develop strategies and practices for RL in their supply chains may find the results valuable. The framework may serve as guidance related to aspects that are critical to consider in developing RL systems in general. Also, even though the suggested framework is tested on a specific furniture manufacturer, case insights may be useful also for managers in other furniture manufacturing companies or RL service providers handling furniture.

This research is based upon a single case, with focus on one furniture manufacturer. More research is needed to further validate the framework, for instance by a multiple case study including several furniture manufacturers. Since RL practices are deployed to a limited extent in the furniture industry, there are only few examples of relevant systems addressed in research. There is a need for new knowledge of how to develop RL systems that contribute with high value in the supply chain in terms of business, environment, and people, that may support the further adoption of RL systems and related business models.

ACKNOWLEDGEMENTS

We would like to thank the reviewers for their valuable feedback regarding improvements of this chapter. Also, we are grateful for the financial support to this research from the Research Council of Norway (the BIA programme, project number 282012). Last, but not least, we would like to thank all our informants for valuable discussions and insights about the challenges and opportunities of reverse logistics for a more circular future.

REFERENCES

Agrawal, S., Singh, R. K., & Murtaza, Q. (2015). A literature review and perspectives in reverse logistics. *Resources, Conservation and Recycling*, 97, 76–92.

Alshamsi, A., & Diabat, A. (2015). A reverse logistics network design. *Journal of Manufacturing Systems*, 37(3), 589–598.

Altekin, F. T., Kandiller, L., & Ozdemirel, N. E. (2008). Profit-oriented disassembly-line balancing. *International Journal of Production Research*, 46(10), 2675–2693.

Cannella, S., Bruccoleri, M., & Framinan, J. M. (2016). Closed-loop supply chains: What reverse logistics factors influence performance? *International Journal of Production Economics*, 175, 35–49.

Das, K., & Chowdhury, A. H. (2012). Designing a reverse logistics network for optimal collection, recovery and quality-based product-mix planning. *International Journal of Production Economics*, 135(1), 209–221.

De Angelis, R., Howard, M., & Miemczyk, J. (2018). Supply chain management and the circular economy: Towards the circular supply chain. *Production Planning & Control*, 29(6), 425–437.

De Brito, M. P., & Dekker, R. (2004). A framework for reverse logistics. In R. Dekker, M. Fleischmann, K. Inderfurth, & L. N. van Wassenhove (eds.), *Reverse Logistics: Quantitative Models for Closed-Loop Supply Chains*. Berlin: Springer, 3–27.

Dekker, R., Fleischmann, M., Inderfurth, K., & van Wassenhove, L. N. (eds.) (2004). *Reverse Logistics: Quantitative Models for Closed-Loop Supply Chains*. Berlin: Springer.

Desai, A., & Mital, A. (2003). Evaluation of disassemblability to enable design for disassembly in mass production. *International Journal of Industrial Ergonomics*, 32(4), 265–281.

Ellen MacArthur Foundation (2019). *Completing the Picture: How the Circular Economy Tackles Climate Change*. http://www.ellenmacarthurfoundation.org/publications.

Ene, S., & Öztürk, N. (2014). Open loop reverse supply chain network design. *Procedia Social and Behavioral Sciences*, 109, 1110–1115.

European Commission (2019). *Sustainable Products in a Circular Economy: Towards an EU Product Policy Framework contributing to the Circular Economy*. https://ec.europa.eu/environment/circular -economy/pdf/sustainable_products_circular_economy.pdf.

Forrest, A., Hilton, M., Ballinger, A., & Whittaker, D. (2017). *Circular Economy Opportunities in the Furniture Sector*. Brussels: European Environmental Bureau.

Galbreth, M. R., & Blackburn, J. D. (2006). Optimal acquisition and sorting policies for remanufacturing. *Production and Operations Management*, 15(3), 384–392.

Geissdoerfer, M., Morioka, S. N., de Carvalho, M. M., & Evans, S. (2018). Business models and supply chains for the circular economy. *Journal of Cleaner Production*, 190, 712–721.

Govindan, K., Soleimani, H., & Kannan, D. (2015). Reverse logistics and closed-loop supply chain: A comprehensive review to explore the future. *European Journal of Operational Research*, 240(3), 603–626.

Guide, & Van Wassenhove, L. N. (2009). The evolution of closed-loop supply chain research. *Operations Research*, 57(1), 10–18.

Kokkinaki, A., Zuidwijk, R., van Nunen, J., & Dekker, R. (2004). Information and communication technology enabling reverse logistics. In R. Dekker, M. Fleischmann, K. Inderfurth, & L. N. van Wassenhove (eds.), *Reverse Logistics: Quantitative Models for Closed-Loop Supply Chains*. Berlin: Springer, 381–405.

Krumwiede, D. W., & Sheu, C. (2002). A model for reverse logistics entry by third-party providers. *Omega*, 30(5), 325–333.

Kumar, S., & Putnam, V. (2008). Cradle to cradle: Reverse logistics strategies and opportunities across three industry sectors. *International Journal of Production Economics*, 115(2), 305–315.

Masi, D., Day, S., & Godsell, J. (2017). Supply chain configurations in the circular economy: A systematic literature review. *Sustainability*, 9(9), 1602.

Morgan, T. R., Richey, R. G., & Autry, C. W. (2016). Developing a reverse logistics competency: The influence of collaboration and information technology. *International Journal of Physical Distribution & Logistics Management*, 46(3), 293–315.

OECD (2016). *Extended Producer Responsibility: Updated Guidance for Efficient Waste Management*. Paris: OECD Publishing.

Olorunniwo, F. O., & Li, X. (2010). Information sharing and collaboration practices in reverse logistics. *Supply Chain Management: An International Journal*, 15(6), 454–462.

Özceylan, E., & Paksoy, T. (2013). Reverse supply chain optimisation with disassembly line balancing. *International Journal of Production Research*, 51(20), 5985–6001.

Rubio, S., Chamorro, A., & Miranda, F. J. (2008). Characteristics of the research on reverse logistics (1995–2005). *International Journal of Production Research*, 46(4), 1099–1120.

Rubio, S., & Jiménez-Parra, B. (2014). Reverse logistics: Overview and challenges for supply chain management. *International Journal of Engineering Business Management*, 6, 1–7.

Sangwan, K. S. (2017). Key activities, decision variables and performance indicators of reverse logistics. *Procedia CIRP*, 61, 257–262.

Shaharudin, M. R., Govindan, K., Zailani, S., & Tan, K. C. (2015). Managing product returns to achieve supply chain sustainability: An exploratory study and research propositions. *Journal of Cleaner Production*, 101, 1–15.

10. Exploring shared value creation in circular food systems: the case of a Norwegian food bank

Heidi C. Dreyer, Luitzen De Boer, Marte Lønvik Bjørnsund and Anna Pauline Heggli

INTRODUCTION

By feeding the world's population, securing health and good living conditions, and encouraging wealth and economic growth, the food system provides value for a significant part of society. Paradoxically, there is a surplus of food created in the food system, leading to high levels of food waste (Gustavsson et al. 2011). At the same time, a high percentage of people struggle to feed themselves and their families because they cannot access provision of food regularly. This is the so-called *paradox of scarcity in abundance*, where even in rich countries, abundance and scarcity coexist (Winne 2008). This offers the potential to reuse and increase the value of the produce in the food system (Vlajic et al. 2018).

Food banks (FBs) act as centres for the redistribution of eligible surplus food from the food system (Ataseven et al. 2020) to frontline organizations that offer food assistance to people in need (Martins et al. 2019; González and Coque 2016). Originally, FBs had a social profile aiming to feed people (Ataseven et al. 2018), but have since also been strongly related to the redistribution of surplus food and reduction of food waste (Ataseven et al. 2020). FBs are an intermediary in the circular supply chain, which coordinates supply from the food system with demand from beneficiaries. FBs can be framed as a social innovation enabling circular economy (CE) in the food system, responding to beneficiaries and the levels of surplus food in the industry (Tikka 2019). While the circularity of FBs concerns the value of eligible food direct reuse (Reike et al. 2018; Kirchherr et al. 2017) or redistribution (Vlajic et al. 2018), the social aspect is related to the contributions from collaborative non-profit and profit organizations (Hebinck et al. 2018).

Even with an increased demand for food assistance, competition for donations increases because the food industry actively engages in reducing surplus food (Ataseven et al. 2020; De Angelis et al. 2018). Although food banking is increasing and strongly contributes to the CE transition of the food system (De Angelis et al. 2018; Hebinck et al. 2018), the growth of FBs is reliant upon the access to surplus food, the ability to efficiently redistribute food (Ataseven et al. 2020) and being able to demonstrate the value created.

CE literature does not say much about the role of supply chain management (SCM) towards a transition to CE, particularly about the value created (Batista et al. 2018; De Angelis et al. 2018). A growing volume of SCM studies shed light on food banking, but mainly from an efficiency and food waste perspective (Ataseven et al. 2020; Martins et al. 2019; Vittuari et al. 2017; González-Torre and Coque 2016). The number of empirical studies is small (Vegter et al. 2020; Vlajic et al. 2018), and to the best of our knowledge, only a few studies address FBs from a CE perspective.

Hence, the aim of the chapter is to explore the potential of FBs as a vehicle for shared value creation (SVC) and gain a better insight into the relationship between SVC and CE principles. To understand the CE system, supply chain management acts as a framework for defining the system, while the theory of SVC is applied as the theoretical lens. The study contributes to the CE literature by providing empirical insights into the supply chain management operations of FB and linking them to SVC.

The remainder of the chapter is divided into the following sections: theoretical background, methodology, findings, discussion and conclusion.

THEORETICAL BACKGROUND

CE Value in the FB Supply Chain

From a supply chain management perspective, FB is a supply chain aiming to efficiently match the demand from people in need of food with the supply of surplus food. The enabler is logistics (Sehnem et al. 2020) and a network of organizations such as municipalities, finance institutions, member agencies and volunteers (Ataseven et al. 2020; Vittuari et al. 2017). Unlike the food system, FBs operate a more complex supply chain with tight constraints (Ataseven et al. 2018). On the supply side, FBs are less formal and institutionalized, while the demand side has a high number of volunteers to run its operations. FBs lack the organizational and managerial mechanisms of for-profit organizations (Ataseven et al. 2020; McLachlin and Larson 2011). Performance is measured by the amount of food redistributed and does not fully reflect the value created. By focusing on the social and food assistance dimension, the innovative potential and novel value created by FBs lies in the energy released among those who are involved in providing the aid (Hebinck et al. 2018).

In CE, perspectives are changed from considering used materials as waste to recognizing the value of those materials and the opportunity to recover and generate new value out of used materials (Farooque et al. 2019; Reike et al. 2018). Circular material flows are facilitated by innovative supply chain ecosystems and the supply chain is configured with the aim to regenerate waste to recover value (Farooque et al. 2019; De Angelis et al. 2018). CE aims to preserve as much of the quality of the used material at its highest possible utility and value and to minimize the value loss. FBs regenerate surplus food at a high level in the waste hierarchy, with a minimum value loss. For fresh food Vlajic et al. (2018) identified that the higher the residual value of the product, the more likely a high-value recovery strategy would be chosen.

CE contributes to the triple bottom line of economic, environmental and social aspects (Martins et al. 2019). While economic and environmental aspects are the most explored in the CE literature, a transition to CE also needs to consider social aspects. By innovations CE aims to transform profit-driven business models to effect persistent and wide-ranging changes in production and consumption patterns (Schöggl et al. 2020; Vegter et al. 2020). Examples show that when the motivation is to reach social goals, non-profitability reuse systems exist in the supply chain (Ataseven et al. 2020). Vlajic et al. (2018) found that financial value from food recovery is not a necessary condition for the creation of a circular flow in the food supply chain. Still, the social aspects remain underrepresented or are even neglected in most studies.

The Concept of SVC

A circular supply chain is enabled by close collaboration with partners within and beyond their immediate industrial boundaries (De Angelis et al. 2018). Given the explicit focus in the literature on the concept of value creation in FBs and the underlying circular business models they are based on, it seems reasonable to apply Porter and Kramer's (2011) general discussion of SVC as our main theoretical framework for later empirical analysis.

At the core of SVC lies the premise that the prosperity of firms and the local communities they operate in are closely intertwined: healthy firms need healthy communities and vice versa. Porter and Kramer argue that over time, many firms have lost sight of this relationship and have taken the well-being of communities for granted. Thus, they are not concerned with social and environmental problems in their environments and how these may affect them negatively.

SVC is about reinstating the awareness of the mutual dependency between firms and their communities and employing the power of profit-driven firms to address the communities' challenges. Porter and Kramer (2011, p. 6) define SVC as "policies and operating practices that enhance the competitiveness of a company while simultaneously advancing the economic and social conditions in the communities in which it operates". More specifically, they identify three ways in which SVC may be achieved:

1. Reconceiving products and markets, identifying how the firm's current products are or could be related to societal needs, tapping into new markets and serving unmet needs;
2. Redefining productivity in the supply chain, assessing how each primary and supportive process in the firms – and the wider supply chain – affects societal challenges and how changes in these processes and the way they are organized may simultaneously create business and social value;
3. Enabling local network development, identifying novel opportunities for collaboration with local organizations, thereby creating value for both firms and the local community.

Immediately, we can see links between each of these three forms of SVC and FBs, as shown in Table 10.1.

Food products are no longer only targeted towards the original customer segment, but also towards socially disadvantaged customers who would otherwise not have the means to purchase the products. The creation of a surplus supply chain can be seen as redefining productivity in the supply chain, and clearly, by involving local NGOs and the establishment of the

Table 10.1   *Relationships between shared value creation (SVC), food banks (FBs) and CE*

SVC level	Application to FBs	Corresponding CE principle/aspect
Reconceiving products and markets	Targeting socially disadvantaged beneficiaries	Avoid loss of value (if initial customers do not buy the product), additional value components
Redefining productivity in the supply chain	Creating and adding surplus food channels to existing linear food chain	Innovative logistics and supply chain ecosystems, additional value components
Enabling local network development	Local retailers, producers, government and non-profit organizations working together	Regenerate value by utilizing surplus food and reducing waste, create new value from by-products, additional value components

FB, local network development is taking place. In our analysis of the empirical case, we shall consider the role of the three forms of SVC.

Whilst many examples of applications of SVC can be found (see http://www.sharedvalue .org), the concept has also received criticism (see, for example, Crane et al. 2014) and in a later publication Kramer and Pfitzer (2016) acknowledge the existence of barriers for achieving SVC, underlining the importance of an ecosystem perspective to SVC and deriving five critical success factors:

1. Agreeing on a common agenda and shared vision among the organizations.
2. Agreeing on a shared measurement system.
3. Making sure that the organization's activities are mutually reinforcing.
4. Creating a system for constant communication.
5. Establishing an independent backbone organization.

We shall return to these critical success factors in the discussion of our empirical case.

METHODOLOGY

This study explores food banking as a CE redistribution strategy and is conducted by means of a semi-systematic literature review and a single, in-depth, longitudinal case study of a Norwegian FB. The semi-structured literature review has combined keywords and snow-balling techniques, searching for literature in Google Scholar and Scopus. It became clear that very few studies discussed FB and CE, and only a few of these looked at value creation in the supply chain.

The unit of analysis is the flow of surplus food in the supply chain of an anonymized FB, FBT, and the value added by the organizations in the supply chain (Figure 10.1).

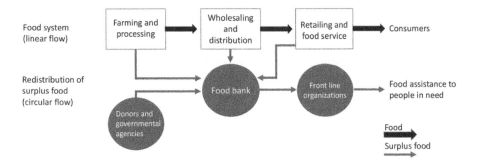

Figure 10.1   The flow of surplus food in an anonymized food bank supply chain

The explorative aim of the research led to the selection of a longitudinal single case study which is a recommended strategy (Yin 2009). A case study contributes to a deep and authentic understanding by revealing the underlying mechanisms, structures and relationships that produce the phenomenon (Ellram 1996). FBT was selected as a case because of its supply chain operations and access to rich data due to geographical closeness and collaboration with

Table 10.2   Overview of data collection

Source of data	Partner/role
Observations/mapping	NA
Interviews	Eight 1-hour long interviews with FBT (CEO), Producer (operations manager), Wholesaler (CEO), Municipality (senior adviser), Bank (chairman of the board), Workforce agency (CEO), Two frontline organizations (senior executives)
Extractions from IT system of FBT	Suppliers. Receivers. Volumes/kg in/out from the warehouse. Food category
Logistics mapping/analysis	FBT (CEO)
Mapping of information flow	FBT (CEO)
Strategic documents FBT	Strategies, plans

the university. The data cover the period from February 2019 to September 2020, which gives a thick description of the unit of analysis (Denzin and Lincoln 2011). Multiple data sources are combined which together with the timespan strengthen the validity of the single case. Table 10.2 summarizes the data sources.

Organizations were selected for interview on the basis of their roles, contributions and the type of frontline organization offering food assistance.

The data coding and analysis is structured according to the supply chain setup in Figure 10.1. CE values are operationalized according to economic (product money value), environment (CO_2 emissions) and social (input/output gains, potential and barrier) aspects (Martins et al. 2019). The quantitative data indicate resource utilization for food that would alternatively become waste. The social dimension is captured qualitatively. The findings are discussed using SVC as the theoretical lens.

FINDINGS

FBT was established in 2016 after a process in which charity organizations, politicians and the municipality recognized the need to provide a system for offering food to beneficiaries. The vision is "giving food, people and environment a new possibility" by a business model whereby surplus food and funding are donated by suppliers (producers, wholesalers, municipality and private organizations) and redistributed to frontline organizations such as the Salvation Army and volunteer centres which provide food assistance (see Figure 10.1). The main operations of the FBT are logistics and supply chain management aiming to fulfil the sustainable development goals (SDGs) of no poverty and hunger, good health, reduced inequalities, sustainable cities and communities, responsible production and consumption, and partnership for the goals (United Nations n.d.).

The activity level of FBT is illustrated in Table 10.3. In the period August 2019 to July 2020, 29 suppliers donated 327 tons of food.

Fifty-five frontline organizations received 232 tons of food and served 2,890 people (80 kg per person). Fifty-five per cent of the food is refrigerated products which is a high share but can be related to the short shelf life of this category and a high supply of fresh surplus food. Not all beneficiaries receiving food have cooking facilities and prefer ready-made meals. The discrepancy between food received and distributed is the stock level in FBT. Approximately 10 per cent of the food in FBT becomes obsolete, which is 6 per cent lower than the average level in the retail sector (Matvett.no, n.d.).

Table 10.3   Volumes received and redistributed by FBT: number of suppliers, member organizations and consumers

Aug. 2019 – July 2020		Weight (kg)
Food received	29 suppliers	326,583
Food distributed	55 frontline organizations	231,828
Refrigerated goods		127,824
Dry goods		53,821
Frozen goods		30,590
Fruit and vegetables		19,593
Beneficiaries	2,890 people	

Table 10.4   Monetary and CO_2 resource utilization (instead of landfill)

Aug. 2019 – July 2020 Food distributed	Weight (kg)	CO_2 emissions (kgCO_2)	Value (NOK)
Refrigerated goods	127,824	799,347	7,308,911
Dry goods	53,821	80,732	3,077,457
Frozen goods	30,590	222,593	1,749,121
Fruit and vegetables	19,593	9,797	1,120,318
Total	231,828	1,112,469	13,255,806

The volume of food redistributed is exhibited in Table 10.4. It is converted to monetary value and CO_2 emissions level, which express the resource efficiency of the food that is consumed instead of being sent to a landfill. The monetary value has been calculated based on the total food waste in Norway in 2018 and the associated financial loss, which corresponds to approximately 57 NOK/kg food waste (Stensgård et al. 2019). The financial loss is based on the market value of the food and does not include costs related to waste management. While calculating the CO_2 emissions level, average values of carbon equivalent per kg product (kgCO_2) were extracted from extant lifecycle assessment literature (Dreyer et al. 2019; Oort and Andrew 2016). Typical product groups and their share were identified for each category and used to calculate the CO_2 emissions level per category.

Table 10.4 shows that food for 13.3 MNOK has been redistributed by FBT to beneficiaries by a team of two employees. The value created per employee is 6.6 MNOK, which is higher than the Norwegian grocery sector, where value created per employee is 1.7 MNOK (Virke 2020). Refrigerated goods are the category with the highest value share (55 per cent of the total value created).

The CO_2 emissions level for the surplus food consumed instead of being sent to a landfill in Table 10.4 is 1,113 tons, which equals 4.8 kgCO_2 per kg food redistributed, or 385 kgCO_2 by each beneficiary. The level of kgCO_2 found in our case study is high compared to Scholz et al. (2015). This might be because of the high level of refrigerated food in this case study causing a high carbon footprint. The CO_2 emissions level in Norway is 8.3 tons per capita (2018). The contribution of FBT by utilizing the food corresponds to the annual emissions of 134 Norwegian inhabitants (Friedlingstein et al. 2019). One thousand kg of CO_2 corresponds to the food waste of an average Norwegian household for a year (Framtiden.no 2020). In Table 10.5 the qualitative values captured from the organizations in the supply chain are presented.

Table 10.5   Value created in the supply chain of FBT

		Values	Value potential	Barriers for increasing value
Suppliers and donors	Wholesaler	*Input*: food. Transport/logistics services. Monetary funding. *Output/gains*: reduced food waste. Publicity and positive market value.	Increase food volumes. Increase the market value of donating food. Product labels showing that FB donations are done when buying the product.	Capacity limitations at FBT when volume of surplus food is high because of campaigns/end of seasons. Organization structure and centralized decisions at the wholesaler.
	Producer	*Input*: food. Transport/logistics services. Monetary funding. *Output/gains*: reduced food waste. Realizing SDG goals. Food donations are positive for employees.	Increase the volume of food redistributed and the company's market value.	Periodic capacity limitations at FBT. Centralized decisions at the producer.
	Municipality	*Input*: initiator. Adviser, discussant and knowledge provider. Network (public and private sector). Monetary funding. Publicity/dissemination. *Output/gains*: realization of SDG goals; poverty, food waste, environment, food provision and integrating immigrants.	Increase competence/knowledge about food among children/young adults. Cooperation with production kitchen.	The role of FBT: to secure the outreach to vulnerable beneficiaries. Limited public funding sources.
	Bank	*Input*: monetary funding and network/contacts. *Output/gains*: publicity and positive market value. Reduced food waste and CO_2. Realizing CE. Showcase.	Increase the capacity, number of food suppliers and assortment. Attract interest from new funding sources.	NA
	Workforce agency	*Input*: strategic, managerial and recruitment competence and time. Network. Technology (app for coordinating of volunteers). *Output/gains*: SDGs experience and competence. Food waste knowledge.	Increase the number of volunteers. Establish production kitchen. Work recruitment to the food industry. Supplier integration and increase no. of suppliers. Logistics system development. Increasing publicity about FBT.	Engaging volunteers is demanding. Limited capacity to train volunteers. Lack of channels for reaching out to beneficiaries.

	Values	Value potential	Barriers for increasing value
FBT	*Input*: supply chain operations, infrastructure (building, equipment, systems and technology). Assortment. Management, food and training competence. Network. Employees and volunteers. *Output/gains*: collecting and redistribution surplus food. Waste reduction and CO_2 emissions utilized, SDGs. Competence (food, work life, sense of achievement). Communication and dissemination.	Donation of food through voluntary stores. Production kitchen. Communities though cooking together. Meaningful work for unemployed. Awareness about reducing food waste. Innovation inspiration to start new projects.	Reduced access to surplus food and new suppliers. Efficient SC operations. Higher costs for less food. Budget reduction. Reduction in frontline organizations.
Two frontline organizations	*Input*: food collection/distribution. Demand/ preferences from beneficiaries. *Output/gains*:work training. Offering food, nutrition and quality food that beneficiaries other vice could not afford. Release funds for other purpose. Increases dignity. Reduces criminality. Reduces food waste. Food competence. Social contact/exercise (practising deaf language). Immigrants' integration. Information source of beneficiaries' condition.	Redistribute more food by meeting the preferences from beneficiaries.	NA

Three observations can be made from Table 10.5. First, the organizations consider value creation to be bi-directional since they both provide and receive value. Second, there is complementarity in the role of creating value by the organizations, as well as distinctions in the values created by them, such as the logistics role of FBT. Third, the qualitative values provided to the beneficiaries are much more than just food and the importance of the social impact and the ripple effect of food becomes clear in the narratives given. Fourth, there is a potential to increase the activity in FBT, particularly the volumes, assortment and funding. The main barrier is the capacity, level of surplus food and organizational mechanisms of the food industry.

DISCUSSION

The case suggests that the FB supply chain may provide a fruitful basis for creating shared circular value in terms of monetary, CO_2 resource utilization and social aspects (Ataseven et al. 2020). Although the value obtained for each organization may differ, the underlying business case seems to hinge on creating circular business results in terms of improved resource utilization (money and CO_2), increased market value, and social results through contributing to several SDGs related to reducing poverty and hunger, improving health and equality and utilizing resources. Still, the results will depend on how invested time and funding provided by the producer, wholesaler and FBT will compare to the cost reduced and the increase in sales. Upon closer examination, however, the case raises some interesting questions in relation to Porter and Kramer's (2011) original SVC concept.

First, who takes the initiative for SVC? Porter and Kramer's work takes a firm's perspective, yet in our case, the initiative came from local politicians and the municipality rather than from the producers or wholesalers. Even though the latter have become actively involved, and each of the three forms of SVC as shown in Table 10.1 (and applied to FBT) can be recognized in our case, they seem to follow from responding to the initiative taken by the frontline organizations, politicians and municipality, rather than deliberately designed strategy by the companies. Inspired by the experience, this may lead to the development of more deliberate, innovative SVC circular strategies in the future. For example, the wholesaler expressed the idea of product promotions specifically targeted to supporting the food bank and the idea by the workforce solution to create an apprenticeship scheme in the food bank to supply the food industry with labour, which would be a more deliberate approach to reconceiving products and markets (Porter and Kramer 2011). A similar example of SVC developing from an emergent to a more deliberate strategy was observed as part of the research project Sustainable Innovation through SVC in Norwegian Industry (SISVI) in 2018 (see Halvorsen et al. 2018).

Secondly, could it be that the successful development of SVC through an FB will progress through different stages? A clear challenge mentioned by most of the interviewees is scaling up the FB. It seems that the FB in its existing form has reached a certain ceiling in terms of capacity, funding and access to volunteers. The producer, wholesaler and bank all mention increasing the scale of operations and product range offered as a value creation potential. The initiative may be taken by a municipality, successfully raising it to a certain level, but 'breaking through' to a next level may require a stronger role and commitment of the organizations involved, or deeper mutual insight into additional innovative forms of value creation. Two examples of such value creation emerged from the interviews. FBT may serve as a feedback channel for the producers and wholesalers providing specific information about how they perceive the products and their needs, and feedback to the municipality by providing more accurate information about the conditions of the beneficiaries and assistance they need from the municipality. It is interesting that these examples were mentioned by the frontline organizations themselves and not by the firms and the municipality and this supports Ataseven et al. (2018) in arguing that the need for innovation can be even higher for such actors than for commercial organizations.

Finally, we consider the case in the light of Kramer and Pfitzer's (2016) five critical success factors for SVC. Regarding the presence of a common agenda and shared vision, it seems that the involved organizations have similar views on what can be achieved. Still, the producer and the wholesaler are part of larger corporate concerns and indicate that decisions taken at a higher, more centralized levels may provide a barrier to further development. So even though there may be a shared vision at the local level, if organizations are also part of larger national structures, this may no longer be the case. However, De Angelis et al. (2018) argue that structural flexibility and localness can be utilized as a driver for CE implementation.

We did not find evidence of a shared measurement system, but according to the mandate of the FB it keeps accounts of the amount of incoming and distributed food and how this is broken down into different categories. The amount of food redistributed may be converted relatively easily into a rough measure of the amount of CO_2 emissions utilized. Still, measuring the other forms of value created – both 'business value', such as positive publicity and improved market value, and social value', such as contributing to less poverty – may be less straightforward. Furthermore, if we view the FB as a potential information hub and feedback channel for the users to provide useful information about their situation and needs, how could the value of that information be measured?

The activities of the different organizations are clearly complementary and reinforcing, but the FB's limited operative capacity and possibilities for additional funding constitute barriers to further development. Moreover, the case study also illustrates a typical paradox when devising strategies for CE: on the one hand, organizations wish to scale up the activities of the FB, while on the other hand, ultimately the objective is to reduce food waste, which in a way undermines the scaling strategy. When producers get better at reducing surplus food, the incoming amount of food of these producers will decrease and have higher variety since surplus food resulting from campaigns and seasonality is increasing. The FB must therefore broaden its scope, find new suppliers and streamline its operations.

The case study data regarding communication and the presence of a backbone organization are limited, but the FB seems to fulfil an important role in coordinating with and facilitating interplay between the other organizations. The workforce agency organization reported that engaging more volunteers becomes demanding due to the required coordination and that it lacks distribution channels for reaching out to users of the FB.

All in all, we can see the contours of the five factors being addressed, but there are challenges related to each of them. Applying Kramer and Pfitzer's framework would therefore suggest that the potential for SVC has not been fully captured yet and that the strategies for further progress in achieving SVC through the FB concept should address each of the factors.

CONCLUSION

The study shows that the FB provides a promising foundation for creating shared value (SVC), echoing the results from previous studies (Hebinck et al. 2018). Food banking in the case, particularly the social aspects (Schöggl et al. 2020).

An implication for practice is that the study reveals the potential for CE innovations and transformative change if food banking becomes a deliberate strategy by the food industry and the industry removes centralized organizational and managerial barriers. Further, in order to further exploit CE, in this case it seems that expansion and upscaling are needed, particularly the supply from the food industry. SVC can play a crucial role, particularly in realizing social innovations exemplified by initiatives such as apprenticeship schemes and learning and information-sharing hubs. Next, to be able to demonstrate and communicate the CE potential of SVC in food banking there is a need for innovative measurement and performance systems in the supply chain, particularly for capturing social value.

Our study is not absolved of limitations, which also opens paths for future research. First, the study relies on data from one single FB. Extending the data with more cases can lead to new insights by allowing a cross-case analysis. These case studies could also be designed so as more comprehensively map how FB deal with Kramer and Pfitzer's (2016) five critical success factors over time. Second, more cases would allow exploring contingency factors such as the impact of the local food system and its produce and the impact on SVC and CE. Third, increasing the number of organizations, particularly from the food industry, will enrich the dataset about their role in SVC.

REFERENCES

Ataseven, C., Nair, A., & Ferguson, M. (2018). An examination of the relationship between intellectual capital and supply chain integration in humanitarian aid organizations: a survey-based investigation of food banks. *Decision Sciences*, 49(5), 827–862.

Ataseven, C., Nair, A., & Ferguson, M. (2020). The role of supply chain integration in strengthening the performance of not-for-profit organizations: Evidence from the food banking industry. *Journal of Humanitarian Logistics and Supply Chain Management* 10(2), 101–123.

Batista, L., Bourlakis, M., Smart, P., & Maull, R. (2018). In search of a circular supply chain archetype: A content-analysis-based literature review. *Production Planning & Control*, 29(6), 438–451.

Crane, A., Palazzo, G., Spence, L. J., & Matten, D. (2014). Contesting the value of "creating shared value". *California Management Review*, 56(2), 130–153.

De Angelis, R., Howard, M., & Miemczyk, J. (2018). Supply chain management and the circular economy: Towards the circular supply chain. *Production Planning & Control*, 29(6), 425–437.

Denzin, N. K., & Lincoln, Y. S. (eds.) (2011). *The Sage Handbook of Qualitative Research*, 4th edition. Thousand Oaks, CA: Sage Publications.

Dreyer, H. C., Dukovska-Popovska, I., Yu, Q., & Hedenstierna, C. P. (2019). A ranking method for prioritising retail store food waste based on monetary and environmental impacts. *Journal of Cleaner Production*, 210, 505–517.

Ellram, L. M. (1996). The use of the case study method in logistics research. *Journal of Business Logistics*, 17(2), 93–138.

Farooque, M., Zhang, A., & Liu, Y. (2019). Barriers to circular food supply chains in China. *Supply Chain Management: An International Journal*, 24(5), 677-696.

Framtiden.no (2020). *Hva får jeg for et tonn CO2?* https://www.framtiden.no/gronne-tips/spor-oss/hva-far-jeg-for-et-tonn-co2.html.

Friedlingstein, P., Jones, M., O'Sullivan, M., Andrew, R., Hauck, J., Peters, G., ... & Le Quéré, C. (2019). Global carbon budget 2019. *Earth System Science Data*, 11(4), 1783–1838.

González-Torre, P. L., & Coque, J. (2016). How is a food bank managed? Different profiles in Spain. *Agriculture and Human Values*, 33(1), 89–100.

Gustavsson, J., Cederberg, C., Sonesson, U., Van Otterdijk, R., & Meybeck, A. (2011). *Global Food Losses and Food Waste*. Rome: FAO Rome.

Halvorsen, H. K., Hermundsdottir, F., & Levang, E. A. (2018). *Innovation and Shared Value Creation: A Social Elephant in the Room? A Qualitative Case Study of How a Norwegian Industry Company Uses Product Innovation to Create Shared Value.* Norwegian University of Science and Technology.

Hebinck, A., Galli, F., Arcuri, S., Carroll, B., O'Connor, D., & Oostindie, H. (2018). Capturing changes in European food assistance practices: A transformative social innovation perspective. *Local Environment*, 23(4), 398–413.

Kirchherr, J., Reike, D., & Hekker, M. (2017). Conceptualizing the circular economy: An analysis of 114 definitions. *Resources, Conservation and Recycling*, 127, 221–232.

Kramer, M. R., & Pfitzer, M. W. (2016). The ecosystem of shared value. *Harvard Business Review*, October, 1–11.

Martins, C. L., Melo, M. T., & Pato, M. V. (2019). Redesigning a food bank supply chain network in a triple bottom line context. *International Journal of Production Economics*, 214, 234–247.

Matvett.no. (n.d.). *Om Matsvinn*. https://www.matvett.no/bransje/om-matsvinn.

McLachlin, R., & Larson, P. D. (2011). Building humanitarian supply chain relationships: Lessons from leading practitioners. *Journal of Humanitarian Logistics and Supply Chain Management*, 1(1), 32–49.

Oort, B. van, & Andrew, R. (2016). *Climate Footprints of Norwegian Dairy and Meat: A Synthesis*. Oslo: CICERO Report.

Porter, M. E., & Kramer, M. R. (2011). Creating shared value: How to reinvent capitalism – and unleash a wave of innovation and growth. *Harvard Business Review*, 89(1–2).

Reike, D., Vermeulen, W. J. V., & Witjes, S. (2018). The circular economy: New or refurbished as CE 3.0? Exploring controversies in the conceptualization of the circular economy through a focus on history and resource value retention option. *Resources, Conservation and Recycling*, 135, 246–264.

Schöggl, J. P., Stumpf, L., & Baumgartner, R. J. (2020). The narrative of sustainability and circular economy: A longitudinal review of two decades of research. *Resources, Conservation and Recycling*, 163, 105073.

Scholz, K., Eriksson, M., & Strid, I. (2015). Carbon footprint of supermarket food waste. *Resources, Conservation and Recycling*, 94, 56–65.

Sehnem, S., Ndubisi, N. O., Preschlak, D., Bernardy, R. J., & Santos Jr, S. (2020). Circular economy in the wine chain production: Maturity, challenges, and lessons from an emerging economy perspective. *Production Planning & Control*, 31(11–12), 1014–1034.

Stensgård, A. E., Pettersen, I., & Grønlund, A. (2019). *Samfunnsøkonomisk analyse av halvering av matsvinn i henhold til bransjeavtalen om redusert matsvinn – Klimakur 2030*. NIBIO Report.

Tikka, V. (2019). Charitable food aid in Finland: From a social issue to an environmental solution. *Agriculture and Human Values*, 36(2), 341–352.

United Nations (n.d.). *The 17 Goals*. https://sdgs.un.org/goals.

Vegter, D., van Hillegersberg, J., & Olthaar, M. (2020). Supply chains in circular business models: Processes and performance objectives. *Resources, Conservation and Recycling*, 162, 105046.

Virke (2020). *Dagligvarehandelen 2019/2020*. https://www.virke.no/Statistikk-Rapporter/dagligvarehandelen-2019-2020/.

Vittuari, M., De Menna, F., Gaiani, S., Falasconi, L., Politano, A., Dietershagen, J., & Segrè, A. (2017). The second life of food: An assessment of the social impact of food redistribution activities in Emilia Romagna, Italy. *Sustainability*, 9(10), 1817.

Vlajic, J., Mijailovic, R., & Bogdanova, M. (2018). Creating loops with value recovery: Empirical study of fresh food supply chains. *Production Planning & Control*, 29(6), 522–538.

Winne, M. (2008). *Closing the Food Gap: Resetting the Table in the Land of Plenty*. Boston: Beacon Press.

Yin, R. K. (2009). *Case Study Research: Design and Methods*, 4th edition. Thousand Oaks, CA: Sage Publications.

11. How waste becomes value: the new ecology of surplus heat exchange in Norwegian industry

Jens Petter Johansen and Jens Røyrvik

INTRODUCTION

Circular economy (CE) is a concept that has gained increased traction in policy, academia and business (Hobson and Lynch 2016). Essential to this is the idea of closing energy and material loops in order to increase competitiveness of industries, as well as reduce the environmental impact (Baldassarre et al. 2019). Thus, a transition from a linear to a CE involves redefining waste as a resource (Ellen MacArthur Foundation 2013). On a practical and local level, this often requires inter-firm innovation processes, in order to assign this resource a value, as well as enable its circulation by establishing organizational and technical structures. However, valuating what was previously regarded a waste is in many contexts a new endeavour, and rarely a straightforward task, as this chapter will illustrate with the case of utilizing *surplus heat*.

Surplus, excess, or waste heat, is an interesting by-product in the context of CE. It is a by-product of almost any production process such as refrigerators in shops and restaurants or server parks in data centres. In most cases, this heat goes through cooling systems, which themselves consume more energy, and out into the ambient environment. Several studies have shown the significant possibilities of directing surplus heat into other useful applications, such as space heating in offices or homes, or industry processes requiring heating such as greenhouses, onshore fish farms, and asphalt production (Enova 2009; Miró et al. 2015). Utilizing surplus heat in this way means consuming energy more efficiently, since it reduces outtake of primary energy. Furthermore, it represents an economic opportunity for both parties. The heat provider saves money on cooling systems and compensation for the delivered energy, while the heat user receives energy that is often cheaper than primary energy sources. These multiple benefits are increasingly being recognized, such as in the Renewable Energy Directive (European Commission 2016). Yet, despite the significant potential of this waste resource, the utilization rate is still low in European countries (Lygnerud and Werner 2018).

As a commodity, surplus heat has some 'extreme case' properties and limits to use, which makes it particularly interesting to investigate as an example of CE. Surplus heat is recovered from industry processes by heat exchangers and transported to its destination as heated water (or gas) through pipelines. This requires costly infrastructure for energy recovery, transportation and end-use technologies, as well as a responsible party in charge of operations and maintenance. Compared to material waste products, heated water cannot travel far before its temperature, which essentially is its significant quality, starts degrading. Because of this, surplus heat is a local resource, bounded in time as well as space. Furthermore, firms that want to exchange surplus heat need to construct technical and organizational structures between them in order to facilitate the trade. Essentially, they need to innovate new ways of delivering, consuming, buying, selling, giving or receiving energy. These properties make it an interesting case of how by-products are valuated differently across localities, and can thus provide further insight and contextualization into barriers and drivers for CE innovation (e.g. Jakobsen and Steinmo, Chapter 13 this volume) and sustainable business models (Bocken et al. 2019).

This chapter explores different ways of framing, valuating and organizing surplus heat as a resource in local CE. We start by providing a short overview of previous research, theoretical perspectives on valuation processes and our methodological approach. Drawing on qualitative case studies from a Norwegian industry context, we show different modes of valuating surplus heat. In conclusion, we discuss the opportunities for integrating valuation perspectives in research on innovation and CE and conclude with practical recommendations.

DRIVERS AND BARRIERS FOR SURPLUS HEAT UTILIZATION

The main focus in social science research on surplus heat has traditionally been on identifying *drivers and barriers* towards utilization in district heating (DH) networks (Broberg Viklund 2015; Enova 2009; Werner 2017) and case studies of local heat markets (Päivärinne et al. 2015; Webb and Hawkey 2017). Päivärinne et al. (2015) combine insights from *industrial symbiosis* (Chertow 2000) with a business model perspective to identify financial, technical and organizational drivers and barriers towards excess heat collaborations. They find that aspects such as mutual economic benefits, available technological solutions, trust and embedded networks between the participants are important preconditions for establishing heat exchanges between heat provider and DH companies. The importance of social ties for enabling local resource exchanges is also highlighted in the wider literature on industrial symbiosis (Walls and Paquin 2015).

Previous studies have identified barriers such as lack of attention in policy and awareness in firms, regulations and the need for framing surplus heat as an energy source (Fontaine and Rocher 2021). At the site level, the most notable barriers are economic factors, agreeing on the price of surplus heat and the business model for exchanging it (Fontaine and Rocher 2021). For example, the heat provider and the DH company often hold different views of the quality of the heat and what its price should be (Lygnerud and Werner 2018, p. 431). However, while lack of agreement on price is a known barrier towards adoption, the processes of how waste resources become a commodity and achieve (different) value in (different) local contexts have largely gone unrecognized. Furthermore, there is a need to examine the particular local contexts that favour or hamper realization of surplus heat concepts (Fontaine and Rocher 2021). We address these gaps from a bottom-up perspective through exploring how actors make sense of the value of surplus heat.

THEORETICAL FRAMEWORK: CIRCULATION OF THINGS

In order to analyse the fundamental issues of transforming by-products into resources with a value, we draw on the concept of *entification* (Larsen 2010). This refers to processes where a phenomenon (e.g. heat escaping an industrial site) takes shape and is framed as an *entity* (e.g. surplus heat). With this understanding as a basis, we elaborate on studies exploring how entities are transformed into commodities or gifts, which circulate in communities based on different logics (Çalışkan and Callon 2009).

The separation between commodities (something you buy) and gifts (something you receive) forms the basis for different systems of circulation. Commodification involves the transformation of goods, people or services into objects of trade (see e.g. Lock 2001). An illustrative example in climate policy is MacKenzie's (2009) study of how the permission to emit a certain amount of greenhouse gases has been made into a commodity (carbon credits) that circulates between firms in carbon markets. As such, commodification entails assigning goods, which previously had none, an economic value, and through this enable its circulation.

Other goods, such as gifts, circulate in communities despite *not* having an economic value. Gifts change hands between people (and organizations) as a gesture, symbolic communication or a reciprocal act. Mauss (2002) describes how gifts establish and affirm continued relationships between actors. This, he argues, is because expectations of continued giving are inherent in the gift. In comparison, the relationship between actors trading commodities ends with each trade. As Çalışkan and Callon (2009, p. 387) explain, 'a gift circulates while preserving the presence of its giver embedded within it, while a commodity erases that connection'. In other words, some things circulate based on the relationship and networks between people (or firms), while others are de-contextualized and involve only the trade itself. Thus, the dynamics of circulation linked to reciprocal gift exchange obey alternative logics to the instrumental rationality corresponding with bartering and trading of commodities in markets.

While commodities versus gifts serves as a useful distinction, Çalışkan and Callon (2009) argue that there is a variety of such *modes of valuations* (e.g. pure gifts, part gifts, counter gifts). Furthermore, the function of gifts between formal organizations is inherently different from those between people. A key characteristic of the former is that a variety of actors compete to participate in defining goods and valuing them (Çalışkan and Callon 2010, p. 8). Fixing a price on a commodity is always the outcome of a struggle between agencies trying to impose their modes for measuring a commodity's value and qualities (Stark 2011). In order to understand how particular things are valuated and circulate, we must therefore investigate how actors negotiate their meaning and apply them in local contexts.

These insights have inspired a few empirical analyses on how waste resources are valuated differently and entered into different forms of circulation. Webb and Hawkey (2017) draw on 'modes of valuations' in their study of how intermediaries in the UK failed to assemble markets for heat network infrastructure. They show that negotiations and controversies over the value of surplus heat became inseparable from a market framing, which dissolved any notion of 'public good'. They argue that risks of economic short-termism, the reliance on price as a proxy for value, and failure to encompass the societal value of innovation for clean energy, need to be at the core of negotiations about the structuring of markets. A similar argument is proposed by Hobson and Lynch (2016, p. 22), that the social and cultural meanings of 'exchange' require further exploration and expansion within the CE research, since also non-monetary forms of sharing and swapping goods, ideas and experiences are essential to a truly transformative agenda. Building on these insights, this chapter explores how actors valuate surplus heat, and how these valuations structure how the exchanges are organized.

METHODOLOGICAL APPROACH

To obtain an understanding of the multiple ways of valuating and organizing surplus heat exchanges, we draw on case studies from three industry-research projects in the period

2011–20. The topic of these projects was *energy efficiency*, with utilization of surplus heat as the main technological focus. Our role, as social scientists, was to facilitate innovation processes and investigate regulatory issues, barriers, and enablers towards implementation of technologies. As the projects were technology and industry driven, we gained access to several existing, ongoing and even failed attempts at establishing surplus heat exchanges. Thus, this chapter builds on a multi-case study of 14 surplus heat initiatives (Figure 11.1).

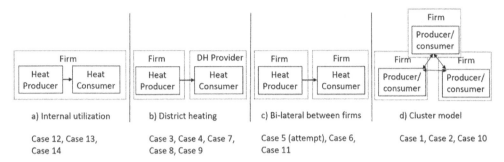

Note: Cases of internal utilization (a) are included here for contextual purposes, and not analysed in the chapter.

Figure 11.1   Four concepts for utilizing surplus heat

The studies included site visits, workshops, focus group studies, document analysis and a total of 53 interviews. The informants included representatives from firms at the supplying and receiving end of the surplus heat exchange, and intermediary actors facilitating the exchange. We also interviewed representatives from DH providers in relevant cases as well as local authorities (e.g. municipality, county council). Municipalities are in charge of area regulations for new industries, and are usually the owner of the DH company. In addition, we interviewed representatives from national authorities to improve our contextual understanding of the frame conditions. We conducted two workshops in 2018 and 2019, specifically discussing challenges with surplus heat utilization with firm representatives, technical researchers and policy makers. As such, the analysis builds on a broad range of perspectives from various actors in the Norwegian setup. We anonymize firm names and refer to case numbers when using quotes.

We analysed documents and interview transcripts to uncover challenges with framing surplus heat as a resource (e.g. regulatory issues), and how surplus heat was valuated across the cases (e.g. market price, free of charge). This involved an analysis where we identified the actors' perspectives on the exchange. Through this, we extrapolated different modes of valuating surplus heat, each carrying different principles for organizing the exchange. We also identified the main barriers towards continued operations particular to the different modes. This resulted in three archetypal modes of valuating surplus heat.

FINDINGS

In the following, we first report on key issues of framing surplus heat as a resource, and continue with presenting the different modes of valuating surplus heat. We present these as archetypes to enable comparisons with different types of industrial innovation processes and CE contexts.

Framing Surplus Heat as a Resource

Identifying and matching heat sources with possible heat users is not a straightforward task. Onshore fish farms and greenhouses are examples of industries with heating demands where it could be economically profitable to utilize surplus heat to reduce primary energy consumption. A barrier reported by several informants is the need to establish such industries close enough to surplus heat sources: 'When something is established in Norway, there is no overview or checklist on existing opportunities for exchanges' (C-5).

In Norway, municipalities oversee area regulations as well as energy planning, and could play an important role in facilitating this match-making process. Despite existing regulations, that states new firms and buildings must connect to nearby DH networks, these are not always enforced: 'We only hear about it when the factory is already established' (C-5).

We also found regulations counteracting increased utilization of surplus heat. Previously, buildings in Norway could achieve high energy- and environmental ratings by connecting to DH networks. Today, the heat source must be located *within* the organizational boundaries of the firm (or building) in order to achieve zero-emission or passive house certification. As reported by our informants, it is now more difficult to achieve good ratings when utilizing surplus heat from other firms or DH networks: 'It is an extremely sub-optimal way of doing it and it undermines the collective system […] if you are really interested in the climate effects, you would look at it holistically' (C-7).

This reported lack of attention from municipal actors shows the need for *framing* surplus heat as a resource, and heat demand as an opportunity. These barriers spring out of an institutional framing disfavouring, or not considering, surplus heat as a resource.

Valuating Surplus Heat

While there are many existing surplus heat exchanges in Norway, considering surplus heat as *valuable* is still a relatively new idea. One recurring issue is the (practical *and* philosophical) question of 'who is doing whom a service', as surplus heat exchange benefits both heat producer and user. Thus, agreeing on its value is neither uniform nor obvious to the various actors. Local actors sometimes value this commodity differently, or do not think of it as a commodity at all. We have identified several ways of valuating, as well as legitimizing the value, of surplus heat in local collaborations, which can be expressed through three different archetypes presented below.

Valuating surplus heat as a market commodity

A common notion is that surplus heat should be a commodity with a competitive price. One informant from a processing plant reasoned that the main issue with 'triggering increased utilization of surplus heat' (C-11) was the need to 'price surplus heat correctly' (C-11). If this is done, the commodity could compete with alternative energy sources and facilitate demand from potential users. Case 1 illustrates how surplus heat can be valuated in this way as a *market commodity* and organized in a local market where the participants negotiate the price structure (Box 11.1).

BOX 11.1 A CASE OF VALUATING SURPLUS ENERGY AS A MARKET COMMODITY

In Case 1, a metal and processing plant delivered surplus energy to two nearby firms, as well as peak load capacity for the DH network. The informants argued that ensuring a competitive price was essential for the collaboration: 'Prices on alternative energy sources are changing. Therefore, we have to ensure that our product is favoured when it comes to price.'

The firms organized the exchange with a set price on energy, contracts spanning three years, and with a third party in charge of operations and maintenance. While contracts between producer and consumer of heat were bi-lateral, the price was equal for all parties, resembling that of a market. The receiving companies argued that this was necessary to accommodate eventual changes: '[…] a three-year horizon is good. So if there are drastic changes in subsidies from the government, CO_2 compensation or the carbon credit prices change drastically, it might be tempting to do something else.'

The informants mentioned external events such as changing energy prices, legislations or companies exiting, as the main barriers for the exchange. For example, when the price on alternative energy sources for heating plummeted a few years previous, it led to re-negotiations of the price of surplus energy. The manager of one of the receiving companies argued that even though changing energy source would disrupt the 'cluster concept', 'that is just how it is; it's the costs that matter'.

We find similar valuations in Cases 1, 7 and 11, where the informants argue that competitive energy prices are the key motivation of the exchange. Here, the mode of valuation revolves around organizing the exchange with formal contracts assigning it an *economic value* and organizing its trade by establishing local heat markets. As argued by the informant above, this is a viable way to ensure that the receivers achieve competitive prices of surplus energy. Such framings highlight how playing into the hands of economic rationalities can potentially increase utilization rates. This also illustrates the main barrier of this way of organizing surplus heat exchange, as changing circumstances affecting how surplus energy is valuated can put pressure on the collaborations and lead to *re-valuations* of the commodity or potentially disrupt the exchange.

Valuating surplus heat as a common good

In other cases, the informants spoke less of economic value, but rather emphasized the mutual benefits of exchanging surplus heat. As shown in Case 2, the valuation of surplus heat can also be grounded in the relationship between individuals and firms (Box 11.2). The collaboration between the firms framed the way they valuated and organized the surplus heat exchange.

BOX 11.2 A CASE OF VALUATING SURPLUS HEAT AS A COMMON GOOD

In Case 2, three companies established a local network of utilizing surplus heat in 2010. The energy exchanges involved surplus heat from an industrial dairy and a poultry processing plant to a nearby greenhouse. In addition, two of the companies utilized the CO_2 from their natural gas combustion in the photosynthesis in the greenhouse. In sum, the circulation of surplus heat and CO_2 significantly reduced the environmental impact of the cluster as a whole. The firms agreed on a mutual beneficial price structure on surplus heat that was equal for all companies, and distribution of costs where all parties covered infrastructure on their own property: 'We have had the basic idea that as long as there are no net costs, we are in. In terms of how much money we make on it, we will see.'

Here, the valuation of surplus heat was not merely an economic price of the commodity, but was also a token of reciprocity and shared values between the stakeholders in the firms: '… it is exactly like he always says, no one can "insert the straw", it has to be "win-win".'

The exchange relied on a form of self-organization with no centralized party enforcing the exchange, nor constant re-negotiations of prices. While there were formal agreements on price, ownership and operations concept, informal relations and trust were essential as well: 'It has to be an open and transparent system where they can trust us, and we can trust them. And it has been exactly like that.'

The informants also argued that this way of organizing the exchange was dependent on maintaining a good relationship between the firms, as well as key personnel: such as 'I think that with or without him is the difference' and 'If you get a crossing of interests, projects like this will strand'. This highlights the importance of inter-organizational networks and trust in order to facilitate, establish and maintain such relationships over time.

This kind of valuation highlights the 'common good' and illustrates how a whole can be greater than the sum of its parts. While these cases are rare in our material (Cases 2 and 10), they are interesting both because they show another way of valuating surplus heat and prove that this approach can be very successful as long as the informal organizational challenges involved are addressed.

Valuating surplus heat as regional anchoring of industrial plants

Many DH networks in Norway are the result of long-term collaborations between local municipalities and 'cornerstone' metal and processing companies providing surplus heat. In several of these cases, we found that the firms deliver the heat free of charge or at a reduced price, to a DH provider often owned by the municipality. 'Our free outtake of surplus heat is based on a historical agreement […] the DH company achieved the rights on surplus heat from the ovens at the plant indefinitely, which we administer' (C-8).

Delivering the surplus heat free of charge does not mean that it is without value. Rather we find that it is valuated in non-economic terms serving other purposes, such as supporting the local community, achieving political goodwill, as well as environmental purposes as mentioned by one informant: 'Our motivation for giving it away free is also about the environmental perspective. We wish to have an as environmentally friendly factory as possible, and utilizing the energy in an efficient way is positive' (C-6).

In most of these cases, there is an interdependency between the company and community, not just in terms of energy supply, but also the survivability of the community and firm. 'Yes, it is very good [that we get it for free], but it depends on whether the industry is able to survive, that their local frame conditions are good' (C-8).

We find similar argumentation in Cases 3, 4, 6, 8 and 9, where the companies provide the heat cheap or without charge. The rationale for providing low cost (or free) surplus heat is a regional anchoring of an industrial plant in the local community, as illustrated in Case 3 (Box 11.3).

BOX 11.3 A CASE OF REGIONAL ANCHORING INDUSTRIAL PLANT IN A LOCAL COMMUNITY

Case 3 involves a 'cornerstone' metal and processing firm localized in a small town. The company uses large amounts of electricity, thereby producing a vast amount of surplus heat. The available heat was the basis for establishing the DH network, owned by the municipality through a DH company. There was so much surplus heat that only the heat from one of the factory's four stoves was needed, finding new uses for the heat was therefore a goal especially for the municipality and the DH company.

From the firm's perspective, the informant argued that they provide the heat almost free of charge: 'we sell it for a symbolic sum' (C-3), with the benefits mostly concerning political goodwill and contributing to a well-functioning community. Although the factory, and thus the municipality, consumed large amounts of energy (with significant carbon emissions), it was regarded as a 'Green Municipality' in government documents because the factory's surplus heat supplied the entire community with DH. While the low-cost surplus heat was beneficial for the community, they were at the same time completely dependent on the company's survival. Conversely, the firm were dependent on services and personnel from the community.

Modes of Valuating Surplus Heat

Establishing local CE for utilizing surplus heat involves processes of framing and valuating it as an entity. Actors hold different opinions on *what kind of entity* surplus heat is, and what it is (and should be) worth. Our cases illustrate how the first step for surplus heat to be treated as a commodity or gift is that it needs to be framed as an entity by the industry actors that are to utilize it. The second step is to specify this entity as a scientific object, separated from all other objects by its measurable characteristics (e.g. kWh, degrees Celsius, price, etc.). The third step is to legally and formally assign the object an ownership, so that it can be given as a gift or sold as a commodity. These valuations and ways of organizing waste products differ across localities, firms and people. As such, there is a variety of possible modes of valuations and circularity. Table 11.1 presents these as archetypes of modes of valuation, principle of circulation and main barriers.

In some cases, surplus heat is valuated as a commodity with a price structure resembling alternative energy costs in the market. This mode of valuation is also visible in studies highlighting economic opportunities and barriers (e.g. Jakobsen and Steinmo, Chapter 13 this volume), and business models perspectives (Päivärinne et al. 2015). Surplus heat can also be

Table 11.1   Archetypes of utilization concepts of surplus heat

	Market commodity	Common good	Regional anchoring
Mode of valuation	Market commodity de-contextualized from the relationship between firms and individuals	Contextualized commodity or part-gift, embedded with cultural and social values	Commodity or part-gift where the value lies in legitimizing the firm and region as sustainable and making them inter-dependent
Principle of circulation	Market relations and economic rationalities	Inter-organizational networks, trust and shared values (win-win) between participants	Formal long-term contracts ensuring local embeddedness of company
Main challenges	External or internal events can trigger re-valuations of commodity and potentially disrupt collaboration	Valuation dependent on relations between individuals. Sensitive to changes over time	Power asymmetry between heat provider and consumer (community). Exit of company would be detrimental
Cases	Cases 1, 7, 11	Cases 2, 10	Cases 3, 4, 6, 8, 9

valuated as a contextualized commodity (or part-gift), where the exchange is rooted in mutual exchange between parties and reifies the collaboration. While previous studies of industrial symbiosis have shown the importance of networks and trust (Walls and Paquin 2015), this finding shows how social ties explicitly connect with how firms valuate waste products. Finally, surplus heat can be valued as a 'gift' between a firm and the local community. In several of our cases, the community and firm are interdependent, and the non-monetary exchange of surplus heat contributes to the mutual benefits and prosperity of both. In line with Hobson and Lynch (2016), this finding shows a form of non-monetary exchange, which has received less attention in CE.

These archetypes are not necessarily mutually exclusive, nor exhaustive. However, different valuations between parties can potentially be conflicting. In line with Webb and Hawkey (2017), we find that applying models grounded in market framings can make it difficult to gather actors around a common good framing of heat networks. This illustrates the challenges of assigning surplus heat an objective value *across* localities or 'constructing a national heat market' (C-11) as suggested by one of our informants. The different framings and valuations of surplus heat are rarely complementary. While there is certainly evidence of learning across cases, for example through participation in industry-research projects, valuations must nevertheless be made and remade each specific exchange. These findings substantiate Fontaine and Rocher's (2021) call for the need to better understand the local contexts that favour or hinder realization of surplus heat concepts. The importance of this local co-production goes to the essence of the findings in this chapter. There is no one-size-fit-all concept, deducible to a generic business model or economic device. Rather, our analysis shows the importance of facilitating local collaborations and innovation processes by providing stakeholders with tools and best-practice examples, in order to develop utilization concepts and valuations to fit local needs.

CONCLUSION

This chapter has explored different processes of how waste energy is valuated. While the case of surplus heat constitutes a limited and practical example, the findings have a broader relevance for research on innovation for a CE. Valuation processes are imperative also for other by-products. Earlier studies have highlighted the need for novel sustainable business models for CE (Bocken et al. 2019). Our study complements these perspectives, in opening up the 'black box' on how negotiating value is an integral part of innovation processes. As such, we argue for the importance of directing attention towards the local grounding of valuations, work of local entrepreneurs and their institutional and social context. This is in line with studies highlighting the importance of informal networks and trust between entrepreneurs in facilitating CE innovations (see e.g. O'Shea et al., Chapter 12 this volume).

In line with Webb and Hawkey (2017), our findings also indicate that there can be a tension between different modes of valuating waste energy and materials. Future research could investigate such tensions further and whether they constitute a barrier for innovative utilization of by-products. These findings also feed into literature that focuses on barriers and drivers for innovation for a CE. For example, Jakobsen and Steinmo (Chapter 13 this volume) show how drivers and barriers to industrial symbiosis changes over time. Our findings contribute to this literature by showing how different modes of valuating waste resources across localities can produce successful results, but also articulate different barriers. Exploring and theorizing barriers and drivers for innovation for a CE *dynamically*, such as (1) over time, (2) across localities, and (3) the particularities of different waste products, are promising avenues for further research.

Implications

This chapter is a first effort of investigating surplus heat exchanges across wide data material, and there is certainly room for more in-depth analysis. Still, the chapter provides some spe-cific recommendations for firms, public actors and policy makers to unleash the potential for utilizing by-products. Our findings suggest that institutional framings and policies somewhat disfavour surplus heat through energy certifications and focus on energy efficiency within buildings. There is also a need for considering such exchanges when localizing new industrial plants (both heat producers and consumers). Here, local municipalities or energy companies can take a leading role, which is already done by some. Regional mapping of waste sources and end-use can be a valuable tool to this end. Local and regional government actors should have a role in facilitating inter-organizational networks lowering collaboration barriers towards CE. Lastly, while business models ensuring mutual economic benefits are essential to trigger exchange of by-products, our findings also indicate opportunities for considering non-monetary forms of exchange and incorporating the social values of innovations.

REFERENCES

Baldassarre, B., Schepers, M., Bocken, N., Cuppen, E., Korevaar, G., & Calabretta, G. (2019). Industrial symbiosis: Towards a design process for eco-industrial clusters by integrating circular economy and industrial ecology perspectives. *Journal of Cleaner Production*, 216, 446–460.

Bocken, N., Boons, F., & Baldassarre, B. (2019). Sustainable business model experimentation by under-standing ecologies of business models. *Journal of Cleaner Production*, 208, 1498–1512.

Broberg Viklund, S. (2015). Energy efficiency through industrial excess heat recovery: Policy impacts. *Energy Efficiency*, 8(1), 19–35.

Çalışkan, K., & Callon, M. (2009). Economization, part 1: Shifting attention from the economy towards processes of economization. *Economy and Society*, 38(3), 369–398.

Çalışkan, K., & Callon, M. (2010). Economization, part 2: A research programme for the study of markets. *Economy and Society*, 39(1), 1–32.

Chertow, M. R. (2000). Industrial symbiosis: Literature and taxonomy. *Annual Review of Energy and the Environment*, 25(1), 313–337.

Ellen MacArthur Foundation (2013). *Towards the Circular Economy: Economic and Business Rationale for an Accelerated Transition*. Cowes: Ellen MacArthur Foundation.

Enova (2009). *Potensialstudie for utnyttelse av spillvarme fra norsk industri*. Oslo: Enova.

European Commission (2016). *The Revised Renewable Energy Directive*.

Fontaine, A., & Rocher, L. (2021). Energy recovery on the agenda. Waste heat: A matter of public policy and social science concern. *Journal of Environmental Planning and Management*, 64(8), 1392–1407.

Hobson, K., & Lynch, N. (2016). Diversifying and de-growing the circular economy: Radical social transformation in a resource-scarce world. *Futures*, 82, 15–25.

Larsen, T. (2010). Acts of entification: The emergence of thinghood in social life. In N. Rapport (ed.), *Human Nature as Capacity: Transcending Discourse and Classification*. New York: Berghahn Books, 154–178.

Lock, M. (2001). *Twice Dead: Organ Transplants and the Reinvention of Death*. Berkeley: University of California Press.

Lygnerud, K., & Werner, S. (2018). Risk assessment of industrial excess heat recovery in district heating systems. *Energy*, 151, 430–441.

MacKenzie, D. (2009). Making things the same: Gases, emission rights and the politics of carbon markets. *Accounting, Organizations and Society*, 34(3–4), 440–455.

Mauss, M. (2002). *The Gift: The Form and Reason for Exchange in Archaic Societies*. Abingdon: Routledge.

Miró, L., Brückner, S., & Cabeza, L. F. (2015). Mapping and discussing industrial waste heat (IWH) potentials for different countries. *Renewable and Sustainable Energy Reviews*, 51, 847–855.

Päivärinne, S., Hjelm, O., & Gustafsson, S. (2015). Excess heat supply collaborations within the district heating sector: Drivers and barriers. *Journal of Renewable and Sustainable Energy*, 7(3), 033117.

Stark, D. (2011). *The Sense of Dissonance: Accounts of Worth in Economic Life*. Princeton, NJ: Princeton University Press.

Walls, J. L., & Paquin, R. L. (2015). Organizational perspectives of industrial symbiosis: A review and synthesis. *Organization & Environment*, 28(1), 32–53.

Webb, J., & Hawkey, D. (2017). On (not) assembling a market for sustainable energy: Heat network infrastructure and British cities. *Journal of Cultural Economy*, 10(1), 8–20.

Werner, S. (2017). District heating and cooling in Sweden. *Energy*, 126, 419–429.

12. The circular water economy and the 'seven C's'

Greg O'Shea, Seppo Luoto, Sanne Bor, Henri Hakala and Iben Bolund Nielsen

INTRODUCTION

In Chapter 1 of this book, the editors emphasize that there is a lack of knowledge about the institutional and societal transformations needed to implement circular practices, particularly those requiring radical changes at societal and institutional level, and therefore there is an urgent need for a more comprehensive understanding of how such circular economy (CE) innovations can be achieved. This chapter tries to add some understanding of system or ecosystem level enablers for circular economy innovation focused on the perspectives and experiences of entrepreneurs trying to enter the circular economy with innovative products and services. It is based on the study of an eco-industrial park, called 'EcoSairila', in the Finnish city of Mikkeli. Mikkeli is located c. 230 km north east from the capital Helsinki, in the Saimaa lake area and has a population of c. 55,000 people.

EcoSairila is boosting the regional circular water economy, around the recycling of wastewater, based on the logic of industrial symbiosis and related innovative, new businesses. We studied this case to better understand what conditions within the local, sustainability-focused, entrepreneurial ecosystem would energize entrepreneurs to enter the CE. Although large cities have been studied, to our knowledge no research exists addressing the transition to a CE in small and medium sized towns and cities such as Mikkeli. EcoSairila is a cornerstone of Mikkeli's smart specialization strategy. By 2030 the goal is to generate new, Mikkeli based, symbiotic start-ups and SMEs with a collective turnover of over €100m.

EcoSairila's goal is challenging on many levels. Any business opportunity identification, in particular novel CE opportunities, is difficult (Bechtel et al. 2013; Rizos et al. 2016). Several authors note that there is often a general lack of technologies, knowledge and technical skills for more 'advanced technical' options (Rizos et al. 2016). CE businesses also typically involve multiple stakeholders and a need for suitable partners (Bechtel et al. 2013), and hence, challenges in collaboration within some form of an ecosystem are further accentuated. Prior research has highlighted that some form of external support from the entrepreneurial ecosystem is crucial to entrepreneurial success, in particular for sustainable entrepreneurship (Cohen 2006). However, a grand challenge for sustainable entrepreneurial ecosystem stakeholders is that the nature of the interactions within an ecosystem and the conditions for creating a supportive entrepreneurial ecosystem remain unclear (Cohen 2006). Similarly, the perspective of the entrepreneurs themselves is rarely considered when designing and improving such support systems (Hakala et al. 2020; O'Shea et al. 2021).

In order to support EcoSairila to attract and grow innovative CE start-ups and SMEs, we posed the following research question as central to our case study: *What enablers need to exist within the local sustainability focused entrepreneurial ecosystem to engage and support innovative CE focused entrepreneurs?* While we conducted a case study of EcoSairila with specific practical aims, we also contribute to the literature on sustainable entrepreneurial ecosystem development by developing a framework for ecosystem enablers that encourages entrepreneurs to focus their efforts on innovating for a local circular water economy. The seven identified enablers are: *competences, customers, connectors, collaboration, coordination, culture* and *centre*, which we term collectively 'the Seven C's'.

ENABLERS FOR CIRCULAR ECONOMY ENTREPRENEURSHIP

To identify the relevant enablers and to construct an initial conceptual framework for our study we scouted the existing literature for enablers in CE focused ecosystems (Bechtel et al. 2013; Rizos et al. 2016) and regional CE development referring mainly to studies focusing on local eco-industrial parks (Mathews and Tan 2011; Ghisellini et al. 2016). Added to these, we also perceived other related topics such as sustainable entrepreneurial ecosystems and generic entrepreneurial ecosystems literature (Cohen 2006; Mason and Brown 2014). Related to CE, prior studies have focused mainly on Chinese regions and towns, but some studies also consider European countries such as the UK, the Netherlands, Denmark and Germany (Ghisellini et al. 2016).

From these studies, we searched especially for *key components and actors* within these systems (Cohen 2006; Mason and Brown 2014) which then allowed us also to decode the core enabling components. First, a clear enabling component relates to *competences* that the entrepreneurs have themselves. In particular, access to various 'sustainability competences' (Eizaguirre et al. 2019), technologies, knowledge, information and technical skills, that help the entrepreneurs to identify, assess and implement 'advanced technical' options for their business (Rizos et al. 2016; Bechtel et al. 2013).

In previous studies, another important enabling component is the presence of customers who offer piloting opportunities for new products and create market demand for sustainable business ideas (Rizos et al. 2016). Business to business (B2B) customers inside the system can provide extremely valuable symbiotic relationships (Chertow 2007).

Within ecosystems, the importance of a *connector* role is also highlighted (Shane and Cable 2002). For instance, the use of experienced business people (Mason and Brown 2014), researchers acting as diplomats, missionaries and knowledge brokers (Haarla et al. 2018), and organizations acting as agents or brokers in the innovation process (Kanda et al. 2018).

Another key enabler is *collaboration*, which increases productivity, reduces R&D costs and creates shared sense-making (O'Shea et al. 2021) around new opportunities. Collaboration also enables the finding and developing of suitable partnerships (Bechtel et al. 2013), understanding and contacting markets and customers efficiently (Rizos et al. 2016), and distributing new ideas in the ecosystem (DiVito and Ingen-Housz 2021).

Coordination within the ecosystem leads to increasing efficiency, coherence of activities and prevention of overlapping functions and roles (Jacobides et al. 2018). This can mean for instance coordinated decisions and integration of sustainability product concepts into businesses (O'Shea et al. 2021). Coordination is also about clarity, e.g. around ecosystem identity, its shared goals, policies and governance (Hakala et al. 2020). Previous studies use the term 'entrepreneurial *climate*' or 'entrepreneurial *culture*' to describe an important part of entrepreneurial ecosystems (Malecki 2018). But besides being entrepreneurial, the *culture* can also embrace the idea of the CE as a whole (Mathews and Tan 2011) and allow shared sustainability orientation amongst the stakeholders (O'Shea et al. 2021; DiVito and Ingen-Housz 2021). Finally, according to previous studies the idea of a *centre*, a physical and virtual place, is important as a visible symbol for the existence of the ecosystem. The real value of the centre is created by its function that unites various supporting resources, partly enhances the supportive culture and makes related services more accessible for entrepreneurs (Spigel 2016).

METHODOLOGY AND CASE DESCRIPTION

The Mikkeli Blue Economy Water Hub, also known as 'EcoSairila', is a CE business park which functions as a center of excellence in water circularity research, processes, and business. The €100m investment includes local communications and transport structures as well as funding for 'blue economy'[1] research and development by local universities. A Membrane Bioreactor (MBR), wastewater treatment plant and water reclamation plant have been built 40 metres deep in the bedrock adjoining Mikkeli city and Lake Saimaa and the park incorporates research and pilot facilities, and a biorefinery producing biogas and organic nutrients. EcoSairila is in a privileged position in that it is closely connected with water separation scientists at two local universities and other water treatment partners on site. There are also other excellent support resources within the ecosystem including a regional development agency, the resources of the city itself and of the regional (county) council acting as coordinator for EU funding.

For the purposes of the study we undertook 45 user-stakeholder interviews, conducted between spring 2019 and summer 2020. The respondents were 28 individuals from 10 different organizations within the EcoSairila ecosystem including SMEs, pre-start-ups, development agencies, research labs, civil servants and EcoSairila itself. The interviews lasted between 45 and 60 minutes. The transcripts and meeting notes comprised c. 350 pages of data.

The overall goal was to develop a framework for various stakeholders such as regional development organizations and the local members of a research and education cluster when building an entrepreneurship focused CE. Finally, to understand the practical implications of our framework, we tested its logic on a start-up within EcoSairila. This start-up is a brewery company that wants to be amongst the world's first to use waste (sewage) water to brew its beer. This short example is also included later in this chapter to show how the final model can be applied to a case.

FINDINGS AND ANALYSIS

Our analysis is data-driven and theory-based around these clusters, developing the model through theory-practice iterations, conceptualized eventually as the Seven C's: *Competences, Customers, Connectors, Collaboration, Coordination, Culture* and *Center.*

Competences

Our data highlights that CE-related competences were acquired elsewhere than in the Mikkeli region, or if in the region, in some other working life context than as an entrepreneur. In several examples, the entrepreneur had moved to the area because of a close connection to the region or other contacts already in the area. Most often the entrepreneurs had built their "sustainability orientation" (O'Shea et al. 2021) in the Helsinki region where access to various "sustainability competences" (Eizaguirre et al. 2019) had opened. For example:

> I guess I have held quite long these green values and thought about my idea ... but it helped me that the Mikkeli area is a good area to live a healthy life near the nature ...

Some entrepreneurs had personal ties, such as family, friends and other informal networks, which they favoured as a partner competence over the ability to set up a business (D'Hont et al. 2016). Sometimes this access to crucial competences had been found amongst trusted friends with shared values and "sustainability orientations" (O'Shea et al. 2021). In terms of formal organizational competences used for entrepreneurial concept support, the city development agency was mentioned several times:

> The biggest thing was that there was only one person ... [I could get help and advice for] everything ... starting the business and getting funding, or legal advice or anything like that via one contact person.

For water circularity expertise, Mikkeli has two university research groups of 'water separation' scientists that are relatively large and highly qualified in their area globally. There is also further technology and process expertise within the EcoSairila park itself. Mentors, university alumni and other experienced actors with social capital also act as an enabler. However, the access to network competences is something in which respondents would like to see improvements; they felt that the system needs more and different experts to be readily accessible. Recent new ventures have relied on venture coaches and innovation agents being sourced from a green innovation centre in a different town. While this has been helpful it was felt that this dependence on experts from a neighbouring region was not an optimal solution:

> One of our challenges in Mikkeli, if we want to do something similar like in many places already, is to have someone who helps researchers and businesses to collaborate, the so called (green) innovation expert.

Customers

This enabler refers to the demand for products and services both inside and outside the ecosystem. The EcoSairila ecosystem is fortunate in that there is a company that manages the whole water treatment cycle, which provides a market outlet and other customer possibilities for other entrepreneurs in the field. Respondents felt that EcoSairila could offer a good context where new sustainable business ideas could emerge also in B2B (Pastakia 1998) in the symbiotic relationships:

> LP company, which is the biggest barley producer in Finland, they have an interest to build this full circle so that the end-waste from EcoSairila biogas-plant would go to the fields of the barley farmers [as fertilizers]. So, it would make the full circle.

For customers outside of the ecosystem, several respondents were positive that nationally there is and will be "green customer potential" (Gleim et al. 2013) increasing in the future:

I guess in that respect we are relatively lucky in Finland that we have some systems [for recycling / circularity] already … and people don't naturally just throw trash on the floor, and these kind of things …

Connector

The enabler importance was highly visible in the interviews. It was used for example to describe persons working in MIKSEI, Mikkeli city council or the Mikkeli University Consortium (MUC):

Mr M also sees the Mikkeli University Consortium as a part of the discussions around regional development, helping to build coherence strategy within the ecosystems, that different organizations have different roles, so one important thing it does is host meetings, gathering people to meet.

It was also used to refer to the need for a facilitator (Gliedt et al. 2018; Howells 2006; Kanda et al. 2018; Kivimaa and Martiskainen 2018) to work in the system as 'innovation intermediaries' or specialists (Patala et al. 2020) facilitating innovation processes and creating new opportunities.

Collaboration

The need for collaboration, like the 'connector' enabler, is something that most respondents were very aware of. Collaboration can enable the finding and developing of suitable partnerships (Wooi and Zailani 2010), contacting markets and customers efficiently (Rizos et al. 2016) and distributing ideas efficiently among different actors in the ecosystem (DiVito and Ingen-Housz 2021):

MIKSEI, has had discussions with all the universities … they have constant discussions with the local businesses, they do that work.

At a strategic level, six or seven core stakeholders meet regularly, but still there is a feeling that more enabling, dense collaboration could take place:

We have been discussing that we should have more meetings … We are trying to get closer.

At an operational level, respondents would like stakeholder collaboration to also focus on researchers and graduate students, to bridge the gap between sustainable entrepreneurship ideas and turning those ideas into start-ups:

We have had some meetings trying to find some businesses from students, and … we (currently) lack … straight line from the student idea to the business, and the support.

One issue appears to be that the overriding shared sustainability intent (O'Shea et al. 2021) is not yet powerful enough and that ecosystem collaborators are not having "the sense of urgency" to support a systemic regional approach in CE business development, versus a pre-occupation with their individual roles:

Maybe we all have too much to do in our own work and do not have time for this type of exercises.

While Mikkeli city has enabled many things to support local CE entrepreneurship, still, respondents mentioned that more openness is needed; if collaboration is weak, or non-systematic, then trust among different parties will not grow to the level needed.

Coordination

This enabler has not naturally emerged in the Mikkeli CE. The city council recognizes this and the director for development explains the city's role as facilitating openness and more coordination within the ecosystem. However, CE entrepreneurs within the system would like to see this done more formally:

> Seems that no one is controlling the system level …

Some respondents would like the regional organizations to be more focused and coordinated:

> The spill-over effect that would come from, for example the research done by the university water research groups … maybe there could be some kind of coordination in the means of research done by these organizations.

At the same time, several users would also like to see more clarity (in how the system fits together and how it works for their interest) and more formal coordination:

> I know that MIKSEI is there and some other players, but it is very hard to get the overview. Who does what and how do different parts fit together … right now I think they do not necessarily fit together?

Culture

Components of the culture enabler are still relatively underdeveloped. EcoSairila is taking its first steps in development and attempts to build a CE brand to persuade entrepreneurs to establish their businesses locally. Many interviewees saw that regional "entrepreneurial culture" has been advancing through the presence of the MIKSEI development agency and EcoSairila. However, more needs to be done to develop this entrepreneurial culture and this specific cluster where a new business could fit as:

> it requires rather than an individual or even small company thinking, it requires cluster thinking to be able to, to take [–] and there for the circle and the circle economy, just to repeat, doesn't take place at the individual or even small groups, small business.

Centre

Many of the respondents considered that the centre, the actual place of activity was an important enabler for the ecosystem, particularly in terms of the CE. The investment on the CE park site has been significant at €100m and the resulting infrastructure and water purification facilities provide piloting and prototyping possibilities as a foundation for technology start-ups:

> Plants need to start first … we need the big stuff first so to speak … then the SMEs will come …

However, SME respondents stated that there does not exist a single centre in the traditional physical building sense. Even if respondents had identified some shared events between different stakeholders in the ecosystem, the importance of the physical centre was brought up in some interviews:

> Even though it was very helpful to achieve concrete and very valuable help by MIKSEI and having one person to talk to all the time ... in overall I guess it would be helpful to have one physical recognized place for start-ups in the area.

We summarize our findings and analyses in Table 12.1, which provides an overview of the Seven C's model or framework as the main contribution from this chapter.

CONCEPTUAL FRAMEWORK

The proposed framework on sustainable entrepreneurial ecosystems and its propositions provide practical insights for sustainable entrepreneurs concerning their interactions with stakeholders of sustainable entrepreneurial ecosystems. Strong stakeholder relationships, multi-stakeholder partnerships and extensive support can in turn facilitate the operations of a sustainable small enterprise.

This model can be applied as a starting point for sustainable entrepreneurial ecosystem development, and then as a reflector of status along the developmental path of the ecosystem. Here (Table 12.2), we illustrate how the framework relates to a CE start-up brewery based in EcoSairila aiming to utilize the purified wastewater in their beer production.

The main theoretical contribution of this study is the Seven C's model. As far as we know, this model is the first attempt to unite, into a theoretical and practical model, different enablers identified both in generic and sustainable entrepreneurship ecosystem research and the literature around CE focused ecosystems and regional CE development (the local eco-industrial parks). Even if not exhaustive, we consider this model as a good starting point when beginning to theorize sustainable ecosystem enablers around large eco-developments like EcoSairila. For strengthening this entrepreneur-centred and in-depth view we would highlight the importance of analysing user experiences of future entrepreneurs with various service design techniques (for instance Helkkula et al. 2012), focused on these ecosystem enablers.

CONCLUSIONS

This case study was about EcoSairila, in the city of Mikkeli, Finland. This chapter puts forward a framework or model of enablers which support entrepreneurial engagement in the circular economy. This model is founded on the process view of ecosystems, placing the entrepreneur as a key user of the process. In our view it is important to build an in-depth understanding of enablers, within an ecosystem, for entrepreneurs to be confident enough to take CE opportunities.

Table 12.1   CE enablers from the entrepreneur's perspective

CE enablers	Relevant literature on enablers	Key findings in the case study
Competence availability: (1) of entrepreneur(s) themselves; (2) through the system	Especially various 'sustainability competences' (Eizaguirre et al. 2019), technologies, knowledge, information and technical skills, enabling 'advanced technical' options for their business (Rizos et al. 2016; Bechtel et al. 2013).	- Often acquired outside the region; sustainability linked to pre-existing values; informal networking; region attractive for living. - Key development agency support; but lack of innovation expertise.
Customer availability	Industrial symbiosis (Chertow 2007) and especially focusing on green values and practices of consumers (Gleim et al. 2013).	Already Business to Business opportunities – green business especially fitting with EcoSairila, and overall supposed Business to Consumer green customer potential.
Connector availability	Conversants (Shane & Cable 2002) experienced business people (Mason & Brown 2014), researchers (Haarla et al. 2018), third-party, broker, and facilitator (Gliedt et al. 2018; Howells 2006; Kanda et al. 2018; Kivimaa and Martiskainen 2018).	Some connector support already existing, such as a development agency, city council, university consortium.
Collaboration inside the ecosystem	Increases productivity and reduces costs (Acs et al. 2008); collaborative sense-making (O'Shea et al. 2021); partnerships (Wooi & Zailani 2010), contacts to customers (Rizos et al. 2016) and distributing ideas in the ecosystem (DiVito & Ingen-Housz 2021).	Identified as something which is needed more, but it has the classical problem of investment need without the certainty of useful outcomes, and trust needs to develop. Support is available as connectors host meetings, gather people, and organize networking hubs.
Coordination: system level fitting the parts of the ecosystem together	Shared goals, and policies boundaries and governance (Hakala et al. 2020); efficiency and coherence (Jacobides et al. 2018); co-sensemaking and co-integration (O'Shea et al. 2021).	Desire is to get an actor to take a more formal role to coordinate different parts of the ecosystem. The current system is informal and 'facilitated' by the city council through 'nudging' activities.
Culture: an innovation oriented and sustainability willing or demanding culture	Both entrepreneurial culture (Malecki 2018) and culture promoting circular economy (Mathews & Tan 2011) and shared sustainability orientation amongst the stakeholders (O'Shea et al. 2021; DiVito & Ingen-Housz 2021).	There already exists a sustainability willing culture. EcoSairila is developing the brand image as an EU centre of water excellence. It has persuaded some entrepreneurs to establish their businesses in the CE park.
Centre: a physical and virtual place	Unites various supporting resources, enhances the supportive culture and makes related services more accessible for entrepreneurs (Spigel 2016).	EcoSairila is growing as a physical centre of excellence for water circularity and research, but a clear and visible centre is needed for creating access for specific resources.

This model can be of value to existing and aspiring sustainable entrepreneurs, those working as intermediaries, and stakeholder support organizations, in the following ways:

- For regional sustainable innovation and CE policy makers to gain a better overview of the existing collaboration and support mechanisms for sustainable entrepreneurship.
- By using this model as a benchmark to identify specific areas of an ecosystem which are in need of further development or which require additional stakeholder support for sustainable entrepreneurship.
- For 'connectors' and intermediaries to use as a diagnosis model to see where their contributions are needed (Kanda et al. 2018).
- An audit tool for individual stakeholder organisations, to review how they participate and collaborate and support local CE entrepreneurship.

- This model could be utilized in practice as a tool for CE ecosystem development facilitation (Kanda et al. 2018), for example in stakeholder workshops.

Overall, our findings will encourage the establishment of extended collaboration and support mechanisms for entrepreneurs with a specific focus on sustainability, such as sustainable investments, sustainability education or sustainability-focused governmental incentives. Enhanced stakeholder support can ultimately influence larger institutional structures and norms leading to institutional change towards sustainability. Through increased engagement in sustainable entrepreneurship, stronger sustainable entrepreneurial ecosystems could further pave the road towards a more sustainable future.

Table 12.2   CE enablers from the entrepreneur's perspective

CE enabler	Case study application
Competence availability	Sustainability competences and related knowledge for water circulation are present in EcoSairila and in the university water circulation lab. From the founding partners, one came with some brewery experience and the other is a business school graduate. The brewery received key development agency support related to funding, piloting, and legitimizing in its early phase.
Customer availability	The established 'Saimaa' brewery is based in Mikkeli and there is already a brand for mainstream Mikkeli beer. Organic microbreweries themselves have a local and national market. Finnish supermarkets and consumers provide a nationally available 'green customer potential'.
Connector availability	The director of EcoSairila has himself been the main connector for the brewery and the CE ecosystem support functions, especially the development agency, Miksei.
Coordination	For the brewery, a high level of clarity of the ecosystem exists, as they are closely connected to EcoSairila and its director, physically and mentally.
Coordinated collaboration	Enabled via the main connector person, the director of EcoSairila.
Culture	The brewery benefits from the water circularity brand of EcoSairila and aims to be the first all circular economy brewery in the world. There is also a subculture of craft beer enthusiasm in the area due to the other relatively successful craft brewery in the city, as well as due to national and international trends. EcoSairila is developing a CE brand image and has persuaded current and nascent entrepreneurs to establish their businesses in the CE park. It is also growing into an EU centre of excellence for water circularity and the city is known for its CE technology and processes. University research units also hold open research conferences/research impact activities with EcoSairila.
Centre	The brewery is based in the CE park which houses the 'centre' water treatment, biogas, and fertiliser plants. Business support available in city centre is only 3 km away. The business park functions as a physical centre of activity and the centre of service, knowledge and support is in the city centre.

NOTE

1. By this concept we refer to better stewardship of our natural water resources. Like in the concept of 'green economy', the blue economy model aims for improvement of human well-being by promoting circular economy and significantly reducing environmental risks (modified from: https://thecommonwealth.org/blue-economy).

REFERENCES

Acs, Z., Desai, S., & Hessels, J. (2008). Entrepreneurship, economic development and institutions. *Small Business Economics*, 31(3), 219–234.

Bechtel, N., Bojko, R., & Völkel, R. (2013). Be in the loop: Circular economy & strategic sustainable development. Master's thesis, Blekinge Institute of Technology, Karlskrona, Sweden.

Chertow, M. R. (2007). "Uncovering" industrial symbiosis. *Journal of Industrial Ecology*, 11(1), 11–30.

Cohen, B. (2006). Sustainable valley entrepreneurial ecosystems. *Business Strategy and the Environment*, 15(1), 1–14.

D'Hont, L., Doern, R., & Delgado García, J. (2016). The role of friendship in the formation and development of entrepreneurial teams and ventures. *Journal of Small Business and Enterprise Development*, 23(2), 528–561.

DiVito, L., & Ingen-Housz, Z. (2021). From individual sustainability orientations to collective sustainability innovation and sustainable entrepreneurial ecosystems. *Small Business Economics*, 56, 1057–1072.

Eizaguirre, A., García-Feijoo, M., & Laka, J. P. (2019). Defining sustainability core competencies in business and management studies based on multinational stakeholders' perceptions. *Sustainability* 11(8), 2303.

Ghisellini, P., Cialani, C., & Ulgiati, S. (2016). A review on circular economy: The expected transition to a balanced interplay of environmental and economic systems. *Journal of Cleaner Production*, 114, 11–32.

Gleim, M. R., Smith, J. S., Andrews, D., & Cronin Jr, J. J. (2013). Against the green: A multi-method examination of the barriers to green consumption. *Journal of Retailing*, 89(1), 44–61.

Gliedt, T., Hoicka, C. E., & Jackson, N. (2018). Innovation intermediaries accelerating environmental sustainability transitions. *Journal of Cleaner Production*, 174, 1247–1261.

Haarla, A., Hakala, H., & O'Shea, G. (2018). Re-imagining the forest: Entrepreneurial ecosystem development for Finnish cellulosic materials. In J. Leitão, H. Alves, N. Krueger & J. Park (eds.), *Entrepreneurial, Innovative and Sustainable Ecosystems*. Cham: Springer, 191–214.

Hakala, H., O'Shea, G., Farny, S., & Luoto, S. (2020). Re-storying the business, innovation, and entrepreneurial ecosystem concepts: The model-narrative review method. International Journal of Management Reviews, 22(1), 10–32.

Helkkula, A., Kelleher, C., & Pihlström, M. (2012). Characterizing value as an experience. *Journal of Service Research*, 15(1), 59–75.

Howells, J. (2006). Intermediation and the role of intermediaries in innovation. *Research Policy*, 35(5), 715–728.

Jacobides, M. G., Cennamo, C., & Gawer, A. (2018). Towards a theory of ecosystems. *Strategic Management Journal*, 39(8), 2255–2276.

Kanda, W., Hjelm, O., Clausen, J., & Bienkowska, D. (2018). Roles of intermediaries in supporting eco-innovation. *Journal of Cleaner Production*, 205, 1006–1016.

Kivimaa, P., & Martiskainen, M. (2018). Innovation, low energy buildings and intermediaries in Europe: Systematic case study review. *Energy Efficiency*, 11(1), 31–51.

Malecki, E. J. (2018). Entrepreneurship and entrepreneurial ecosystems. *Geography Compass*, 12(3), e12359.

Mason, C., & Brown, R. (2014). Entrepreneurial ecosystems and growth oriented entrepreneurship. Background paper prepared for the workshop organized by the OECD LEED Programme and the Dutch Ministry of Economic Affairs, The Hague, Netherlands.

Mathews, J. A., & Tan, H. (2011). Progress toward a circular economy in China: The drivers (and inhibitors) of eco-industrial initiative. *Journal of Industrial Ecology*, 15(3), 435–457.

O'Shea, G., Farny, S., & Hakala, H. (2021). The buzz before business: A design science study of a sustainable entrepreneurial ecosystem. *Small Business Economics*, 56, 1097–1120.

Pastakia, A. (1998). Grassroots ecopreneurs: Change agents for a sustainable society. *Journal of Organizational Change Management*, 11(2), 157–173.

Patala, S., Salmi, A., & Bocken, N. (2020). Intermediation dilemmas in facilitated industrial symbiosis. *Journal of Cleaner Production*, 261, 121093.

Rizos, V., Behrens, A., Van Der Gaast, W. et al. (2016). Implementation of circular economy business models by small and medium-sized enterprises (SMEs): Barriers and enablers. *Sustainability*, 8(11), 1212.

Shane, S., & Cable, D. (2002). Network ties, reputation, and the financing of new ventures. *Management Science*, 48(3), 364–381.

Spigel, B. (2016). Developing and governing entrepreneurial ecosystems: The structure of entrepreneurial support programs in Edinburgh, Scotland. *International Journal of Innovation and Regional Development*, 7(2), 141–160.

Wooi, G. C., & Zailani, S. (2010). Green supply chain initiatives: Investigation on the barriers in the context of SMEs in Malaysia. *International Business Management*, 4(1), 20–27.

13. Drivers and barriers for industrial symbiosis: the case of Mo Industrial Park

Siri Jakobsen and Marianne Steinmo

INTRODUCTION

The circular economy (CE) – the concept of closing material and energy loops to extract their utilization – has started gaining momentum as a solution to address sustainable development. Replacing a linear model of production, where goods are manufactured from raw materials, used and disposed of (Saavedra et al. 2018), a circular system maintains the value of resources, products and materials in the economy as long as possible (Merli et al. 2018). CE can be defined as "an economy constructed from societal production-consumption systems that maximize the service produced from the linear nature-society-nature material and energy throughput flow" (Korhonen et al. 2018, p. 39).

Several authors argue that the CE transition needs to be interpreted at three levels (e.g. Fang et al. 2007; Jackson et al. 2014; Sakr et al. 2011): changes in social and economic dynamics at a *macro* level; implementation of circular processes such as product design and consumption at the *micro* level; and industrial symbiosis between firms at a *meso* level (Merli et al. 2018). Adapting the meso level, this chapter explores a key strategy for CE, namely, the *industrial symbiosis* between actors in an industrial park, where the aim is to create physical links between actors through the exchange of energy, materials, water and by-products (Hardy and Graedel 2002; Prosman et al. 2017). Industrial symbiosis is found to be more sustainable than most other manufacturing concepts because it comprises more innovation targets and mechanisms (Geissdoerfer et al. 2017; OECD 2009). This chapter joins this debate of *change* (Damanpour 1991) as an important attribute of innovation for industrial symbiosis. The change towards industrial symbiosis (IS) is connected to a set of barriers and drivers, as these factors require cooperation between actors, capital and intellectual input. Numerous drivers and barriers of IS are recognized in the literature and mainly capture technical aspects, such as water treatment, optimization models and product flows (Bacudio et al. 2016). This chapter responds to calls to examine IS from a social science point of view (Lindkvist and Baumann 2014) and for longitudinal case studies on the development of drivers and barriers in IS (Zhu and Ruth 2014). Hence, we address the following research question: *How have the drivers and barriers to IS developed in Mo Industrial Park over a decade?*

We start with a theoretical presentation of the drivers and barriers to innovation of IS before we present the case of the Mo Industrial Park and the methods. Next, the findings of the drivers and barriers to IS development are discussed in relation to the literature.

DRIVERS AND BARRIERS TO IS DEVELOPMENT IN AN INDUSTRIAL SYSTEM

Industrial symbiosis refers to energy and material exchanges between actors located in geographic proximity (Ehrenfeld and Gertler 1997) and was originally defined as "traditionally separate industries in a collective approach to competitive advantage involving physical exchange of materials, energy, water and by-products" (Chertow 2007, p. 12). Chertow (2007) mentions three main connections of resource exchanges: (1) the reuse of by-products as substitutes for products or raw materials, (2) sharing of infrastructure, use and organization of resources such as energy, water and wastewater, and (3) a common supply of services, such as transport, food and fire stations. The goal of industrial symbiosis is that cooperation between actors increases the efficiency of the system as a whole, and although some of the actors in the system are less environmentally focused, the whole system can be environmental because of the connections between the actors (Ehrenfeld and Gertler 1997).

Table 13.1   *Drivers and barriers of industrial symbiosis*

	Drivers	Barriers
Economic	– Increased revenue (Giurco et al. 2011) – Lower input costs (Van Beers et al. 2007)	– Operational costs and revenues (Giurco et al. 2011) – Lack of funding (Bacudio et al. 2016; Fang et al. 2011; Li et al. 2015) – Insufficient financial support from banks (Su et al. 2013) – Investments in extended production systems (Van Beers et al. 2007)
Regulations	– New pollutant targeted regulations (Giurco et al. 2011) – Strong government engagement (Mathews & Tan 2011; Zhu & Ruth 2014) – Government-initiated policies (Behera et al. 2012)	– Environmental regulations (Giurco et al. 2011) – Inadequate public tax incentives (Su et al. 2013)
Cooperation	– Between stakeholders (Geissdoerfer et al. 2017) – Social ties (Zhu & Ruth 2014)	– Lack of willingness to collaborate (Bacudio et al. 2016) – Lack of cooperation and information sharing (Gibbs & Deutz 2007; Golev et al. 2015) – Lack of trust among locators (Gibbs & Deutz 2007)
Knowledge and technology	– Specific knowledge that actors acquire through experience and learning of IS in their system (Boons et al. 2011) – Technical knowledge (Zhu and Ruth 2014)	– Technological challenges (Li et al. 2015) – Lack of technology infrastructure readiness (Costa & Ferrão 2010; Li et al. 2015)
Management	– Corporate sustainable focus in the firm (Giurco et al. 2011) – Proactive management (Geissdoerfer et al. 2017)	– Cultural changes within firms (Giurco et al. 2011) – Lack of awareness of IS (Bacudio et al. 2016; Chiu & Yong 2004) – Lack of top management support (Bacudio et al. 2016; Chiu & Yong 2004)
Resources	– Availability of resources (Zhu & Ruth 2014) – Staff mobility between different industries (Van Beers et al. 2007)	– Resource scarcity (Giurco et al. 2011)
Location	– A facilitator in the system (Behera et al. 2012)	– Distances between companies (Giurco et al. 2011)

More recent studies have focused on the role of innovation as a tool for IS and green growth (Taddeo et al. 2017). This chapter joins this debate by focusing on *change* (Damanpour 1991) as an important attribute of innovation for IS. More precisely, we examine the changes in the drivers and barriers to IS in an industrial system. Table 13.1 highlights the key drivers and barriers in the IS literature, classified in terms of economics, regulations, resources, cooperation, knowledge and technology, locations and management.

As these studies are mainly cross sectional and quantitative, calls have been made for studies that examine how IS networks grow for longer periods using complementary methods such as case studies (Zhu and Ruth 2014). We respond to these shortcomings through a longitudinal case study of IS development in Mo Industrial Park and thereby contribute new insights into the content of CE that remain largely unexplored (Korhonen et al. 2018).

THE CASE OF MO INDUSTRIAL PARK

BOX 13.1 CASE DESCRIPTION: MO INDUSTRIAL PARK

1. Situated in the city Mo i Rana in Northern Norway.
2. Continuation of the state-owned company Norsk Jernverk that was built after the Second World War, as the government saw the need for steel production in Norway.
3. When Norsk Jernverk was dissolved in 1988, it was replaced as an industrial park with several new companies within steel production, maintenance, civil engineering solutions, ICT, accounting, engineering, aquaculture, logistics, special waste storage, and handling and transport.
4. The industrial park is based on the individual companies concentrating fully on their own business ideas but shares infrastructure and services with other firms in the park.
5. MIP AS was established as an infrastructure company that owns most of the infrastructure such as roads, piping system and buildings.
6. Today, MIP consists of 108 companies, 2,500 employees, and a total turnover of 7.5 billion NOK (whereby 5.5 billion in exports).

This study is based on a single case study of IS development in Mo Industrial Park, which is a critical case for understanding IS development between actors in an industrial system (Flyvbjerg 2006). We aim for insight into this single case in depth and over time rather than generalizing beyond this case. This study is a longitudinal analysis of interviews with the main actors of the industrial symbiosis in the Mo Industrial Park as the main source (see Table 13.2). The interviews were conducted in 2010 and 2020, providing a unique opportunity to map both the physical changes of IS and the firm drivers and barriers associated with them. We also interviewed external actors relevant for IS development. In 2010, these were mainly governmental actors, whereas in 2020, knowledge actors were the most important external actors.

The interviews were conducted at the informants' offices and lasted approximately 45 minutes on average. To uncover critical drivers and barriers of IS development, we showed the informants the IS overview (Figure 13.1) and encouraged them to freely reflect upon the development and changes from 2010 to 2020 (Patton 2015). We also used a semi-structured

Table 13.2   *Data collection*

Actors	Characteristics	2010	2020
Celsa Armeringsstål AS	Produce steel reinforcements, where iron and steel scrap is the most important raw material Production capacity: 1.5 million tons pr. year.	Size: 294 Ownership: Celsa Group (Spanish) Informant(s): CEO Environmental manager	Size: 315 Ownership: Celsa Group Informant: CEO
Vale Manganese Norway AS (2010) Ferroglobe (2020)	Produce ferromanganese with a capacity of 120,000 tons/year.	Size: 80 Ownership: Vale Manganese Norway (Brazilian) Informant: CEO	Size: 91 Ownership: Ferroglobe (Spanish) Informant: CEO
Ruukki Profiler AS	Manufacture basic metals and fabricated metal products.	Size: 110 employees Ownership: Ruukki Profiler AS (Finnish) Informant: CEO	Closed down in 2010
Fesil Rana Metall AS (2010) Elkem Rana AS (2020)	Produce ferrosilicon with a capacity of 90,000 tons/year.	Size: 85 Ownership: Fesil Rana Metall AS (Norwegian) Informant: CEO	Size: 100 Ownership: Elkem Rana AS (Chinese) Informant: CEO
Ranfjord Fiskeprodukter AS (2010) Kvarøy Smolt AS (2020)	Produce salmon fry by utilizing waste heat from the metals producing firms.	Size: 11 Ownership: Ranfjord Fiskeprodukter (Norwegian) Informant: CEO	Size: 14 Ownership: Kvarøy Smolt AS (Norwegian) Informant: Owner
Mo Industrial Park AS (MIP AS)	Property and infrastructure company. Main tasks are to manage, develop and carry out operation of properties, infrastructure, facilities and equipment in the industrial park and adapt for new establishments and market the industrial park as an establishment location.	Size: 62 Ownership: Norwegian Informant: CEO Communication manager	Size: 67 Ownership: Informant: CEO, COO, vice president marketing
Mo Fjernvarme (CEO)	District heating company that uses excess heat from the process industry as the main source (99.4% in 2020) of heat production. Produce 40 GWh.	Size: 3 Ownership: MIP AS and Helgeland Kraft Informant: CEO	Size: 4 Ownership: MIP AS and Helgeland Kraft Informant: CEO
MIP Environmental Group (2010) MIP Sustainability (2020)	Coordination of environmental efforts within the park.	Informant: Manager	Informant: Manager
External actors		Informant: Environment manager, Rana municipality Senior adviser, Climate and Pollution directorate (KLIF)	Informant: CEO, science park of Helgeland, Technical research institute

interview guide to help the informants reflect on critical IS changes (Yin 2013). Secondary sources, such as press articles, presentations and industry conference participation, are used for contextual understanding. We followed an inductive data analysis approach, where both authors coded the data to ensure shared meanings (Miles and Huberman 1994). Firm names are made visible with the acceptance of the participants; however, firm-related quotes by participants are labelled as being from 'firm informants' to secure the informants' privacy.

INDUSTRIAL SYMBIOSIS IN MO INDUSTRIAL PARK

Figure 13.1 illustrates the IS between firms in Mo Industrial Park in 2010.

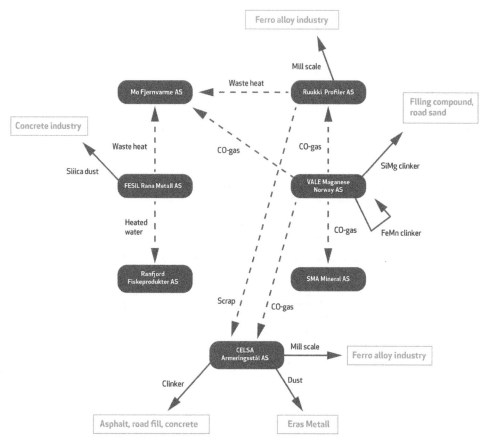

Source: Adapted from Jakobsen and Steinmo (2010).

Figure 13.1   Industrial symbiosis in Mo Industrial Park 2010

At the core of the energy and material exchanges are the metal-producing firms Fesil, Vale, Celsa and Ruukki, where Vale and Fesil are the largest distributors of by-products in terms of CO gas and excess heat. CO gas is used as input in the production processes in four other firms within the park: SMA Minerals, Celsa, Mo Fjernvarme and Ruukki. From Fesil, excess heat is used by Mo Fjernvarme, a district heating company that sells heat to a large number of municipal and apartment buildings. Municipal regulations demand that new buildings over 1,000 square metres are connected to district heating where possible, and 80 per cent of their input heat came from Fesil in 2010. In addition, cooling water from Fesil is used by a nearby salmon smolt (young salmons) facility, where the cooling water has an ideal temperature for smolt farming. A third distributor of by-products in the park in 2010 was Ruukki Profiler, which sold iron scrap from their production to Celsa, which produced iron reinforcement from the scrap. Mo Fjernvarme also used heat from Ruukki for district heating (3 MW), although Fesil was their main heat provider. In times of very cold weather, Mo Fjernvarme used oil in addition to the excess heat from Fesil and Ruukki.

The main changes in the IS between 2010 and 2020 were that Ruukki was closed down, Celsa lost a source of high-quality and close-range scrap, and Mo Fjernvarme lost a heat source. Mo Fjernvarme has adapted to the situation and made several investments over the years to increase its percentage of renewable energy, which today is over 99 per cent, but surprisingly, we cannot observe many new ISs in 2020 compared to 2010. However, we do observe some significant changes in the drivers and barriers to IS development, as discussed below.

DRIVERS AND BARRIERS TO IS DEVELOPMENT IN MO INDUSTRIAL PARK

Table 13.3 summarizes the main drivers and barriers to IS development in Mo Industrial Park in 2010 and 2020, which the following discussion refers to.

Industrial Symbiosis in Mo Industrial Park, 2010: 'Harvesting Low-Hanging Fruit'

Analysing the drivers and barriers to IS development, we describe the situation in 2010 as 'harvesting low-hanging fruit'. This is because most of the by-product exchanges within the park took advantage of the existing infrastructure of buildings, pipelines and roads, which was built when the entire park was one state-owned facility.

From Table 13.3, it is obvious that the main IS driver in 2010 was economic gains, as illustrated by an informant who explains that they use CO gas (by-product from Vale) as long as it is cheaper than the alternative: "We would prefer to use CO gas, but it is a financial question regarding emission trading. If the price of CO gas and emission permits were lower compared to the use of oil, we would choose the gas. If not, we would use oil. It is as simple as that." This finding is in line with recent publications within the CE literature that highlight economic prosperity as the main aim of CE activities (Kirchherr et al. 2017), and because infrastructure for distributing excess heat and gas is available at a low price, firms benefit from using each other's by-products. However, further investments in extended production systems were considered a great IS barrier (Van Beers et al. 2007). Firms are reluctant to participate in long-term investments for circularity, which underscores that the role of the government is extremely important for enabling eco-industrial initiatives (Mathews and Tan 2011). With existing infrastructure and access to by-products, the park becomes more attractive for new establishments, which is the case for Ranfjord Fiskeprodukter, which uses heated water to produce salmon fry.

Furthermore, we observe that environmental regulations act both as a driver and a barrier to industrial symbiosis in 2010. On the one hand, regulations motivate circular activities because firms expect stricter environmental regulations. This is in line with studies on environmental innovation that show that firms respond proactively to the expectation of future regulations (Borghesi et al. 2015). On the other hand, several firms experienced regulations as a barrier to circularity (Moors et al. 2005), especially regarding emissions trading. They would prefer

Table 13.3   Drivers and barriers of IS development in Mo Industrial Park in 2010 and 2020

Economy		Drivers	Barriers
	2010	**About a by-product they give away for free, rather than pay to deposit:** "It is something we do not make a profit on. It costs us to get rid of it" (Firm informant) "First and foremost, we would prefer the CO gas as our energy source, but it is an economic question." (Firm informant) "It is costly to deposit waste; if we rather make new products from it, we will make a profit" (Firm informant) "We can accept a lower cost-benefit relationship if there are significant environmental benefits, but the economic investment demands are strict" (Firm informant)	**Investment cost:** About plans for thermic power plant: "There have been plans for this for the last 10–12 years, however, MIP [the infrastructure owner/builder] wants 30-year contracts and we cannot promise that" (Firm informant) **The firms' main concern is short-term cost saving:** "Firms are mainly concerned with short-term and cost-efficient solutions, which restrain their long-term investments" (Firm informant) "What is important [for IS] is solely cost-efficient operations" (Firm informant)
	2020	**Increased awareness on long term benefits from IS investments:** "We now observe that several firms view investments in IS as valuable in the long-term" (Firm informant) "There is an increased awareness of revenues associated with by-products, and green competitiveness through IS" (Firm informant)	**Low price:** "They are looking at alternative use of the CO gas. To not just use it fuel purposes, but to make use of the molecules for something else. However, it is relatively low priced" (Firm informant) **Access to capital:** "We have proposed to add more money to the pool because I know that if we increase our internal funds and generate good ideas, we can multiply that funding.... so the ambitions are high, but we are not able to follow up with enough resources. In addition, then everything is just a little bit too weak" (Firm informant)

		Drivers	Barriers
Regulation	2010	**An incentive to be in front of regulations:** *"The environmental focus is much stronger from the owners than it is from the Norwegian authorities"* (Firm informant) *"They [talking about emission reduction regulations] force us to find new ways of reducing our emissions"* (Firm informant)	**Strong focus on regulations related to climate offset:** *"The paradox is that the gas we use is excess gas from Vale which should have been given free emission permits, however the government does not share our view. We actually have to pay a fee in order to recycle"* (Firm informant) **About the price of emission permits:** *"Their permits are very expensive, and it is sometimes cheaper to use oil instead. This is an economic question ... If Vale has to burn their gas, it will damage the environment. However, if we have to buy emission permits, it might be more profitable for us to use propane in order to reduce our greenhouse emissions"* (Firm informant) *"It should and shall be a shortage of emission permits in order to gain emission reductions ... In principle carbon emissions have a price and firms have to start including carbon prices in their finances"* (Firm informant)
	2020	**Increased governmental pressure:** *"Firms are more proactive [in developing IS] as they experience that it provides long-term competitiveness. That would not have been possible without governmental pressure"* (Firm informant)	**Regulations impose uncertainty:** *"Regulations have slowed down several of our IS initiatives»* (Firm informant) *"Changes in regulatory frameworks cause insecurity in a time where we shall build new industry"* (Firm informant)

		Drivers	Barriers
Cooperation	2010	**Established an environmental group:** "We established an environmental group with representatives from all the largest firms that cooperate on initiatives to reduce air and water emissions." (Firm informant) **Vale and Fesil were a part of a research association where Vale is part of a research project:** "The by-product we work on in the research project will not be profitable for us to re-manufacture alone. It is therefore essential for us to be part of this association in order to develop knowledge on this." (Firm informant)	**Limited cooperation with actors outside the park:** "We do not have a culture for cooperating with research institutions. We want things to go fast, and we want them to be good. That is not always a good combination. In addition, research institutions must be trained. It takes them time to get to know our processes and problems." (Firm informant) "The Environmental group has not discussed the possibility of including permanent members from outside the park ... I am not sure if any of the firms are interested in that." (Firm informant) "We have tried to get involved in environmental discussions with the industry, especially when we feel that we can contribute with something ... There are challenges outside the park as well." (Rana municipality)
	2020	**Increased R&D cooperation for circular innovativeness:** "We believe that new establishments will come from research and development." (Firm informant) "I believe that we have 7–8 projects: large projects with SINTEF [research institute] and such. What I am saying is that we cannot handle any more. Even though we are a small organization, we are part of many projects" (Firm informant) "And then we work through HighEFF [research centre] in order to use the heat to produce electrical power, because then we have solved the problem. New technologies. That is one of our main motivations in HighEFF." (Firm informant) "We cooperate to a large extent with customers and suppliers. There is little secrecy in what we do." (Firm informant)	**Initiative overload where firms finds it challenging to navigate and choose between several circular initiatives:** "We have thought that because there are so many initiatives, we have to land some of them, right? Make it happen. It is new establishments we are interested in." (Firm informant) "It [MIP sustainability] is the programme to become a world-class green industrial park. As you know there are many initiatives under that umbrella, but we try to limit the number of new initiatives and rather make some of them materialize." (Firm informant) "In a period there where so many initiatives and requests that we were unable to handle it. It wore the process firms down that we invited them to many things. They had trouble meeting up and felt that they answered the same questions over and over" (Firm informant)

		Drivers	Barriers
Infrastructure	2010	**Geographical proximity and existing infrastructure:** "We are located here [the industrial park] because it provides us with the right temperature from Fesil" (Firm informant) "The piping system [to exchange energy and materials between actors] is already there, which clearly is an advantage of being located here" (Firm informant)	**Lack of a facilitator in the system that mobilize to IS development:** "Back then, the focus was on attracting large industrial customers who were offered reasonable infrastructure services" (Firm informant)
	2020	**Mobilizing activities from knowledge actors:** "We have worked on numerous mobilizing projects over the years, especially through a programme for mobilizing research-driven innovation." (Science park) "We have contributed to the establishment and of course we believe in it [about establishment of local research institute]" (Firm informant) **Establishment of a local research institute:** "They have accelerated our development. They have made their mark in our region and changed how firms perceive R&D institutions. They initiate and enable the use of a range of instruments for research-based innovation." (Firm informant)	**A proactive facilitator in the park:** "It is important that we, who own the infrastructure, facilitate increased IS through new establishments within the park, something we have succeeded with." (Firm informant) **Consequences of Ruukki's close down:** "We had one of those heat exchangers on the roof there, which obviously is out of use after Ruukki closed down" (Firm informant) "Because Ruukki closed down, the flow of CO gas to Ruukki disappeared. Hence, there are only three CO users today" (Firm informant)

to use excess CO gas from Vale, but they argue that due to the price of emission permits, they sometimes had to choose other (virgin) sources of energy with lower total costs.

IS studies highlight cooperation between stakeholders as imperative to reach circular/ sustainable goals (Geissdoerfer et al. 2017; Zhu and Ruth 2014). In 2010, there was limited cooperation, both between actors within the park and between actors in the park and actors outside the park, such as academic institutions, other firms or governments/municipalities. The municipal environmental department desires more cooperation (see Table 13.3), but the firms are reluctant to include outsiders in their environmental group. Regarding cooperation with R&D institutes, two firms are involved in an industry association that conducts joint industry research; however, there are no joint research or innovation projects within the park. This is reflected in firms' production-oriented mindset, as stated by one of the firm informants: "production will always triumph [over] research".

Taken together, in 2010, Mo Industrial Park was characterized by taking advantage of existing win-win situations where exchanges between firms were initiated because they were expected to provide economic profits. They were simply picking the fruits from governmental infrastructure investments made decades before.

Industrial Symbiosis in Mo Industrial Park, 2020: 'Sowing New Seeds'

Although no new symbiosis exchanges are identified in the period from 2010 to 2020, we observe some important IS changes in 2020 compared to 2010, where the park has entered a phase of 'sowing new seeds'. Our data identify several new IS initiatives and an observable change in the mindset of the firms regarding further development of the symbiosis. In this situation, the IS drivers and barriers are different in 2020 than they were in 2010.

First, we find that the studied firms in Mo Industrial Park have put environmental and climate concerns high on their agendas and incorporated them into their strategies to a much higher extent than in 2010. An example is the overall vision of MIP AS to become "a world-class industrial park that creates value through a focus on environmentally friendly and energy-efficient services and solutions" (mip.no). With a more strategic emphasis on IS development, we observe that firms are much more willing to invest in new IS innovation projects. These initiatives originate and develop in cooperation between several actors within and outside the park. The motivation for these initiatives is a belief that IS will increase their competitiveness. This is illustrated by the quote: "I hoped we could be able to build competitive advantage in the process industry by initiating circular economy projects." This attitude is quite different from what we observed in 2010, and we see that there are three important factors that influence this change. First, where there was practically no cooperation with academic institutions in 2010, in 2020, there are a number of R&D projects with universities and research centres, where the most important change is the establishment of a local research institute. The firms value the research institute that has established IS R&D initiatives based on firm needs, which is illustrated by the quote: "We are starting to get 'a good model' of [the local research centre] because they understand our industry and what we need for further development" (Firm informant).

Second, several cooperative innovation initiatives have been formalized. A key initiative to become more circular oriented is the establishment of the innovation cluster, the Arctic Cluster Team (ACT), where several of the firms within the industrial park participate to increase their innovativeness and sustainability. The initiative came from the process firms within the park and resulted in widespread cooperation between firms and academic institutions from the whole northern region. A firm representative explains the ACT establishment: "We were four firms at the beginning. We met and had a specific topic that we discussed each time. When Elkem entered the park, they became a driver for increased cooperation, and with the help from KPH [science park], we applied for the Arena project [cluster programme], which formalized the cooperation and made it larger." We find that ACT has been a trigger in strengthening the circular mindset of several firms, which has led to a collective commitment towards IS development, as explained by one of the firm informants: "If we are to succeed with the circular economy, we have to connect different firms and different industries. Because the solution lies across different industries." We further observe 'mobilizing activities from knowledge actors' as a driver for innovation for circularity, particularly by the local science park that has worked on several initiatives towards the industry: "We [science park] work with strengthening firms' competence and innovative ability, enhancing openness and trust between industry actors – they should know each other and trust each other in order to open up and cooperate on common problems" (Science park).

Third, we observe that the infrastructure owner, MIP AS, has taken a much more proactive role in the overall development of the park, particularly in mobilizing firms in the park to develop new circular solutions. Where MIP AS in 2010 harvested the fruits of governmental investments and took little initiative for new development, they are now coordinating several of the R&D initiatives and making circular investments. One example is that MIP AS has bought an industrial area on the coast where they facilitate new IS across sectors.

Regarding the barriers, we observe that the economy is still the main barrier for innovation for new IS exchanges. The informants highlight low prices on by-products and limited access to capital as the main economic barriers. This barrier is in line with recent research that highlights that IS initiatives require large capital investments, but as IS initiatives are associated with high risk, there is insufficient financial support from banks and inadequate public tax incentives (Su et al. 2013), which calls for financial innovations for further development of IS (Mathews and Tan 2011).

Second, our data also show the effect of losing an actor in a system. When Ruukki closed down, several exchanges vanished, as they were both a user and a supplier of by-products. Hence, the closure of one firm affects the environmental performance of other firms in the system, and they have not yet been able to replace the firm with new initiatives.

Last, we observe that there are many new IS initiatives, but the park seems to suffer from an 'initiative overload' where the firm informants feel that they use too much time on new initiatives and less on actually putting them to life. This initiative overload could be partly explained by the firms' limited experience in R&D and innovation, where they struggle to decide what initiatives would potentially leverage most benefit over time. Although firms' R&D and innovation orientation has increased significantly since 2010, firms are still in their infancy related to their ability to develop more radical solutions, which are essential for the circular economy (Ritzén and Sandström 2017). As such, local knowledge actors play an important role in facilitating R&D and innovation initiatives together with firms, as mentioned as one of the key drivers of IS.

CONCLUSION AND IMPLICATIONS

By investigating the IS changes in Mo Industrial Park from 2010 to 2020, we contribute longitudinal insights into the development of drivers and barriers in IS (Zhu and Ruth 2014) and thereby add to the content of CE (Korhonen et al. 2018).

We find that developing a circular industry through IS is a long-term process that requires open innovation efforts. Here, academic institutions are essential in mobilizing firms by involving them in cooperative initiatives to obtain a collective direction towards circularity. The main barrier for IS, both in 2010 and 2020, is the economy, where firms lack access to risk capital to invest in research-based IS solutions associated with uncertainty and are reluctant to choose IS solutions if they are less profitable. Furthermore, due to limited R&D and innovation experience, firms also experience an initiative overload in which they find it challenging to choose relevant initiatives to invest resources.

To overcome the barriers of the economy and limited R&D activity, we suggest that firms establish collaborations with R&D institutions and other firms to pool their resources and share the risk associated with IS. Because of global awareness of sustainability and stricter requirements of all business activities to become circular, we strongly advise firms not to sit on the fence waiting for IS to become profitable but to act now to gain a competitive advantage in a more circular future. In this process, policy-makers should establish more innovative support systems for circular solutions, for risk-sharing, to facilitate cross-industry collaboration and reward the use of by-products over virgin materials. Finally, our findings show the importance of a 'proactive facilitator' (Behera et al. 2012), such as MIP AS in this study, that facilitates and stimulates collaboration between actors in a system.

REFERENCES

Bacudio, L. R., Benjamin, M. F. D., Eusebio, R. C. P., Holaysan, S. A. K., Promentilla, M. A. B., Yu, K. D. S., & Aviso, K. B. (2016). Analyzing barriers to implementing industrial symbiosis networks using DEMATEL. *Sustainable Production and Consumption*, 7, 57–65.

Behera, S. K., Kim, J.-H., Lee, S.-Y., Suh, S., & Park, H.-S. (2012). Evolution of 'designed' industrial symbiosis networks in the Ulsan Eco-Industrial Park: 'Research and development into business' as the enabling framework. *Journal of Cleaner Production*, 29, 103–112.

Boons, F., Spekkink, W., & Mouzakitis, Y. (2011). The dynamics of industrial symbiosis: A proposal for a conceptual framework based upon a comprehensive literature review. *Journal of Cleaner Production*, 19(9), 905–911.

Borghesi, S., Cainelli, G., & Mazzanti, M. (2015). Linking emission trading to environmental innovation: Evidence from the Italian manufacturing industry. *Research Policy*, 44(3), 669–683.

Chertow, M. R. (2007). "Uncovering" industrial symbiosis. *Journal of Industrial Ecology*, 11(1), 11–30.

Chiu, A. S., & Yong, G. (2004). On the industrial ecology potential in Asian developing countries. *Journal of Cleaner Production*, 12(8–10), 1037–1045.

Costa, I., & Ferrão, P. (2010). A case study of industrial symbiosis development using a middle-out approach. *Journal of Cleaner Production*, 18(10–11), 984–992.

Damanpour, F. (1991). Organizational innovation: A meta-analysis of effects of determinants and moderators. *Academy of Management Journal*, 34(3), 555–590.

Ehrenfeld, J., & Gertler, N. (1997). Industrial ecology in practice: The evolution of interdependence at Kalundborg. *Journal of Industrial Ecology*, 1(1), 67–79.

Fang, S.-R., Chang, Y.-S., & Peng, Y.-C. (2011). Dark side of relationships: A tensions-based view. *Industrial Marketing Management*, 40(5), 774–784.

Fang, Y., Cote, R. P., & Qin, R. (2007). Industrial sustainability in China: Practice and prospects for eco-industrial development. *Journal of Environmental Management*, 83(3), 315–328.

Flyvbjerg, B. (2006). Five misunderstandings about case-study research. *Qualitative Inquiry*, 12(2), 219–245.

Geissdoerfer, M., Savaget, P., Bocken, N. M. P., & Hultink, E. J. (2017). The circular economy: A new sustainability paradigm? *Journal of Cleaner Production*, 143, 757–768.

Gibbs, D., & Deutz, P. (2007). Reflections on implementing industrial ecology through eco-industrial park development. *Journal of Cleaner Production*, 15(17), 1683–1695.

Giurco, D., Bossilkov, A., Patterson, J., & Kazaglis, A. (2011). Developing industrial water reuse synergies in Port Melbourne: Cost effectiveness, barriers and opportunities. *Journal of Cleaner Production*, 19(8), 867–876.

Golev, A., Corder, G. D., & Giurco, D. P. (2015). Barriers to industrial symbiosis: Insights from the use of a maturity grid. *Journal of Industrial Ecology*, 19(1), 141–153.

Hardy, C., & Graedel, T. E. (2002). Industrial ecosystems as food webs. *Journal of Industrial Ecology*, 6(1), 29–38.

Jackson, M., Lederwasch, A., & Giurco, D. (2014). Transitions in theory and practice: Managing metals in the circular economy. *Resources*, 3(3), 516–543.

Jakobsen, S., & Steinmo, M. T. (2010). *Mo Industripark-et industrielt økosystem?* Høgskolen i Bodø.

Kirchherr, J., Reike, D., & Hekkert, M. (2017). Conceptualizing the circular economy: An analysis of 114 definitions. *Resources, Conservation and Recycling*, 127, 221–232.

Korhonen, J., Honkasalo, A., & Seppälä, J. (2018). Circular economy: The concept and its limitations. *Ecological Economics*, 143, 37–46.

Li, J., Pan, S.-Y., Kim, H., Linn, J. H., & Chiang, P.-C. (2015). Building green supply chains in eco-industrial parks towards a green economy: Barriers and strategies. *Journal of Environmental Management*, 162, 158–170.

Lindkvist, M., & Baumann, H. (2014). *A Review of Social Science in Five Industrial Ecology Journals*. Chalmers University of Technology, Gothenburg.

Mathews, J. A., & Tan, H. (2011). Progress toward a circular economy in China. *Journal of Industrial Ecology*, 15(3), 435–457.

Merli, R., Preziosi, M., & Acampora, A. (2018). How do scholars approach the circular economy? A systematic literature review. *Journal of Cleaner Production*, 178, 703–722.

Miles, M. B., & Huberman, A. M. (1994). *Qualitative Data Analysis*. London: Sage Publications.

Moors, E. H. M., Mulder, K. F., & Vergragt, P. J. (2005). Towards cleaner production: Barriers and strategies in the base metals producing industry. *Journal of Cleaner Production*, 13(7), 657–668.

OECD (2009). *Sustainable Manufacturing and Eco-Innovation Framework, Practices and Measurement – Synthesis Report*. Paris: OECD.

Patton, M. Q. (2015). *Qualitative Evaluation and Research Methods* (4th ed.). Thousand Oaks, CA: Sage Publications.

Prosman, E. J., Wæhrens, B. V., & Liotta, G. (2017). Closing global material loops: Initial insights into firm-level challenges. *Journal of Industrial Ecology*, 21(3), 641–650.

Ritzén, S., & Sandström, G. Ö. (2017). Barriers to the circular economy: Integration of perspectives and domains. *Procedia CIRP*, 64, 7–12.

Saavedra, Y. M., Iritani, D. R., Pavan, A. L., & Ometto, A. R. (2018). Theoretical contribution of industrial ecology to circular economy. *Journal of Cleaner Production*, 170, 1514–1522.

Sakr, D., Baas, L., El-Haggar, S., & Huisingh, D. (2011). Critical success and limiting factors for eco-industrial parks: Global trends and Egyptian context. *Journal of Cleaner Production*, 19(11), 1158–1169.

Su, B., Heshmati, A., Geng, Y., & Yu, X. (2013). A review of the circular economy in China: Moving from rhetoric to implementation. *Journal of Cleaner Production*, 42, 215–227.

Taddeo, R., Simboli, A., Ioppolo, G., & Morgante, A. (2017). Industrial symbiosis, networking and innovation: The potential role of innovation poles. *Sustainability*, 9(2), 169.

Van Beers, D., Bossilkov, A., Corder, G., & Van Berkel, R. (2007). Industrial symbiosis in the Australian minerals industry: The cases of Kwinana and Gladstone. *Journal of Industrial Ecology*, 11(1), 55–72.

Yin, R. K. (2013). *Case Study Research: Design and Methods*. Thousand Oaks, CA: Sage Publications.
Zhu, J., & Ruth, M. (2014). The development of regional collaboration for resource efficiency: A network
perspective on industrial symbiosis. *Computers, Environment and Urban Systems*, 44, 37–46.

PART IV

TYPES OF CIRCULAR ECONOMY INNOVATIONS

14. Simultaneous adoption of circular innovations: a challenge for rapid growth of the circular economy

Arild Aspelund, Martin Fredrik Olsen and Ottar Michelsen

INTRODUCTION

Population and consumption growth over the past decades have left us in a situation where we exploit more resources than the planet can regenerate (UNEP 2011). This can be illustrated by the 'Earth Overshoot Day', which represents the day where we have consumed more resources than the planet can regenerate over a year. In 2020, 'Earth Overshoot Day' fell on 22 August and after this date we mined resources that did not regenerate within the year. Hence, we borrow resources from future generations and this is not a sustainable development by definition (Brundtland 1987). The UN's International Resource Panel warns that the current global resource consumption will have significant negative environmental, social and economic consequences (IRP 2019).

According to the United Nations Environmental Programme (UNEP 2011) and many others, the solution to the resource problem is a transition to a circular economy. In addition to solving the global resource challenge, a transition to a circular economy would also deliver promising economic benefits. According to the European Commission (2020) a transition to a circular economy can create 700,000 new jobs and annual business savings of €600 bn. The UN, independent consultancy houses, and NGOs support the European Commission's positive economic prospects for a circular economy (Ellen MacArthur Foundation and McKinsey Center for Business and Environment 2015; IRP 2019) and expect that a circular transition can deliver unprecedented economic resource productivity, new jobs, products, services, and business opportunities.

Even though the business case for the circular economy remains convincing, the actual adoption has been limited. In Norway, where this study is conducted, only 2.4 per cent of materials are recycled into the economy (Circle Economy 2020b). The global numbers are 8.6 per cent in 2020, down from 9.1 per cent in 2018 (Circle Economy 2020a). Hence, so far the transition to a circular economy has been too limited to counter an overexploitation of planetary resources. This negative trend is also echoed in the recent Global Sustainable Development Report (2019). The authors of that report find that the global waste streams are growing and SDG 12 (Sustainable Consumption and Production measured in absolute material footprint and domestic material consumption) is on a negative long-term trend, and unlikely to be met by 2030. To add to the pain, the International Resource Panel (2019) finds that material intensity is similar to that of the 1980s. Resource efficiency has not been improved over the last 40 years!

This leaves us with an intriguing question. If circular innovations can deliver economic value to the extent found by the UN, European Commission, independent think-tanks and consultancy houses, then why is the adoption so limited and slow?

We argue that there exists a coordination problem in the circular transition that can contribute to answering this question. The coordination problem occurs because circular transition requires simultaneous and coordinated adoption of circular innovations from multiple actors within, and often even across, value chains. We conceptualize the problem by using game theory and show how coordination games offer us valuable insight into how a more rapid and outspread circular transition can be facilitated for the future.

The contribution of this chapter is to show that in the absence of resourceful actors that can ensure simultaneous and coordinated adoption of circular innovation, then non-adoption would be a more expected outcome than adoption.

This chapter proceeds with a presentation of the theoretical background of the coordination problem and game theory from economics. We then explain how the coordination problem occurs as a consequence of the requirement of simultaneous adoption in a transition towards a circular economy. A practical empirical illustration is presented from the fish farming industry before we discuss the theoretical, managerial and policy implications.

THEORETICAL FRAMEWORK

Transition to Circular Economy

In order to create a circular economy, we need a transition away from the linear economy that dominates today (Bocken et al. 2016; Bouton et al. 2016) and to a circular economy, commonly defined as "a circular economy is restorative and regenerative by design, and aims to keep products, components, and materials at their highest utility and value at all times" (Moreau et al. 2017, p. 498). A circular transition can be defined as the shift from open to closed loops of materials and energy (Ghisellini et al. 2016); a transition away from the take-make-dispose logic, and into a circular economy as defined by Moreau et al. as above (2017, p. 498). This is what we mean by a circular transition. From this, we can similarly define circular innovations as innovations that contribute to close open material or energy loops and keep materials and energy at their highest utility and value at all times.

Transitions are multi-level and multi-actor activities where whole systems change (Geels 2011). However, it is not likely that all actors will benefit from the transition. Hence, as market actors remain concerned about the economic outcome, it is important to bear in mind that corporate profit should be maintained, and preferably increased, if market actors are to maintain motivation to develop and adopt innovation that are necessary (Ghisellini et al. 2016; Markard et al. 2020). Market actors will compare the expected outcome of a circular transition with the competing certain outcome of status quo of the current economic system (Korhonen et al. 2018). This gives emerging circular business models a disadvantage since the linear structures already are in place with business working with known figures.

We also know that circular innovations are not developed in a vacuum, but often developed in an ecosystem of actors with common economic interests. Moreover, when one company adopts a circular innovation it will in most cases also influence upstream and downstream actors who need confidence that they will maintain or increase profitability in the new terrain

(Markard et al. 2020). Consequently, we are talking about a transition that involves multiple actors that can choose to adopt an innovation, and where the economic outcome for one actor is dependent on the decision of others. This the characteristics of a coordination problem.

Game Theory and the Coordination Problem

The coordination problem is a classical economic problem that dates back centuries. Simply stated, game theory conceptualizes decision-making of a set of rational and non-rational actors as participating in a game where the outcomes depend on the actors' decisions or behaviour. The coordination problem occurs when there exists one collective action that produces a common collective good, but simultaneously there exists actions that individual actors might take to improve their individual outcome even if the collective will suffer (Hardin 1971).

Oxford philosopher Toby Ord argues that the existence of humanity can be conceptualized as a coordination game. Humanity can potentially last for millions, or even billions of years, but in order to realize that potential global perils such as atomic weapons, global warming and the resource challenge need to be overcome by coordinated global efforts (Ord 2020). However, there will always be motivation for individual nations to defect from the coordinated solution. To illustrate, the COP21 Paris Agreement is an example of a coordinated global effort to deal with the emerging climate challenge. The former US president (Donald Trump) withdrew the country from the Paris Agreement arguing it did not serve the best interests of the USA, and hence, disrupted the common agreement. This is known as the 'tragedy of the commons' (Hardin 1968).

To illustrate the challenges in this study, we will introduce a game referred to as the Stag Hunt. The Stag Hunt has its origin in *Discourse on Inequality* by Jean-Jacques Rousseau in 1755 (Skyrms 2001) and illustrates two hunters that together can hunt a stag. They cannot successfully hunt the stag alone, but if they collaborate they are likely to succeed. Stag hunting represents the highest collective good (see Figure 14.1). However, if one hunter leaves his post to hunt a hare that passes by, he might get the hare, but no one will get the stag. If they both abandon their posts to go hunting for hare, they can expect to do well, but not as well as if they stayed in the Stag Hunt.

Both stag hunting and hare hunting are equilibria, but what is rational for one player depends on his beliefs about what the other will choose (Skyrms 2001, p. 3). There are great benefits from coordination and doing whatever the other actor is doing, both individually and collectively. In other words, there is a coordination problem.

		Hunter 1	
		Stag	Hare
Hunter 2	Stag	4 / 4	0 / 3
	Hare	3 / 0	3 / 3

Figure 14.1   The Stag Hunt: revenues for the hunters

Adoption of Circular Innovations

In order to understand the relevance of the Stag Hunt and game theory for the transition to a circular economy, we need to get a deeper understanding of the nature of a circular transition and what circular innovations it entails in practice for industrial actors. Typically, it entails innovations on the production or product level, the business model level, and the value chain or ecosystem level (Konietzko et al. 2020). Hence, in the case of industrial process by-products and waste streams, like in our case, it will typically entail three innovations on these levels.

First, it often entails industrial process innovations (Avraamidou et al. 2020). The industrial processes that have been developed to optimize production efficiency and minimize transaction costs of a linear industrial model are probably not the same as those that are optimized to restore and regenerate products, components and materials through a closed loop. It might require substantial investments to develop and implement new circular processes. It is also well known from innovation management research that incumbents might be reluctant to make these investments because they have vested interests in conserving the status quo (Christensen and Raynor 2013).

Second, it is likely to entail business model innovation and new ways of creating economic value (Bocken et al. 2016). Previous research on the circular economy shows that the circular economy opens up opportunities for new business models and new ways of creating value that disconnect use of resources from value creation.

Finally, it entails innovations in terms of the composition of new circular value chains and ecosystems (Rashid et al. 2013). Existing linear value chains that start with taking resources out of the planet and end with disposal, are probably not efficient in a closed circular system or likely to contain the same industrial actors.

Common for all these innovations are that they require investments on behalf of all actors, adoption needs to be coordinated to ensure that adopted innovations are compatible, and adoption needs to be simultaneous to ensure that investment in circular innovations remains unproductive in terms of new resource use.

This shows why a circular transition can be conceptualized as the Stag Hunt. In the Stag Hunt there is an outcome that is economically better for all parties – hunting the stag – but it requires coordinated and dedicated participation and investments from multiple parties simultaneously. A transition to a circular economy holds the promises of sustainable above-average economic rent where value creation is disconnected from increased use of resources. However, there is also a second equilibrium (hunting hares) represented by the status quo (staying with the linear paradigm). Due to sustainability challenges this solution is expected to be less economically rewarding in the long run (UNEP 2011; IRP 2019), but might be tempting enough in the short term, especially if actors are uncertain of the intentions of others.

However, the worst option is when somebody adopts while others defect. The ones that defect (not adopting circular innovations) will still make economic rents from the traditional linear system, while the actors that adopt circularity and make the investments will not be able to gain economic rent from them. These two solutions to the game also show the necessity of simultaneous adoption. The hunt will not be successful if one party shows up a week late.

METHODS

This study adopted an abductive approach (Dubois and Gadde 2002) where researchers go between the empirical and the model domain, continuously adopting research issues and frameworks to fit with the reality they observe. The initial motivation for the study was to understand the seemingly slow adoption of circular innovations. However, as this topic is little treated in the literature, we initially adopted a 'blank page' approach (Eisenhardt 1989) and a single case study, which is appropriate to explore a new phenomenon (Yin 2017). As the case study developed, game theory became the dominant framework of interpretation. As such, the intention of this chapter is not to deduct theory from the case, but rather to introduce a new way of conceptualizing a problem related to adoption of circular innovations, and explore its validity and implications in a realistic and practical setting.

In order to be data efficient, the study chose a case company that was central to the circular innovation adoption argument in question. We had the following case selection criteria:

1. An industry with significant resource streams, where circular innovation is not a total novelty.
2. A focal actor that delivers circular innovations, such as products or services for the industry to be able to close external resource loops.
3. An actor that fully depends on its circular business activities, to avoid larger actors that manage circular innovations as real options in a broader portfolio of activities that also include typical linear operations in the same sector.

Based on these criteria we selected a case from the Norwegian fish farming industry. Circular innovations are relatively novel in the fish farming industry, but common in bio-based industries in general. There is also strategic intent from many of the actors in this industry to adopt circular innovations to profit from large quantities of valuable by-products and waste. The fish farming industry is one of the largest producers of plastic waste in Norway (Hognes and Skaar 2017).

The business idea of the company is to be an enabler for a circular transition in the fish farming industry and facilitate closing resource loops within and across supply chains. They are a small, newly founded firm (17 employees, established in 2016) with no other business activities outside of this domain. Given that the research focus is on the outcome of adoption decisions of circular innovations provided by the focal firm – not the rationale for the decisions – we find it sufficient to draw empirical data from a single focal case firm for the purpose of the study.

We gathered data from three sources – interviews, online information and field observations. The use of multiple sources assists the research by helping avoid post-hoc rationalizations and contribute to increase reliability and validity (Eisenhardt 1989). Collection of online material and field observations on processing sites were done early in the data collection and served as a source for understanding the extent of change that actors had to undergo in order to adopt the circular innovations of the focal case firm.

Subsequently, we went back to the model and developed a semi-structured interview guide and interviewed the CEO, CTO and CQO of the firm. The interviews were transcribed and the analyses started by extracting information from the transcribed raw data and creating a within-case analysis.

With this approach, the findings from the study do not exclusively come from data or theory, but rather from a combined view of the case in the empirical world and the theoretical framework in the conceptual world (Dubois and Gadde 2002). The findings of an abductive study are the result of the co-evolution of theoretical concepts and empirical investigations.

EMPIRICAL BACKGROUND

The Industry and the Actors

Aquaculture in Norway dates back hundreds of years, but it was not until the early 1970s that fish farming was scaled up to industrial levels. The 1970s, 1980s and 1990s saw much experimentation in fish farming techniques, which led to significant growth of the industry. A traditional linear value chain was developed (see Figure 14.2) and Norwegian salmon farming grew from 380,000 tons in 1998 to 1.25 million tons in 2012 (Steinset 2017).

However, in 2009 the Norwegian Ministry of Fisheries published a report that voiced serious concerns about the long-term sustainability of the fish farming industry (Norwegian Ministry of Fisheries 2009). The report argued that the linear value chain with current fish farming techniques and scale led to unmanageable environmental challenges in the form of sea lice, diseases, escaped fish and waste streams. The following year the fish farming industry in Chile collapsed. Production fell from 400,000 tons to 60,000 tons due to an outbreak of Infectious Salmon Anaemia (ISA). The collapse was an eye opener for Norwegian authorities and fish farmers as the production technologies in Chile were predominantly the same as in Norway.

As a response the Norwegian authorities stopped issuing new production licences in 2012 and the growth flattened out (Steinset 2017). Still, the aim of the Norwegian government is a growth by a factor of five before 2050 (Olafsen et al. 2012). In order to achieve this on a sustainable trajectory, new sustainable innovations need to be developed and implemented. The government's solution to motivate the industry is twofold. First, significant research funds are made available for sustainability research in the food industry (approximately 1,000 million NOK annually for sustainability innovation research in the agriculture and aquaculture sectors

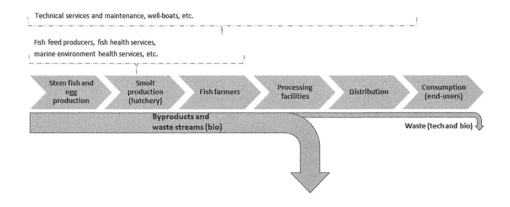

Figure 14.2   Traditional value chain in fish farming

combined). Secondly, from 2013 the Ministry of Fisheries tied new production licences to sustainability innovations. Traditionally, new licences were awarded from a bidding process, however, with the establishment of 'green licences' in 2013 and 'development licences' in 2017, new production licences were offered for free to projects with significant sustainability innovations. The licences were granted with an option of converting them to permanent licences if the innovations proved successful. The programmes have served as major boost for sustainable development of the industry and many of these innovations are currently being implemented.

The Case Company

The case company – hereby denoted KM – seeks to be a central actor in the emerging circular fish farming industry by facilitating the establishment of circular supply chains by closing resource loops vertically and horizontally across relevant supply chains. KM initially targeted both the biological and technical by-product and waste streams from the fish farming industry. They seek to become the focal broker company that creates the link between the fish farming supply chain and other supply chains that utilize by-products or waste for new production. Although there are similarities between the strategic approaches to the two research streams, the outcomes are so different that we will present the two stories separately. Figure 14.3 shows the role of KM in the emerging circular value chain.

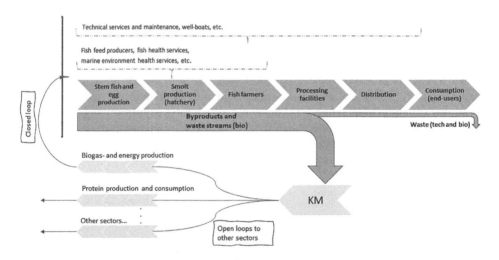

Figure 14.3   The role of KM in the new circular value chain

KM Bio: the business model and market offering

KM continuously innovated their business model since starting in 2016 by changing and adding new activities, products and services. Business models based on trade in by-products and recycling of waste are, in principle, attractive as brokers such as KM will get paid both to receive materials (upstream customers) as well as selling them on (downstream customers). For KM Bio, the market offering consists of three elements.

First, KM offers collecting, transporting, storing, and processing of biological materials through its fleet of trucks, trailers, and ships. KM supplies these materials to biogas plants, incineration plants, and producers of fish oil and protein concentrate.

Second, KM contributes to increased value creation for both upstream and downstream customers by offering resource handling at customers' sites to optimize material quality and cost efficiency. This service is provided by sensors and software for live tracking and measuring by-product and waste streams.

Finally, KM offers consultancy services and provides advice on routines, methods, and product development that adds value to by-products and waste streams. These services often enable new business opportunities for KM to develop and deliver new products and services for existing customers.

These value propositions can only create value if both upstream and downstream customers adopt the circular innovation simultaneously and form a coordinated new circular supply chain. Alternatively, there will be unmet asymmetric demand and inefficiencies. In this case, simultaneous adoption of the circular bio innovation was partly due to strategic intent and partly fortunate coincidences. There was strategic intent in the sense that fish farmers were looking for more sustainable alternative use for growing biological waste streams. However, it was also fortunate in the sense that there was a growing downstream demand for biological waste for energy production and protein and oil production for both human and animal consumption. Customers from those industries saw bio waste from the fish farming industry as an attractive resource for further growth.

KM Bio: new industrial processes

KM's circular innovation required development of new industrial processes and equipment. As a small and new actor, KM has adopted an open innovation processes involving many different actors. Predominantly, KM works with fish farmers, egg or smolt producers, but they also cooperate with academic institutions to develop new knowledge, methods, and technology related to value retention throughout the lifecycle of biological materials.

"One of the projects we work on with scientists at NTNU explores how bacteria cultures in the silage evolve, because they may develop resistance to the treatment methods we use", said the CTO. KM engages in continuous dialogue with its partners and customers, seeking to develop routines, methods, technology, and skills that can enable increased levels of circularity. Not only because it is environmentally responsible, but because it is highly profitable.

KM also stresses that frequent interaction with partners and customers improves the performance of the circular innovations after implementation. The CTO explains: "We used to get rejected much more frequent when we arrived at the biogas plants with new batches, due to low quality of the silage in terms of total solids percentage and other particles contaminating the batch." She explains that KM succeeded with increasing the quality of these batches through improving methods and routines in cooperation with their partners and customers: "These days, however, we get rejected very rarely because we have worked closely with them to improve routines and develop systems that ensure the quality of the batches."

Many of KM's circular innovation projects have received support from the Research Council of Norway (RCN). KM believes that their current research portfolio, where sponsorship from RCN is widespread, can contribute significantly to increase the degree of circularity in fish farming.

However, the Norwegian Food Safety Authority (NFSA) has been instrumental for the commercial success. NFSA created a categorization of biological waste from fish farming. The categorization effectively defines the technical interface between actors in the new circular value chain, and provides specifications for process and product development. Maybe most important, it provides incentives for managing waste in such a fashion that it retains high quality and value since the categorization ranges from high value by-products that can be used for human consumption to the lowest which should be disposed. Hence, KM and its upstream customers are incentivized to ensure the highest possible categorization since the better the quality of the recycled material, the higher the profit potential.

KM Bio: the new circular value chain

As found in previous research (Rashid et al. 2013), the establishment of a new circular value chain means creating a new industrial network within and across established value chains. This was also the case for KM. CEO and founder of KM argues that the new industrial network has been key for the success the firm has today. "In KM, we find ourselves in the crossroads between fish farmers, regulators, and R&D initiatives, and therefore act as an interface and active agent between these actors by showing them that much of the category 2 by-products can be used for better purposes. […] communication and cooperation on these issues are even in the contracts."

More than just having a well-functioning circular value chain and industrial network, the size of the network matters. Specifically, hub-storage capacity is scarce and represents a logistical challenge as quality, and hence value, is reduced if left unmanaged. Therefore, it is beneficial to have access to an industrial network of some scale to ensure flexibility and efficiency in operations. For this reason, KM has established a network of industrial actors in Norway, Sweden, and Finland, that can receive batches at short notice. A larger and steadily growing network also ensures increased efficiency since monopoly situations are avoided and an efficient market with standardized contracts develops.

KM plastics: sometimes hare hunters prefer to continue hunting hares

As mentioned above, the aquaculture sector is the largest producer of plastic waste in Norway and stricter regulations are expected (Hognes and Skaar 2017). During start-up in 2016, KM developed a similar business model for technical waste as the one proved successful for bio-waste, including material handling, information infrastructure and consultancy. Recycling of marine plastics is technically challenging, but KM succeeded in developing an innovative method called 'Miljøhugging', a term which in Norwegian conveys the idea of environmentally friendly caretaking and recycling of plastic fish farming pens.

However, KM was never able to establish a circular value chain surrounding the circular innovations. The upstream customers, typically fish farmers, would not adopt the innovation as there were "no incentives for them to pay large sums for getting rid of it" (CEO KM). Instead they continued less sustainable practices such as local disposal. As for downstream customers, KM was able to identify potential actors. However, turning recycled marine plastics into new products requires investments in production and downstream customers were reluctant to take this investment unless they could be assured of sufficient supply of materials.

By 2017, KM realized that these factors hampered a circular value chain for technical materials. First, it would require significant investment to continue innovating and developing methods and equipment. Second, there was little or no willingness to pay among upstream customers and capacity issues among downstream customers. Finally, there was a lack of governmental regulation that could effectively help to coordinate adoption. Hence, KM closed down these efforts in 2017 pending more favourable conditions.

DISCUSSION

The case study shows two outcomes. In the first on biological waste, we observed a simultaneous and coordinated adoption of the circular innovation from both upstream and downstream customers. We also observed that a third party – national authorities – was instrumental in facilitating simultaneousness and coordination. Moreover, we see that a profitable industry has been created out of biological waste streams that only a few years ago went to disposal. This is the Stag Hunt – a coordinated adoption of a circular innovation that ensures the most valuable outcome for all actors.

The case for technical waste is different. Here only the focal company developed and adopted the circular innovation. Up- and downstream customers did not adapt, nor was simultaneousness or coordination facilitated by external parties. This is the failed Stag Hunt; some actors adopt the circular innovation, but not sufficiently enough to establish a well-functioning and competitive circular value chain. In this case, the circular innovators will not be able to earn rent on investments. We can call this 'the curse of the circular innovator'. On the other hand, those who opted for status quo and the 'hunting hares' outcome are expected to do reasonably well – at least in the short term.

As such, the case illustrates that the adoption of circular innovations in an industry is a game with multiple actors where the outcome of the game is dependent on the coordinated and simultaneous efforts of these actors. It shows that adoption of circular innovations holds the same characteristics as a coordination game with multiple actors as described by the Stag Hunt (Hardin 1971).

Game theory provides valuable insight into why the adoption of circular innovations and practices are so slow. The Stag Hunt is a game with two equilibria (Skyrms 2001). In our case, all incumbents start the game in the position of one of the equilibria, namely the 'hunting hares' equilibrium that illustrates the linear paradigm. Hence, very convincing economic or strategic motivation is needed in order for them to leave this equilibrium to go hunting stags. The motivation to remain in status quo and not adopt the circular innovation is enhanced by the knowledge that the success of circular adoption is dependent on a sufficient number of other actors making the same decision at the same time. This will potentially generate a competitive complete circular value chain, but actors are likely painfully aware that there could be significant first mover disadvantages if the establishment fails.

However, the Stag Hunt conceptualization has its limitations. First of all, even though recent research suggests that sustainability innovations in general are profitable (Hermundsdottir and Aspelund 2021), it is hard to establish a priori whether adopting a circular innovation will result in an overall beneficial economic system. The Stag Hunt conceptualization relies on the assumption that the circular economy structure will be more sustainable and profitable in the long run (European Commission 2020), but in some cases idiosyncratic characteristics might violate that assumption.

Nor is it reasonable to assume that the Stag Hunt game theory approach applies to all sustainability innovations. There are numerous examples where actors adopt sustainability innovations independently and without simultaneous or coordinated adoption from others. An example from the fish farming industry is that fish farmers are seeking to solve the issues of lice and escaped fish by building facilities that can be placed in the open sea. They can implement this sustainability innovation without coordinated activities from other actors. The Stag Hunt conceptualization only applies when the circular innovation deals with closing of external material or energy loops that includes integrated action from external independent actors.

Despite its limitations the framework is still applicable. The theoretical assumptions are wide and the case from the Norwegian fish farming industry shows the typical traits of adoption of circular innovations as we know them from previous research. We see that adoption depends on development of new business models that are better suited to effectively create value from closing resource loops or extending use of resources (Bocken et al. 2016). We also see that adoption requires a reformation of value chains (Rashid et al. 2013) and development of new industrial processes, specialized equipment and software (Avraamidou et al. 2020). These changes and developments require investments from all actors that seek to be a part of the emerging circular supply chains. We argue that lack of systematic regulatory systems for ensuring simultaneousness and coordination are major contributors to the failure of rapid and extensive adoption of circular innovations among market actors. But what are the political and managerial implications?

First, the realization that coordination and simultaneousness represent significant hurdles for adoption of circular innovations provides us with insight in policy priorities. We acknowledge that circular value chains can form naturally in the marketplace with little influence from regulators when resourceful actors in the market are economically motivated and can coordinate and make sure adoption is fairly simultaneous. As the opportunity arose, actors voluntarily established a stag hunting team in the biological waste example in this study. It was sufficient for regulators to coordinate through the establishment of the categories that effectively standardized the interface between actors in the emerging circular value chain.

However, in the absence of powerful and economically motivated actors it is less likely that a circular industrial system will emerge. This is what we observed in the story of the failure to establish a circular value chain for marine plastics. As upstream customers lacked motivation, the first mover into the circular value chain failed to earn any rents on early investments and ultimately the investments were lost. In this case, the stag hunting team were not established before the investments were made. In these cases, regulators might see it as effective to take the responsibility to form and coordinate the Stag Hunt.

In the latter case, regulators can use a broad range of tools. The study does not provide insight into which regulatory tools are most efficient, but it does provide insight into what should be effective goals. They are threefold:

1. Make sure the relative difference between 'hunting stags' and 'hunting hares' is significant enough to motivate resourceful actors. This objective can be achieved by either increasing the value of circular transformation or reducing the value of linear status quo.
2. Facilitate the establishment and coordination of the stag hunting team. There are multiple ways this can be achieved. The present study highlights the importance of coordinating roles and interfaces between actors in the emerging circular value chain to make the transition simple and transaction cost efficient.

3. Facilitate simultaneousness to make the stag hunting team go hunting on the same day and thereby avoid that motivated actors lose early investments because other actors are playing the waiting game.

The Stag Hunt rationale also applies for practitioners. The implications can be summed up in two broad points:

1. Work with resourceful actors to join the stag hunting team. The present study shows that adoption is more likely in the presence of powerful actors that reduce risk for others, set standards for trade and quickly take commercial activities to scale. The latter is crucial because scale drives transaction cost efficiency of markets and also helps overcome potential cost disadvantages of the circular solution versus the incumbent linear system.
2. Make sure you gather the stag hunting team before significant investments are made. This is especially important for smaller actors and entrepreneurs as their resource base leaves them vulnerable if others play the waiting game.

Limitations and Further Research

The findings in this chapter are based on a single case study. Consequently, there are methodological shortcomings and the general applicability is limited by the factors mentioned above. The strength of the study is that it provides a conceptual framework that provides both intuitive explanatory power and new insight into how circular innovations are adopted in an industrial system. However, we call for more research on adoption decisions of circular innovations in general, and game theory approaches in particular in order to evaluate the robustness and boundaries of the game theory conceptualization. We believe that further investigation on investment and adoption decisions is important to understand the limited adoption of circular innovations.

CONCLUSIONS

This chapter departed from the need for a rapid and extensive transition to a circular economy in order to solve the global resource challenge. The main contribution of this study is to conceptualize adoption of circular innovation as a coordination game. The game theory approach helps us understand why circular adoption stands at a strategic disadvantage to non-adoption in the absence of resourceful actors that can ensure simultaneous and coordinated adoption across actors that can form a full competitive circular supply chain.

We have used the case of KM – a typical industrial company that employs a circular business model to close resource loops within and across value chains related to the Norwegian fish farming industry. The study concludes that the game theory conceptualization provides intuitive explanatory power and valuable new insight into adoption of circular innovations and practices. In particular, there are three elements of the Stag Hunt coordination game that provide new insight. First, it is about the assembly of a capable stag hunting team. Chances for successful adoption of circular innovations are much higher if one can assemble a dedicated and resourceful team of actors that can form a complete and competitive circular supply chain, and that do not deviate if other business opportunities arise elsewhere. Gather the hunter team before making significant investments! Second, like stag hunts, adoption of circular innovations requires coordination to be successful predominantly because the emerging circular value chain needs to be transaction efficient. Finally, adoption needs to be simultaneous. The stag hunting team needs to go hunting on the same day. Actors that adopt circular innovations before the emerging circular value chain can be completed with other efficient actors will most likely lose their investments.

REFERENCES

Avraamidou, S., Baratsas, S. G., Tian, Y., & Pistikopoulos, E. N. (2020). Circular economy: A challenge and an opportunity for process systems engineering. *Computers & Chemical Engineering*, 133, 106629.

Bocken, N. M., de Pauw, I., Bakker, C., & van der Grinten, B. (2016). Product design and business model strategies for a circular economy. *Journal of Industrial and Production Engineering*, 33(5), 308–320.

Bouton, S., Hannon, E., Rogers, M., Swartz, S., Johnson, R., Gold, A., & Staples, M. (2016). The circular economy: Moving from theory to practice. *McKinsey Center for Business and Environment. Special edition.*

Brundtland, G. H. (1987). *Our Common Future.* Report for the World Commission on Environment and Development, United Nations. New York: Oxford University Press.

Christensen, C., & Raynor, M. (2013). *The Innovator's Solution: Creating and Sustaining Successful Growth.* Boston, MA: Harvard Business Review Press.

Circle Economy (2020a). *The Circularity Gap Report.*

Circle Economy (2020b). *The Circularity Gap Report – Norway.*

Dubois, A., & Gadde, L.-E. (2002). Systematic combining: An abductive approach to case research. *Journal of Business Research*, 55(7), 553–560.

Eisenhardt, K. M. (1989). Building theories from case study research. *Academy of Management Review*, 14(4), 532–550.

Ellen MacArthur Foundation and McKinsey Center for Business and Environment (2015). *Growth Within: A Circular Economy Vision for a Competitive Europe.*

European Commission (2020). *EU Circular Economy Action Plan.*

Geels, F. W. (2011). The multi-level perspective on sustainability transitions: Responses to seven criticisms. *Environmental Innovation and Societal Transitions*, 1(1), 24–40.

Ghisellini, P., Cialani, C., & Ulgiati, S. (2016). A review on circular economy: The expected transition to a balanced interplay of environmental and economic systems. *Journal of Cleaner Production*, 114, 11–32.

Global Sustainable Development Report (2019). *The Future is Now.* https://sustainabledevelopment.un .org/content/documents/24797GSDR_report_2019.pdf.

Hardin, G. (1968). The tragedy of the commons. *Science*, 162, 1243–1248.

Hardin, R. (1971). Collective action as an agreeable n-prisoners' dilemma. *Behavioral Science*, 16(5), 472–481.

Hermundsdottir, F., & Aspelund, A. (2021). Sustainability innovations and firm competitiveness: A review. *Journal of Cleaner Production*, 280, 124715.

Hognes, E. S., & Skaar, C. (2017). *Avfallshåndtering fra sjøbasert havbruk.* http://hdl.handle.net/11250/ 2477326.

International Resource Panel (IRP) (2019). *Global Resources Outlook.* Nairobi: United Nations Environmental Programme.

Konietzko, J., Bocken, N., & Hultink, E. J. (2020). A tool to analyze, ideate and develop circular innovation ecosystems. *Sustainability*, 12(1), 417.

Korhonen, J., Honkasalo, A., & Seppälä, J. (2018). Circular economy: The concept and its limitations. *Ecological Economics*, 143, 37–46.

Markard, J., Geels, F. W., & Raven, R. (2020). Challenges in the acceleration of sustainability transitions. *Environmental Research Letters*, 15(8), 081001.

Moreau, V., Sahakian, M., van Griethuysen, P., & Vuille, F. (2017). Coming full circle: Why social and institutional dimensions matter for the circular economy. *Journal of Industrial Ecology*, 21(3), 497–506.

Norwegian Ministries of Fisheries (2009). *Strategi for en miljømessig bærekraftig havbruksnæring* [Norwegian]. https://www.regjeringen.no/no/dokumenter/strategi-for-en-miljomessig-barekraftig-/id571066/.

Olafsen, T., Winther, U., Olsen, Y., & Skjermo, J. (2012), *Verdiskaping basert på Produktive hav i 2050* [Norwegian]. Norwegian Academy of Technological Sciences. https://www.sintef.no/siste-nytt/2012/verdiskaping-basert-pa-produktive-hav-i-2050/.

Ord, T. (2020). *The Precipice: Existential Risk and the Future of Humanity*. Paris: Hachette Books.

Rashid, A., Asif, F. M., Krajnik, P., & Nicolescu, C. M. (2013). Resource conservative manufacturing: An essential change in business and technology paradigm for sustainable manufacturing. *Journal of Cleaner Production*, 57, 166–177.

Skyrms, B. (2001). The stag hunt. Paper presented at the Proceedings and Addresses of the American Philosophical Association.

Steinset, T. A. (2017). Frå attåtnæring til milliardindustri [Norwegian]. *Samfunnsspeilet*, 1.

UNEP (2011). *Decoupling Natural Resources Use and Environmental Impacts from Economic Growth*. https://www.resourcepanel.org/reports/decoupling-natural-resource-use-and-environmental-impacts-economic-growth.

Yin, R. K. (2017). *Case Study Research and Applications: Design and Methods*. Los Angeles, CA: Sage Publications.

15. Business model innovation for a circular economy: adapting to create value

Maria Figueroa-Armijos

BUSINESS MODELS AND THE CIRCULAR ECONOMY

The linear economy is in trouble. Global exponential consumption and depletive extraction of natural resources is reaching a point of no return (Ellen MacArthur Foundation 2014). Market volatility and regulatory forces, including sanitary measures, are further exacerbating the urge to transition to a circular economy (CE). Reducing consumption of raw materials and avoiding or minimizing waste at the source are rapidly becoming essential for business survival and growth (Planing 2018). Moreover, the COVID-19 pandemic shaking most of 2020 and half of 2021 emphasizes the unprecedented disruptions of our 'new normal' (Wuyts et al. 2020) which require systemic solutions such as radical new business strategies (Circularity20 2020) and systemic innovations that "may open up whole new markets" (Antikainen and Valkokari 2016, p. 6). Indeed, a circular economy has the potential to offer strategic and operational benefits "with huge potential for innovation, job creation and economic growth" that can no longer go unnoticed (Ellen MacArthur Foundation 2014, p. 12).

The concept of circular economy has progressively transcended the boundaries of the natural sciences where it was born (Lahti et al. 2018) to make its leap to various business domains, including strategy, innovation, operations, and technology management (Centobelli et al. 2020; Urbinati et al. 2017). Most notable advances at this crossroads involve our enhanced understanding on the dynamics of value creation and value capture (Bocken et al. 2016, 2019; Lewandowski 2016), and on the design of value propositions that promise a competitive advantage (Linder and Williander 2017; Urbinati et al. 2017; Zucchella and Previtali 2019). However, we still lack a fundamental business model framework (Antikainen and Valkokari 2016; Planing 2018) that can successfully adapt our current linear economy designs towards higher material and resource efficiency (Ellen MacArthur Foundation 2015; Stahel 2014) – a global economic savings estimated at over a trillion dollars a year by 2025 (Ellen MacArthur Foundation 2014).

Albeit ideal, adhering to circular economy principles entails a structural redesign of existing business models and their dimensions (Bocken et al. 2019; Lüdeke-Freund et al. 2019) to adapt to ongoing transformations, including revamping the value proposition, revisiting relationships with supply chain partners and customers, and revising the cost structure. Extant business model frameworks (for the most prominent see Osterwalder and Pigneur 2010, and Ries 2011) lack a systematic connection with dynamic circular economy principles. Indeed, current business models are fixed canvases that allow to plan but not to methodically evolve as progress towards circularity is made at the firm and ecosystem level. Current efforts lack a theoretical unison (Lüdeke-Freund and Dembek 2017) and a cumulative empirical probe (Foss and Saebi 2017), such that we continue to observe varied business model applications across contexts (Dentchev et al. 2018).

In principle, current business models are widely applied and effective at guiding startups and business growth. In fact, several reviews exist that propose a framework adapted for the CE (for examples see Bocken et al. 2019, Pieroni et al. 2019, and Antikainen and Valkokari 2016). In practice, small businesses and corporations alike are devising their own versions of current business models to adapt to their unique needs and situations, each enduring their own trial-and-error path. Collaborative platforms, alliances and summits emerge every year to further advance a collective pursuit (for the prime example in North America see Circularity21, Verge, and NetZero events at GreenBiz). Hence, despite multiple efforts to transform current business models for a circular design, a baseline framework that can be widely implemented and adapted to various settings is still underway.

Furthermore, research on business model innovation (BMI) oriented for a circular economy is still nascent, with most articles on the topic published between 2015 and 2020 (Diaz Lopez et al. 2019). Despite this growth, however, most of this research still focuses on concept development (Linder and Williander 2017; Lewandowsky 2016; Nußholz 2017). This chapter seeks to offer a systematic cross-disciplinary review of current efforts at the intersection of research and practice on circular economy business model innovation (CE-BMI), using a business and economics multidisciplinary lens. The goal is to identify critical inter-disciplinary linkages that unveil an emergent innovative framework, intended as a cumulative empirical tool for everyday use in the classroom and in practice. The incremental design of this framework might be particularly helpful for college startups and young entrepreneurs who are eager to propose CE solutions for current global challenges. This population has no lack of enthusiasm but is rather easily discouraged by complicated scholarly models and conceptual comparisons. This adaptable framework aims to facilitate the development of a logical CE rationale behind their anchor purpose and value proposition.

EXAMINING BARRIERS IN BUSINESS MODEL INNOVATIONS FOR THE CIRCULAR ECONOMY: ARE WE CREATING AND CAPTURING VALUE?

The business model construct emerged half a century ago and was initially mostly associated with IT system modelling (Pieroni et al. 2019). Since then, scholars in various business disciplines progressively became interested in its capability to explain the basic dynamics of business (Magretta 2002). Yet, both in theory and practice, various interpretations of business models exist, leading to an imprecise construct (Gassman et al. 2016). More recent definitions conceptualize a business model as the "design [...] of the value creation, delivery, and capture mechanisms" (Teece 2010, p. 172) or the value generation logic of a reference system composed of various pieces (Wirtz et al. 2016). The most successful attempt at simplifying the business model construct is the one-page canvas proposed by Osterwalder and Pigneur (2010), which streamlines the business plan into a static construct with nine elementary building blocks – key partners, key activities, key resources, cost structure, value propositions, customer relationships, channels, customer segments, and revenue streams. This static but rather highly executed canvas can be further divided into three umbrella sections: 'value proposition', 'value creation and delivery', and 'value capture' (Richardson 2008).

Beyond the foundations offered by the business model (BM) construct there is the notion of business model innovation. BMI has become a prominent stream of research, attracting increasing interest from management scholars and practitioners (Foss and Sibae 2017; Spieth et al. 2014; Zott et al. 2011). Drivers of innovations in our current business models include the constant rise and volatility of raw materials (Planing 2018) and an increasingly prevalent transformation in consumer behaviour (Ellen MacArthur Foundation 2014). Although the BM concept itself has evolved (Wirtz et al. 2016) to be acknowledged as a complement to product, process, and organizational innovation (Zott et al. 2011), a theoretical conceptualization of BMI remains nascent (Foss and Saebi 2017) with limited systematic research reviews (Spieth et al. 2014) to advance this evolutionary discovery process.

Although a distinct theory of BMI is still to be defined (Zott et al. 2011), a few theoretical attempts exist. At the ecosystem level, Osterwalder and Pigneur (2010, p. 5) propose that a "business model innovation is about creating value, for companies, for customers, and society". Antikainen and Valkokari (2016) further add the consideration of trends and drivers and stakeholder involvement. At the organizational level, Foss and Saebi (2017, p. 201) define it as "designed, novel, nontrivial changes to the key elements of a firm's business model and/ or the architecture linking these elements". Other works explain organizational innovation as a response to both internal and external triggers that incentivize changes in the business model to create, diversify, acquire, or transform (Geissdoerfer et al. 2018, 2020). Thus, in essence, the business model can serve as the playground where innovations flourish (i.e., process, product or service) or as the innovation 'itself' to achieve competitive advantage (Boons et al. 2013).

In practice, empirical research from the last two decades points to BMIs as fundamental reference points for innovation, value creation, sustained growth (IBM Global Business Services 2006), and positive firm performance (Cucculelli and Bettinelli 2015; Zott and Amit 2007) because as one CEO points out "there is no growth without changing ourselves and the industry itself" (IBM Global Business Services 2006, p. 15). At its core, the *innovation* dimension of the BM implies a "significant positive change" (Berkun 2010, p. xvii) in any of the dimensions of the original BM, which introduces something *new to the firm* (Björkdahl and Holmén 2013) and *new to the customers* (Planing 2018), always aligned to the firm's strategic vision (Wirtz et al. 2016) and level of innovation intensity (Foss and Saebi 2017).

Overall, the accelerated search for CE-BMIs is facilitated by myriad factors, most notably the enabling dynamic advances in information technology (Planing 2018), the emergent demand to establish return and recovery networks (Mentink 2014; Planing 2018), and the rise in consumer-driven business models such as access, performance, or results-based business models (i.e., as opposed to ownership-based only) that have revolutionized the market in the last 20 years (for examples see Bakker et al. 2014; Cinquini et al. 2013; Evans 2014; Lacy et al. 2013; Sempels 2014). As current trends indicate, the optimization of current CE-BMIs to truly adapt to CE principles requires the design of a holistic value proposition that includes both rational and non-rational motives of consumer behaviour.

AN ADAPTABLE-DIMENSIONS FRAMEWORK FOR BUSINESS MODEL INNOVATION FOR THE CIRCULAR ECONOMY

A CE-BMI involves a systemic (Antikainen and Valkokari 2016; Geissdoerfer et al. 2020) and trans-disciplinary (Sakao and Brambila-Macias 2018) integration of circular economy principles into the design and structure of the business model (Pieroni et al. 2019). The ideal CE-BMI would approach the product and economic value creation from an efficiency and effectiveness framework (Bocken et al. 2016, 2019; Den Hollander and Bakker 2016), integrating business strategies that seek a 'fully circular' approach (i.e., downstream and upstream; Urbinati et al. 2017). However ideal, a CE-BMI also involves many complexities and uncertainties beyond those of the typical non-CE-BMI (Pieroni et al. 2019). For instance, a CE-BMI must include reverse logistics for return and recovery of resources which involves a dynamic calculation of timing on top of quantity and quality (Bocken et al. 2019; Bocken et al. 2018). Beyond the operational model, a CE-BMI must also consider customer perceptions (Bocken et al. 2018) for products that have been transformed to follow the principles of the CE, and innovations regarding product design and the value creation chain that considers digital technologies (Geissdoerfer et al. 2018) and other critical resources.

Although a handful of practical frameworks or outlines have been proposed to the public at a price (for an example see BS 8001 in BSI 2017) or for free (for examples see Ellen MacArthur Foundation 2016 or WRAP 2020) in the last few years, we still lack a systematization of the proposed methodologies (Geissdoerfer et al. 2020; Pieroni et al. 2019). In this section, following an exhaustive literature review, cross-check and analysis, I propose an 'adaptable-dimensions framework for CE-BMI'. Departing from any of the practical frameworks available in the market (e.g., business model canvas proposed by Osterwalder and Pigneur 2010), Table 15.1 offers a synthesis of the most critical dimensions for CE identified in the literature and in practitioner outlets. The columns in the table seek to offer a user-friendly approach to adjust any practical business model from the market to the evolving needs of a circular economy. Firms and industries differ and transform as they achieve various dynamic stages of their progress to become more circular. As such, Table 15.1 is expected to serve as a guideline (a checklist) to remind the user of critical dimensions that must be considered for each type of business model. References for each dimension are provided for greater detail.

Table 15.1 includes adaptable dimensions for two broad types of business models. Each type is unique in its application and involves a differing relationship with stakeholders – primarily the customer and suppliers – therefore requiring a dedicated approach. The first broad type of business model 'access/performance/results/use-based BM' applies to cases where the customer does not buy a product from the firm, but rather pays for the service that such product provides to solve a problem. As an example in this type of business model, if the customer's problem is the need to wash their clothes, the customer can lease a washing machine for a fixed period of time (access or use BM; see Sempels 2014), lease a washing machine for a fixed number of washing cycles (performance-based BM; see Cinquini et al. 2013), or alternatively the customer can pay for a pick-up and delivery washing service (results-based BM; see Sempels 2014). The second type of business model – 'ownership-based BM' – is the archetypal pre-twenty-first century BM where the client purchases the washing machine and owns it for as many desired cycles or an indefinite period of time (Planing 2015).

CONCLUSIONS AND IMPLICATIONS FOR RESEARCH AND PRACTICE

In the last decade, practitioners and scholars alike have become accustomed to applying various versions of the business model canvas to classroom and coaching activities. Paired with the lean startup (Ries 2011) revolution and other emerging approaches (e.g., no code), these simplified tools have rapidly engaged the public in a realm that had formerly seemed

Table 15.1   An adaptable-dimensions framework for business model innovation for the circular economy (CE-BMI)

Type of business model	Adaptable BMI dimensions for the circular economy			
	Modify this dimension	Add to this dimension	Create a new dimension	Transform this dimension (requires changes in infrastructure to adapt to two-way flow)
Access/performance/results/use-based BM[vw]	Value proposition[gsqu] Customer value,[f] collaboration,[h] and perceptions[j] Critical resources (efficiency and longevity[ai] including resource security,[m] dynamic capabilities,[de] and digital technologies[k] Supply and distribution networks[hr] Revenue schemes (short-term and long-term)[alpq] Key Activities[bqtu]	Cost structure[lo]	Shared value creation[bc] System boundaries[bc]	Return/recovery networks (reverse logistics, take-back systems)[aflr] Strategic partners' relationships[hnqr]
Ownership-based BM[s]	Strategic partners' relationships[hnqr] Revenue schemes (short-term and long-term)[alpq] Key Activities[bqtu]	Value proposition[gsqu] Cost structure[lo]	Shared value creation[bc] Return/recovery networks (reverse logistics, take-back systems)[aflr] System boundaries[bc]	Critical resources (efficiency and longevity)[ai] including resource security,[m] dynamic capabilities,[de] and digital technologies[k] Customer value,[f] collaboration,[h] and perceptions[j]

Note: [a]Pieroni et al. 2019; [b]Boons and Lüdeke-Freund 2013; [c]Wirtz et al. 2016; [d]Demil and Lecocq 2010; [e]Foss and Saebi 2017; [f]Urbinati et al. 2017; [g]Sustainn 2017; [h]Ellen MacArthur Foundation 2016; [i]Díaz Lopez et al. 2019; [j]Bocken et al. 2019; [k]Bocken et al. 2018; [l]Mentink 2014; [m]Stahel 2014; [n]Antikainen and Valkokari 2016; [o]Subramanian and Gunasekaran 2015; [p]Van Ostaeyen et al. 2013; [q]Van Renswoude et al. 2015; [r]Ellen MacArthur Foundation 2014, 2015; [s]Planing 2015; [t]Lacy et al. 2014; [u]Laubscher and Marinelli 2014; [v]Sempels 2014; [w]Cinquini et al. 2013.

risky and unattainable, especially for the young generations sporting grand dreams and ambition, but who hold at times little technical understanding of the challenges of venture creation. Fortunately, despite the lack of a systematic scholarly framework (Antikainen and Valkokari 2016; Geissdoerfer et al. 2020) for business model design and implementation, local, regional, and supranational collaborative pursuits and legislation (see Singularity University 2020 and the European Commission's 2020a Entrepreneurship Action Plan and 2020b EU Circular Economy Action Plan as examples) have injected the market with a level of collective enthusiasm and interest for entrepreneurship, innovation, and venture financing. Most notably, the twenty-first century has birthed the exponential discovery of unicorns, gazelles, and other variations (Aldrich and Ruef 2018) that have further garnered the interest of young entrepreneurs around the world.

Furthermore, the emergence of the Chief Sustainability Officer (CSO) position in 2004 (Fu et al. 2020) drove a substantial new labour demand for entrepreneurial leaders who can "think and act like a CEO" on matters of environmental and social sustainability (Luijkenaar and Spinley 2007, p. 2). The progressive evolution from basic corporate compliance that positioned sustainability issues as a luxury or a marketing tactic, to seeing social and environmental sustainability applications as a fundamental human right (Antikainen and Valkokari 2016) exacerbated the need for innovation in the already lacking business model frameworks.

Research on BMI oriented for a circular economy is still nascent, with most articles on this particular topic published between 2015 and 2020 (Diaz Lopez et al. 2019). Despite this growth, however, most of this research still focuses on concept elaboration and development (Geissdoerfer et al. 2020; Linder and Williander 2017; Lewandowsky 2016; Nußholz 2017). Whereas rising scholarly research on business model innovations in the last five years (Diaz Lopez et al. 2019) has stagnated around the development of a construct (Linder and Williander 2017; Lewandowsky 2016; Nußholz 2017) with mostly incremental progress, the market has addressed this gap with makeshift frameworks (for examples see BSI 2017; Ellen MacArthur Foundation 2016 or WRAP 2020) that partly address the urgent need for direction.

In the absence of a systematization of the various proposed methodologies, this chapter aimed to propose an 'adaptable-dimensions framework for CE-BMI' intended as an adaptable empirical tool for new startups and young entrepreneurs in the classroom and in practice. The design of this framework might be particularly helpful for college startups and entrepreneurs who are eager to propose CE solutions for current global challenges. For example, this framework may be especially suitable for the needs of student startups and early-stage firms in master's programmes in entrepreneurship, innovation, strategy or related fields, where students are required to design a year-long business plan as a master's thesis.

The proposed 'adaptable-dimensions framework for CE-BMI' may also be used by practitioners, including coaches, and consultants as a checklist to guide the transition of any firm with a business model towards the integration and implementation of circular economy principles in business model innovations. This tool is intended as a sketch framework that can be enhanced incrementally as new scholarly and practical evidence surfaces. The end result is a CE-BMI capable of addressing urgent needs at the very foundation of the purpose that anchors the firm to renew and enhance the social, environmental, and ethical conditions of their stakeholders. The 'adaptable-dimensions framework for CE-BMI' proposed here is also a first modest attempt at building bridges between academics in the business and sustainability-sciences fields.

REFERENCES

Aldrich, H. E., & Ruef, M. (2018). Unicorns, gazelles, and other distractions on the way to understanding real entrepreneurship in the United States. *Academy of Management Perspectives*, 32(4), 458–472.

Antikainen, M., & Valkokari, K. (2016). A framework for sustainable circular business model innovation. *Technology Innovation Management Review*, 6(7).

Bakker, C., den Hollander, M., van Hinte, E., & Zijlstra, Y. (2014) *Products That Last: Product Design for Circular Business Models*. Delft: TU Delft Library.

Berkun, S. (2010) *The Myths of Innovation*. Beijing: O'Reilly.

Björkdahl, J., & Holmén, M. (2013). Business model innovation: The challenges ahead. *International Journal of Product Development*, 18(3), 213–225.

Bocken, N., de Pauw, I., Bakker, C., & van der Grinten, B. (2016). Product design and business model strategies for a circular economy. *Journal of Industrial and Production Engineering*, 33(5), 308–320.

Bocken, N. M., Schuit, C. S., & Kraaijenhagen, C. (2018). Experimenting with a circular business model: Lessons from eight cases. *Environmental Innovation and Societal Transitions*, 28, 79–95.

Bocken, N., Strupeit, L., Whalen, K., & Nußholz, J. (2019). A review and evaluation of circular business model innovation tools. *Sustainability*, 11(8), 2210.

Boons, F., & Lüdeke-Freund, F. (2013). Business models for sustainable innovation: State-of-the-art and steps towards a research agenda. *Journal of Cleaner Production*, 45, 9–19.

Boons, F., Montalvo, C., Quist, J., & Wagner, M. (2013). Sustainable innovation, business models and economic performance: An overview. *Journal of Cleaner Production*, 45, 1–8.

BSI (2017). BS 8001:2017. *Framework for Implementing the Principles of the Circular Economy in Organizations – Guide.*

Centobelli, P., Cerchione, R., Chiaroni, D., Del Vecchio, P., & Urbinati, A. (2020). Designing business models in circular economy: A systematic literature review and research agenda. *Business Strategy and the Environment*, 29(4), 1734–1749.

Cinquini, L., Di Minin, A., & Varaldo, R. (eds.) (2013). *New Business Models and Value Creation: A Service Science Perspective*. Milan: Springer

Circularity20 (2020). Accelerating the circular economy. https://events.greenbiz.com/events/circularity/online/2020.

Cucculelli, M., & Bettinelli, C. (2015). Business models, intangibles and firm performance: Evidence on corporate entrepreneurship from Italian manufacturing SMEs. *Small Business Economics*, 45, 329–350.

Demil, B., & Lecocq, X. (2010). Business model evolution: In search of dynamic consistency. *Long Range Planning*, 43, 227–246.

Den Hollander, M., & Bakker, C. (2016). Mind the gap exploiter: Circular business models for product lifetime extension. In *Proceedings of Electronic Goes Green 2016+*. Berlin: Fraunhofer IZM Berlin, 1-8.

Dentchev, N., Rauter, R., Jóhannsdóttir, L., Snihur, Y., Rosano, M., Baumgartner, R., ... Jonker, J. (2018). Embracing the variety of sustainable business models: A prolific field of research and a future research agenda. *Journal of Cleaner Production*, 194, 695–703.

Diaz Lopez, F. J., Bastein, T., & Tukker, A. (2019). Business model innovation for resource efficiency, circularity and cleaner production: What 143 cases tell us. *Ecological Economics*, 155, 20–35.

Ellen MacArthur Foundation (2014). *Towards the Circular Economy: Accelerating the Scale-Up across Global Supply Chains*. Cowes, Isle of Wight: Ellen MacArthur Foundation.

Ellen MacArthur Foundation (2015). *Towards a Circular Economy: Business Rationale for an Accelerated Transition*. https://www.ellenmacarthurfoundation.org/assets/downloads/TCE_Ellen-MacArthur-Foundation_9-Dec-2015.pdf.

Ellen MacArthur Foundation (2016). *The Circular Design Guide*. https://www.circulardesignguide.com.

European Commission (2020a). *The 2020 Entrepreneurship Action Plan*. https://ec.europa.eu/growth/smes/promoting-entrepreneurship/action-plan_en.

European Commission (2020b). *EU Circular Economy Action Plan*. https://ec.europa.eu/environment/circular-economy/pdf/new_circular_economy_action_plan.pdf.

Evans, J. (2014) *The Circular Economy Toolkit*. University of Cambridge, Institute for Manufacturing (IfM). http://circulareconomytoolkit.org/.

Foss, N. J., & Saebi, T. (2017). Fifteen years of research on business model innovation: How far have we come, and where should we go? *Journal of Management*, 43(1), 200–227.

Fu, R., Tang, Y., & Chen, G. (2020). Chief sustainability officers and corporate social (ir)responsibility. *Strategic Management Journal*, 41(4), 656–680.

Gassmann, O., Frankenberger, K., & Sauer, R. (2016). *Exploring the Field of Business Model Innovation.* London: Palgrave Macmillan.

Geissdoerfer, M., Morioka, S. N., de Carvalho, M. M., & Evans, S. (2018). Business models and supply chains for the circular economy. *Journal of Cleaner Production*, 190, 712–721.

Geissdoerfer, M., Pieroni, M. P., Pigosso, D. C., & Soufani, K. (2020). Circular business models: A review. *Journal of Cleaner Production*, 277, 123741.

IBM Global Business Services (2006). *Expanding the Innovation Horizon: The Global CEO Study 2006.*

Lacy, P., Keeble, J., McNamara, R., Rutqvist, J., Haglund, T., et al. (2014). *Circular Advantage: Innovative Business Models and Technologies to Create Value in a World without Limits to Growth.* Chicago: Accenture.

Lacy, P., Rosenberg, D., Drewell, Q., & Rutqvist, J. (2013). *Five Business Models That Are Driving the Circular Economy.* https://www.fastcompany.com/1681904/5-business-models-that-are-driving-the-circular-economy.

Lahti, T., Wincent, J., & Parida, V. (2018). A definition and theoretical review of the circular economy, value creation, and sustainable business models: Where are we now and where should research move in the future? *Sustainability*, 10(8), 2799–2818.

Laubscher, M., & Marinelli, T. (2014). Integration of circular economy in business. In *Going Green—CARE INNOVATION.* 7th International Symposium and Environmental Exhibition, Vienna.

Lewandowski, M. (2016). Designing the business models for circular economy: Towards the conceptual framework. *Sustainability*, 8(1), 43.

Linder, M., & Williander, M. (2017). Circular business model innovation: Inherent uncertainties. *Business Strategy and the Environment*, 26(2), 182–196.

Lüdeke-Freund, F., & Dembek, K. (2017). Sustainable business model research and practice: Emerging field or passing fancy? *Journal of Cleaner Production*, 168, 1668–1678.

Lüdeke-Freund, F., Gold, S., & Bocken, N. M. (2019). A review and typology of circular economy business model patterns. *Journal of Industrial Ecology*, 23(1), 36–61.

Luijkenaar, A., & Spinley, K. (2007). *The Emergence of the Chief Sustainability Officer: From Compliance Manager to Business Partner.* Chicago: Heidrick & Struggles International.

Magretta, J. (2002). Why business models matter. *Harvard Business Review.* https://hbr.org/2002/05/why-business-models-matter.

Mentink, B. A. S. (2014). *Circular Business Model Innovation: A Process Framework and a Tool for Business Model Innovation in a Circular Economy.* Delft: TU Delft Library.

Nußholz, J. L. (2017). Circular business models: Defining a concept and framing an emerging research field. *Sustainability*, 9(10), 1810.

Osterwalder, A., & Pigneur, Y. (2010). *Business Model Generation: A Handbook for Visionaries, Game Changers, and Challengers.* Hoboken, NJ: Wiley & Sons.

Pieroni, M. P., McAloone, T. C., & Pigosso, D. C. (2019). Business model innovation for circular economy and sustainability: A review of approaches. *Journal of Cleaner Production*, 215, 198–216.

Planing, P. (2015). Business model innovation in a circular economy reasons for non-acceptance of circular business models. *Open Journal of Business Model Innovation*, 1(11), 1–11.

Planing, P. (2018). Towards a circular economy: How business model innovation will help to make the shift. *International Journal of Business and Globalisation*, 20(1), 71–83.

Richardson, J. (2008). The business model: An integrative framework for strategy execution. *Strategic Change*, 17, 133–144.

Ries, E. (2011). *The Lean Startup: How Today's Entrepreneurs Use Continuous Innovation to Create Radically Successful Businesses.* New York: Crown Business.

Sakao, T., & Brambila-Macias, S. A. (2018). Do we share an understanding of transdisciplinarity in environmental sustainability research? *Journal of Cleaner Production*, 170, 1399–1403.

Sempels, C. (2014). Implementing a circular and performance economy through business model innovation. In K. Webster (ed.), *A New Dynamic: Effective Business in a Circular Economy.* London: Ellen McArthur Foundation Publishing.

Singularity University (2020). About us – Leadership. https://su.org/about/leadership/.

Spieth, P., Schneckenberg, D., & Ricart, J.E. (2014). Business model innovation: State of the art and future challenges for the field. *R&D Management*, 44, 237–247.

Stahel, W. R. (2014). The business angle of a circular economy: Higher competitiveness, higher resource security and material efficiency. In K. Webster (ed.), *A New Dynamic: Effective Business in a Circular Economy*. London: Ellen MacArthur Foundation, 46–60.

Subramanian, N., & Gunasekaran, A. (2015). Cleaner supply-chain management practices for twenty-first-century organizational competitiveness: Practice-performance framework and research propositions. *International Journal of Production Economics*, 164, 216–233.

Sustainn (2017). *Circularity Canvas: Methodology to Outline Circular Business Models*. http://www.wearesustainn.com/en/2017/03/circularity-canvasmethodology-circular-business-models/.

Teece, D. J. (2010). Business models, business strategy and innovation. *Long Range Planning*, 43, 172–194.

Urbinati, A., Chiaroni, D., & Chiesa, V. (2017). Towards a new taxonomy of circular economy business models. *Journal of Cleaner Production*, 168, 487–498.

Van Ostaeyen, J., van Horenbeek, A., Pintelon, L., & Duflou, J.R. (2013). A refined typology of product-service systems based on functional hierarchy modeling. *Journal of Cleaner Production*, 51, 261–276.

Van Renswoude, K., Wolde, A. T., & Joustra, D. J. (2015). Circular business models. Part 1: An introduction to IMSA's circular business model scan. Amsterdam: Instituut voor Milieu- en Systeemanalyse Amsterdam. https://groenomstilling.erhvervsstyrelsen.dk/sites/default/files/media/imsa_circular_business_models_-_april_2015_-_part_1.pdf.

Wirtz, B. W., Pistoia, A., Ullrich, S., & Gottel, V. (2016). Business models: Origin, development, and future research. *Long Range Planning*, 49, 36–54.

WRAP (2020). *Innovative Business Models*. http://www.wrap.org.uk/content/innovativebusiness-models-1.

Wuyts, W., Marin, J., Brusselaers, J., & Vrancken, K. (2020). Circular economy as a COVID-19 cure? *Resources, Conservation, and Recycling*, 162, 105016.

Zott, C., & Amit, R. (2007). Business model design and the performance of entrepreneurial firms. *Organization Science*, 18, 181–199.

Zott, C., Amit, R., & Massa, L. (2011). The business model: Recent developments and future research. *Journal of Management*, 37, 1019–1042.

Zucchella, A., & Previtali, P. (2019). Circular business models for sustainable development: A "waste is food" restorative ecosystem. *Business Strategy and the Environment*, 28(2), 274–285.

16. Exploring the entrepreneurial landscape and systemic barriers of circular business models

Even Bjørnstad and Jorunn Grande

INTRODUCTION: THE NEEDED SUSTAINABILITY TRANSITION

The circular economy (CE) has emerged as a central approach in addressing the sustainability challenge described in the introduction to this volume. Its key role in the European Green Deal is illustrative in this respect (EC 2019). China (Merli et al. 2018) and several individual countries and regions in Europe (ECESP 2020) have also presented explicit CE strategies. Still it seems that the CE concept lacks a clear unifying framing to form a basis for strategic policies and for establishment of robust business models at the micro level. Kirchherr et al. (2017), in their analysis of this issue, identified 95 different definitions among the 114 reviewed. Although a common core of ideas is present in these definitions, their variation in approach and emphasis is apparent. This width in approaches paves the road for a range of initiatives and practices under the CE umbrella that are not necessarily coherent, possibly even contradictory. The fact that the current global economy is growing even less circular, as pointed out in the 2020 circularity gap report (De Wit et al. 2020), gives reason to pause and ask why this urgently needed CE transition is not happening.

The focus in this chapter is on the opportunities and barriers observed at business level that define the entrepreneur's ability and incentives to innovate and develop circular and sustainable business models. We suggest that there exist both physical and systemic issues that pose fundamental challenges to the transition to a circular economy, that are under-communicated, perhaps even misunderstood, in the research and policy debate on the circular economy. We believe that these issues help explain why the emergence of the CE is slow from a macro-economic perspective, and also why individual businesses find it difficult to innovate into truly sustainable circular business models (CBMs). The nature of these issues is such that the discussion must combine both business level and system level perspectives. In short, the aim of our analysis is to contribute to a clarification of this complex landscape, and to identify key issues that society must address in the transition to a sustainable circular economy.

After a short note on the CE concept, the chapter proceeds by discussing the mentioned physical and systemic issues, and how the businesses at micro level seem to adapt to CE and sustainability issues. From this we expand on the CE strategies to derive a framework model which maps the opportunity space for entrepreneurship within the circular economy. This map identifies a critical region where political, entrepreneurial and research efforts must concentrate in order to transition to a truly circular economy.

MAIN ELEMENTS OF A CIRCULAR ECONOMY

The sustainability challenge is succinctly captured by what Stahel (2019) refers to as the Linear Industrial Economy (LIE), or the 'make-use-dispose' logic. External to this economic value creating logic are the costs from resource depletion and ecosystem destruction at the start of the value chain, and environmental disruptions, including climate change, at its end. Addressing this sustainability challenge is at the very core of the CE. Kirchherr et al. (2017) demonstrate that a majority of CE definitions relate to activities of reducing, reusing and recycling materials, and with a main aim of economic prosperity. The ReSOLVE framework (Ellen MacArthur Foundation 2015) captures these strategies, as do different 'R'-models (3R, 4R, even 9R) found in the CE literature (see also Ghisellini et al. 2016). Hereafter we refer to CE strategies as 'R strategies'. These strategies have historical roots, some of them can be recognized in the so-called 'waste-hierarchy' and similar strategies that have been part of the environmental and waste policy debate since at least the 1980s (Brataas 1999, p. 50).

The novelties that the CE brings to the table, are the prospects of a 'redesign' of the industrial logic at a more systemic level that could open for economic prosperity while reducing the negative resource and environmental impacts. Seminal in this respect are the three volumes of *Towards the Circular Economy* from the Ellen MacArthur Foundation (2013a, 2013b, 2014) that set an agenda for CE as a vehicle for a more general transition to a sustainable economy. Disconnecting economic activity from wasteful resource use ties the principles of the CE to the centre of the *decoupling* hypothesis, which is the fundamental idea upon which current resource and climate policies are built. Decoupling, it is assumed, will allow a continued expansion of global economic activity, while simultaneously reducing resource inputs and negative environmental impacts, and eliminating carbon emissions. The vision for the EU Green Deal (EC 2019, p. 2), with its Circular Economy Action Plan (EC 2020) is a telling example in this respect. Further, the United Nations Environment Programme's circularity platform postulates that "disconnecting natural resource use and environmental impacts from economic activity and human well-being is essential" in achieving a sustainable future (UNEP 2020).

These principles of circularity seem like a good idea, both for individual businesses and for society as a whole. However, almost 50 years after the Club of Rome's 'Limits to Growth', decades of environmental and waste policies promoting the waste hierarchy and R-principles, and an exponential proliferation of automation and resource efficient digitalization and communication technologies: the hard empirical facts still do not indicate that such a necessary decoupling and transition to circularity is happening. The global economy, in its 'normal' state of operation, is simply not responding to the sustainability challenge. The reasons for this must be understood and dealt with, in order for the CE to do its job. In investigating these reasons, we propose to summarize them in two themes: the physics of the economy and the 'growth imperative', to be discussed next.

THE PHYSICS OF ECONOMIC VALUE

In order to better understand the limits and potentials of a circular economy, we must recognize the *material* nature of economic activity. Economic value is, generally, created from the 'first' surplus or rent, made possible by the supply of some physical resources that happen to possess desirable properties. The sectors of the economy referred to as 'primary industries' contribute, in a suitable combination with labour and technological inputs, to this basic surplus by utilizing useful resources from land, forest, sea and other physical sources. These surpluses form the basis for and feed the complex web of value chains that the economy consists of. In our context of a circular economy, it is necessary to clarify more in principle the quality that makes these resources so essential in value creation. This important insight follows from a study of thermodynamics. Unfortunately, these fundamental physical laws are largely ignored by standard economic theory, regardless of the important economic insights they give. The following brief account is inspired by the pioneering contributions on this issue by Boulding (1966) and Georgescu-Roegen (1971).

In a CE context, the first and second laws of thermodynamics are central. Assuming a properly defined system of analysis, the first law states that energy and matter are constant. Neither matter nor energy can be created or destroyed, although they can be transformed during an economic process. Physical resources that are inputted to the economy, will always remain in some form and some place in the system that is being analysed. This first law is straightforward and can be demonstrated by a study of materials and energy flows in an economy.

The second law, the entropy law, is much more subtle and difficult to grasp. It is the entropy law that gives insights to the creation of economic value and sets the physical limits to the potentials of the CE. The implication of the second law is that the running of any process, either in nature or within the economic system, requires a 'fuel'. This generalized concept of a 'fuel' can be understood as a quality inherent in the material characteristics of the process in question. This fuel, or quality, is referred to as 'exergy'. It is the available exergy that enables the system to produce work or value in some form. An economic process is typically designed such as to utilize available exergy to produce a desirable outcome. Exergy is often understood as 'free energy' and it is a central concept in energy system analyses and similar applications (Wall 1977; Ayres and Warr 2010; Science Europe 2016).

The exergy driving a process can only be used once. The inherent 'quality' of the system that the exergy represents, is consumed as the process unfolds, and it cannot be recovered or recycled. An automobile, for example, produces mobility (work) by a transformation of energy in the form of gasoline into movement of the car and its passengers. This energy ultimately ends up as waste heat that is dissipated in the air. Although the energy in the gasoline is not lost after being combusted in the car engine, its ability to do further work is lost. This inevitable reduction in energy quality and the subsequent lost ability of the dispersed energy to reproduce the work done, is a fundamental implication of the second law.

The concept of exergy is also applied to describe and quantify the similar quality of non-energy material resources and objects (Capilla and Delgado 2014). Materials and their physical quality (exergy) are necessary inputs to the economic process in order to facilitate a range of desired functions within society. It is the facilitating quality of these materials in products and economic processes that makes them valuable, and which is reduced during use and lost when the product is discarded. To illustrate, a smartphone needs around 70 of the elements of the periodic table to work (Rohrig 2015).

The key insight from the second law of thermodynamics is that an economic process requires the input of high exergy resources (for energy or materials), and that a net consumption of exergy always results. This is a non-negotiable physical fact that sets an absolute limit for technological systems and economic processes. A logical consequence is that economic value cannot be created without the expenditure of exergy. All economic value creation requires input of exergy in some form, and some of this exergy will be consumed in the process and can never be recovered. In essence, the second law effectively refutes the hypothesis of absolute decoupling between economic value creation and resource use. The consequences for CE entrepreneurship of this insight will be discussed in a subsequent section.

THE GROWTH IMPERATIVE

In addition to its undeniable material basis, the concept of *economic growth* is a determining characteristic of the globalized economic system. Economic output is measured by the gross domestic product (GDP), and economic growth is usually understood as an increase over time of the inflation-adjusted GDP. Growth in economic activity has different sources. Population growth is a 'natural' source of economic growth, since more people means increasing demands for life's necessities. Population growth also represents an increased supply of labour in the economy. Technological development plays a key role in economic growth, enabling new and more efficient modes of production. Increasing labour productivity is one important effect of technological shifts, freeing labour resources to be employed in other economic activity. Improved technologies also generate economic surplus (rents) that are reinvested in new economic activity (Acemoglu 2012; Saad-Filho and Johnston 2005).

In addition to its 'natural' sources, economic growth also has a political dimension. Technological systems and infrastructure represent capital that requires returns. Such returns are generated by increasing economic value creation. Owners of capital thus depend on economic growth to maintain asset value and profits over time. The labour force receives its share of economic output via wages, and a high degree of employment is needed to maintain social stability in an economy. A labour force challenged by labour efficiency enhancing technologies, perhaps also by net growth in the labour stock, will require a general increase in economic activity to remain occupied. The political desire to maintain full employment thus also requires economic growth (Jackson 2017).

This systemic need to generate ever increasing economic value, is referred to as the 'growth imperative' (Wilhite 2016), and it represents the main driving force in creating the problems that the CE is addressing. The LIE (Stahel 2019) follows as a logical consequence of the growth imperative, in that its high throughput of exergy is necessary to create the economic surpluses that perpetuate the needed economic growth. The degree of compatibility of the CE strategies with this reigning growth imperative is a fundamental issue in understanding the sustainability challenge, and it represents a key framework condition for CE entrepreneurship.

CHALLENGES AT SYSTEMIC AND ENTREPRENEURIAL LEVEL

The CE literature has circled in on a family of *strategies* to guide innovation into relevant business models, exemplified by the 'nine Rs' model proposed by Potting et al. (2017). A *business model* is an overall plan and rationale for an organization in realizing its goal, whether it be sustained profits or other objectives (Jørgensen et al. 2019). A *circular business model* represents, in this context, the value proposition and plan for an entrepreneur to realize an innovation into a competitive business within a relevant R strategy. Successful innovation in this domain depends not only on characteristics of the entrepreneur and her relevant entrepreneurial support system, but also on the compatibility of the business model with the more general economic and political context. This can be a challenging landscape for the entrepreneur.

CE Opportunities and Barriers at Business Level

Small businesses are necessary to complement political change in addressing resource and climate actions. Yet we find that the entrepreneur and small businesses have received little attention in such change processes. The improvisational actions of entrepreneurs may provide unconventional solutions to many social and environmental issues (York et al. 2016). From the fields of eco-innovation, environmental and sustainable entrepreneurship (Alos-Simo et al. 2020; De Bernardi and Pedrini 2020) we can get some insight on what triggers and hinders circular entrepreneurial and firm actions.

First of all, a critical issue at firm level seems to be the ability to recognize and develop CE opportunities. Patzelt and Shepherd (2010) suggest that entrepreneurs are more likely to discover sustainable development opportunities the greater their knowledge of the natural and communal environment is. This is supported by Eide et al. (2020), who found that intellectual leadership induced more beneficial sustainable strategies. Firms and entrepreneurs are likely to take on more proactive environmental stances if they believe or have knowledge that such opportunities exist. They will then look more actively for such opportunities and have a greater chance of discovering them (Hart and Dowell 2011).

Second, it must be beneficial to firms to invest in such opportunities. Even if eco-innovation may be "a strategic enabler of entire value-chain transformations" as explained by De Jesus and Mendonça (2018, p. 77), studies investigating its influence on firm performance are indecisive (Alos-Simo et al. 2020). Studies indicate that sustainability strategies focusing on resource efficiency are likely to influence firm performance positively due to reduced cost (Eide et al. 2020). Also, if it is a competitive advantage to be 'environmentally friendly' (for instance by capturing conscious consumers) such strategies are more easily adapted. However, more radical changes, where the initial benefits are less obvious and outcome is uncertain, are likely to be more difficult to induce. This is typical of CE-needed transitions.

Third, a lack of alternative business models is found to limit transition to CE (Millette et al. 2020). Traditional business model thinking builds on three main parts: creating, delivering and capturing value (Jørgensen et al. 2019). In each part there will be a CE opportunity and/ or barrier, and the choice of business model will influence the impact on environment and society. In addition, there are barriers related to the perceived 'greenness' of products, processes or systems labelled as green innovation (Abdullah et al. 2016).

The 'R'-strategies are well established within the CE literature. From a business entrepreneur's perspective, however, it is not clear how these different strategies represent a viable fundament for a competitive business model. The viability of a CE strategy, and of the derived business models, depends on the wider political and economic framework and the degree to which this framework acts, on a structural level, as a facilitator or a barrier to the business models in question. This is closely connected to the need of radical innovations to enable transition into true CBMs (Hofmann and Jaeger-Erben 2020). Here, Merli et al. (2018) explain that 'closing the loops' strategies have been more widely studied, whereas less is known about 'slowing the loops' CE strategies. The latter require much more radical change both in product development and in consumption. Also, as previously discussed, linear business thinking and acting are often deeply rooted in dominant patterns of business decision-making and organizational communication (Hofmann and Jaeger-Erben 2020). Firm owners might also perceive CE as a distraction in the creation of wealth of individual businesses, since it is perceived as a socially responsible activity (Millette et al. 2020).

Truly circular business models will often imply radical changes to the business and its operation, which is likely to be a steep barrier for single businesses to overcome. CE business innovation is very much an experimental process, during which businesses face great risk and uncertainties (Chen et al. 2020). It often implies great financial, economic, and knowledge-based barriers (Millette et al. 2020). Furthermore, Lewandowski (2016) suggests that the fit between implementation of CE and handling factors hindering this process is a critical point in building CE business models. Also, the solutions might be outside the business' product or production line, and in need of new technology and knowledge. In these situations it is relevant to look at the impetus of the wider political and economic framework in supporting CBMs.

Governmental Regulation and Facilitation

The challenges at individual business level mean that collaborative, supportive and regulative efforts are much needed. As of now, De Jesus and Mendonça (2018) found CE globally to be driven primarily by 'soft' social, regulatory or institutional factors. Thus, public agencies have a crucial role in institutional framing, from institutional infrastructures to legal set-ups, as well as in R&D support and increasing social awareness. For instance, Hart and Dowell (2011) found that stakeholder integration, higher order learning and continuous innovation were important for establishing more proactive environmental attitudes. This is supported by Millette et al. (2020), who stress the need of multiple stakeholders to interact in order to provide information needed for CE entrepreneurship. Thus, networks, collaboration and supporting mechanisms emerge as important facilitators.

Governmental agencies and collective efforts through support system arrangements may reduce barriers. Doh et al. (2019) hold forth collective environmental entrepreneurship as a promising tool to respond to grand environmental challenges. This is understood as "the process through which businesses, government, and NGOs work as partners to leverage and combine their sector-specific competencies to discover, develop, and scale innovative adaptive responses to environmental challenges" (Doh et al. 2019, p. 451).

The lack of acceptance or neglect of scientific knowledge is often a challenge. The exchange of knowledge between scientists, government and communities is of critical importance but may not be prioritized by any of them (Millette et al. 2020). This unshared knowledge may contain important information and opportunities for CE entrepreneurs. But, if businesses themselves don't see the opportunities or can't afford to take collaborative actions, governmental incentives are critical in facilitating such processes.

CE-focused business incubators are another example of collaborative efforts that may aid individual firms in developing more CE business models (Millette et al. 2020). A CE incubator can collect and disseminate important information related to CE from many participants and facilitate related collaborative business opportunities. Examples include industrial coordination, creating projects for increased cooperation, and other incentives aimed at identifying, evaluating and inducing new interaction. Intermediary actors such as business consultants, can help individual firms to identify other partners and relevant stakeholders to 'solve problems' as well as facilitating knowledge transfer and participation in R&D projects (Nauwelaers 2011).

THE CE ENTREPRENEURIAL LANDSCAPE

The previous section is a sample of the many barriers that are faced by CE entrepreneurs, and illustrates the observed inertia against CE business entrepreneurship. To frame this complex picture, we propose a simple model of the CE entrepreneurial landscape (Figure 16.1). It aims to structure the relationship between the different CE strategies with their relevant business models, and the general political and economic context. This 'systemic context' consists of society's motivations for CE solutions, and the principal political means applied to achieve them. Further, the model also captures the influence of the two overarching framework issues discussed above – the physical basis of the economy and the growth imperative – on the economic context of CE business innovations. By locating the prospective CE business model within this entrepreneurial landscape, the entrepreneur and the actors in her support network will be better able to sort out the nature of the barriers and opportunities they are facing, and identify the best ways to proceed in realizing the business case.

CE Motivations and Strategies

Our model defines a two-dimensional landscape. The horizontal dimension describes society's motivation for pursuing increased circularity (the Whys): 'Damage prevention', 'Value creation' and 'Sustainability'. The vertical dimension represents policy tools or responses available for society to achieve its circularity goals (the Hows): 'Regulation', 'Business innovation' and 'Policy innovation'. The colours of brown, blue and green further differentiate the Whys.

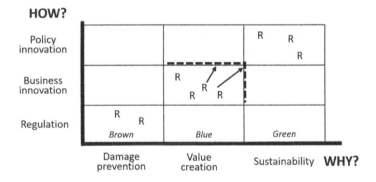

Figure 16.1   *The CE entrepreneurial landscape*

For illustration, we have plotted some R strategies in the landscape. The logic of the model suggests that relevant Rs will cluster along the main diagonal upwards and to the right. In the lower left rectangle we expect to find most of the 'Damage prevention' CE strategies. These Rs are mainly motivated by avoiding or reducing external costs related to the end stage of the linear material chains, and are found in waste policies and environmental regulation. Regulation is the main policy instrument in this domain of damage prevention. These are the 'brown' strategies, and associated business models are often developed and operated within the public sphere (e.g. municipalities).

The centre rectangle is a domain characterized by the 'Value creation' category on the horizontal axis. These are the blue CE strategies. This domain represents activities aimed to capture economic value from products or materials that would otherwise be lost. Such materials may be recyclable clean fractions, by-products and wastes related to production processes, or they could be products suitable for repair or reuse in a second-hand or remanufacture context. Blue CE strategies represent local 'loops' in the exergy flow that generate new value adding activities, and represent a response to society's desire to create new business activities, value added, jobs and economic growth. These strategies are compatible with business innovation policies within competitive market contexts.

The third category of Whys is 'Sustainability' – green strategies. This class of CE strategies, logically clustered in the upper right part of the model, is motivated by society's stated need to reduce, in absolute terms, the current wasteful and harmful overuse of natural resources. Green CE strategies thus represent an alternative at a more fundamental level to the prevailing economic logic promoting the LIE. Sustainability, by way of green CE strategies and business models, logically represents the ultimate goal for proponents of a circular economy.

Most CE strategies (Rs) are found at various locations along the diagonal of the model. A certain strategy, e.g. 'Reuse of materials', may be applied both in a regulatory municipal 'brown' context (within the waste handling system), and in a commercial 'blue' context (say, within an industrial park). The economic logic – rules of the game – may differ substantially between a regulatory setting in the brown case, and a purely competitive market environment in the blue case. Thus, although the CE strategy is the same, the dynamics of innovation and business model development may differ widely between the two contexts.

More generally, the way the different R strategies serve as a framework for business innovation, will depend on the specific strategy and on the political and economic context within which it is applied. And, as demonstrated by other contributions to this book, several of the CE strategies may be assumed to work in a variety of contexts. This illustrates how crucial it is, in an entrepreneurial setting, to acquire full information on all relevant regulatory, market and other important aspects of the context innovation takes place within. To realize the sustainability potential of the CE, Rs and their business models must be aimed at the upper right part of the landscape.

The Fundamental Systemic Barrier

Most importantly, however, we hypothesize that there exists a strong barrier (indicated by the thick dotted line) against entering the upper right domain of sustainable CE strategies and business models. This barrier exists as long as the 'growth imperative' continues to be the dominant economic logic of the global society. True sustainability oriented (green) business models will not work within a growth oriented economic market context. From a micro level perspective, a business model that aims at exergy conservation and slow material flows will not be competitive in a LIE environment. The rules of the economic game simply do not promote such businesses. From a macro perspective, an economic logic that aims for resource (and thus exergy) conservation, will necessarily generate less total economic value, and therefore conflict fundamentally with the growth imperative. This barrier, we hypothesize, is the main reason why CE business models still are so limited.

Breaking this barrier requires not only innovations at the business level, but also, and more fundamentally, a radical revision of the 'rules of the economic game'. We denote this 'Policy innovation' at the How dimension. How to break the 'growth imperative' and thereby open the playing field for truly green CE strategies and business models, is not clear. But we know, from the discussion of the entropy law, that such an economy necessarily must generate less economic activity than a growth economy, it must be focused on satisfying key societal needs at minimal exergy expenditure rather than maximizing economic value, and it must ensure a fair distribution of the jobs and economic value created. Key hallmarks of such an economy are that the absence of economic growth does not necessarily constitute a crisis, and that it brings about real progress towards a sustainable future.

From a CE innovation perspective, the transition interface between blue and green strategies and business models really is where efforts should be focused. It represents one of the determining missions of our time, and a wide-open space for important innovations at many levels. Policy innovations are needed to prepare the structural level of society for green business models, and wide-ranging innovations at the business level will be needed. In addition, the business support actors and stakeholders in general, including research and knowledge suppliers, must reorientate towards the green logic. We round off this section with a brief look at how this transition barrier could be attacked.

Managing the CE Transition

The Missions framework of the EU's research and innovation policy (Mazzucato 2018) and transition management and the multilevel perspective (Loorbach 2007; Geels 2011), are examples of higher level approaches that could address society's grand challenges, including sustainability. The possibility of framing these policy and transition approaches around the barriers of the green CE strategies would be an effort worth exploring at the macro level.

At the level of the entrepreneur and the entrepreneurial system, we find the *ecosystem* approach to be a promising framing. With a focus on the entrepreneurial context, it still embraces the wider set of actors and agencies deemed necessary in this transition. Entrepreneurial ecosystems focus on "the alignment structure of the multilateral set of partners that need to interact in order for a focal value proposition to materialize" (Adner 2017, p. 40). This focal value proposition may thus be the innovation system needed in order to realize green CE business models. Ecosystem thinking is particularly useful when there is a need for coordination that cannot be dealt with in markets and classical value systems (Jacobides et al. 2018). The heart of an ecosystem consists of the network of entrepreneurs, leadership, finance, talent, knowledge and support service, and a social context that enables interaction (Adner 2017). The orchestration and coordination of a complex set of partners is naturally critical in order to achieve the innovation objective and focal value proposition (Yaghmaie and Vanhaverbeke 2020).

CONCLUSION AND WAY FORWARD

Our model frames a complex barrier structure facing CE entrepreneurs aspiring to develop innovative business models within the truly sustainable green CE strategies. We find that the challenges of CBM innovation increase as the entrepreneur moves closer to the green region of the CE landscape. That is, those strategies inspired by reducing, slowing or even entirely avoiding resource flows. Business models developed around 'slowness' and resource efficient value chains fail to create sustainable business value in a fiercely competitive marketplace where growth, speed and volume are criteria of success. Individual businesses and entrepreneurs must play by the rules of the game, and a true circular economy requires different 'rules'. Micro level business entrepreneurs may not be in possession of agency to change these rules. Governmental support and collaborative efforts may aid entrepreneurs to transform into more circular business strategies. However so far these seem to be stuck in linear thinking and too slow a pace on changes. Prospective CBMs are often trapped by conflicting interests: sustaining traditional industry and jobs on the one hand, and the need of radical innovations for more circular and sustainable future economy on the other. Lowering these barriers will be particularly important for developing a truly sustainable economy.

The development of green circular business models therefore requires a rearrangement of the economic framework conditions at a systemic level that create the incentives and business logics that are required for a resource efficient circular economy to evolve. This endeavour is embedded in the urgently needed sustainability transition, and it must be broadly anchored and legitimized across the spectrum of actors and institutions in society. New ideas and innovations within many domains and levels of society are needed to achieve this transition.

On our way forward we find that governmental policies, support systems and intermediary actors play a crucial role, not only in nudging individual business towards CE, but also as facilitators of the more radical changes needed in industrial and entrepreneurial ecosystems. The importance of these actors may be underestimated, and to increase knowledge on this issue we suggest more research on the role of different stakeholders in such collaboration and transition.

REFERENCES

Abdullah, M., Zailani, S., Iranmanesh, M., & Jayaraman, K. (2016). Barriers to green innovation initiatives among manufacturers: The Malaysian case. *Review of Managerial Science*, 10(4), 683–709.

Acemoglu, D. (2012). Introduction to economic growth. *Journal of Economic Theory*, 147(2), 545–550.

Adner, R. (2017). Ecosystem as structure: An actionable construct for strategy. *Journal of Management*, 43(1), 39–58.

Alos-Simo, L., Antonio J., Verdu-Jover, A. L. J., & Gomez-Gras, J. M. (2020). Does activity sector matter for the relationship between eco-innovation and performance? Implications for cleaner production. *Journal of Cleaner Production*, 263, 121544.

Ayres, R., & Warr, B. (2010). *The Economic Growth Engine: How Energy and Work Drive Material Prosperity*. Cheltenham, UK and Northampton, MA, USA: Edward Elgar Publishing.

Boulding, K. E. (1966). The economics of the coming Spaceship Earth. In H. Jarrett (ed.), *Environmental Quality in a Growing Economy*. Baltimore, MD: Johns Hopkins University Press, 3–14.

Brataas, J. (1999). *Miljøledelse. Hvordan møter bedriften miljøutfordringene?* Kristiansand: Høyskoleforlaget.

Capilla, A. V., & Delgado, A. V. (2014). *Thanatia: The Destiny of the Earth's Mineral Resources. A Thermodynamic Cradle-to-Cradle Assessment*. Singapore: World Scientific Publishing.

Chen, L.-H., Hung, P., & Ma, H.-W. (2020). Integrating circular business models and development tools in the circular economy transition process: A firm-level framework. *Business Strategy and the Environment*, 29, 1887–1898.

De Bernardi, C., & Pedrini, M. (2020). Entrepreneurial behaviour: Getting eco-drunk by feeling environmental passion. *Journal of Cleaner Production*, 256, 120367.

De Jesus, A., & Mendonça, S. (2018). Lost in transition? Drivers and barriers in the eco-innovation road to the circular economy. *Ecological Economics*, 145, 75–89.

De Wit, M., Hoogzaad, J., & Von Daniels, C. (2020). *The Circularity Gap Report 2020*. Amsterdam: Ruparo.

Doh, J. P., Tashman P., & Benischke, M. H. (2019). Adapting to grand environmental challenges through collective entrepreneurship. *Academy of Management Perspectives*, 33, 450–468.

EC – European Commission (2019). *The European Green Deal*. Brussels, 11 December, COM(2019) 640 final.

EC – European Commission (2020). *A New Circular Economy Action Plan. For a Cleaner and More Competitive Europe*. Brussels, 11 March, COM(2020) 98 final.

ECESP – European Circular Economy Stakeholder Platform (2020). Strategies. https://circulareconomy .europa.eu/platform/en/strategies?page=1.

Eide, A. E., Saether, E. A. & Aspelund, A. (2020). An investigation of leaders' motivation, intellectual leadership, and sustainability strategy in relation to Norwegian manufacturers' performance. *Journal of Cleaner Production*, 254, 120053.

Ellen MacArthur Foundation (2013a). *Towards the Circular Economy Vol. 1: An Economic and Business Rationale for an Accelerated Transition*.

Ellen MacArthur Foundation (2013b). *Towards the Circular Economy Vol. 2: Opportunities for the Consumer Goods Sector*.

Ellen MacArthur Foundation (2014). *Towards the Circular Economy Vol. 3: Accelerating the Scale-Up across Global Supply Chains*.

Ellen MacArthur Foundation (2015). *Growth Within: A Circular Economy Vision for a Competitive Europe*.

Geels, F. W. (2011). The multi-level perspective on sustainability transitions: Responses to seven criticisms. *Environmental Innovation and Societal Transitions*, 1(1), 24–40.

Georgescu-Roegen, N. (1971). *The Entropy Law and the Economic Process*. Cambridge, MA: Harvard University Press.

Ghisellini, P., Cialani, C., & Ulgiati, S. (2016). A review on circular economy: The expected transition to a balanced interplay of environmental and economic systems. *Journal of Cleaner Production*, 114, 11–32.

Hart, S. L., & Dowell, G. (2011). Invited editorial: A natural-resource-based view of the firm: Fifteen years after. *Journal of Management*, 37(5), 1464–1479.

Hofmann, F., & Jaeger-Erben, M. (2020). Organizational transition management of circular business model innovations. *Business Strategy and the Environment*, 29, 2770–2788.

Jackson, T. (2017). *Prosperity without Growth? The Transition to a Sustainable Economy* (2nd ed.). London: Routledge.

Jacobides, M. G., Cennamo, C., & Gawer, A. (2018). Towards a theory of ecosystems. *Strategic Management Journal*, 39(8), 2255–2276.

Jørgensen, S., Pedersen, L. J. T., & Skard, S. E. R. (2019). Eksperimentering for bærekraftig forretnings-modellinnovasjon. *Magma*, 5, 51–59.

Kirchherr, J., Reike, D., & Hekkert, M. (2017). Conceptualizing the circular economy: An analysis of 114 definitions. *Resources, Conservation and Recycling*, 127, 221–232.

Lewandowski, M. (2016). Designing the business models for circular economy: Towards the conceptual framework. *Sustainability*, 8(1), 43.

Loorbach, D. (2007). Transition management: New mode of governance for sustainable development. Dutch Research Institute for Transitions (DRIFT).

Mazzucato, M. (2018). *Missions. Mission-Oriented Research & Innovation in the European Union. A Problem-Solving Approach to Fuel Innovation-Led Growth*. Luxembourg: Publications Office of the European Union.

Merli, R., Preziosi, M., & Acampora A. (2018). How do scholars approach the circular economy? A systematic literature review. *Journal of Cleaner Production*, 178, 703–722.

Millette, S., Hull, C. E., & Williams, E. (2020). Business incubators as effective tools for driving circular economy. *Journal of Cleaner Production*, 266, 121999.

Nauwelaers, C. (2011). Intermediaries in regional innovation systems: Role and challenges for policy. In P. Cooke et al. (eds.), *Handbook of Regional Innovation and Growth*. Cheltenham, UK and Northampton, MA, USA: Edward Elgar Publishing, 467–481.

Patzelt, H., & Shepherd, D. A. (2010). Recognizing opportunities for sustainable development. *Entrepreneurship Theory and Practice*, 35(4), 631–652.

Potting, J., Hekkert, M. P., Worrell, E., & Hanemaaijer, A. (2017). *Circular Economy: Measuring Innovation in the Product Chain* (No. 2544). The Hague: PBL Publishers.

Rohrig, B. (2015). *Smartphones: Smart Chemistry*. American Chemical Society. https://www.acs .org/content/acs/en/education/resources/highschool/chemmatters/past-issues/archive-2014-2015/ smartphones.html.

Saad-Filho, A., & Johnston, D. (eds.) (2005). *Neoliberalism: A Critical Reader*. Chicago: University of Chicago Press.

Science Europe (2016). *In a Resource-Constrained World: Think Exergy, not Energy*. D/2016/13.324/5. Brussels.

Stahel, W. R. (2019). *The Circular Economy: A User's Guide*. London: Routledge.

UNEP – United Nations Environment Programme (2020). *UNEP Circularity Platform*. https:// buildingcircularity.org.

Wall, G. (1977). *Exergy – A Useful Concept within Resource Accounting*. Report 77-42, Chalmers University of Technology and University of Göteborg.

Wilhite, H. (2016). *The Political Economy of the Low Carbon Transformation: Breaking the Habits of Capitalism*. London and New York: Routledge.

Yaghmaie, P., & Vanhaverbeke, W. (2020). Identifying and describing constituents of innovation eco-systems: A systematic review of the literature. *EuroMed Journal of Business*, 15(3), 283–314.

York, J. G., O'Neil, I., & Sarasvathy, S. D. (2016). Exploring environmental entrepreneurship: Identity coupling, venture goals, and stakeholder incentives. *Journal of Management Studies*, 53(5), 695–737.

17. How innovations catalyse the circular economy: building a map of circular economy innovation types from a multiple-case study[1]

Anil Engez, Valtteri Ranta and Leena Aarikka-Stenroos

INTRODUCTION

In the field of environmental sustainability, the circular economy (CE) has attracted global interest concerning resource efficiency, conservation of natural resources, and increasing carbon neutrality (Ghisellini et al. 2016). The CE has been identified as a concrete means of implementing sustainability into business (Ghisellini et al. 2016) and is strongly driven by innovation, as it requires firms to introduce novel products and processes that adhere to CE principles (Prieto-Sandoval et al. 2018). In the CE, the value of materials and products is maintained to reduce demand for virgin natural resources (Geissdoerfer et al. 2018). Thus, it may require companies to adapt or replace their current business models (Prieto-Sandoval et al. 2018) and innovate in diverse ways (Mariadoss et al. 2011) to generate innovation that catalyses the CE.

Environmentally sustainable innovations have been framed as eco-innovations (De Jesus and Mendonça 2018; Hellström 2007; Prieto-Sandoval et al. 2018; Rennings 2000) and product and CE business model innovations (Bocken et al. 2016; den Hollander et al. 2017; Vasiljevic-Shikaleska et al. 2017). Eco-innovations are socio-technical solutions that preserve resources by allowing for the recovery of resources and mitigate environmental degradation (De Jesus and Mendonça 2018). Thus, they provide a foundation for CE innovations. Studies have highlighted the potential of eco-innovations to contribute to environmental sustainability but have under-explored the related aspects of innovation management. The consequent research gap regards the innovation types that enable the CE and the sustainability issues that those innovations aim to solve. To address this gap, the present chapter examines the diversity of CE innovations through innovation management lenses to illuminate the innovation needs of firms, which range from technology to business development for sustainability and the CE. To this end, it maps CE innovation types and their characteristics to uncover innovation diversity in the CE in theory and to guide managers and practitioners in their innovation efforts to develop sustainable solutions. The study considers three research questions (RQs):

RQ1: What are the CE innovation types from the technology and innovation management perspective?

RQ2: Which sustainability issues are addressed by the CE innovations?

RQ3: Which benefits do CE innovations pursue?

We apply an analysis framework that differentiates between four organizational innovation types: product, process, service, and business model innovations (Crossan and Apaydin

2010). We further divide each innovation type into three sub-types based on our analysis. Following this categorization, we provide examples for each sub-type with references to CE innovations developed by various companies. Our study not only introduces a new, nuanced, and explicit categorization of CE innovations with comprehensive sub-types but also explores the pursued sustainability implications and the pursued benefits of the various types. While similar studies have been limited to the descriptive and explorative level and focused on the product design and business model strategies (Bocken et al. 2016; den Hollander et al. 2017; Vasiljevic-Shikaleska et al. 2017), this research extends the CE innovation categorization approach by presenting the process and service innovation categories along with the relational aspect of CE innovations and sustainability issues. Consequently, the study connects the CE with technology and innovation management research streams.

This chapter is structured as follows. After the introduction, the second section discusses the innovation types in the CE to explain the theoretical background of the study. The third section then presents the research design. Subsequently, the fourth section examines product, process, service, and business model innovations and their sub-types through company offerings. The final section concludes the chapter and specifies the theoretical contribution, practical implications, and future research avenues.

INNOVATION IN CE: INNOVATION TYPES

The CE is a restorative and generative economic system that aims to maintain the value of products, materials, and resources by reducing, reusing, recycling, and recovering materials in production/distribution and consumption processes (Kirchherr et al. 2017; Ranta et al. 2018). In CE, innovations are developed to slow and close resource loops (Bocken et al. 2016). Slowing resource loops refers to the process of decreasing the rate of material flows from production to recycling. It can be achieved by extending a product's lifespan through the use of durable materials and a design that is repairable, reusable, upgradable, and suitable for disassembly and reassembly (Bocken et al. 2016; Stahel 2016). Meanwhile, closing resource loops refers to a recycling process that utilizes materials from products that are no longer usable. Therefore, it seeks to close the loop between post-use waste and production (Stahel 2016). These two approaches are dominant in CE innovation literature. To expand this view and ground CE innovations in innovation management literature, we review the innovation types of product, process, service, and business model innovations (Crossan and Apaydin 2010) within their CE context.

Product Innovations

Product innovation is realized as an assembled product that is sold to a customer once it is manufactured and which evokes perceived newness, novelty, originality, uniqueness, and usefulness of the innovation (Henard and Szymanski 2001). When developing product innovations for the CE, it is important to apply sustainability principles at an early stage in the product design process. These principles include designing for a technological cycle (emphasizing the cycle of the products of service), a biological cycle (using materials that can biodegrade through e.g. composting), disassembly and reassembly, product-life extension, and long-lasting products (Bocken et al. 2016; Vasiljevic-Shikaleska et al. 2017). Another approach to classify CE product innovations considers the integrity and recycling aspects in the product design (den Hollander et al. 2017). Designing for integrity focuses on preventing obsolescence at the product/component level, while designing for recycling applies such focus at the material level.

Process Innovations

Process innovation refers to the implementation of "new production methods, new management approaches, and new technology that can be used to improve production and management processes" (Wang and Ahmed 2004, p. 305), which describes processes that enable internal value creation for a firm (Crossan and Apaydin 2010). A process innovation may lead to the emergence of new products or enhance an existing product's performance, design, and cost attributes or the materials/components of which it is composed (Maine et al. 2012). Therefore, process innovations are not only internal to one firm but can also be commercialized and transferred to other firms.

Service Innovations

A service is an asset that serves a customer need and provides a benefit to the customer. Thus, it is an inherent value that is transferred from the provider to the recipient (O'Sullivan et al. 2002). Service innovation emphasizes the development of new service offerings and concepts and intertwines tangible (e.g. product forms) and intangible (e.g. processes, knowledge) aspects of an innovation (Kindström and Kowalkowski 2014), in which information technology is influential. As the digital era departs from the goods-dominant logic of value creation, service innovations need to be network-centric, information-centric, and experience-centric to remain competitive in the market (Lusch and Nambisan 2015). This need requires firms to realign their dynamic capabilities of sensing opportunities and threats, seizing opportunities, and reconfiguring their resources (Kindström et al. 2013; Teece 2007). The service-dominant logic dictates that firms must concentrate on actor-to-actor networks, digitize information, and densify and integrate their resources (Lusch and Nambisan 2015). In the CE, services can reduce the overall use of resources by allowing multiple users to share underutilized resources or helping to optimize the use of resources by a single user (Ranta et al. 2020). Furthermore, services contribute to closing loops through recycling (Stahel 2016).

Business Model Innovations

A firm's business model consists of three main elements: the value proposition to customers, value creation and delivery, and value capture (Teece 2010). Business model innovation entails changes in an organization's business model elements, which concern the target segments, the offering, value chain organizations, revenue capture mechanisms, and the value proposition itself. Business model innovation complements the traditional subjects of process, product, and service innovations by devising a novel way of creating, delivering, and capturing value (Foss and Saebi 2016). In the CE, circular business models aim to generate profits from the flow of materials and products over time (Bocken et al. 2016).

RESEARCH DESIGN

Since the current literature on innovations in the field of CE is nascent, we employed an explorative approach to fulfil our objective. Specifically, we conducted a multiple-case study of 27 firms from Finland with 27 innovative offerings that have been introduced to domestic and global markets to catalyse the CE. To sample forerunners and suppliers with innovative offerings, we selected our cases from a compilation by the Finnish Innovation Fund (SITRA), which is a national leader and independent expert organization in promoting awareness of CE and the technology industries of Finland. The offering descriptions include suppliers' explanations of new features of the offering (i.e. innovation reflecting the sustainability transition) and the value that the offering imparts to customers and the provider. Following our strategy for gathering a comprehensive and inclusive data set, the offerings are based on a variety of innovations, including unprecedented usages of recycled materials, new services for lengthening product lifecycles, novel and more sustainable production processes, and new business models for reusing and sharing products. Thus, they cover each of the innovation types identified in the literature.

As our units of analysis, we used the four aforementioned innovation types. The analysis chart lists the following aspects: the main innovation types, three sub-types, innovation examples per sub-type, the company that developed the innovation, the main sustainability issue addressed by the innovation, and the pursued benefit/value. The final framework synthesizes the chart into a conceptual figure that depicts the CE innovations and their sub-types in the form of a tree diagram.

FINDINGS

Our analysis of 27 innovative offerings by forerunner firms in the Finnish CE ecosystem encompasses the four innovation types and their value in terms of sustainability. The analysis informed a map of the main CE innovation types and their sub-types (see Figure 17.1).

The next sections detail our findings per CE innovation type with examples. Table 17.1 contains an overview of the CE innovation types and their corresponding sub-types, example offerings from companies, explanations of the main sustainability issues that the innovations address, and the pursued benefits. A detailed analysis follows.

Product Innovations

Recyclable products that are suitable for return to circulation
As an example of this innovation type, Honkajoki produces fertilizers made from organic waste from local communities and industrial operators. In industrial plants, animal-based waste is converted into raw materials for the energy, cosmetics, fertilizer, and animal feed industries. A second example is the biochar product by Carbons/Carbofex. The pyrolysis process produces biochar along with gas, pyrolysis oil, wood vinegar, and heat. The latter can be distributed in the district heating network. Because of its high water and nutrient absorption capacity, biochar is effective as a biofilter in stormwater management systems and a growing medium in agriculture and for the treatment of seepage water runoff. A third example is Durat's production of recycled interior design materials from plastic waste, which uses recy-

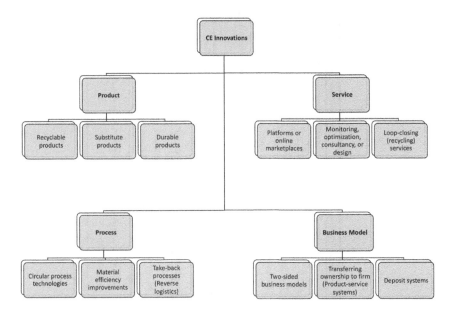

Figure 17.1   The main CE innovation types and their sub-types

cled post-industrial plastics to create interior materials, such as kitchen and bathroom sinks and kitchen worktops. Recycling reduces the demand for virgin raw materials.

Substitute products that are more sustainable than their traditional alternatives
Substitute products intend to replace current unsustainable products. An example is Gold & Green's range of plant protein products made from oats and legumes as alternatives to meat-based products. Meat production is inherently unsustainable due to the high greenhouse gas emissions that result from methane production by livestock (Steinfield et al. 2006). Similarly, bio-based renewable materials intend to replace non-renewable materials, such as plastics. One example is Sulapac's development of biodegradable packaging products that use wood- and plant-based binders, such as wood chips and cellulose. The reusability, recyclability, and biodegradability attributes of these renewable materials define them as a sustainable alternative to plastics.

Durable products with a long lifespan
Durable products have a long utilization period. Durable products include high-quality materials and components that last longer without breaking down or becoming worn out, which extends the product's lifespan. An example of this innovation is a laser coating created by Kokkola LCC that increases the durability of metal parts in the metal, energy, and process industries. Durable products require fewer repairs and component replacements over time, which slows resource loops by eliminating new raw material usage. They also enable users to reduce repair and maintenance costs, although their purchase price might exceed that of regular products.

Table 17.1   *Circular economy innovation types*

Innovation type	Sub-type	Example	Company	Sustainability issue addressed	Pursued benefit/value
Product	(1) Recyclable products	Biochar to be used as growing medium and as biofilters	Carbons/Carbofex	Low nutrient recycling and eutrophication	A sustainable improvement for soil quality, acting as a carbon sink
		Fertilizers and raw materials from animal by-products	Honkajoki	Low nutrient recycling and eutrophication	Turning animal-based waste into pure and safe raw materials (e.g. pet foods, biofuels, and pharmaceuticals)
		Solid recyclable surface material containing recycled post-industrial plastics	Durat	Low recycling rate of interior materials (e.g. worktops, sinks)	Durable sustainable products made from recycled plastics
	(2) Substitute products	Plant protein products from oats and legumes	Gold & Green	Meat production and consumption (greenhouse gas emissions)	Replacing meat products that have significant emissions and land footprints with plant-based alternatives
		Biodegradable packaging using wood-based materials as raw materials	Sulapac	Non-renewable plastic materials	Replacing plastic packaging with biodegradable wood-based packaging
	(3) Durable products	Reducing maintenance costs and increasing durability with laser coating	Kokkola LCC	Unnecessary consumption of raw materials	Lengthening component and product lifecycles

Innovation type	Sub-type	Example	Company	Sustainability issue addressed	Pursued benefit/value
Process	(1) Circular process technologies	Vegetable oil refining process to produce renewable diesel fuel	Neste	Fossil fuels (greenhouse gas emissions)	Replacing non-renewable, fossil fuel-based oil products with bio-based renewable alternatives
		Technology for producing textile fibre from cellulose	Spinnova	High water consumption in current textile fibre production	Replacing polluting and water-intensive cotton and synthetic materials production with wood-based textile fibre
		Extraction and purification of used alkaline batteries to make fertilizers	Tracegrow	Low circulation of zinc and manganese in soil	Extracting otherwise wasted valuable materials, producing recycled nutrients
		Process for turning industrial waste into geopolymer-based construction materials	Betolar	Low utilization of industrial waste	Replacing high CO_2 footprint cement-based concrete with environmentally friendly geopolymer concrete using industrial waste as raw material
	(2) Material efficiency improvements	New uses for by-products and use of barley husk for energy production instead of peat	Altia	Low utilization of industrial waste	Reducing industrial waste through improved utilization of by-products
	(3) Take-back processes (Reverse logistics)	Take-back process for cardboard, glass, plastic, and metal packaging	Rinki	Low packaging recycling	Enabling source separation for recyclables, improving recycling rates, and preventing incineration of waste
		Take-back process for reusable delivery packaging for online retailers	RePack	Non-renewable plastic materials	Halting the growth of packaging waste from online sales by providing reusable postal packaging

Innovation type	Sub-type	Example	Company	Sustainability issue addressed	Pursued benefit/value
Service	(1) Platforms or online marketplaces	Online marketplace that convenes the sellers and buyers of used goods	Tori.fi	Low circulation of reusable consumer goods	Providing a convenient marketplace for trading used products
		Online marketplace for surplus food	ResQ Club	Food waste	Ability for grocery stores and restaurants to capture revenue from expiring products, access to discounted products for consumers
		Battery optimization	Bamomas	Misuse of batteries and lack of information on battery usage rates	Lengthening product lifecycles and optimizing value gained from the product by customers
	(2) Monitoring, optimization, consultancy, or design	Waste management optimization	Enevo	Low digitalization in waste management operations	Inefficient logistics causing both unnecessary greenhouse gas emissions and overflow of waste collection containers
		Supply and optimized spreading of nutrients on soil	Soilfood	Low nutrient recycling	Improving soil quality with nutrients made from recycled materials
		Predictive real-time maintenance	Konecranes	Unnecessary maintenance visits and early replacement of spare parts	Lengthening product lifecycles
	(3) Loop-closing (recycling) services	Energy recycling in the form of district heating from excess industrial waste heat	Calefa	Transferring excess heat into air or water instead of recovery and recycling	Improving the energy efficiency of the system, reducing greenhouse gas emissions

Innovation type	Sub-type	Example	Company	Sustainability issue addressed	Pursued benefit/value
Business model	(1) Two-sided business model	Acquiring label waste and turning it into new products for sales	UPM	Low utilization of industrial waste	Turning waste into a product, reducing incineration of waste, and replacing virgin raw materials with recycled ones
		Buy-back of old spare parts to repair and resell them	Ponsse	Low utilization of reusable old spare parts	Lengthening product lifecycles and preventing product components from becoming waste
		Solar power as a service	NAPS	Fossil fuels (greenhouse gas emissions)	Replacing non-renewable, polluting energy sources with clean, renewable alternatives
	(2) Transferring product ownership from customer to the firm (Product-service systems)	Work uniform and textile-leasing model	Lindström	Textile waste	Reducing textile waste and need for new products through reuse and maintenance of products
		Shared mobility on pay-per-minute basis	Voi/Tier	Fossil fuels (greenhouse gas emissions)	Reducing the need for owning own products through a service-based business model
	(3) Deposit systems	Managing and developing beverage package return and deposit systems	Palpa	Low packaging recycling	Ensuring high recycling rates for beverage packaging, incentivizing consumers to return beverage packaging
		Remanufacturing used tractor gearboxes and managing and developing their return and deposit systems	Valtra	Low recycling rate of used tractor gearboxes	Lengthening product lifecycles, providing an affordable, cost-efficient alternative for new products through remanufacturing

Process Innovations

Circular process technologies that enable novel and efficient processing of a certain type of waste or used product

An example in this category is the hydrotreated vegetable oil (HVO) refinery process by which Neste produces diesel fuel. This process employs several forms of waste and residue as raw materials (e.g. used cooking oil, animal fat from food industry waste, and vegetable oil processing waste and residues). Generating diesel from renewable materials results in up to a 90 per cent reduction in greenhouse gas emissions compared to fossil diesel production. Another example is Spinnova's process of producing textile fibre from cellulose. The company partners with a eucalyptus pulp producer, an expert company in cellulose fibre, and several clothing brands. Other examples in this category include Betolar's transformation of industrial waste into geopolymer-based construction materials and Tracegrow's extraction and purification of used alkaline batteries to produce organic fertilizers.

Material efficiency improvements to increase utilization rate

Material efficiency improvement processes aim to maximize the utilization rate of a material by modifying the material or its use process. Because the material can be used for longer periods, the higher utilization rate reduces carbon dioxide emissions and costs by eliminating the need for new raw material production/usage and providing energy savings. An example in this category is the usage of barley husk as the main fuel for steam energy production in Altia's Koskenkorva distillery. The plant uses barley grain to manufacture the spirit and produces starch and animal feed as sidestreams. In this process, carbon dioxide is captured and employed in greenhouse farming, and ashes are given to farmers to use as fertilizer, which results in a material efficiency of 99 per cent.

Take-back processes for products that are no longer in use (reverse logistics)

In this category, firms take back usable materials or parts of a product and return them to the market for reuse, optionally after remanufacturing or recycling them. Producers benefit from this process through profits generated from the reuse, remanufacture, or recycling processes of reclaimed products and materials. An example is the eco take-back point network of Rinki, which has over 1,850 take-back points for cardboard, glass, and metal packaging and over 500 take-back points for plastic packaging. The collected packaging waste materials are processed into raw materials for new products. Another example is RePack's reusable delivery packaging for online retailers. The take-back process starts when end users return empty packages by post for free. They are rewarded for returning the packages, which enables a high return rate. Apart from packaging, batteries, cars, and electronics are other consumer products that are widely considered suitable for take-back processes and further refurbishing or recycling.

Service Innovations

Platforms/online marketplaces on which people can connect and share or sell used products

An example of this innovation is Tori's online platform, which facilitates consumer-to-consumer (C2C) sales and thus slows resource loops by encouraging the reuse of goods. As another example, ResQ Club targets the issue of food waste by offering a location-based online platform on which restaurants and supermarkets can sell their surplus or nearly expired food products at a discount at the end of the day. Once the food products are posted on the platform, end-users can pay the reduced price online and collect the food from the restaurant or super-market. This service allows restaurants and supermarkets to generate additional revenue from surplus food that would otherwise be wasted. Additionally, it enables customers to save time on cooking and enjoy restaurant-quality food.

Monitoring, optimization, consultancy, or design services

As an example in this category, the company Soilfood, which specializes in nutrient recycling, offers soil improvement services to its clients. The company supplies and spreads recycled nutrients on soil according to the soil properties. By using recycled nutrients as organic ferti-lizers, farmers can improve crop yields while minimizing fertilizer costs. Another example in this category is Bamomas' extension of the lifespan of industrial batteries through optimiza-tion. This service uses sensors for measuring the voltage, current, temperature, and water refill levels of the batteries to pursue more efficient use of batteries through maintenance and the detection of end-of-life batteries for replacement. A third example is Enevo's collection of data from waste management operations for optimization analysis. The company installs sensors inside waste containers to monitor the fullness of the container. This information allows waste collection once a container is completely full, which lowers logistics costs. The sensors are key to monitoring and optimization services, as both cases employ them in providing their services. A fourth example in this category is the predictive real-time maintenance service of Konecranes, which eliminates unnecessary maintenance visits and early replacement of spare parts. The service benefits both suppliers and customers, as both parties can save on time and costs. The services in this category can be diversified by using different types of sensor, such as vision and imaging, temperature, proximity, position, pressure, or humidity sensors.

Loop-closing (recycling) services

As an example in this category, Calefa recycles energy from excess industrial waste heat to convert into district heating. Recycling the waste heat reduces costs and carbon dioxide emis-sions, as the captured heat can be sold or reused in buildings, and it minimizes the additional heat generation requirement. The company closes the loop by recovering and recycling the excess heat instead of transferring it into the air or water.

Business Model Innovations

Diversification of the business model through a two-sided design

In this category, a single firm provides waste management services to obtain the required raw materials and then produces new products from those materials. For example, the forest industry company UPM offers recycling services for self-adhesive label by-products and then transforms them into magazine paper, paper liner, composite material, or energy. The company maintains a two-sided business model that establishes a waste management service for customers of its label business alongside an entirely new business of producing and selling products that are made from the label waste. As another example in this category, the business model of Ponsse, which specializes in forestry vehicles and machinery, entails buying back its old spare parts to later repair and resell them. This approach increases the utilization rate of reusable old spare parts.

Transferring product ownership from customer to firm (product-service systems)
These innovations replace the one-time product purchase fee for customers with continuous service fees throughout the use of the product. Lindström has adopted this business model in leasing work uniforms and equipment to its clients for a certain period. With this service, companies can avoid spending a large lump sum on work uniforms, and they can focus on their core business activities while the provider company assumes responsibility for clothing maintenance and ensures that the equipment is in good condition and has a long lifespan. Another example is the design, implementation, and maintenance of photovoltaic systems (e.g. solar panels) for clients by NAPS. The company generates revenue by periodically billing its clients, who only pay for the photovoltaic power produced on their roofs. A final example in this category is the rental of electric scooters by Voi/Tier via a mobile application, where users pay on a per-minute basis.

Deposit systems where customers reclaim deposit amount upon returning used products
An example in this category is a bottle return system by Palpa. The broad range of the beverage bottle recycling network in Finland facilitates a beverage container recycling rate of over 90 per cent. When a customer buys a beverage from a supermarket, its price includes a deposit for the bottle, which can be reclaimed by returning the empty bottle to an automated reverse vending machine. The machine transfers the bottle to the respective container for its material (e.g. glass, plastic, or can), which it identifies by scanning the barcode of the bottle. The machine automatically compresses the collected plastic bottles and cans to accommodate more returns and increase the cost efficiency of transportation. Once the materials are transported to the recycling centre, they are further processed into raw materials for new beverage bottles. The recycling of cans is highly sustainable; because of the lightness and durability of aluminium, it consumes only 5 per cent of the energy of the first manufacturing process. Meanwhile, coloured plastic bottle flakes can be repurposed as raw material for the textile industry. The whole process is carried out by the non-profit company Palpa. Cooperation among the manufacturers and importers of beverages, consumers, stores and supermarkets, logistics companies, and operators is vital to realize an efficient recycling process.

Another example is the innovation of Valtra, which specializes in tractor and agricultural machinery manufacturing, in its deposit scheme for used tractor gearboxes. In this model, the company remanufactures used tractor gearboxes, and it manages and develops their return and deposit systems. Remanufactured gearboxes are sold at a price that is 30–40 per cent lower than that of new products. In addition to the purchase price of the remanufactured gearbox, the customer pays for an additional deposit that amounts to approximately 50 per cent of the gearbox price. If the purchased gearbox breaks down after the one-year warranty period, the customer can return it to the company and reclaim the deposit. The company will then take back the broken gearbox, fix it, and remanufacture it for the next customer. Remanufacturing requires nearly 85 per cent less energy than manufacturing a brand new gearbox.

DISCUSSION AND CONCLUSIONS

Studies on sustainability and CE transition have strongly emphasized the role of 'eco-innovations' (De Jesus and Mendonça 2018; Hellström 2007; Rennings 2000). This chapter has employed the term 'CE innovations' to highlight the recirculation of resources in reuse, recycling, and renewal processes to slow and close resource loops (Bocken et al. 2016). The term also stresses the significance of the circularity aspect of the innovations for sustainability. We have divided CE innovations into four types and three sub-types for each for a total of 12 CE innovation sub-types. Our categorization is based on Crossan and Apaydin's (2010) framework of organizational innovation as an outcome and thus connected the CE and technology and innovation management stream, which supports a clearer understanding of the CE for organizations that are at the forefront of advancing the CE (Vasiljevic-Shikaleska et al. 2017). Our analysis reveals four innovation types in the CE (product, process, service, and business model) and provides insight into their benefits and sustainability impacts. The CE innovation types are here considered as categories in a typology (not a taxonomy), in which each type is kind of archetype. Therefore, the types can overlap and interact (e.g. technological process innovation can lead to a business model innovation), and an empirical case can hold characteristics of several CE innovation types.

Theoretical Contributions

The examination of the main CE innovation types in this study contributes to innovation literature in the areas of eco-innovation and sustainable innovation (De Jesus and Mendonça 2018; Hellström 2007; Rennings 2000). To build on the typology of innovation forms by Crossan and Apaydin (2010), the study has cited examples of CE innovations and further categorized them into their corresponding innovation type. Therefore, the study has devised a new typology for CE innovations that can increase raw material availability, energy savings, and product/material utilization rates over the lifecycle as well as reduce carbon emissions. This study has extended beyond the descriptive and explorative level of previous literature (Bocken et al. 2016; den Hollander et al. 2017; Vasiljevic-Shikaleska et al. 2017), to establish a CE innovation categorization that considers the process and service innovation types alongside the relational aspects of the CE innovations and sustainability issues. Thus, it offers a new, nuanced, and explicit categorization of CE innovations and comprehensive sub-types while addressing ongoing global sustainability issues that can be mitigated by innovating within those categories.

Practical Implications

The identified CE innovation types and sub-types can guide managers in (re-)designing their customer value propositions and approaches to creating, delivering, and capturing value in line with sustainable development goals. Sustainable design is essential to improve resource efficiency and reduce the negative environmental impacts of products and services. Companies must transform their linear business models into circular ones to meet the urgent demand for sustainable innovations that can combat the acceleration of global warming. The categorization in this study can act as a guide for emerging innovations to be designed taking into account their environmental impact.

The refined categorization of innovation types reveals innovations that enable the introduction of the CE into a firm's operations. Thus, it provides managers with a clear set of options for use in planning. Managers can also apply the categorization to consider the interplay of different types of innovation; for example, business managers who are designing a business model for a technological innovation that supports efficient reuse of products should be interested in the process and business model innovations that facilitate profitable implementation of the technological innovation. Meanwhile, technology managers should consider the technological CE process capabilities under development within a firm in light of other potentially necessary types of innovation. Our CE innovation categorization clarifies the CE and can inform idea generation at the beginning of the innovation process.

Future Research Avenues

This study has explored innovation examples from numerous companies. Future research could examine the dynamics of the relationship between firms and stakeholders in successful introductions of CE innovations. Such findings could deliver crucial guidance for firms in collaborating with stakeholders and for stakeholders in supporting the introduction of the CE in firms.

ACKNOWLEDGEMENTS

This work is supported by the Academy of Finland's 'Circular Economy Catalysts: From Innovation to Business Ecosystems (CICAT2025)' research funding (grant ID 320194), the Academy of Finland's 'Profi4 – Urban Platform for the Circular Economy (UPCE)' research funding (grant ID 318940), and the research grant that was awarded to Anil Engez by the Jenny and Antti Wihuri Foundation.

NOTE

REFERENCES

Bocken, N. M. P., de Pauw, I., Bakker, C., & van der Grinten, B. (2016). Product design and business model strategies for a circular economy. *Journal of Industrial and Production Engineering*, 33(5), 308–320.

Crossan, M. M., & Apaydin, M. (2010). A multi-dimensional framework of organizational innovation: A systematic review of the literature. *Journal of Management Studies*, 47(6), 1154–1191.

De Jesus, A., & Mendonça, S. (2018). Lost in transition? Drivers and barriers in the eco-innovation road to the circular economy. *Ecological Economics*, 145, 75–89.

den Hollander, M. C., Bakker, C. A., & Hultink, E. J. (2017). Product design in a circular economy: Development of a typology of key concepts and terms. *Journal of Industrial Ecology*, 21(3), 517–525.

Foss, N. J., & Saebi, T. (2016). Fifteen years of research on business model innovation: How far have we come, and where should we go? *Journal of Management*, 43(1), 200–227.

Geissdoerfer, M., Morioka, S. N., de Carvalho, M. M., & Evans, S. (2018). Business models and supply chains for the circular economy. *Journal of Cleaner Production*, 190, 712–721.

Ghisellini, P., Cialani, C., & Ulgiati, S. (2016). A review on circular economy: The expected transition to a balanced interplay of environmental and economic systems. *Journal of Cleaner Production*, 114, 11–32.

Hellström, T. (2007). Dimensions of environmentally sustainable innovation: The structure of eco-innovation concepts. *Sustainable Development*, 15(3), 148–159.

Henard, D. H., & Szymanski, D. M. (2001). Why some new products are more successful than others. *Journal of Marketing Research*, 38(3), 362–375.

Kindström, D., & Kowalkowski, C. (2014). Service innovation in product-centric firms: A multidimensional business model perspective. *Journal of Business and Industrial Marketing*, 29(2), 96–111.

Kindström, D., Kowalkowski, C., & Sandberg, E. (2013). Enabling service innovation: A dynamic capabilities approach. *Journal of Business Research*, 66(8), 1063–1073.

Kirchherr, J., Reike, D., & Hekkert, M. (2017). Conceptualizing the circular economy: An analysis of 114 definitions. *Resources, Conservation and Recycling*, 127, 221–232.

Lusch, R. F., & Nambisan, S. (2015). Service innovation: A service-dominant logic perspective. *MIS Quarterly: Management Information Systems*, 39(1), 155–175.

Maine, E., Lubik, S., & Garnsey, E. (2012). Process-based vs. product-based innovation: Value creation by nanotech ventures. *Technovation*, 32(3–4), 179–192.

Mariadoss, B. J., Tansuhaj, P. S., & Mouri, N. (2011). Marketing capabilities and innovation-based strategies for environmental sustainability: An exploratory investigation of B2B firms. *Industrial Marketing Management*, 40(8), 1305–1318.

O'Sullivan, J., Edmond, D., ter Hofstede, A., Benatallah, B., & Casati, F. (2002). What's in a service? *Distributed and Parallel Databases*, 12(2), 117–133.

Prieto-Sandoval, V., Jaca, C., & Ormazabal, M. (2018). Towards a consensus on the circular economy. *Journal of Cleaner Production*, 179, 605–615.

Ranta, V., Aarikka-Stenroos, L., Ritala, P., & Mäkinen, S. J. (2018). Exploring institutional drivers and barriers of the circular economy: A cross-regional comparison of China, the US, and Europe. *Resources, Conservation and Recycling*, 135, 70–82.

Ranta, V., Keränen, J., & Aarikka-Stenroos, L. (2020). How B2B suppliers articulate customer value propositions in the circular economy: Four innovation-driven value creation logics. *Industrial Marketing Management*, 87, 291–305.

Rennings, K. (2000). Redefining innovation: Eco-innovation research and the contribution from ecological economics. *Ecological Economics*, 32(2), 319–332.

Stahel, W. R. (2016). The circular economy. *Nature*, 531(7595), 435–438.

Steinfeld, H., Gerber, P., Wassenaar, T., Castel, V., Rosales, M., & de Haan, C. (2006). *Livestock's Long Shadow, Environmental Issues and Options. Livestock, Environment, and Development Initiative*. Rome: United Nations Food and Agriculture Organization.

Teece, D. J. (2007). Explicating dynamic capabilities: The nature and microfoundations of (sustainable) enterprise performance. *Strategic Management Journal*, 28(13), 1319–1350.

Teece, D. J. (2010). Business models, business strategy and innovation. *Long Range Planning*, 43(2–3), 172–194.

Vasiljevic-Shikaleska, A., Gjozinska, B., & Stojanovikj, M. (2017). The circular economy: A pathway to sustainable future. *Journal of Sustainable Development*, 7(17), 13–30.

Wang, C. L., & Ahmed, P. K. (2004). The development and validation of the organisational innovativeness construct using confirmatory factor analysis. *European Journal of Innovation Management*, 7(4), 303–313.

18. Salmon farming firms moving towards resource circularity: a typology of resource loop innovations

Karin Wigger, Thomas Lauvås, Siri Jakobsen and Marianne Steinmo

INTRODUCTION

Firms play a central role in the movement towards resource circularity through innovation activities where 'take-make-use-dispose' resource flows are redesigned into resource loops (Buijs 2003; De Jesus and Mendonça 2018; Pieroni et al. 2019). These resource loops as a result of accumulation would lead to more resource circularity within and between firms and thus, circular industries. Resource loop innovations are a concrete means for the transformative change towards a circular economy aimed at minimizing the harms firms inflict on nature (van der Laan and Aurisicchio 2020). In particular, resource circularity minimizes and eliminates negative externalities and overexploitation of resources, and can increase the productivity of scarce resources such as natural resources.

The role of firm innovation in the movement towards resource circularity has gained increased scholarly attention, where prior studies particularly have contributed with insights of product design innovations (Bocken et al. 2016) and innovations related to feedback-rich collaboration systems (Antikainen and Valkokari 2016; Pieroni et al. 2019), such as business model innovations (e.g. De Jesus and Mendonça 2018; Pieroni et al. 2019; Planing 2015) and supply chain innovations (e.g. Genovese et al. 2017; Govindan and Hasanagic 2018). As research on resource circularity and circular economy in general is over-represented by system-level studies (Homrich et al. 2018), this chapter responds to the call for more firm-level research (Werning and Spinler 2020), and more precisely calls for studies on how circular economy principles could be applied and implemented to firms' operations (Lieder and Rashid 2016; Murray et al. 2017). In this chapter, we focus on the resources and innovations undertaken by firms to move towards resource loops, and ask: *What type of resource loop innovations do firms develop to move towards circularity?* This research question is critical for scholars, policy makers and practitioners as resource loop innovations contribute to address grand challenges, such as environmental degradation, climate change, and resource scarcity.

We apply the Penrosean resource-based logic to abductively conceptualize types of resource loop innovations developed by Norwegian salmon farming firms; creating three primary contributions to the literature on innovation for resource circularity. First, we expand the resource loop perspective of circular innovations (Buijs 2003) drawing on the Penrosean resource-based logic and particularly the versatility of resources (Penrose 1959/2009). This allows us to carve out seven types of resource loop innovations regarded as a win–win situations where circularity and resource productivity complement each other, meaning that these types of innovations contribute to both environmental and economic value creation.

Second, we expand on prior research on resource circularity which has mainly focused on feedback-rich systems (Geissdoerfer et al. 2018) by offering a typology matrix that presents our seven types of resource loop innovations from the perspective of how firms develop resource loop innovation. Understanding the dynamics of resource loop innovations within firms is crucial given the central role firms play in implementing resource circularity. Third, the typology matrix addresses the locus of the resources (i.e. inbound, inhouse, and outbound) and the approach for resource productivity (i.e. reconfiguring, minimizing, and expanding), which provides more nuanced insight on how firms develop resource loop innovations (e.g. Hobson 2016) concerning whether the resources are flowing in or out of the firms or staying inside the firms.

THEORETICAL BACKGROUND

Innovation, the Versatility of Resources, and Resource Approach

Firms consist of a heterogenous bundle of productive resources (Foss et al. 2008; Penrose 1959/2009), which are deployed to provide services contributing to the firm's final products or services. The Penrosean resource-based logic assumes that firms generally aim to "use the most valuable specialized services of its resources as fully as possible" (Penrose 1959/2009, p. 63). To maximize the productivity of resources, firms innovate (Weiss et al. 2013), for example in the form of business expansion to avoid inefficiency in resource use (Penrose 1959/2009), reconfiguration of resources towards more productive services (Dothan and Lavie 2016), or novel resource combinations to create new values (Haynie et al. 2009), which we refer to as approaches for resource productivity. From the Penrosean resource-based logic, innovation for increased resource productivity aims at maximizing the productive services of the resource bundle a firm uses to provide its services and final products. This type of innovation could be both product innovation and process innovation, meaning that innovation aimed at increasing resource productivity can for example have an outcome in the form of a new or modified product/service or a new change process.

For environmental innovation, such as innovation for a circular economy, the productivity of resources may not only be considered in pure economical, but also environmental terms (Jakobsen and Clausen 2016). Prior research has shown that the two-fold value dimension of environmental innovation comes with challenges (Marin et al. 2015; Polzin et al. 2016). Examples are conflicting environmental and financial goals and the double externality issue resulting in conservative environmental policies at the firms and fewer environmental innovation projects (Garcia et al. 2019). These challenges are rooted in the assumption that firms strive to use resources in the most productive way to grow and flourish in the long term (Penrose 1959/2009; Sirmon et al. 2011).

The versatility of resources provides firms with combinative possibilities, which firms can take advantage of (Nason and Wiklund 2018); that is, resources can be reallocated and assigned new purposes to minimize resource unproductivity (Penrose 1959/2009). Negative externalities, for example, by-products and overexploitation caused by unsustainable resource use are examples of unproductive resource use. Following this line of thinking, the approach of resource circularity can, but does not necessarily have to, address resource unproductivity, meaning that the circularity and efficiency principles are in line. This chapter therefore considers that circular innovations, such as resource loop innovations, are most likely those where resource productivity and resource circularity represent a win–win situation.

Resource Loop Innovations

Resource loop innovation is a distinct type of innovation for a circular economy, which in this chapter is deemed as a distinct resource innovation aimed at moving from a linear resource process following a take-make-use-dispose approach to closed resource loops (Hobson 2016). As such, we follow the circular economy principles, where resources assigned different services go through a loop of resource use while retaining as much value as possible to increase its utilization and productive service range (MacArthur 2013; Merli et al. 2018).

These resource loops can either circulate within a firm or between actors in an external environment (Chertow 2007; Foss et al. 2008). In particular, the organizational environment consists of other firms, institutions and organizations (Foss et al. 2008), and the natural environment comprises geology, animals and other features and products of the earth (George et al. 2015). The resources acquired and deployed by firms, which traverse the external environment come with environmental issues such as degradation of resources and negative externalities, for example in the form of waste and pollution (Sauvé et al. 2016). The principle of circularity is to minimize and avoid such issues by keeping the resources in the loop of productive resource services (Camilleri 2018). Given the critical role firms play in the transformation towards circularity, we need to learn more about what type of resource loop innovations firms actually implement.

METHODOLOGY

Strategic Research Site

Norwegian salmon farming firms act as the empirical setting to explore resource loop innovations in this study because they already have implemented initiatives to transform towards a circular economy (Boye 2019). The production of salmon comes with negative externalities on the marine environments (Sandvik 2016), and the salmon farmers are interested to innovate to become more environment-friendly. While the salmon farmers in the early stages focused on how to keep the salmon alive and increase the production volume (Osland 1990), environment-friendly production is nowadays a top priority (interview with the director and co-owner of fish farm 2).

Principles of circularity, where resources are kept in use as long as possible (Prieto-Sandoval et al. 2018), are regarded as a direction towards a sustainable salmon farming industry. For example, the director of fish farm 1 explains, "it is not like that we change ships and cars every second year, just because there is a new model. We like to use what we have before we buy something new." Similar principles are applied at fish farm 2, where they want to reuse what they have. While the salmon farming firms point out the positive aspects of resource circularity, they also stress that these sets of innovations must be economical. The sustainability manager at fish farm 3 explains, "this [circular economy innovation] must also be economical, this is the way to go." These statements from our case firms show that they apply and reflect over circular economy principles and strategies. Hence, we regard the Norwegian salmon farming industry as an adequate research site to study what kind of circular economy innovations our case firms develop.

Research Design and Data Collection

We use data material that the authors collected as part of a large research project focusing on innovation and collaboration within the Norwegian salmon farming industry (henceforth referred to as the project). An abductive research design is applied to provide us with in-depth understanding of the innovation projects the salmon farmers develop. This allows us to explore innovations that follow the principles of circularity within our strategic research site (Chouinard et al. 2019). Thereby, we gain a more profound understanding of what kind of resource loop innovations firms develop.

In the project, we apply a multi-case study design. The case unit is the salmon farming firm and we used secondary data (e.g. newspaper articles, reports from research institutions and a large database on innovation projects in Norway) to identify relevant case firms. For this chapter, we have selected 12 case firms that operate in the same geographical area (county of Nordland and Trøndelag) but vary in size and type of organization. This case selection enables a broader exploration of a variety of resource loop innovations developed by several firms (Eisenhardt 1989), which in turn strengthens the validity of our findings (Yin 2009).

We use a semi-structured interview guide to learn about innovation in the Norwegian salmon farming industry. We asked the case firms about current and past innovation projects, where the ideas for these innovation projects came from the innovation process involved. In this chapter, we make use of 23 interviews, of which 5 are group interviews. Thirteen of the interviews were conducted with fish farmers (i.e. case firms), of which only 1 case firm has been interviewed twice; 4 interviews were conducted with suppliers and 6 with research and governmental institutions. All the interviews were conducted with a minimum of two interviewers. The interviews have been recorded and transcribed.

Data Analysis

We use an abductive data analysis approach, meaning that we first observe and identify the circular innovations within our strategic research site and then inspired by circular economy literature and Penrosean resource-based logic we predict the type of resource loop innovation firms use. We used a recursive step-wise data analysis strategy (Saldaña 2015), starting by going through the interviews to identify the single innovation projects. Thereafter, we identified resource loop innovations within these projects, inspired by the circular economy literature (e.g. Bocken et al. 2016; Buijs 2003). We ended up with 34 innovation projects, which we then grouped according to their outcomes of resource loop innovations. Inspired by literature on innovation for a circular economy and the Penrosean resource-based logic we further developed a typology-matrix of resource loop innovation according to the resource outcome. The matrix is divided into approaches for resource productivity (i.e. reconfiguring, minimizing, and expanding) and the locus of resource (i.e. inbound, inhouse and outbound resources). This process resulted in a matrix with seven types of innovation defined by their outcome (see Table 18.1).

Table 18.1   A typology of resource loops innovation

Locus of resources	Approach for resource productivity		
	Reconfiguring	Minimizing	Expanding
Inbound	Reallocate unproductive resources into novel input resources	Minimize the use of unproductive natural resources	–
Inhouse	Re-utilize underutilized resources	–	- Simultaneously use non-consumptive resource services - Extend the productive services of resources
Outbound	Extract new resource services for value creation	Eliminate unproductive resource outflows	–

FINDINGS

In the following sections, we elaborate on the typology matrix with the seven identified types of resource loop innovations the salmon farming firms in this study have developed to move towards circularity. We first present our typology of resource loop innovations (Table 18.1), which summarizes and groups the identified innovations into seven innovation types. These innovations are grouped on the horizontal axis, into three approaches for resource productivities: (1) reconfiguring, (2) minimizing and (3) expanding. The vertical axis reflects the locus of resources: (1) inbound, (2) inhouse (3) outbound. Table 18.1 guides the discussion, following the locus of resources.

Inbound Resource Loop Innovation

The salmon farming firms mobilize resources from their external environment (organizational and natural environment). Our case firms use resources from other organizations, such as feed for the salmon, or make use of natural resources, such as sea water. These resources are part of a resource flow that, from the perspective of our case firms, involves the inflow of resources. Our analysis shows that firms innovate towards circularity aimed at reallocating unproductive resources into novel input resources through reconfiguration of resource services and exchanging less productive natural resources with more productive natural resources, which allows to create resource loops replacing resource flows.

Reallocating unproductive resources into novel input resource

The firms innovate to turn resource flows into resource loops meaning that the innovations lead to a reconfiguration of resources, which currently are unproductive (i.e. waste and end-of-life resources), into new productive resource services. The CEO of fish farm 4 explains that they use feed that is made from "waste from the salmon, but also the whitefish industry. Earlier this has been dumped in the ocean—I mean backbones, heads and so on. But these are important proteins [to feed the salmon]." Feed producer A adds, "this is feed which is locally sourced and sustainable because we use the waste from the salmon production to produce more salmon." Hence, the salmon farming firms reconfigure unproductive resources and assign them new services to keep the resources in circulation.

Minimizing the use of unproductive natural resources

Further, our case firms innovate to replace non-renewable energy sources, such as cruel oil and diesel into energy generated from renewable sources. The director of fish farm 1 explains, "we constantly develop ourselves in the direction of, for example moving away from fossil fuels, and perhaps taking an even clearer position in the circular economy, so to say." Concrete innovation examples from the Norwegian salmon farming industry are to use hybrid feed barges as the director and co-owner of fish farm 2 points out, and land-based electricity supply as the sustainability manager at fish farm 3 indicates: "by doing so we can exchange electricity from diesel generator sets with land-based electricity supplies".

Another example is fish farm 4 that has bought two fully electrical vessels that are considerably more expensive than traditional diesel vessels. A representative from fish farm 4 comments the on vessels' purchase: "We [the fish farmers] have always strived to be as environment-friendly as we can be. Adopting new technologies helps us to take care of the resources we manage in a better way." These examples show that the industry replaces fossil fuels with renewable resources, such as electrical energy from hydropower; 96 per cent of the Norwegian electricity is from hydropower plants (Energy Facts Norway 2019). Thereby, firms contribute to move towards a circular industry by selecting renewable resources and thus move towards productive resource loops.

Inhouse Resource Loop Innovation

Moreover, we have identified innovation projects leading to more inhouse resource circulation. This means that the salmon farming firms innovate to keep resources in circulation within the firm's boundary. We identify three idiosyncratic inhouse innovation outcomes towards a circular economy: re-utilizing underutilized resources, simultaneously using non-consumptive resource services, and extending the productive services of resources.

Re-utilizing underutilized resources

The case firms innovate to put underutilized resources into use, keeping them circulating in the production system. For example, to minimize negative externalities and avoid production disturbance, the salmon farming firms are considering moving the production from open sea-cages[1] to land, and produce in a closed production facility. The innovation manager at fish farm 3 stresses, "the technology to build large farming facilities onshore—closed facilities—are extremely costly. Moreover, it will use large amount of land resources and large areas." The CEO and owner of fish farm 5 is more optimistic and believes in the innovations to produce salmon onshore. He details, "We work with concrete land-based fish farming projects for three locations", whereas fish farm 7 has gone further and invested in a land-based fish farming project. The CEO explains the investment: "if future fish farming shall have less environmental impact, secure the welfare of the fish and provide better production terms; the solution will probably be both traditional fish cages, land-based facilities and facilities out at the sea."

While moving the entire production onshore is still under consideration, the salmon farming industry already grows smolt on land and has developed recirculation plants to keep the water in circulation. These recirculation plants use recirculating aquaculture systems and the CEO and owner of fish farm 5 states, "We build recirculation plants, which reuse 90 per cent of the water." Fish farm 7 is part of an aquaponics project, where the idea is to use the excretions from their smolt production facility to grow vegetables. This project is at an early stage, but is an illustrative example of how to put waste to new use.

Simultaneously using non-consumptive resource services

Moreover, we identified resources that provide services without consuming resources. The previous example of keeping the water circulating in the recirculation plants is an example of non-consumptive resource use. Such non-consumptive use of resources allows to use the resource providing multiple services simultaneously. The director at fish farm 1 explains that the water they use at the recirculation plant is also used to produce electricity. This electricity is then used to warm the water inside the recirculation plant. Another example of innovations from the salmon farming industry are visitor centres, which the salmon farmers have established in the last years. While the salmon are growing in the cages, visitors can take a boat trip to the cages and learn about the salmon and watch how the fish are jumping and moving around. The simultaneous use of non-consumptive resources allows to make use of different services from the same resource and thereby minimize resource use.

Extending the productive services of resources

Extending the productive service range of resources inhouse is another innovation outcome the salmon farmers aim at to enhance resource circularity. Our analysis shows that our case firms create new products from the waste of the main product and thereby extend their product portfolio. The director of fish farm 1 mentions the following example: "at the hatchery we have built a biogas plant to make use of the sludge. Well, this is still at a development stage." This example shows that fish farm 1 expands its business and diversifies its portfolio as an outcome of innovation to make use of negative externalities from the production process. Another example is that the salmon farming firms have built their own fish oil plants and protein plants to use the waste from the slaughter and fillet factory. By doing so, the salmon farming firms extend their resource loops inhouse, which is a concrete means towards circularity.

Outbound Resource Loop Innovation

Lastly, we identified resource loop innovations aimed at extracting new resource services for value creation and eliminating unproductive resource outflows. While the latter is an example of eliminating resource outflows, the former focuses on closing resource loops, which involves third parties. Both approaches facilitate the transition towards sustainable resource practices.

Extracting new resource services for value creation

The case firms also innovate to close resource loops within the organizational environment, aiming at reconfiguring the performed service of a resource. The director of fish farm 1 mentioned that they purify the water they use at the recirculation plant and extract the parts, which are rich in phosphorus and are used to make fertilizer pellet. The fish farming firms also use a lot of plastic during their production and currently are involved in innovation projects to makes use of old plastic that is not in use any longer. The CEO of fish farm 4 mentions that worn-out ropes from their production in the sea are now recycled to granules and applied in new products, such as chairs, which he regards as a win–win situation. Fish farm 13 also reuses plastics in cooperation with a local entrepreneur who makes new products out of discarded net pens (e.g. floating piers). Through these kind of innovative initiatives unproductive resources are assigned new values and services. Thereby the resource outflow from the fish farming firms is the start of a new resource loop.

Eliminating unproductive resource outflows
Finally, our case firms are concerned to minimize and eliminate unproductive resource outflows, for example negative externalities from the resources they use. For instance, the CEO of fish farm 6 explains that they are continuously trying to find "possibilities to reduce the use of medications". In particular, salmon lice treatments can be harmful for the wild salmon and other actors of the natural environment. Moreover, the salmon farming firms innovate to eliminate polychlorinated biphenyls (PCB) from the feed. PCB can be harmful for both animals and humans; for example it can cause cancer. The managing director at fish farm 7 stresses that their innovation allows "the opportunity to produce and extract PCB from the cycle of nature. You can take it out directly and in this way nature becomes cleaner." Additionally, several of our case firms mentioned the idea of closed or semi-closed cages. The sustainability manager at fish farm 3 says, "the large innovation projects connected to [name of innovation] and closed-cage production are innovations, which will increase the sustainability because it reduces pollution and minimizes the use of lice-treatments." To conclude, these examples of circular innovations show that there is a great awareness among the salmon farming firms to innovate in order to eliminate the negative impact their production has on nature.

DISCUSSION

Our typology matrix reveals seven types of resource loop innovations and thereby contributes with knowledge on what types of circular innovations firms develop to increase both utilization of inbound, inhouse, and outbound resources to move towards resource circularity, and resource productivity.

Our analysis suggests that firms develop resource loop innovations to reconfigure resource services, minimize the use of unproductive resources, and to expand the range of resource services. These three approaches for resource productivity extend Bocken et al.'s (2016) study, who found that increasing resource productivity comes with narrowing the flow of resources used by a firm and thereby contributes to the transition towards circularity. Narrowing resource loops decreases the amount of resource used, meaning that productivity of resources must be increased in order to maintain the portfolio of services provided by the resource bundle (e.g. by producing a product with fewer resources) (Bocken et al. 2016). Instead, our findings show that the logic of resource productivity, as assumed by the Penrosean resource-based logic (Penrose 1959/2009), applies not only for narrowing, but also closing resource loops and eliminating non-circular resource inflows and outflows, such as non-renewable resources and by-products for example in the form of emissions.

Moreover, our findings suggest that for all three resource loci (i.e. inbound, inhouse and outbound resources) firms innovate to increase resource productivity and circularity, whereas the economic and environmental value can be addressed to different degrees. For example, making outbound resource loop innovations to eliminate harmful resource outflows is a situation where the pressure towards a transition to resource circularity outweighs the firm's sole striving for increased productivity (Meek et al. 2010). In particular, the firms innovate to minimize or even avoid negative externalities caused by the firm's resource use, which at the same time does not affect or even decrease the productivity of resources within the firms, such as the example of replacing non-renewable resource with renewable resources. At the same time, our study shows that resource circularity within the firm's boundaries (i.e. inhouse resources) can also be more productive than the linear approach of resource flow. Prior studies (e.g. Alexopoulos et al. 2018) stress that there are situations where a firm's action to contribute to sustainability is a win–win situation. We found that firms innovate to expand the range of services of a resource in order to move towards more circularity and simultaneously increase the productivity of resources. We therefore suggest that when firms develop resource loop innovations, they aim to increase the accumulated economic and environmental value of resource services instead of only aiming for the most valuable specialized services of a resource (Penrose 1959/2009). Hence, we suggest that the resource loop innovations for circularity developed by firms are those that come with external pressure for a circular movement and internal motivation of increased resource productivity.

Our findings have important implications for firms, policy makers, and future research on how to facilitate resource loop innovation. First, as our findings show that resource loop innovation captures both economic and environmental values, we would advise firms to include resource loop innovation in their innovation portfolio for the movement towards circularity. As such, firms ought to identify resources that could be utilized either internally or by other firms. Second, to share the risk associated with resource loop innovations we suggest policy makers provide incentives for firms to implement circular innovations, which increases or at least maintains the productivity of the firm's resource bundle.

As the transformation of the Norwegian salmon farming firms towards a circular industry is at an early stage (Boye 2019), we need more research focusing on industries that have gone further in the process to move towards circularity in order to gain more insight as to whether the innovation behaviour, in particular the focus on innovation for increased productivity, also applies at later stages or whether the process towards circular economy commences with innovations that are win–win situations. Further, it would be interesting to compare different industries that pursue circular innovations. We therefore call for further research to examine if, and in which ways, resource loop innovations are an idiosyncratic type of environmental innovations in order to understand the mechanism behind innovations for a circular economy more broadly.

CONCLUSION

By investigating how Norwegian salmon farming firms innovate for resource circularity, we offer a typology matrix consisting of seven types of resource loop innovations, and thereby this chapter extends the debate on firm-level innovation for a circular economy (Lieder and Rashid 2016; Murray et al. 2017). We find that the resource loop innovations developed by firms are those creating or capturing environmental value while at the same time increasing the productivity of firm's resource services or minimizing the use of unproductive resources. Specifically, our study shows that while the transformation towards circularity is often externally driven (e.g. De Jesus and Mendonça 2018; Govindan and Hasanagic 2018), the firms' innovation behaviour remains guided by the striving for increased productivity (Penrose 1959/2009). Therefore, the innovation behaviour of firms must be considered in the movement towards circular industries.

NOTE

1. Open sea-cages have two main issues: salmon escape and salmon lice outbreaks, which are considered to have negative externalities on wild trout and salmon. See *Skattlegging av havbruksvirksomhet* (2019): http://www.regjeringen.no.

REFERENCES

Alexopoulos, I., Kounetas, K., & Tzelepis, D. (2018). Environmental and financial performance. Is there a win–win or a win–loss situation? Evidence from the Greek manufacturing. *Journal of Cleaner Production*, 197, 1275–1283.

Antikainen, M., & Valkokari, K. (2016). A framework for sustainable circular business model innovation. *Technology Innovation Management Review*, 6(7), 5–12.

Bocken, N. M. P., de Pauw, I., Bakker, C., & van der Grinten, B. (2016). Product design and business model strategies for a circular economy. *Journal of Industrial and Production Engineering*, 33(5), 308–320.

Boye, E. (2019). *Sirkulær framtid—om skiftet fra linær til sirkulær økonomi*. Framtiden i våre hender.

Buijs, J. (2003). Modelling product innovation processes, from linear logic to circular chaos. *Creativity and Innovation Management*, 12(2), 76–93.

Camilleri, M. A. (2018). Closing the loop for resource efficiency, sustainable consumption and production: A critical review of the circular economy. *International Journal of Sustainable Development*, 21(1–4), 1–17.

Chertow, M. R. (2007). "Uncovering" industrial symbiosis. *Journal of Industrial Ecology*, 11(1), 11–30.

Chouinard, U., Pigosso, D. C., McAloone, T. C., Baron, L., & Achiche, S. (2019). Potential of circular economy implementation in the mechatronics industry: An exploratory research. *Journal of Cleaner Production*, 239, 118014.

De Jesus, A., & Mendonça, S. (2018). Lost in transition? Drivers and barriers in the eco-innovation road to the circular economy. *Ecological Economics*, 145, 75–89.

Dothan, A., & Lavie, D. (2016). Resource reconfiguration: Learning from performance feedback. In T. B. Folta, C. Helfat, & S. Karim (eds.), *Resource Redeployment and Corporate Strategy*. Advances in Strategic Management, vol. 35. Bingley: Emerald Group Publishing, 319–369.

Eisenhardt, K. M. (1989). Building theories from case study research. *Academy of Management Review*, 14(4), 532–550.

Energy Facts Norway (2019). Electricity production. https://energifaktanorge.no/en/norsk -energiforsyning/kraftproduksjon/.

Foss, N. J., Klein, P. G., Kor, Y. Y., & Mahoney, J. T. (2008). Entrepreneurship, subjectivism, and the resource-based view: Toward a new synthesis. *Strategic Entrepreneurship Journal*, 2(1), 73–94.

Garcia, R., Wigger, K., & Hermann, R. R. (2019). Challenges of creating and capturing value in open eco-innovation: Evidence from the maritime industry in Denmark. *Journal of Cleaner Production*, 220, 642–654.

Geissdoerfer, M., Morioka, S. N., de Carvalho, M. M., & Evans, S. (2018). Business models and supply chains for the circular economy. *Journal of Cleaner Production*, 190, 712–721.

Genovese, A., Acquaye, A. A., Figueroa, A., & Koh, S. C. L. (2017). Sustainable supply chain management and the transition towards a circular economy: Evidence and some applications. *Omega*, 66, 344–357.

George, G., Schillebeeckx, S. J., & Liak, T. L. (2015). The management of natural resources: An overview and research agenda. *Academy of Management Journal*, 58(6), 1595–1613.

Govindan, K., & Hasanagic, M. (2018). A systematic review on drivers, barriers, and practices towards circular economy: A supply chain perspective. *International Journal of Production Research*, 56(1–2), 278–311.

Haynie, J. M., Shepherd, D. A., & McMullen, J. S. (2009). An opportunity for me? The role of resources in opportunity evaluation decisions. *Journal of Management Studies*, 46(3), 337–361.

Hobson, K. (2016). Closing the loop or squaring the circle? Locating generative spaces for the circular economy. *Progress in Human Geography*, 40(1), 88–104.

Homrich, A. S., Galvao, G., Abadia, L. G., & Carvalho, M. M. (2018). The circular economy umbrella: Trends and gaps on integrating pathways. *Journal of Cleaner Production*, 175, 525–543.

Jakobsen, S., & Clausen, T. H. (2016). Innovating for a greener future: The direct and indirect effects of firms' environmental objectives on the innovation process. *Journal of Cleaner Production*, 128, 131–141.

Lieder, M., & Rashid, A. (2016). Towards circular economy implementation: A comprehensive review in context of manufacturing industry. *Journal of Cleaner Production*, 115, 36–51.

MacArthur, E. (2013). Towards the circular economy. *Journal of Industrial Ecology*, 2, 23–44.

Marin, G., Marzucchi, A., & Zoboli, R. (2015). SMEs and barriers to eco-innovation in the EU: Exploring different firm profiles. *Journal of Evolutionary Economics*, 25(3), 671–705.

Meek, W. R., Pacheco, D. F., & York, J. G. (2010). The impact of social norms on entrepreneurial action: Evidence from the environmental entrepreneurship context. *Journal of Business Venturing*, 25(5), 493–509.

Merli, R., Preziosi, M., & Acampora, A. (2018). How do scholars approach the circular economy? A systematic literature review. *Journal of Cleaner Production*, 178, 703–722.

Murray, A., Skene, K., & Haynes, K. (2017). The circular economy: An interdisciplinary exploration of the concept and application in a global context. *Journal of Business Ethics*, 140(3), 369–380.

Nason, R. S., & Wiklund, J. (2018). An assessment of resource-based theorizing on firm growth and suggestions for the future. *Journal of Management*, 44(1), 32–60.

Osland, E. (1990). *Bruke havet-: pionertid i norsk fiskeoppdrett*. Oslo: Samlaget.

Penrose, E. T. (1959/2009). *The Theory of the Growth of the Firm* (4th ed.). Oxford: Oxford University Press.

Pieroni, M. P., McAloone, T. C., & Pigosso, D. C. (2019). Business model innovation for circular economy and sustainability: A review of approaches. *Journal of Cleaner Production*, 215, 198–216.

Planing, P. (2015). Business model innovation in a circular economy reasons for non-acceptance of circular business models. *Open Journal of Business Model Innovation*, 1(11), 1–11.

Polzin, F., von Flotow, P., & Klerkx, L. (2016). Addressing barriers to eco-innovation: Exploring the finance mobilisation functions of institutional innovation intermediaries. *Technological Forecasting and Social Change*, 103, 34–46.

Prieto-Sandoval, V., Jaca, C., & Ormazabal, M. (2018). Towards a consensus on the circular economy. *Journal of Cleaner Production*, 179, 605–615.

Saldaña, J. (2015). *The Coding Manual for Qualitative Researchers*. London: Sage Publications.

Sandvik, K. (2016). *Under overflaten: en skitten historie om det norske lakseeventyret*. Copenhagen: Gyldendal.

Sauvé, S., Bernard, S., & Sloan, P. (2016). Environmental sciences, sustainable development and circular economy: Alternative concepts for trans-disciplinary research. *Environmental Development*, 17, 48–56.

Sirmon, D. G., Hitt, M. A., Ireland, R. D., & Gilbert, B. A. (2011). Resource orchestration to create competitive advantage: Breadth, depth, and life cycle effects. *Journal of Management*, 37(5), 1390–1412.

van der Laan, A. Z., & Aurisicchio, M. (2020). A framework to use product-service systems as plans to produce closed-loop resource flows. *Journal of Cleaner Production*, 252, 119733.

Weiss, M., Hoegl, M., & Gibbert, M. (2013). The influence of material resources on innovation projects: The role of resource elasticity. *R&D Management*, 43(2), 151–161.

Werning, J. P., & Spinler, S. (2020). Transition to circular economy on firm level: Barrier identification and prioritization along the value chain. *Journal of Cleaner Production*, 245, 118609.

Yin, R. K. (2009). *Case Study Research: Design and Methods*, 4th edition. Thousand Oaks, CA: Sage Publications.

PART V

TECHNOLOGY AND DIGITALIZATION FOR A CIRCULAR ECONOMY

19. Experimenting with new business model strategies for the circular economy

Nancy Bocken, Christiaan Kraaijenhagen, Jan Konietzko,
Brian Baldassarre, Phil Brown and Cheyenne Schuit

1.   BACKGROUND

The circular economy has been positioned as a possible lever for sustainability and economic prosperity (Geissdoerfer et al. 2017). It seeks to narrow, slow, close and regenerate resource flows (Bocken et al. 2016; Konietzko et al. 2020b; Stahel 1994). With support from business, policymakers and other societal actors (Ghisellini and Ulgiati 2020), the circular economy can help close the idea–action gap of sustainable innovation (Baldassarre et al. 2020).

As part of a circular economy, companies need to shift from linear to circular business models (Sarisini and Linder 2018). A business model consists of a value proposition (product offering), value creation and delivery (how this value is provided) and value capture mechanisms (how money and other forms of value are captured) (Bocken and Short 2016; based on Richardson 2008). These elements can be changed, for example, so that a company can provide its product as a service. It then retains ownership of the product and has an incentive to increase durability to keep operating costs low, which can slow the associated resource flows (Bocken et al. 2016). This helps to shift the dominant linear logic of business models: from volume-driven to value-driven models, and from take-make-use-dispose to value retention of materials and products.

To make this shift, companies need to invest time to develop new strategies and experiment (Chesbrough 2010; McGrath 2010) with new circular business models (Bocken et al. 2018; Weissbrod and Bocken 2017). Experimentation is a process that allows a company to gather information about how a new business model might be realized in practice with the goal to de-risk and accelerate the transition (Bocken et al. 2018). The first part of the experimentation process usually entails qualitative forms of data collection, like customer interviews or co-creation workshops to ideate new value proportions (Brown 2008; Osterwalder and Pigneur 2009). This information can then be used to design experiments that deliberately vary a business model element to test and validate the different outcomes. After first experiments have been conducted, a series of sequential experiments can be conducted under a pilot. During this process, it is important to keep track of potential environmental impact reductions (Baldassarre et al. 2020). This is essential to serve the customer, but also to create positive impact on society and the environment (Stubbs and Cocklin 2008).

How to experiment with new business models in the context of a circular economy is a new field (Antikainen et al. 2017; Bocken et al. 2017). Some tools and approaches have already been developed (Bocken et al. 2019; Pieroni et al. 2019). But more research is needed to better understand how these tools can be used during the circular and sustainable business model experimentation process. In particular, it is not clear what kinds of practices can help, and when, to do this kind of experimentation (Bocken and Snihur 2019). This chapter, therefore, addresses the following research question: *What types of experimentation practices do companies adopt in the transition to a circular business model?*

1.1   Framework: Iterative Circular Business Model Experimentation Process

Business literature (e.g. Chesbrough 2010) suggests that approaches such as effectuation (Sarasvathy 2009), lean start-up (Ries 2011) and design thinking (Brown 2008) might be used and combined in the business model experimentation process. Effectuation is about entrepreneurs using 'what is available' here and now, to make the most out of a challenging and uncertain business environment (Sarasvathy 2009). Lean start-up is about formulating hypotheses or assumptions about the future business and testing these in practice with real customers (Ries 2011). This can be done by building minimum viable products (very early iterations of a business model), services or solutions, iteratively testing them, measuring their impacts, and learning to iterate on the way forward (Ries 2011). Design thinking is a collection of methods focused on meeting people's needs and desires in a technologically feasible and strategically viable way (Brown 2008). Earlier work on circular business experimentation shows that design thinking, lean start-up and effectuation are being used in parallel for circular business model experimentation (e.g. Bocken and Antikainen 2018; Bocken et al. 2017). Within this, approaches and practices such as focus groups, interviews and paper prototypes are being used (Baldassarre et al. 2017; Schuit et al. 2017). However, much of the former work on circular business model experimentation focuses on a limited number of company interactions and more empirical data is needed to gain an understanding of the practices that may be used for circular business model experimentation.

As a starting point for this study, we propose an iterative framework for a circular business model experimentation process, developed based on earlier work (see Figure 19.1). It starts with the business purpose (Bocken et al. 2018; Kraaijenhagen et al. 2016) and value proposition (Osterwalder and Pigneur 2010), which is followed by an iterative experimentation process (Ries 2011). During this process, the desirability, viability, feasibility, and circularity are tested (Brown 2008; Baldassarre et al. 2020) focusing on further aspects such as how value is created and delivered, and captured (Richardson 2008) in addition to the value proposition which typically remains under scrutiny during the whole experimentation process (Schuit et al. 2017). Smaller experimentation practices would then be followed by larger pilots with the customer coming increasingly closer to 'business reality'. This offers an approach that aligns the specific practice used to the ideation or testing stage to support practitioners to advance their idea (Mansoori and Lackéus 2020). This conceptual framework serves as a starting point to understand the circular business model experimentation process. The present study focuses on understanding the tools, methods and practices within this process.

While the work by Ries (2011) and later studies on sustainability and business model experimentation (e.g. Baldassarre et al. 2017; Schuit et al. 2017) identified generic practices such as digital and paper prototyping, custom tools have been developed by the authors specifically for circular business model innovation. These include the Circularity Deck (Konietzko et al. 2020b); Circular Collaboration Canvas (Brown et al. 2019), the Sustainable and Circular Business Model (SBM) Pilot Canvas (Baldassarre et al. 2020) and Metrics cards (Konietzko et al. 2020a). Such tools help to keep the focus of experimentation on circularity.

The Circularity Deck (Konietzko et al. 2020b) is a card deck-based tool that challenges innovators to take a broad perspective on the circular economy. It aims to keep circularity

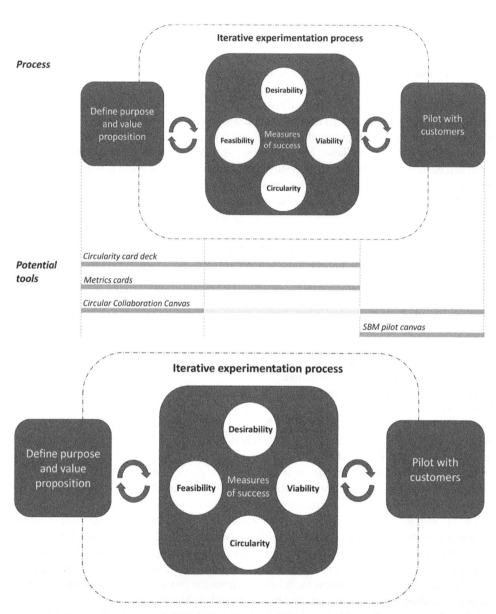

Source: Developed in this study, based on Baldassarre et al. (2020), Bocken et al. (2018), Brown (2008), Konietzko et al. (2020a, 2020b), Osterwalder and Pigneur (2010), Ries (2011).

Figure 19.1　Iterative circular business model experimentation process

in focus throughout the business experimentation process by supporting organizations to analyse, ideate and develop the circularity potential of their innovation ecosystem. The tool is based on a collection of circular oriented innovation principles, and practical examples that show how these principles have been applied. The principles are organized according to the intended circular strategy outcome that they pursue (i.e. narrow, slow, close, regenerate and inform material and energy flows), and the extent of the innovation perspective that is needed to operationalize a principle (i.e. product, business model, or ecosystem innovation).

The Circular Collaboration Canvas (Brown et al. 2019) is a poster template used within a workshop setting. It gets users to think in detail about a circular value proposition. The canvas aims to keep circularity in focus throughout the experimentation process by guiding collaborating organizations through key topics. These include trigger questions that create discussion and ideation upon the challenge at hand, the resources the team has and needs, who the customers or users are and their problems and what solution might overcome these. Crucially the tool explores which partners can aid and bring value to the circular innovation to support a viable circular proposition. The canvas challenges users to identify value for potential partners and challenges within the circular idea. This aids the quick identification of knowledge gaps, assumptions and required actions to improve the desirability, feasibility and viability of a circular value proposition by bringing in an early focus on partners within the ideation process.

The Sustainable Business Model (SBM) Pilot Canvas (Baldassarre et al. 2020) is a tool that helps organizations to co-define, with a range of collaborating stakeholders, how to execute a small-scale pilot. It supports organizations in finding out whether their circular business idea can work in reality. If it does not, the tool nudges the innovator to go back to change the business idea and try again, while focusing on circularity next to desirability, feasibility and viability. The tool is essentially a poster template that allows stakeholders to get around the table, and think about the circular business idea in terms of a prototype that has to be defined, built, and delivered to customers while generating profit and measuring the circular impact that is achieved by doing so. Since 'the devil is in the details' and 'cash is king', the tool will push users to think about specific actions to perform right now, with available knowledge, financial resources and manpower.

Metrics cards (Konietzko et al. 2020a, based on Croll and Yoskovitz 2013; Heikkilä et al. 2016) are cards that let users define the relevant different metrics they will use to track progress during experimentation. The cards are categorized into desirability, viability, feasibility and circularity. They trigger experimenters to keep circularity in focus throughout the business experimentation process. Examples of business model metrics include the 'percentage of active monthly users' in an app to track the desirability of a project, or the 'monthly average revenue per user' to track the viability of a project. Circularity metrics include, for instance, the 'recycling rate' of the used materials to track progress on the 'closing' strategy, or the 'comparative product life extension' achieved to track progress on the 'slowing' strategy. The Metrics cards trigger the participants to track progress on the different business model elements and the circularity of the ideas during experimentation.

The tools are featured in Figure 19.1 where they are most fitting. The conceptual framework and tools form the basis for this study.

The remainder of this chapter is structured as follows. In the next section, we present the method to gather empirical evidence, discussing how the practices of the circular business model experimentation process outlined in Figure 19.1 are collated. Next, we present and discuss our results focusing on the types of tools and practices identified in the process, as well as on the lessons learned along the way. Finally, the conclusions section collates the main outcomes and presents insight for future research and practice on circular business model experimentation.

2.   METHOD

This study uses an action-based research approach (Prendeville et al. 2017; Robson and McCartan 2016; Van de Ven 2007), using "deliberate, exploratory and collaborative methods over time" (Prendeville et al. 2017, p. 1329). Building on Kraaijenhagen et al. (2016), Bocken et al. (2018) and Schuit et al. (2017) we seek to gain insight into the different tools and methods that can be used to move from a linear to a circular business model. The researchers' activities spanned a period of four years (2016–2020) and included interactions with a diverse range of companies – start-up, small or medium sized company (SME), large company, multinational – to advance these companies' transitions to a circular business model. Companies were selected based on their interest in advancing their business models towards the circular economy. Based on their needs, different interactions were agreed upon and conducted. The companies that participated in this study include:

1. **Fresh-R:** Dutch start-up company selling decentralized ventilation systems with heat recovery.
2. **Mud Jeans:** Dutch start-up company in the clothing industry.
3. **Bugaboo:** large Dutch company selling consumer durables, like baby strollers.
4. **Vereijken Hooijer:** a Dutch SME in the agricultural sector (stables and nursing homes for pigs).
5. **Boska Holland:** a Dutch SME selling consumer durables (cheesewares).
6. **Peerby:** a Dutch product sharing platform.
7. **Evides:** a Dutch drinking water and tailored business services company.
8. **Philips (project 1):** multinational electronics company active in health care and personal care. The interaction focused on personal care.
9. **Philips (project 2):** focus on a different proposition for personal care.
10. **Welcome to the Village:** Dutch summer music festival where 10 start-ups in various sectors developed and tested new circular business model ideas.
11. **Adaptive city mobility:** German start-up that has created a combination of lightweight and optimally designed electric vehicles, swappable batteries, renewable energy-as-a-service, and mobility-as-a-service solutions.
12. **Miniloop:** Swiss start-up that provides baby clothing as a service.
13. **Grassrooted:** Swiss start-up that rescues left over and 'ugly' vegetables from farmlands and sells them through a subscription box.
14. **IV-infra:** A large Dutch civil engineering service company.
15. **Unwaste:** A Dutch start-up that turns waste from offices into soap that is re-delivered to the office.
16. **Circular Fashion Games:** circular challenges of Dutch companies executed during boot-camps by students, entrepreneurs and designers, with early stage ideas.
17. **Australian Fashion Council:** Australia coalition of several small and large business organization in the textile/fashion industry. Project collaboration also with several business organizations, the Australian government and academia.

Our work is based on 17 cases, consisting of circular business experimentation projects carried out with over 40 organizations, who in some cases worked collaboratively (cases 10, 16, and 17). The next section lists all the practices that were part of experimentation, including reflections on the process.

3. RESULTS AND DISCUSSION

In Table 19.1, we provide an overview of all the experimentation practices that were conducted in each case. In the table we also specify to what extent the practices contributed to testing desirability, feasibility, viability and circularity, and whether a pilot was conducted. It should be noted that all cases were about circular business model experimentation, but the column 'experimentation focus' highlights which aspects were most prominently tested.

3.1   Observations about the Experimentation Process

The experimentation practices listed in Table 19.1 were relevant in defining business model strategies for the circular economy. From the practices, it transpired that typically, different practices of design thinking (Brown 2008) are performed before starting an experiment. Furthermore, experimentation follows when sufficient insight is gained from this initial stage, although often design thinking practices like customer interviews continue to gain additional insight when experimenting. Finally, after multiple types of experiments, a more elaborate pilot with customers is performed. See Figure 19.2.

In our study, interviews were performed nine times. This helped to gain first insights that could inform the design of experiments. For example, in the Evides case, interviews with multiple stakeholders paved the way for more focused and collaborative co-creation sessions. Indeed, these sessions proved to be essential for the process – to prepare for the design of meaningful experiments. This practice was performed 17 times, allowing stakeholders to generate initial business model strategies, to align on key aspects of their collaboration, and plan a potential pilot. For example, in the Philips (project 2) case, the three co-creation sessions supported by the Circularity Deck (Konietzko et al. 2020a), Collaboration Canvas (Brown et al. 2019), and SBM Pilot Canvas (Baldassarre et al. 2020), brought different departments of the company together. As a result, they could define how to exploit the opportunity to provide electronic products for personal care as a service. Ultimately, the three co-creation sessions led to the definition of a plan for a potential pilot, in line with the lean start-up and effectual approach that lies at the core of experimentation (Blank 2013; Sarasvathy 2009).

Only a few pilots were rolled out in practice (four in total) during our interactions with the companies. Prototyping was essential to support the execution of pilots. For example, in the Welcome to the Village case, two full days of prototyping supported the ten early stage ventures. This helped to create a business model and deliver it, and to assess its profitability and impact. Indeed, prototyping makes a business model tangible and testable. Nevertheless, in order for a pilot to be valid, it is crucial to define circular business model metrics. Defining metrics is crucial during the process. It forces the participants to specify what an experiment is supposed to achieve (e.g. revenue growth per month up by X per cent). Throughout our cases, there was only one explicit test on circularity (case 12). Several sessions made use of circular economy specific tools, but circularity assumptions were not always tested. As highlighted by previous research (Baldassarre et al. 2020), this aspect deserves further attention and dedicated tools.

In order to keep track of circularity, it is critical to start from a baseline, calculated for example through a fast-track life cycle assessment (reference). However, companies did not always do this. Rather, the entrepreneurs relied on their intuition. We found that quantifying environmental and social impacts is difficult and not always a priority within the experimenta-

Table 19.1   Overview of experimentation practices, pilots and circularity checks

Cases	Experimentation practices, tools and methods	Experimentation focus:				
		Desirability	Feasibility	Viability	Circularity	Pilot
1	**Fresh-R**					
	Interviews with school principals and a business centre	X	X	X		
	Co-creation workshop on value proposition and business model	X	X	X		
2	**Mud Jeans**					
	A/B split test on Facebook	X				
	Co-creation workshop		X	X		
3	**Bugaboo**					
	Interviews with retailers		X			
	Interview retailers to discuss and revise ideas		X			
	Co-creation workshop			X		
4	**Vereijken Hooijer**					
	Focus group with ten farmers to test three value propositions and business model	X				
	Co-creation workshop		X	X		
5	**Boska Holland**					
	Facebook community with 'people who love cheese' to collect insights	X				
	Questionnaire to validate four value propositions with the target group	X				
	Co-creation workshop		X	X		
6	**Peerby**					
	Facebook community members were asked questions about the existing platform and how more value could be added	X				
	Co-creation session with ex-retailer to generate ideas for circular value propositions and business models	X				
	Co-creation workshop		X			
	Calculate business case and talk to retailer to explore the potential of the business model			X		
7	**Evides**					
	Facebook community with inhabitants of Rotterdam Lombardijen to collect insights on what can be improved in the neighbourhood and what inhabitants find important	X				
	Interviews with architects of Gebouwd Water, municipality of Rotterdam and neighbourhood manager of Rotterdam to collect insights on their perspective on the water issue and reusing rainwater		X			

	Cases	Experimentation practices, tools and methods	Desirability	Feasibility	Viability	Circularity	Pilot
8	**Philips (project 1)**	Co-creation session between a municipality, a social housing corporation and water experts to help neighbourhoods become more water-resilient		X			
		Call panel members to collect insights as to whether people who did not buy the specific Philips product yet, would be interested in the circular business model	X				
		Interviews with second-hand sellers of the product to collect insights as to why sellers decide to sell this specific product		X			
		Facebook ads to test conversions on different value propositions			X		
		Facebook community with consumers who are taking part in the circular business model to collect real-life insights of what consumers think of the product in combination with the circular business model					X
9	**Philips (project 2)**	Co-creation session with members of different departments (i.e. design, marketing, sustainability and operations) to define a value proposition for providing customers with electronic products for personal care as a service. Tools: Circularity Deck, the Sustainable and Circular and SBM Pilot Canvas	X				
		Follow up co-creation session to define how value creation and delivery might take place around the aforementioned value proposition. Tool: Circular Collaboration Canvas		X			
		Follow up co-creation session to define how value capture might take place and as well as planning different options for potential field experiments and pilots			X		
10	**Welcome to the Village**	Ten co-creation sessions and interviews with ten early stage ventures aiming to ideate various business propositions to support the Welcome to the Village (sustainable music festival and main client/ partner of the ventures) in becoming more circular. For example, during one of these sessions one venture put forward a concept for a biodegradable food packaging to support the festival in producing less waste. Tools: SBM Pilot Canvas, Circular Collaboration Canvas	X				

Cases	Experimentation practices, tools and methods	Desirability	Feasibility	Viability	Circularity	Pilot
	Ten follow up co-creation sessions and interviews with the lead of each venture, to define how value creation and delivery might take place around the aforementioned value propositions. For example, during one of these sessions one venture planned how to create and deliver a dishwashing service for festival visitors in order to avoid the use of plastic disposables		X			
	Ten follow up co-creation sessions and interviews with the lead of each venture, to define how value capture might take place to support the business models of the ventures from a financial standpoint. For example, during one of these sessions one venture defined how to sell sustainable vegan snack to festival visitors, and for what price			X		
	Two full days of prototyping to build product concepts and gear up for executing service concepts to be piloted on the festival grounds. Two full days of testing the aforementioned prototypes and concepts during the music festival. For example one of the ventures built a bench integrated with solar panels in order to allow festival visitors to charge mobile devices with renewable energy					X
11 **Adaptive city mobility**	Prototyping: testing of small-scale cardboard versions of the vehicle and system with potential users	X				
	Several rounds of testing of the electric vehicle and the battery swapping system in the factory		X			
	A pilot with eight vehicles in the city of Munich to test the desirability, feasibility and viability of the service model, software and battery swapping					X
12 **Miniloop**	Test willingness to pay for a veggie box by asking ten potential customers if they are willing to commit the proposed amount for a pilot round. Tools: Metrics cards; experiment configurator	X				
	Life cycle costing to estimate all costs along the entire life cycle of the service model. Circularity was tested by looking at the number of use cycles compared to a general sales model. They found that they could achieve six use cycles, compared to one. Tool: Metrics cards			X	X	

Experimentation focus:

	Cases	Experimentation practices, tools and methods	Experimentation focus:				
			Desirability	Feasibility	Viability	Circularity	Pilot
13	Grassrooted	Test willingness to pay for a veggie box by asking ten potential customers if they are willing to commit the proposed amount for a pilot round. Tool: Metrics cards	X				
		Organize a pilot with 200 veggie boxes through a local food retailer; put offering on the platform; communicate it through social media; organize staff for logistics and packaging					X
14	IV-infra	Come up with several value propositions; test them with internal staff and top management to see which ones are accepted and might be pursued further. Tool: Circularity Deck	X				
15	Unwaste	Joint meetings with several partners within the ecosystem (e.g. offices, waste managers, material processor, soap production partner) to define interests, roles and responsibilities		X			
16	Circular Fashion Games: early stage ideas	Interviews with potential customers to test Value Proposition and/or business model	X				
		Value proposition and business model co-creation session with teams focused on early stage ideas in circular fashion		X	X		
		Value proposition and business model co-creation session with teams focused on early stage ideas in circular fashion			X		
17	Australian Fashion Council	Co-creation session to generate initial ideas on how the stakeholders involved could collaborate to make the fashion industry more circular in Australia. Tool: Circularity Deck	X				

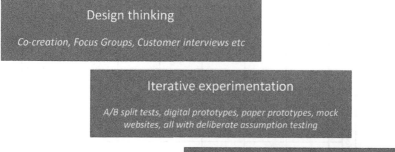

Figure 19.2   Types of activities identified

tion process. This aspect might represent a critical barrier to go beyond mere good intentions for the transition to a circular economy.

Finally, we note that the challenge of the overall process is to design specific experiments, define and maintain a clear goal and purpose, and remain open to spontaneous learning. Moreover, while it may be environmentally desirable to combine different circular economy strategies, this increases the complexity and makes it less actionable for participants faced with the need to include and test various aspects about the future business model.

3.2   Suggestions for Future Tools and Methods

The findings have implications for assessing environmental impacts, partnering and managing complexity during the experimentation process.

First, setting an environmental baseline helps to understand the environmental hotspots and focus points. Furthermore, regular circularity checks and experiments are important to understand where most impacts can be reduced. These can be conducted via fast track life cycle assessments, or heuristic questions like: What can this product or service substitute? What makes it a more circular solution? An ongoing challenge is to assess potential rebound effects (Zink and Geyer 2017). New approaches like the ecologies of business models approach (Boons and Bocken 2018) might help make sense of potential feedback loops in an innovation ecosystem that results from introducing a new solution.

Second, partnering early on seems desirable, particularly when the model includes fundamental assumptions on how such a partner might behave, especially regards perceived value within the future business model. While seemingly obvious, this is a step that was often forgotten. Tools like the Circular Collaboration Canvas (Brown et al. 2019) might help identify these partners early on. Further, the identity and focus of the entrepreneur, whether they are more or less commercially or sustainability focused, can inhibit the types of partners they might think to work with (York et al. 2016). The challenge is to get entrepreneurs to move beyond their initial framing when selecting partners.

Third, complexity seems inevitable but needs to be managed. In some of the sessions, participants developed their own tools, like action templates to manage the complexity and break the complexity down into manageable chunks of action. Future tools could focus on how to bring together multiple aspects of circularity, as well as desirability, feasibility and viability.

4. CONCLUSIONS

The circular economy requires companies to shift their business models from a predominantly linear to a circular model. This study investigated the type of experimentation practices companies can adopt in the transition to a circular business model. First, a conceptual framework for circular business model experimentation was introduced (Figure 19.1). Second, action research with over 40 organizations was conducted. It was found that design thinking practices like interviews and focus groups precede the experimentation process, and iterative experimentation practices would lead to a more complete pilot with customers (Figure 19.2). Thus, iterative experimentation cycles help to build a picture of the whole circular business model. Practices identified in this study include co-creation sessions and interviews with key stakeholders, social media and prototype tests, and to a lesser extent, questionnaires, focus groups and business case calculations (Table 19.1). These practices originate from design thinking (Brown 2008), lean start-up (Ries 2011), and effectuation (Sarasvathy 2009). Experimentation practices focus on testing the desirability, feasibility, viability and circularity of new circular business models. In addition, various custom tools for circular business model innovation were used. These tools aim to keep the circular economy in focus, whilst advancing experimentation to also test desirability, feasibility and viability. Still, future work will need to identify ways to sustain circularity in the implemented business model and to find ways to validate increased positive impacts on society and the environment while minimizing negative impacts. The study was limited by the heterogeneous sample of companies interested in participating. Future research may include longitudinal, observatory and ethnographic methods, in addition to action research.

ACKNOWLEDGEMENTS

We would like to thank all companies for their participation in the experimentation sessions. This research was supported by project Circular X, which received funding from the European Research Council's Horizon 2020 funding scheme under grant agreement no. 850159.

REFERENCES

Antikainen, M., Aminoff, A., Paloheimo, H., & Kettunen, O. (2017). Designing circular business model experimentation: Case study. In *ISPIM Innovation Symposium* (pp. 1–14). The International Society for Professional Innovation Management (ISPIM).

Baldassarre, B., Calabretta, G., Bocken, N. M. P., & Jaskiewicz, T. (2017). Bridging sustainable business model innovation and user-driven innovation: A process for sustainable value proposition design. *Journal of Cleaner Production*, 147, 175–186.

Baldassarre, B., Konietzko, J., Brown, P., Calabretta, G., Bocken, N., Karpen, I., & Hultink, E. J. (2020). Addressing the design-implementation gap of sustainable business models by prototyping: A tool for planning and executing small-scale pilots. *Journal of Cleaner Production*, 255, 120295.

Blank, S. (2013). Why the lean start-up changes everything. *Harvard Business Review*, 91(5), 63–72.

Bocken, N. M., & Antikainen, M. (2018). Circular business model experimentation: Concept and approaches. In *International Conference on Sustainable Design and Manufacturing* (pp. 239–250). Cham: Springer.

Bocken, N. M., De Pauw, I., Bakker, C., & Van Der Grinten, B. (2016). Product design and business model strategies for a circular economy. *Journal of Industrial and Production Engineering*, 33(5), 308–320.

Bocken, N. M., Miller, K., Weissbrod, I., Holgado, M., & Evans, S. (2017). Business model experimentation for circularity: Driving sustainability in a large international clothing retailer. *Economics and Policy of Energy and the Environment*, 38, 85–122.

Bocken, N. M. P., Schuit, C. S. C., & Kraaijenhagen, C. (2018). Experimenting with a circular business model: Lessons from eight cases. *Environmental Innovation and Societal Transitions*, 28, 79–95.

Bocken, N. M., & Short, S. W. (2016). Towards a sufficiency-driven business model: Experiences and opportunities. *Environmental Innovation and Societal Transitions*, 18, 41–61.

Bocken, N., & Snihur, Y. (2019). Lean startup and the business model: Experimenting for novelty and impact. *Long Range Planning*, 53(4), 101953.

Bocken, N., Strupeit, L., Whalen, K., & Nußholz, J. (2019). A review and evaluation of circular business model innovation tools. *Sustainability*, 11(8), 2210.

Boons, F., & Bocken, N. (2018). Towards a sharing economy: Innovating ecologies of business models. *Technological Forecasting and Social Change*, 137(C), 40–52.

Brown, P., Baldassarre, B., Konietzko, J., Bocken, N., & Balkenende, R. (2019). Developing and testing a collaborative partner ideation tool for circular proposition design: Evidence from a circular innovation festival. European Roundtable for Sustainable Consumption and Production (ERSCP), Barcelona, 15–18 October.

Brown, T. (2008). Design thinking. *Harvard Business Review*, 86(6), 84–92.

Chesbrough, H. (2010). Business model innovation: Opportunities and barriers. *Long Range Planning*, 43(2–3), 354–363.

Croll, A., & Yoskovitz, B. (2013). *Lean Analytics: Use Data to Build a Better Startup Faster*. Sebastopol, CA: O'Reilly Media.

Geissdoerfer, M., Savaget, P., Bocken, N. M., & Hultink, E. J. (2017). The circular economy: A new sustainability paradigm? *Journal of Cleaner Production*, 143, 757–768.

Ghisellini, P., & Ulgiati, S. (2020). Circular economy transition in Italy: Achievements, perspectives and constraints. *Journal of Cleaner Production*, 243, 118360.

Heikkilä, M., Bouwman, H., Heikkilä, J., Solaimani, S., & Janssen, W. (2016). Business model metrics: An open repository. *Information Systems and e-Business Management*, 14(2), 337–366.

Konietzko, J., Baldassarre, B., Brown, P., Bocken, N., & Hultink, E. J. (2020a). Circular business model experimentation: Demystifying assumptions. *Journal of Cleaner Production*, 277, 122596.

Konietzko, J., Bocken, N., & Hultink, E. J. (2020b). A tool to analyze, ideate and develop circular innovation ecosystems. *Sustainability*, 12(1), 417.

Kraaijenhagen, C., Van Open, C., & Bocken, N. (2016). *Circular Business: Collaborate and Circulate*. Amersfoort: Circular Collaboration.

Mansoori, Y., & Lackéus, M. (2020). Comparing effectuation to discovery-driven planning, prescriptive entrepreneurship, business planning, lean startup, and design thinking. *Small Business Economics*, 54, 791–818.

McGrath, R. G. (2010). Business models: A discovery driven approach. *Long Range Planning*, 43(2–3), 247–261.

Osterwalder, A., & Pigneur, Y. (2009). *Business Model Generation: A Handbook for Visionaries, Game Changers, and Challengers*. Amsterdam: Self-published.

Pieroni, M. P., McAloone, T. C., & Pigosso, D. C. (2019). Business model innovation for circular economy and sustainability: A review of approaches. *Journal of Cleaner Production*, 215, 198–216.

Prendeville, S. M., O'Connor, F., Bocken, N. M., & Bakker, C. (2017). Uncovering ecodesign dilemmas: A path to business model innovation. *Journal of Cleaner Production*, 143, 1327–1339.

Richardson, J. (2008). The business model: An integrative framework for strategy execution. *Strategic Change*, 17(5–6), 133–144.

Ries, E. (2011). *The Lean Startup: How Today's Entrepreneurs Use Continuous Innovation to Create Radically Successful Businesses*. London: Penguin Books.

Robson, C., & McCartan, K. (2016). *Real World Research: A Resource for Social Scientists and Practitioner-Researchers*. Hoboken, NJ: John Wiley & Sons.

Sarasini, S., & Linder, M. (2018). Integrating a business model perspective into transition theory: The example of new mobility services. *Environmental Innovation and Societal Transitions*, 27, 16–31.

Sarasvathy, S. D. (2009). Effectuation: Elements of Entrepreneurial Expertise. Cheltenham, UK and Northampton, MA, USA: Edward Elgar Publishing.

Schuit, C., Baldassare, B., & Bocken, N. (2017). Sustainable business model experimentation practices: Evidence from four start-ups. *Product Lifetimes and the Environment* (PLATE), 8–10.

Stahel, W. (1994). The utilization-focused service economy: Resource efficiency and product-life extension. In B. R. Allenby & D. J. Richards (eds.), *The Greening of Industrial Ecosystems*. Washington, DC: National Academies Press, 178–190.

Stubbs, W., & Cocklin, C. (2008). Conceptualizing a "sustainability business model". *Organization & Environment*, 21(2), 103–127.

Van de Ven, A. H. (2007). *Engaged Scholarship: A Guide for Organizational and Social Research*. Oxford: Oxford University Press on Demand.

Weissbrod, I., & Bocken, N. M. (2017). Developing sustainable business experimentation capability: A case study. *Journal of Cleaner Production*, 142, 2663–2676.

York, J. G., O'Neil, I., & Sarasvathy, S. D. (2016). Exploring environmental entrepreneurship: Identity coupling, venture goals, and stakeholder incentives. *Journal of Management Studies*, 53, 695–737.

Zink, T., & Geyer, R. (2017). Circular economy rebound. *Journal of Industrial Ecology*, 21(3), 593–602.

20. How digital technologies boost value potential creation and value realization in CE: insights from a multiple case study across industries[1]

Sami Rusthollkarhu, Valtteri Ranta and Leena Aarikka-Stenroos

INTRODUCTION

Digital technologies and technological innovations have been identified as important catalysts for business model innovations that enable value creation while adhering to circular economy (CE) principles (Nascimento et al. 2019; Rosa et al. 2020; Ranta et al. 2021; Bocken et al. 2016). Although the concept of business models has often been used in the CE literature, its primary function has been to showcase a more holistic perspective on how CE principles can be implemented in business (see e.g. Lüdeke-Freund et al. 2019). Thus, the business models in the CE literature have mainly focused on value proposition (Manninen et al. 2018), value creation (Bocken et al. 2016), and value capture (Ranta et al. 2018) activities of companies that enable adhering to CE principles in business. The literature, however, has not given much attention to the models' primary role in describing customer value creation (Teece 2010) and the necessary participation of the customer in value creation (Vargo and Lusch 2004, 2016). In this chapter, we therefore discuss how digital technologies enable and boost customer value creation in CE. We give special attention to not only the effects of digital technologies in creating value potential for customer but also the effects in the customer's possibilities to realize this value.

As with business model innovations, the CE literature has approached digital technologies from a circularity and material efficiency perspective. Technologies have allowed companies to better utilize their supply chain data to track products and materials, potentially improving their ability to retain value (Lopes de Sousa Jabbour et al. 2019) and thus better fulfil the requirement for circularity (Ranta et al. 2020). However, adhering to CE principles does not determine a company's ability to succeed or even exist in the market. For this, the value perceived by the customer is considered fundamental (Slater and Narver 1994). For a business model to be applicable, it must create value for the customer and be able to capture a part of that value (Teece 2010).

The dominant approach to customer value considers it as something determined by the customer (Vargo and Lusch 2004, 2016) and created through interactions between the customer and the supplier (Lindgreen et al. 2009). The supplier is seen as a facilitator (Grönroos and Voima 2013), or proposer (Vargo and Lusch 2004, 2016), of value as well as an organizer of the value process (Aarikka-Stenroos and Jaakkola 2012). The customer realizes the value as co-creator and evaluator (Grönroos 2011; Grönroos and Voima 2013; Prahalad and Ramaswamy 2004; Vargo and Lusch 2016) by interacting with the supplier and using the products and services offered to them (Grönroos and Voima 2013; Vargo and Lusch 2004).

The chapter adopts this dominant approach, in which the customer is seen as the necessary co-creator of value. Customer-perceived value is then determined by two aspects: (1) the value potential created and (2) the customer's ability to realize that potential. We utilize these two aspects to examine the effects of digital technologies on value creation in the CE context. We aim to understand how digital technologies allow companies to develop and redesign their CE business by (1) improving the value potential of CE business and (2) improving the customer's ability to realize that value. Together, these two aspects explain how providers can utilize digital technologies to enhance customer value creation in order to strengthen CE innovations.

We conducted a multiple case study among six companies from different industries. The study examined their CE solutions, in which digital technologies were utilized for both customer value creation and adherence to CE principles. The interview data gathered were categorized according to different digital technologies as well as their effects on value potential and its realization.

This study aims to contribute to the literature on circular and sustainable business, CE innovations, and value creation by exploring the relationship between circularity, digital technologies, and customer value creation. In addition to introducing the topic of customer value creation in CE, this chapter provides managerial guidelines for practitioners in their innovative business endeavours.

VALUE CREATION IN THE CE CONTEXT

A business model's ability to provide realizable value for the customer determines the company's likelihood of remaining in the market (Teece 2010). In this section, we discuss creating and realizing customer value potential in relation to CE principles.

Creating and Realizing Value Potential

Customers have an active role in the process of value creation. The customer realizes value by interacting with the value proposition of the company (Vargo and Lusch 2004) and can also participate in the process in a more extensive manner as a co-producer, designer, developer, or marketer (Aarikka-Stenroos and Jaakkola 2012). The role of the company is to offer value propositions (Vargo and Lusch 2004) and facilitate the value process (Grönroos and Voima 2013). We emphasize that the creation and realization of value propositions take place in an ecosystem, meaning that propositions can be created by multiple actors (Vargo and Lusch 2016).

Furthermore, the customer's process of realizing value is guided by a broad range of inter- and intra-organizational interactions, not just those with value proposition. Thus, the value realized by the customer is not necessarily similar to the value proposition offered by the company (Rusthollkarhu et al. 2020). This is especially relevant in the context of CE, as the function of products and materials differs in different parts of the cycle. For example, recycled or reused goods can have functions for customers distinct from their original purposes (Ranta et al. 2020). To capture a more holistic view of customer-perceived value, we use the concept of value potential, which includes all the potential value the customer can realize while interacting with the physical good or service, including the intended value communicated by the value proposition. Next, we discuss the connection between value potential and CE activities.

Value Potential in CE Business

To understand CE characteristics in value creation, we use the four CE value creation logics described by Ranta et al. (2020): resurrect, share, optimize, and replace value. These logics are consistent with other CE business model categorizations (e.g. Ellen MacArthur Foundation 2015; Bocken et al. 2016; Lüdeke-Freund et al. 2019). However, while the other models primarily focus on improving the circularity of business, the value creation logics explicitly focus on value creation but from the perspective of the company (Ranta et al. 2020). Thus, the crucial activities within these value creation logics provide an understanding of the value-potential-building activities of CE business models. An important aspect of value creation logics is that while each describes core aspects of how certain activities aim to increase value potential, multiple value creation logics can and often are found simultaneously in a CE business model (Ranta et al. 2020).

In the *resurrect value logic*, the company focuses on reintroducing value back into resources, such as products, components, and materials. To leverage this logic, companies need to be able to reintroduce value cost efficiently so that the revitalization of value offers competitive value potential for customers compared to new resources while enabling profitable value capture for the company (Ranta et al. 2020). Crucial CE activities for this logic include the acquisition of the resources with diminished value in the value resurrecting process through, for example, take-back systems (Lewandowski 2016) or circular supply chains (Centobelli et al. 2020); the actual process of resurrecting value, be it maintenance, repairing, remanufacturing, or recycling (Lüdeke-Freund et al. 2019); and the sale of the resources back to the market (Ranta et al. 2018).

In the *share value logic*, the company focuses on enabling customers to move from the ownership of products toward using shared resources, which reduces the amount of resources and, thus, the materials needed to fulfil the needs of the customer base. To leverage this logic, companies need to overcome the existing customer preference for owning their own resources by providing a shared resource alternative with competitive value potential (Ranta et al. 2020). Crucial CE activities, thus, make it convenient and economically viable for customers to discover, access, and use shared resources. Companies can, for example, improve the discoverability of shared resources by implementing online marketplaces and ensuring the accessibility of shared resources. Companies using this logic can either own the resources themselves and fully manage the fleet of shared resources (Ranta et al. 2020), or they can enable resource sharing between customers with excess resources and customers with resource needs, following a sharing economy approach (Belk 2014).

In the *optimize value logic*, the company focuses on providing specialized knowledge and resources for the customer's use, enabling them to create more value with fewer resources. Companies can provide monitoring services that allow customers to identify waste in energy and material usage as well as services that allow customers to improve on identified issues. For example, monitoring data from an industrial machine enables the provision of predictive maintenance services, optimizing the uptime of the machine. To leverage this logic, companies need to have a sound understanding of both the resource for which value creation is to be optimized as well as the business of the customer in order to improve both the value potential of the resource and the customer's realization of that potential (Ranta et al. 2020). Important activities for this logic, thus, include the ones that deepen the customer's understanding of resource use in their value realization process.

In the *replace value logic*, the company focuses on providing an alternative resource that can fulfil the same customer needs as traditionally used resources while fulfilling the emerging sustainability needs related to CE principles. This logic is especially relevant concerning generally unsustainable resources; an example of it is the increasingly popular plant-based meat replacement products that help reduce the environmentally unsustainable levels of meat consumption while offering customers competitive value potential compared to actual meat (Ranta et al. 2020). Crucial activities for this logic involve identifying certain needs of the customer that if left unfulfilled would deter the customer from switching from the traditional resource to the replacement one. Such needs can be properties of the resource itself (e.g. the taste of the plant-based protein product), or they can be the qualities of the resource that make it suitable for the customer to use without other large investments, such as using waste oil-based diesel in the same vehicle as fossil fuel-based diesel. As this logic usually builds upon a novel innovation, research and development activities are often central to it.

Digital Technologies in CE

Digital technologies have been identified as having a key role in enabling CE principles in business (Pagoropoulos et al. 2017) by narrowing, slowing, and closing of resource loops (Ranta et al. 2021). In particular, the product-service systems (PSS) model, in which product-oriented offerings are transformed by supporting services or even by selling the product as a service (Tukker 2015), benefits from the implementation of digital technologies. In this context, digital technologies enable remote monitoring of the product, which, in turn, allows optimizing the provision of maintenance services for the customer, thus lengthening the product's lifecycle. Furthermore, as the product reaches the end-of-life stage, digital technologies enable the PSS provider to collect the product and identify whether reusing, remanufacturing, or recycling of the product is economically feasible through analysing the data collected from the product during the use phase or embedded in the product as a product passport (Alcayaga et al. 2019). Thus, in the PSS model, digital technologies facilitate closing the loop on the products and improving the ability to select the optimal revalorization route when products reach their end-of-life stage.

Five technology groups are identified as relevant in the context of CE: cyber-physical systems (CPS), Internet of Things (IoT), big data and analytics (BDA), additive manufacturing (AM), and simulation (Rosa et al. 2020). CPS refers to the embedded computers and networks used in monitoring physical processes (Lee et al. 2015). IoT technologies utilize modern wireless telecommunications (e.g. radio frequency identification [RFID], sensors, tags, actuators) to enable interaction among people, devices, and objects (Nasiri et al. 2017). BDA is an umbrella term for applications of advanced data analysis techniques applied to big data, including cloud storage and computing as well as AI analysis techniques (Soroka et al. 2017). AM describes technologies that allow production via layering or 3D printing (Dutta et al. 2001). Lastly, simulation refers to a wide range of mathematical programming techniques (Rosa et al. 2020).

RESEARCH DESIGN, CASES, DATA, AND ANALYSIS

To study how digital technologies enable and boost customer value creation in CE, we chose a qualitative multiple case study strategy. This approach enables us to develop a theoretical understanding of the focal phenomenon in its natural setting (Yin 1994) and to integrate conceptual research-based knowledge and empirical insights derived from the cases (Dubois and Gadde 2002). By selecting a multiple case study strategy with six cases from different industries with differing business models, we could uncover differences between the cases regarding how digitalization shapes value creation in the CE setting and identify similar patterns across different company cases. The case companies are headquartered in Northern Europe, although they conduct most of their business globally.

The case selection was purposive. First, by using maximum variation criteria (Patton 1990), we carefully selected cases from various CE-related businesses. These businesses used different business models and came from different industries; they also differed in terms of their size and types of digital tools used. Second, by choosing cases where diverse resource flow strategies and CE principles are followed – including narrowing, slowing, and closing resource flows – we ensured that our findings captured the full spectrum of CE business models. Third, we selected successful cases (see Patton 1990), as we assumed that by focusing on companies running feasible CE-related businesses, we would be able to analyse implemented digital technologies for CE and examine how this shapes value creation for all involved actors (suppliers, customers, other actors). Additionally, to improve case selection, we conducted a preliminary analysis of more than ten cases and then focused our analysis on the six cases (see Table 20.1) from different industries.

We built on both the primary and secondary data sources for each case. The primary dataset comprised 14 semi-structured face-to-face and remote interviews, conducted between July 2019 and January 2020 with key actors, such as business, logistics, technology, software, and project managers as well as experts directly involved in the use of digitalization and business development in the field of CE. The secondary dataset supported and extended each case; these data comprised internal and media-originated data, such as technical documents, articles, companies' websites, and other web pages concerning the solutions, the companies, and their evolving market and business environments.

In our case analysis, we first conducted a within-case analysis as we generated an overview of digital technologies used and their effect on value potential. Next, we conducted a cross-case analysis and generated more synthesized patterns by identifying similarities and differences across the cases. To improve quality of analysis and trustworthiness of the results, we applied a range of tools and tactics, such as a structured coding procedure as well as researcher triangulation with drafted tables and figures, which encouraged discussion among all involved researchers (Flick 2004).

DIGITAL TECHNOLOGIES IN CUSTOMER VALUE CREATION: CREATING AND REALIZING VALUE POTENTIAL IN THE CE CONTEXT

Next, we discuss the results gained from the six company cases. In Table 20.2, we summarize the results. We present the identified digital technologies, short descriptions of how the tech-

Table 20.1   *The cases and their background information*

Case	Company size (revenue)	Industry	Description	Interviews	Secondary data
Construction tool service	5,300 MEUR	Tools/construction	Provider of technologically leading tool products and digital solutions for professional construction sites. Digital solutions aim to improve resource efficiency in construction areas.	Services & software, area sales manager	Company web pages, annual reports
Forest machinery and harvesting	610 MEUR	Machinery	Manufacturer of forest machinery. It utilizes digital tools in harvesting solutions to optimize machine usage and provide maintenance services.	Spare parts manager, HSE manager	Company web pages, annual reports
Waste management	370 MEUR	Waste management (public)	A municipal body that develops resource efficient reuse processes for city waste.	Logistics manager, Landfill field manager, Project manager	N/A
Oil refinery	14,900 MEUR	Oil refinery and technology developer	Oil refinery producing refined oil products from renewable feedstock.	Chief information officer, Head of digital transformation	Company web pages, annual reports, news articles
Fertilizers and infra products	8 MEUR	Forestry and agriculture	Produces fertilizers for forestry and agriculture and products for groundworks and environmental construction from industrial side flows.	Technical sales specialist	Company web and social media pages, industrial area case report
Pulp refinery	10240 MEUR	Pulp refinery	Produces, refines, and markets pulp products and energy solutions. Applies tailored digital solutions to close flows and develops platforms for utilization of industry side flows.	Director of business, Partner company CEO, Partner company, head of circular economy, Partner company environment chief, Partner company, technology platform manager	Technical platform documents

nologies enable the value potential provided by the CE company in each case, and the different interfaces that enable the realization of the provided value potential. The interfaces are categorized as company-provided ones that are managed by the provider and third-party ones that are not owned by the company but through which customers can realize the value potential.

Five different technology categories were indicated in relation to creating value potential: IoT technologies, cloud technologies, enterprise resource planning (ERP) systems, artificial intelligence (AI), and automation. IoT included sensors and systems that enabled information gathering concerning production or customer machine use. Both cloud technologies and ERP were mentioned in the context of integrating information from multiple sources and allowing easy access to it. Because of their learning capabilities, AI tools were utilized in the analysis of vast datasets concerning forecasting tasks. One case company bundled their production technologies under the general term 'automation', including both the software and hardware components that enable autonomous actions in manufacturing. Our findings concerning technology categories are in line with Rosa et al.'s (2020) categorization. CPS, BDA, and simulations present themselves in descriptions of the use of cloud and AI systems. ERP systems were also brought up as a tool for lighter data storage and analysis. AI's forecasting capabilities were used to simulate the material flows in supply chains. AM was the only technology category that was not mentioned in the interviews, as none of the case companies relied on 3D printing/layering technologies in their manufacturing. Furthermore, interviewees highlighted the importance of cloud technology. Although cloud technologies do not form a separate category in Rosa et al.'s (2020) categorization, data storage and computing capabilities, such as cloud technologies, are inherently imbedded in categories of IoT, BDA, and simulation.

DISCUSSION

The Four Roles of Digital Technologies in CE Value Creation

All company cases analysed in this chapter utilize digital technologies for creating value potential, enabling value realization, and adhering to the CE principles, which supports the value logic of the company. Based on our results, we propose four roles for digital technologies in CE value creation: *digital technology acting as an interface, digital technology providing access to value potential, digital technology improving operational efficiency*, and *digital technology helping to understand value realization*. These four roles explain how companies with CE solutions can use digital technologies to enhance the value potential of their offerings and empower their customers in value realization through diverse digital tools.

Digital technology acting as an interface: Digital technology forms the communication interface between the customer and the company or other ecosystem actors. Convenient interfaces for customers are crucial for value realization in all CE value logics. API, mobile, and online interfaces utilized in the cases of construction tool service, forest machinery, and oil and pulp refinery demonstrate the technology's role as an interface. These solutions provide an example of how companies can utilize different digital interfaces to enable value realization in resurrect, share, optimize, and replace value logics.

Digital technology providing access to value potential: Digital technologies ensure that value potential is accessible to the customer through the interface. Cloud, IoT, and ERP technologies utilized in resurrect logics of construction tools and forest machinery and harvesting

Table 20.2   Digital technologies, value potential, and interfaces for value realization in CE setting

Case	Digital technologies	Value logic and technologies' effect on value potential	Link to CE principles	Company-provided interfaces for value realization and customer's actions	Third-party provided interfaces for customer's value realization
Construction tool service *Product-service system operator, tool manufacturer for the construction industry*	**IoT technologies** collect data from machines, providing machine health and location information. **Cloud** technologies integrate and show data to the company and customer, enabling the potential for offering context-specific maintenance services.	**Optimize: IoT** technologyenables tool tracking and data generation. Data allow the company to fulfil the needs of customers with fewer overall tools. Data from construction machines are used to provide higher quality maintenance service at a lower cost. **Resurrect: Cloud** technologies provide customers convenient, timely access to maintenance services, increasing demand and use of services.	**Narrow**[a] resource flows by serving customers with fewer tools and **slow**[b] flows by increasing the demand for maintenance service by making it accessible.	Tools and machines used in construction sites, mobile app, QR tags, online interface. Customer uses tools and interacts with mobile and online interfaces to conveniently access to maintenance services as well as tool location and use information.	Third-party tools and machines used in construction sites

Case	Digital technologies	Value logic and technologies' effect on value potential	Link to CE principles	Company-provided interfaces for value realization and customer's actions	Third-party provided interfaces for customer's value realization
Forest machinery and harvesting *Product service system operator, forestry machine manufacturer*	**IoT** technologies collect machine health and usage data. An **ERP system** integrates data for maintenance and product development operations. The **online ordering system** allows customers to directly order spare parts.	**Optimize: IoT** technologies allow gathering the data on the customer's use of the machine. The data can be utilized in product development to optimize a machine's fuel consumption and make the product more desirable and cost effective for the customer. **Optimize and resurrect: IoT** technologies enable data gathering on machine health and customer's machine usage. The **ERP system** allows data integration into maintenance and product development operations, enabling the provision of high quality and cost effective maintenance services and spare part ordering.	**Narrow** resource flows by optimizing fuel economy and **slow** them by increasing the efficiency of maintenance and spare part services.	Machines, online interface. Customer uses the machines and interacts with online interfaces to access spare part and maintenance services.	Third-party parts
Waste management *Material processor, municipality-owned waste and water management group*	**IoT** technologies provide data from vehicles used in logistics systems.	**Optimize: IoT** technologies enable tracking and data generation of the logistics system. Data can be utilized to identify opportunities for efficiency and cost reductions.	**Narrow** resource flows by increasing operational efficiency of logistics system.	Waste collection bins and stations. Customer interacts with waste collection bins and stations. Efficient logistics ensure that bins and stations are usable at all times.	No identified third-party interfaces

Case	Digital technologies	Value logic and technologies' effect on value potential	Link to CE principles	Company-provided interfaces for value realization and customer's actions	Third-party provided interfaces for customer's value realization
Oil refinery *Material processor, producer of refined products from renewable feedstock in the oil industry*	**IoT** technologies collect data from chemical processes and the supply chain. **Cloud** technologies store, integrate, and analyse large volumes of data. **AI** technologies provide forecasting capabilities.	**Replace: IoT** technologies enable the optimization of production and supply chain processes. This enables production with fewer materials, reducing costs while simultaneously improving the quality of the product. **Replace: Cloud** technologies allow the company to access larger volumes of data from the supply chain, increasing knowledge about its real-time operation, thus enabling a cost-effective, more reliable supply chain. **Replace: AI** technologies allow the company to better forecast supply for waste materials and demand for refined products, developing knowledge for supply chain management and reducing unnecessary warehousing and potential shortages.	**Narrow** and **close** resource flows with more efficient production and supply chain processes.	Distribution substations, online interface for ordering, oil refinery logistics services. Customer uses refined oil products, interacts with online ordering system, logistics services and with distribution substation.	Third-party distribution substations, machines using the product

Case	Digital technologies	Value logic and technologies' effect on value potential	Link to CE principles	Company-provided interfaces for value realization and customer's actions	Third-party provided interfaces for customer's value realization
Fertilizers and infra products *Produces fertilizers for forestry and agriculture and products for groundworks and environmental construction from industrial side flows*	**Manufacturing automation** increases operational efficiency in production processes.	**Replace: Manufacturing automation** enables operational efficiency in production, where industrial side flows are utilized in the manufacturing of fertilizer and groundworks products, closing resource flows. Operational efficiency ensures the low cost of production and enables economic value for customer.	**Close** resource with more efficient production processes.	Fertilizers, infra products Customer uses fertilizers and infra products.	Agricultural and forest machinery/ services, machines and tools used in construction site
Pulp refinery *Producer of pulp and refined products, developing industry-wide platform for utilizing side streams*	**Cloud** technologies store, integrate, and analyse large volumes of data.	**Share: Cloud** technologies allow integrating real-time information on the side streams of individual companies closing resource flows.	**Close** resource flows by allowing shared use of side streams.	Online interface, application programming interfaces (APIs) with ERP and CRM when compatible. Customers interact with online interfaces to access side-stream information and to engage with the side-stream. APIs enable the automation of the interaction.	ERP and CRM systems

Notes: [a] Narrowing resource flows: using fewer resources per product (Bocken et al. 2016); [b] Slowing resource flows: extending the life of a product (Bocken et al. 2016); [c] Closing resource flows: through recycling, closing the loop between post-use and production (Bocken et al. 2016).

demonstrate this role. In these solutions, customers can realize value without interacting with the tools, machines, or service personnel of the company. Conveniently accessible interfaces combined with wide access to value potential allowed case companies to increase the demand for their CE services.

Digital technology improving operational efficiency: Digital technologies increase economic value for customers by lowering production costs. Illustrative examples in our study were production automation in the case of fertilizers and infra products; IoT, cloud, and AI technologies in supply chain efficiency in the case of oil refinery; and IoT technologies in logistics efficiency in the case of the waste management company. The operational efficiency also highlights that CE innovation does not need to be radical to be successful. Improvements in operational efficiency can take place in company processes without radically changing the business model.

Digital technology helping to understand value realization: Digital technologies monitor customer's use of the product or service improving the company's understanding of the customer's value realization process. The data gathered from the customer provides valuable information to guide further development and innovation. The final role is especially crucial to optimize logic, as the value potential in it is directly linked to customers' use of the product/ service. IoT technologies in cases of construction tool service, forest machinery, and harvesting, are examples of digital technologies in enabling customer understanding in optimize value logic.

Practical Implications

The four roles of digital technology in CE value creation generate insights for managers on how to implement diverse digital technologies to develop their CE business and customer value. Therefore, managerial takeaways for each identified role of digital technology are presented. We suggest the four principles of digital CE value creation: relevance of interfaces, accessibility of the value potential, the efficiency of the processes, and analysis of value realization. Practitioners should consider these as guidelines for digital and business innovation in the field of CE.

1. Relevance of interfaces: Identify the interfaces that are most accessible for your customer and build service by utilizing those interfaces. For example, in the case of a construction tool service, the mobile application ensured that every worker on the construction site could interact with the service regardless of time or location.
2. Accessibility of the value potential: Ensure that the customer can realize the highest possible value potential through each interface. For example, in the case of the pulp refinery, cloud technologies ensured that the information on the side streams was accessible through both online and API interfaces.
3. Efficiency of the processes: Ensure a sufficient level of operational efficiency for a low production cost to provide economic value for the customer. For example, in the case of the oil refinery, IoT, cloud, and AI technologies were used to ensure that the supply chain worked efficiently.
4. Analysis of value realization: Build technologies and processes to understand the value realization processes of the customer for continuous improvement and further innovation. For example, in the case of the forest machinery and harvesting, IoT technologies were

used to monitor the customer's usage of the machine. This information was used in R&D and was also provided to the customers to help them optimize their own machine usage.

Theoretical Contributions and Directions for Future Research

Our study provides theoretical contributions to the literature on business and technology innovations in CE, to the literature on sustainable business, to the literature on the role of digital technology in CE business and to the literature on value creation. Prior circular and sustainable business literature covered technology and business innovation from the view of circularity (see e.g. Bocken et al. 2016; Lüdeke-Freund et al. 2019; Manninen et al. 2018; Ranta et al. 2018), leaving the realm of customer value creation unexplored. By taking the customer value approach and revealing aspects of value potential, as well as its realization, this chapter provides conceptualization for future studies focusing on customer value in circular and sustainable business as well as on business and technology innovations in CE.

The literature on the role of digital technologies in CE business has thus far been task and business model centric. These studies describe how various digital technologies enable the circulation of materials and products within CE business models (Pagoropoulos et al. 2017; Rosa et al. 2020) and analyse how the implementation of digital technologies enables incremental and radical sustainability and business model innovations (Ranta et al. 2021). Our study explicitly links digital technologies to the customer value by identifying the four roles of digital technologies in CE value creation. By doing so, the chapter has initiated a discussion for combining the customer value creation and CE principles; it has contributed to the literature on circular and sustainable business as well as to the literature on value creation, which have previously focused on the dynamics between the customer and provider (Aarikka-Stenroos and Jaakkola 2012; Grönroos and Voima 2013; Vargo and Lusch 2004) without explicit focus on the role of digital technologies.

For future research endeavours in the field of value creation in CE, we propose the following themes:

- The relevance of different roles of digital technology: Are all technology roles identified in this study equally relevant in other business environments?
- Customer-centric view on value realization: How is the customer's process of value realization and the customer's engagement with CE business models? Which technologies are used and how? Which actors participate in the value realization process?
- Processes with ecosystem actors: What kinds of roles do interactions with different ecosystem actors have in the creation of value potential or its realization in CE?

ACKNOWLEDGEMENTS

The data generation and writing of this book chapter were supported by the Strategic Research Council, Academy of Finland, through the research projects entitled 'Circular Economy Catalysts: From Innovation to Business Ecosystems' (CICAT2025) (grant ID 320194) and 'Sustainable Industry Ecosystem' (SIE) (grant ID 337722). Special thanks to research assistants Juha-Matti Väisänen, Puja Saha, and Roosa Lahtinen for their efforts in data collection for this study.

NOTE

1. This is an open access work distributed under the Creative Commons Attribution-NonCommercial-NoDerivatives 4.0 Unported (https://creativecommons.org/licenses/by-nc-nd/4.0/). Users can redistribute the work for non-commercial purposes, as long as it is passed along unchanged and in whole, as detailed in the License. Edward Elgar Publishing Ltd must be clearly credited as the rights holder for publication of the original work. Any translation or adaptation of the original content requires the written authorization of Edward Elgar Publishing Ltd.

REFERENCES

Aarikka-Stenroos, L., & Jaakkola, E. (2012). Value co-creation in knowledge intensive business services: A dyadic perspective on the joint problem solving process. *Industrial Marketing Management*, 41(1), 15–26.

Alcayaga, A., Wiener, M., & Hansen, E. G. (2019). Towards a framework of smart-circular systems: An integrative literature review. *Journal of Cleaner Production*, 221, 622–634.

Belk, R. (2014). You are what you can access: Sharing and collaborative consumption online. *Journal of Business Research*, 67(8), 1595–1600.

Bocken, N. M. P., de Pauw, I., Bakker, C., & van der Grinten, B. (2016). Product design and business model strategies for a circular economy. *Journal of Industrial and Production Engineering*, 33(5), 308–320.

Centobelli, P., Cerchione, R., Chiaroni, D., Del Vecchio, P., & Urbinati, A. (2020). Designing business models in circular economy: A systematic literature review and research agenda. *Business Strategy and the Environment*. https://doi.org/10.1002/bse.2466.

Dubois, A., & Gadde, L. (2002). Systematic combining: An abductive approach to case research. *Journal of Business Research*, 55, 553–560.

Dutta, D., Prinz, F. B., Rosen, D., & Weiss, L. (2001). Layered manufacturing: Current status and future trends. *Journal of Computing and Information Science in Engineering*, 1(1), 60–71.

Ellen MacArthur Foundation (2015). *Growth Within: A Circular Vision for a Competitive Europe*.

Flick, U. (2004). Triangulation in qualitative research. In U. Flick, E. von Kardoff, & I. Steinke (eds.), *A Companion to Qualitative Research*. Thousand Oaks, CA: Sage Publications, 178–183.

Grönroos, C. (2011). Value co-creation in service logic: A critical analysis. *Marketing Theory*, 11(3), 279–301.

Grönroos, C., & Voima, P. (2013). Critical service logic: Making sense of value creation and co-creation. *Journal of the Academy of Marketing Science*, 41(2), 133–150.

Lee, J., Bagheri, B., & Kao, H. A. (2015). A cyber-physical systems architecture for Industry 4.0-based manufacturing systems. *Manufacturing Letters*, 3, 18–23.

Lewandowski, M. (2016). Designing the business models for circular economy: Towards the conceptual framework. *Sustainability (Switzerland)*, 8(1), 1–28.

Lindgreen, A., Antioco, M., Palmer, R., & van Heesch, T. (2009). High-tech, innovative products: Identifying and meeting business customers' value needs. *Journal of Business and Industrial Marketing*, 24(3–4), 182–197.

Lopes de Sousa Jabbour, A. B., Rojas Luiz, J. V., Rojas Luiz, O., Jabbour, C. J. C., Ndubisi, N. O., Caldeira de Oliveira, J. H., & Junior, F. H. (2019). Circular economy business models and operations management. *Journal of Cleaner Production*, 235, 1525–1539.

Lüdeke-Freund, F., Gold, S., & Bocken, N. M. P. (2019). A review and typology of circular economy business model patterns. *Journal of Industrial Ecology*, 23(1), 36–61.

Manninen, K., Koskela, S., Antikainen, R., Bocken, N., Dahlbo, H., & Aminoff, A. (2018). Do circular economy business models capture intended environmental value propositions? *Journal of Cleaner Production*, 171, 413–422.

Nascimento, D. L. M., Alencastro, V., Quelhas, O. L. G., Caiado, R. G. G., Garza-Reyes, J. A., Lona, L. R., & Tortorella, G. (2019). Exploring Industry 4.0 technologies to enable circular economy practices in a manufacturing context: A business model proposal. *Journal of Manufacturing Technology Management*, 30, 607–627.

Nasiri, M., Tura, N., & Ojanen, V. (2017). Developing disruptive innovations for sustainability: A review on impact of Internet of Things (IOT). *PICMET 2017 – Portland International Conference on Management of Engineering and Technology: Technology Management for the Interconnected World, Proceedings, 2017 January*, 1–10. https://doi.org/10.23919/PICMET.2017.8125369.

Pagoropoulos, A., Pigosso, D. C. A., & McAloone, T. C. (2017). The emergent role of digital technologies in the circular economy: A review. *Procedia CIRP*, 64, 19–24.

Patton, M. (1990). Designing qualitative studies. In *Qualitative Evaluation and Research Methods* (2nd ed.). Beverly Hills, CA: Sage Publications, 169–186.

Prahalad, C. K., & Ramaswamy, V. (2004). Co-creation experiences: The next practice in value creation. *Journal of Interactive Marketing*, 18(3), 5–14.

Ranta, V., Aarikka-Stenroos, L., & Mäkinen, S. J. (2018). Creating value in the circular economy: A structured multiple-case analysis of business models. *Journal of Cleaner Production*, 201, 988–1000.

Ranta, V., Aarikka-Stenroos, L., & Väisänen, J. M. (2021). Digital technologies catalyzing business model innovation for circular economy: Multiple case study. *Resources, Conservation and Recycling*, 164, 105155.

Ranta, V., Keränen, J., & Aarikka-Stenroos, L. (2020). How B2B suppliers articulate customer value propositions in the circular economy: Four innovation-driven value creation logics. *Industrial Marketing Management*, 87, 291–305.

Rosa, P., Sassanelli, C., Urbinati, A., Chiaroni, D., & Terzi, S. (2020). Assessing relations between circular economy and Industry 4.0: A systematic literature review. *International Journal of Production Research*, 58(6), 1662–1687.

Rusthollkarhu, S., Hautamaki, P., & Aarikka-Stenroos, L. (2020). Value (co-)creation in B2B sales ecosystems. *Journal of Business and Industrial Marketing*. https://doi.org/10.1108/JBIM-03-2020-0130.

Slater, S. F., & Narver, J. C. (1994). Market orientation, customer value, and superior performance. *Business Horizons*, 37(2), 22–28.

Soroka, A., Liu, Y., Han, L., & Haleem, M. S. (2017). Big data driven customer insights for SMEs in redistributed manufacturing. *Procedia CIRP*, 63, 692–697.

Teece, D. J. (2010). Business models, business strategy and innovation. *Long Range Planning*, 43(2–3), 172–194.

Tukker, A. (2015). Product services for a resource-efficient and circular economy: A review. *Journal of Cleaner Production*, 97, 76–91.

Vargo, S. L., & Lusch, R. F. (2004). Evolving to a new dominant logic for marketing. *Journal of Marketing*, 68(1), 1–17.

Vargo, S. L., & Lusch, R. F. (2016). Institutions and axioms: An extension and update of service-dominant logic. *Journal of the Academy of Marketing Science*, 44(1), 5–23.

Yin, R. K. (1994). *Case Study Research: Design and Methods*. London: Sage Publications.

21. The circular economy impacts of digital academic spin-offs

Phuc Hong Huynh and Einar Rasmussen

INTRODUCTION

Digital technologies are often seen as essential enablers for the transition to a more circular economy (CE) (Antikainen et al. 2018; Ranta et al. 2021). New digital technologies, such as the Internet of Things (IoT), additive manufacturing, automation, and artificial intelligence, are transforming the sociotechnical system rapidly (Kopp et al. 2019; Li et al. 2020). The sociotechnical system entails the co-evolution of technology and society in which organizations adopt and adapt technologies into the organization and application contexts (Geels 2004; Li et al. 2020). The trajectory of new digital technologies impacts both the processes and outcomes of innovation and entrepreneurship (Nambisan 2017; Zaheer et al. 2019). Entrepreneurial firms play a vital role in harnessing and exploiting the opportunities of digital technologies to build a broad range of innovative products and services or upgrade production processes (Kraus et al. 2018; Nambisan 2017; Sahut et al. 2021).

Digital entrepreneurship not only promotes growth but may also tackle social and environmental issues (Bocken 2015; Giones and Brem 2017). In recent years, severe resource degradation and environmental pollution problems caused by the linear 'take-make-discard' production model have required an alternative and more sustainable model – the CE (Korhonen et al. 2018). The core of the CE is to transform the economy from a linear 'take-make-dispose' system to a circular 'make-use-return' system in which obsolete materials and goods are maintained, regenerated and restored to narrow, slow, and close the production–consumption loop (Lieder and Rashid 2016). Thus, natural resources are preserved, and waste and emissions are minimized.

Among entrepreneurial firms, academic spin-offs (ASOs) are new ventures initiated in the context of a parent university or research institute to commercialize scientific knowledge and technology (Rasmussen 2011). ASOs are highly knowledge-intensive firms associated with significantly higher inventiveness and growth rates than other firms (Shane 2004). Thus, ASOs are potentially important firms for commercializing digital innovations contributing to the CE transition. Although the economic impacts of ASOs are emphasized in the literature (Mathisen and Rasmussen 2019), little is known about the CE impacts of ASO firms, especially ASO firms that rely on digital technology. Given the potential of digital technologies for the CE (De Sousa Jabbour et al. 2018; Pagoropoulos et al. 2017) and the potential impacts of ASOs (Fini et al. 2018), digital ASOs may contribute to the transition to a CE in several ways. This chapter examines the role of ASOs that introduce digital innovations to potentially benefit the CE. Our research question asks *how ASOs commercializing digital innovations can contribute to the CE.*

LITERATURE REVIEW

The Emergence of Digital Technologies

Over the last decade, the evolution of digital technologies has transformed innovation and entrepreneurial processes, redefined market patterns, and created new markets (Nambisan 2017; Nambisan et al. 2019; Zaheer et al. 2019). There are various types of digital technologies such as the IoT, artificial intelligence, big data, sensors, blockchains, platforms, and software. Nambisan (2017) classified digital technologies into three main categories:

- A digital artefact is a "component, application, media content that are parts of new products or services and offer a specific functionality or value to end-users" (Nambisan 2017, p. 1031; Ekbia 2009;) and they "exist as stand-alone products or as parts of a platform" (Zaheer et al. 2019, p. 2).
- A digital platform is "a shared, common set of services and architects that serves to host complimentary offerings, including artefacts" (Nambisan 2017, p. 1031).
- A digital infrastructure is "digital technology tools and systems that offer communication, collaboration, and computing capacities to support innovation and entrepreneurship" (Nambisan 2017, p. 1031).

The three types may be combined to generate innovative solutions. A popular example is the service provider Airbnb, which combines a digital platform with digital artefacts in the form of a mobile application with app functions to deliver shared accommodation services to end-users.

The Influences of Digital Technology on Entrepreneurship

The advent of digital technologies has shifted both the processes and outcomes of entrepreneurship (Nambisan 2017). The term 'digital entrepreneurship' refers to "all new business ventures and the transformation of existing businesses that drive economic and/or socio values by creating and using novel digital technologies" (European Commission 2015, p. 2). The infusion of digital technologies mitigates the inherent uncertainty of the entrepreneurial processes (i.e., how and when entrepreneurial activities are implemented) and the entrepreneurial outcomes (i.e., the types, scopes, and markets of product and service offerings) (Nambisan 2017).

Digital technologies can improve the product development phase so that it is more quickly created, modified, and repeated (Kraus et al. 2018). Digital infrastructures, such as 3D printing and artificial intelligence, can also make entrepreneurship and innovation processes less predefined and more quickly adopted, modified, and enacted (Nambisan 2017; Ries 2011). Hence, the behaviours of entrepreneurial firms, such as how they collaborate and interact with other actors in the innovation ecosystem, are also altered due to these unique attributes (i.e., openness and generativity) of digital technologies (Nambisan 2017; Zaheer et al. 2019). For example, the blockchain increases the traceability and reliability of shared information, and digital platforms allow more open and interactive communication and collaboration among actors in the ecosystem. The liquidity of cash flow increases due to the flexibility and generativity of digital technologies, which also allow more new ventures to innovate without deadlock investments.

Digital advantages allow more start-ups to lead technological developments, explore unaddressed market demands, and create new markets. Many entrepreneurs find digital-based business models more dynamic than traditional business models (Kraus et al. 2018). For example, Airbnb and Uber are forerunners of the sharing economy by creating new markets for sharing accommodation and transport. The sharing business model is a significant digital-based business model that can benefit the CE (Bressanelli et al. 2018). The model illustrates how digital technologies, when combined with appropriate new business models, can create substantial sustainability impacts such as reduced new demand, reduced resource consumption, and reduced waste. Other entrepreneurial companies rely on, for example, blockchain-based business models to increase traceability or tailored-made business models using 3D printing and artificial intelligence to reduce overproduction, resource consumption, and waste.

Digital Academic Entrepreneurship for a More Circular Economy

Rippa and Secundo (2019) draw attention to the intersection of digital transformation and academic entrepreneurship research. Following the acceleration of digital technologies in academic entrepreneurship, the term 'digital academic entrepreneurship' indicates "the use of new digital technologies to improve the emerging forms of academic entrepreneurship, such as the development of digital spin-offs and alumni start-ups" (Rippa and Secundo 2019, p. 907). Secundo et al. (2020) show that digital innovations impact not only the outcomes but also the entrepreneurial processes of academic start-ups. For example, digital technologies can shift the traditional entrepreneurial incentives of academic entrepreneurship from pure scientific knowledge commercialization to broader socioeconomic values with a higher level of stakeholder engagement (Secundo et al. 2020). We define a digital CE-related ASO as one that commercializes digital innovations with potential CE impacts.

In sustainability transitions such as the CE that may require radical technological shifts and market reforms (Ranta et al. 2021), ASOs may play an important role by initiating necessary changes in the technological trajectory, transferring technology, and infusing knowledge spillovers (Autio 1997). Indeed, small, new firms have a higher likelihood of introducing radical innovations and taking CE actions compared to large incumbents (Henry et al. 2020). Large incumbents tend to innovate by applying marginal changes in their existing systems because of their organizational inertia and risk avoidance (Hockerts and Wüstenhagen 2010; Schaltegger et al. 2016). Despite the potential ability to solve sustainability issues, the roles and impacts of digital academic entrepreneurship have yet to be explored. Zaheer et al. (2019) called for more research on digital entrepreneurship related to social and sustainability issues.

The Influences of Digital Technologies on Sustainability and CE

The CE concept offers alternative solutions for a more sustainable production and consumption system. The CE, designed as a 'make-use-return' system, is replacing the traditional linear business model of 'take-make-dispose', which is causing severe resource degradation, environmental pollution, and waste emission problems (Geissdoerfer et al. 2017). The CE aims to reduce resource consumption; increase the product lifetime by reusing, repairing, and refurnishing; dematerialize physical products; and close the loop using recycling activities (Lieder and Rashid 2016). Therefore, the production and consumption loop is expected to be narrowed, slowed and closed. At the operational firm level, many circular business models involve digital technologies (Bressanelli et al. 2018; Ranta et al. 2021).

Entrepreneurial firms adopt different types of digital innovations in new business models to tackle sustainability challenges (George et al. 2020) and contribute to a more CE. For example, the blockchain decentralizes transaction activities in more transparent, trustworthy, reliable, and informative ways (George et al. 2020) and increases traceability for better recycling and reuse. Artificial intelligence and the IoT allow production automation to achieve resource efficiency by reducing false prototypes. Through digital technologies, decision making based on real-time data becomes more effective, and collaborations between actors in the innovation ecosystem are less geographically bounded.

Several studies examine the role of digital innovation in the CE. Digital innovations optimize material flows and enable reverse material flows (Pagoropoulos et al. 2017), integrate value chains through data collection and sharing (De Sousa Jabbour et al. 2018), and improve traceability and transparency through the product timeline (Antikainen et al. 2018). Digital technologies enhance the knowledge on the locations, conditions, and availability of materials and products, which facilitates predictive maintenance, refurbishment, recycling, and reuse (Antikainen et al. 2018). Hence, consumption patterns are shifted by engaging consumers in the digital system (De Sousa Jabbour et al. 2018). Most studies of digital innovation for the CE are either conceptual or literature reviews, and there are few empirical studies. Additionally, the current stream of the digital innovation CE literature predominantly centres on one type of digital technology, one company, or one CE process. De Angelis and Feola (2020) and Henry et al. (2020) examined spin-offs and start-ups, but those firms did not rely on digital technology; furthermore, other studies did not distinguish the application of digital technologies for CE by different types of firms (i.e., large incumbents, SMEs, and start-ups).

METHOD

We employ an exploratory, inductive multiple-case study of 25 digital CE-related ASOs. Our sample is identified from the population of 374 Norwegian ASOs established during 1999–2011 and by using media coding in a stepwise process, as outlined in Table 21.1. The number of CE-related ASOs is likely to be higher than 25 because of limited media coverage

Table 21.1   The process of identifying the sample of digital CE-related ASOs

Step	Sample	Coding tasks
1	Population of 374 ASOs	Searched the Atekst/Retriever media archive and downloaded 4,252 news articles written on approximately 295 of the ASOs until 2016. The remaining firms were early failures with no media coverage.
2	295 ASOs with media coverage	Trained student assistants read all articles and identified 1,041 articles that provided information on the impact of each ASO and its activity. These articles were re-read to identify 60 CE-related ASOs.
3	60 CE-related ASOs	The CE impacts were coded according to the specific types of CE impacts such as resource efficiency, extending the product lifecycle, reuse, and recycling. The types of technology and innovation were also coded.
4	25 digital CE-related ASOs	We sorted the 60 CE-related ASOs by technologies to obtain a sample of 25 CE-related ASOs using digital technologies.

on many firms. However, for the purpose of our study, this sample allows us to gain new insights into the CE-related activities of the most profiled ASOs in this population.

We conducted qualitative content analysis to analyse the 25 cases. Content analysis is defined as "a research technique for making replicable and valid inferences from texts (or other meaningful matter) to the contexts of their use" (Krippendorff 2018, p. 18). Through the coding stages of content analysis, we examined a total of 195 news articles written on digital CE-related ASOs to find emergent categories from the data and compared the differences and similarities among the cases and the categories for empirical interpretation. The coding analysis involved two research assistants and one author of this chapter. The coders worked independently and in parallel on the same sample to reduce personal biases during the coding process. Another author was involved in cases of disagreement between the coders.

The coding process included two levels. First, the codes consist of direct quotes from the articles concerning CE objectives, digital technologies, and innovation (e.g., product versus process, or novelty). The following example is one first-order code of digital technology.

Badger Explorer ASA, develops an autonomous robot that will drill into the ground to search for oil, without it coming back to the surface (Article 1). Sensors are also mounted in the tool that continuously monitors the mass that is passed through the tool. These sensors can tell if there are hydrocarbons in the mass, and thus indicate that there is oil in the sublayers in which it is drilled. Sensors run on pressure, and temperature can provide information about the mechanical properties of the ground such as pore and fractional pressure. It is important for later well and drilling operations (Article 2).

These codes explicitly explain the type of digital innovation and how digital technologies are used.

At the second level of coding, we identified the keywords that emerged from the first-order codes and then inferred and assigned them to specific categories. The categories include the types of innovation (i.e., incremental, radical product, and process innovation), the types of digital technology (i.e., sensor, automation artificial intelligence, real-time data, and software), the subcategories of digital technology (i.e., digital artefact, infrastructure, platform), CE impacts (i.e., resource efficiency and waste minimization), and performance (i.e., commercialization and survival).

In the previous code example, we identified the keywords '*sensor*' and '*robot*'. According to the predefined literature concepts, we assigned the digital technologies of Badger Explorer AS into the digital infrastructure category. In this study, we refer to the radical innovation of ASOs as the first digital product or process innovation in the market. The incremental innovation of ASOs identifies significant improvements based on existing knowledge or products in the market. For example, in the coding of the company DolphiScan, "this is the first product of its kind configured for composite materials in the market and can be easily used by maintenance personnel" or "the company DolphiScan on a groundbreaking invention: An ultrasonic code reader", the terms 'first product in the market' or 'groundbreaking invention' were defined to refer to digital radical innovation. Another example is the company Kognita with an e-learning platform. The coding "the e-La application will be built upon a current application developed by the entrepreneurs whilst employed at MARINTEK" indicates that this product innovation is built upon some existing application; thus, it is identified as incremental product innovation. Finally, to interpret the results, we compared the similarities and dissimilarities of the coded categories across the 25 cases.

FINDINGS

Among the 60 ASOs found with CE-related businesses (Table 21.1), 25 rely on digital technologies. This indicates that digital innovation holds a central role for ASOs commercializing innovations with potential CE impacts. Table 21.2 provides more details on 10 of the digital CE-related ASOs. These ASOs employed digital platforms, digital artefacts, and digital infrastructure technologies (i.e., sensors, robotics, platforms, software, and data analytics) to introduce digital product and process innovations.

Two main types of digital innovations are found in our sample. First, some ASOs entail digital product innovations by embedding digital platforms and digital artefacts that target final users' experiences. This type of digital product innovation is often known as 'Product-Service Systems (PSS)' (Tukker 2015). PSSs aim to fulfil final users' demands by combining tangible products and intangible services (Tukker 2015) and increasing the ownership sharing of products (Bressanelli et al. 2018). The ASOs in this study introduced e-learning portals, virtual interfaces, or digital laboratories that enable collaboration, interaction, and communication between multiple users. The locus of communication hosted by digital platforms and artefacts is not spatially bounded. Numerous users from different locations, within or outside the organization, can easily access the same platform and the same data to interact with each other in real time. Physical objects such as paper books and laboratory equipment are virtualized and dematerialized to reduce the consumption of energy and material resources and then reduce the logistical waste of physical classrooms and laboratories. Examples are Cyberlab and Smart Energy (Table 21.2). The digital platform and digital artefacts are closely embedded rather than functioning alone. Hence, if the digital platform hosts the users' activities, digital artefacts enable operational activities.

The second type of CE-related ASO involves digital process innovation using digital infrastructure technologies such as sensors, robotics, big data, and the IoT. This type of digital process innovation relates to the concept of Industry 4.0 (De Sousa Jabbour et al. 2018). Digital infrastructure optimizes the production processes by coordinating physical and virtual objects based on real-time data. Smart sensors and data analytics connected via wireless networks allow 'real-time' prediction and decision making. Thus, managers are provided with more precise information to prevent failures and errors because the combination of digital infrastructure technologies can help validate, inform, and verify potential issues in production and logistic processes. This could minimize prototype failures and resource inputs using pre-maintenance instead of repair. In addition, the automation enabled by artificial intelligence and robotics with big data (or so-called cyber-physical systems) substantially increases productivity and efficiency in manufacturing. Examples are Comex, DrillScience, and Thelma (Table 21.2).

CE-related ASOs seem to pursue digital process innovations more often (16 firms) than digital product innovations (9 firms). Nearly all digital process innovations are radical and provide unique solutions to the market. In contrast, digital product innovations are mostly incremental and tended to be built upon knowledge or products that already existed in the market. This ratio of radical versus incremental and product versus process innovation also corresponds to the patent rate. Among the 25 CE-related ASOs, 8 firms patented their innovations. All these patented innovations are radical process innovations based on digital infrastructure technologies whereas no product innovations based on digital platforms and artefacts were patented.

Table 21.2   Illustrative cases of digital CE-related ASOs

ASO	Status	Products/services	Innovation types	CE impacts
Kognita	Established: 2000 Status: Acquired	E-learning platform and application that allows training providers to access a library of online learning materials and promote online courses over the internet.	- Innovation type: incremental product innovation. - Digital technology: digital e-learning platform and digital artefact (i.e., software).	- Reduce the raw material and energy consumption of traditional classes such as paper books and electricity, respectively. - Increase the efficiency of connecting people through a software platform for online teaching. - Reduce the emissions from travels to attend workshops/seminars abroad.
PrediChem	Established: 2001 Status: Changed purpose	- Virtual laboratory software that can be used to integrate and simulate computational chemistry, experimental design and chemometrics for research and development in medicine. Reduces the expensive testing costs of laboratories using a cheaper and easier testing program performed in a virtual laboratory. - First in the market to introduce this innovation.	- Innovation type: radical product innovation. - Digital technology: digital platform (i.e., virtual laboratory platform) and digital artefact (i.e., software).	- Dematerialize physical laboratory to reduce logistic resources such as laboratory material inputs, electricity, and fuels. - Reduce physical lab prototypes and waste. - Increase efficiency and reduce time and costs of laboratory testing and medical product development.
Octaga	Established: 2001 Status: Bankrupted	- Multiple user 3D visualization software for training, simulation, operation and maintenance. Enhances visualization and offers users new ways to communicate and collaborate. - Developed the innovation based on an existing innovation.	- Innovation type: Incremental product innovation. - Digital technology: digital platform and digital artefact (i.e., 3D visualization and software).	Optimize the communication and collaboration process to reduce the consumption of resource inputs.
Pronavis	Established: 2002 Status: Acquired	Multiuser network platform for internal collaboration and interaction in the maritime and offshore logistics. Technology allows everyone to have access to what others are doing and can coordinate with them.	- Innovation type: Incremental product innovation. - Digital technology: Digital platform.	- Optimize the logistic process to reduce fuel consumption and fuel costs up to 10%. - Reduce environmental impacts.
Smart Energy Applications	Established: 2002 Status: Acquired	Wireless device plugged into the power grid to track power consumption and transfer information on power consumption to a portable device such as a cell phone. Helps household consumers and large buildings optimize their electricity consumption.	- Innovation type: Incremental product innovation (a version of the old wattmeter needle). - Digital technology: Digital artefact (the tracking device and software).	Optimize power consumption, reduce the consumption and costs of electricity and energy.

ASO	Status	Products/services	Innovation types	CE impacts
Thelma	Established: 2000 Status: Bankrupted	- Sensor mounted on a fish to record the fish breathing patterns to measure the well-being of the fish because farmed fish are more susceptible to illness when they are stressed. - First in the market to introduce this innovation.	- Innovation type: Radical product innovation. - Digital technology: Digital infrastructure (a tracking device and software).	- Reduce the number of sick fish and enhance fish quality. - Reduce the resource inputs for fish farming and reduce waste because of fish disease.
Comex	Established: 2003 Status: Active	- Sensor-based sorting system for the production and classification of fine powders and optical separation of large particles based on colour, shape, size, surface pattern, thermal, and magnetic properties. Technology can be used in the process of crushing and grinding minerals in the mining industry. - First in the market to introduce this innovation.	- Innovation type: Radical process innovation. - Digital technology: Digital infrastructure (sensor and data).	Makes the mining process less energy intensive by removing waste first with a reduction of approximately 150 terawatt-hours (TWh) if the mining industry uses this technology.
Drilltronic	Established: 2004 Status: Active	- Digital system with AI, a sensor, real-time data, and software to visualize and automate the drilling process and detect the errors and faults in the oil drilling. - Unique drilling technology for complex reservoirs and in more inaccessible and environmentally sensitive areas. - First in the market to introduce this innovation and achieved commercial success.	- Innovation type: Radical process innovation. - Digital technology: Digital infrastructure (AI, sensor, real-time data, and software).	- Optimize process via decentralized real-time data updates. - Significantly reduce downtime and resource consumption in drilling. - Reduce incidents and environmental risks during the drilling process.

ASO	Status	Products/services	Innovation types	CE impacts
Badger Explorer	Established: 2003 Status: Active	Autonomous robot with a sensor that will scan the seabed and drill into the ground to search for oil without it coming back to the surface. These sensors can identify the hydrocarbons in masses and thus indicate the potential oil in the sublayers. The sensors and real-time data can provide information about the mechanical properties of the ground, such as pore and fractional pressure. - First to introduce this innovation in the market.	- Innovation type: Radical process innovation. - Digital technology: Digital infrastructure (AI, robotics, sensor, and real-time data).	- Significantly increase efficiency and productivity. Reduce resource inputs during oil exploration, thus reducing the costs of oil exploration by 50%. - Make the drilling process safer and reduce the environmental impacts of dangerous gas emissions during the oil exploration process.
Franatech	Established: 2008 Status: Active	- Sensor for measuring CO_2 and methane in connection with oil and gas wells. - First in the market to introduce the technology, which was believed to be game-changing technology for subsea leak detection.	- Innovation type: Radical process innovation. - Digital technology: Digital infrastructure (sensor).	Helps offshore operations to map and reduce the emissions of environmental gases and CO_2 in oil wells.

Noticeably, the majority of CE-related ASOs are technology suppliers who took the lead as first-mover innovators in their market. ASOs collaborate with and supply technological solutions to large incumbent firms or public organizations to enhance production and logistic processes. Only a small number of the ASOs in this study directly provide products or services to final users. ASOs are start-up firms that typically lack complex in-house manufacturing systems. Thus, ASOs contribute to the CE with technology and sustainable, circular solutions that can be implemented by larger incumbents. This may be attributed to the fact that ASOs are knowledge intensive and highly innovative firms (Clausen and Rasmussen 2013); thus, ASOs play an important role in leading technological trajectories and incubating radical innovations in their innovation ecosystem (Novotny et al. 2020). These ASOs have strong horizontal integration (with peer research organizations) and vertical integration (with client companies).

Our findings confirm the potential role of technology-based start-ups as sources of innovation and technological initiatives for large incumbents and manufacturers (Autio 1997). Start-up firms with more flexible organizational structures and fewer resources are more incentivized to search for unique market ideas, to innovate, and to quickly respond to disruptive technological changes (Homfeldt et al. 2019). The collaborative role of the CE-related ASOs as technology suppliers and knowledge transferers also aligns with the study of De Jesus et al. (2018) explaining the multilevel CE transition. At the meso level, the CE transition requires more collaboration, integration, and synergy between firms within the value chain, such as through industrial symbiosis; and the CE innovations of one firm may influence other firms in the same network to achieve a joint circular system.

The empirical evidence in this study also reinforces Hojnik and Ruzzier's (2016) findings that market pull factors and cost reductions are important drivers of eco-innovation in both the innovation development and diffusion stages. This pattern also seems to be true for the digital innovations commercialized by ASOs. We also found that most digital CE innovation ideas are derived from the original needs for cost cutting and market demands before the CE objectives are indirectly achieved through resource efficiency. Our empirical evidence also validates the finding of Ranta et al. (2020) that compared to more linear economy suppliers, the customer value propositions of suppliers in the CE tended to be more market-driven and built for radical innovations that involve the close participation of direct customers and other ecosystem actors. These technological changes and CE transitions in the ecosystem of digital ASOs are led by the combined effects of 'technology-push' and 'demand-pull'.

CONCLUSION

The hand-collected dataset based on the population of ASOs established in Norway between 1999 and 2011 allowed us to examine the potential CE-related impacts of 25 ASOs commercializing digital innovations based on digital artefacts, platforms, and infrastructure technologies. We identified two main types of digital CE-related ASOs, which were based on digital product innovation and on digital process innovation. While ASOs commercializing process innovations often introduced radical innovations and new knowledge, ASOs commercializing product innovations were more often based on existing knowledge in the market. Digital process innovations tended to relate to digital infrastructure technologies such as sensors, robotics, big data, and the IoT. In contrast, digital product innovations were likely to entail digital platforms and artefacts such as mobile applications, virtual e-learning platforms, and software. The digital platform acts as the medium to be embedded with either digital infra-structures or digital artefacts.

ASOs contribute to the CE mainly in the role of technology suppliers for other large incumbents and public organizations. They closely collaborate with partners to facilitate both horizontal and vertical integration of their value chain. ASOs may facilitate technological changes in their innovation ecosystem and enable a meso-level industrial symbiosis of the CE. Most digital innovation ideas of ASOs are derived from resolving particular issues of their clients or markets. Hence, ASOs offer solutions to increase resource efficiency, cut costs, and address new market demands. Through economic incentives derived from more efficient processes, the CE impacts are indirectly generated by, for instance, reducing resource consumption, prolonging the product lifecycle, and closing the production-consumption loop.

Among the six circular business models (i.e., Regenerate, Sharing, Optimize, Loop, Virtual, Exchange) of the ReSOLVE framework, which has been most widely used in circular business model classification (Merli et al. 2018), digital CE-related ASOs employ mostly the optimize model and the virtual model. Hence, our findings align with Merli et al. (2018), stating that optimize is the second most popular circular business model, while the most popular circular business model is the Loop concerning the 'reuse' and 'recycle' strategies. To enable a resource-efficient CE, societal and environmental sustainability should be aligned with economic incentives (Ghisellini et al. 2016). This indicates that digital CE-related ASOs can provide important contributions to the CE transition because their original business purposes are often cost savings through advanced production automation and collaborative interaction enabled by radical digital innovations.

Our findings can also be related to the three common Rs of the CE literature, 'reduce, reuse, recycle' (Ghisellini et al. 2016; Prieto-Sandoval et al. 2018), which are attributed to the resource flow of narrowing (by reducing), slowing (by reusing, repairing) and closing (by recycling and recovering) the loop (Bocken et al. 2016). Resource efficiency related to the 'reduce' strategy is one of the essential CE objectives to narrow the loop by lowering resource consumption and emissions and increasing the efficiency of the technical and biological cycles. Compared to slowing and closing the loop, narrowing the loop is a distinct CE strategy because it does not directly influence the speed or cyclicality of the resource flows. However, resource efficiency or narrowing the loop is still considered crucial, especially at the CE microlevel aiming for cleaner production (Ghisellini et al. 2016). We contribute to this growing stream of resource-efficient CE literature by adding knowledge on the role of digital CE-related ASOs as potentially important facilitators of the 'narrowing the loop' strategy by enhancing the efficiency of both the demand (through digital products and services) and supply sides (through digital production processes).

Hofmann (2019) argues that the 'slowing the loop' strategy is irreconcilable and incoherent to our current economy based on growth, ceaseless technological progress, and fast consumerism. "What is truly required to reduce environmental impacts is less production and less consumption" (Zink and Geyer 2017, p. 600). Perhaps digital CE-related ASOs can be forerunners in the transition to a more CE by helping to narrow the loop by orchestrating industrial symbiosis, by optimizing value creation and offering higher efficiency production, by using minimal resources and costs per unit, or by optimizing new demand while maintaining profitability thanks to higher productivity. The condition for this to happen, however, is that the increased efficiency does not lead to a further increase in production and consumption, causing 'circular economy rebound' effects (Zink and Geyer 2017). Hence, the potential role of digital CE-related ASOs in the transition to a CE depends on how they are integrated in a larger transformation of the economy.

REFERENCES

Antikainen, M., Uusitalo, T., & Kivikytö-Reponen, P. (2018). Digitalisation as an enabler of circular economy. *Procedia CIRP*, 73, 45–49.

Autio, E. (1997). New, technology-based firms in innovation networks symplectic and generative impacts. *Research Policy*, 26(3), 263–281.

Bocken, N. M. (2015). Sustainable venture capital: Catalyst for sustainable start-up success? *Journal of Cleaner Production*, 108, 647–658.

Bocken, N. M., De Pauw, I., Bakker, C., & Van der Grinten, B. (2016). Product design and business model strategies for a circular economy. *Journal of Industrial and Production Engineering*, 33(5), 308–320.

Bressanelli, G., Adrodegari, F., Perona, M., & Saccani, N. (2018). Exploring how usage-focused business models enable circular economy through digital technologies. *Sustainability*, 10(3).

Clausen, T. H., & Rasmussen, E. (2013). Parallel business models and the innovativeness of research-based spin-off ventures. *Journal of Technology Transfer*, 38(6), 836–849.

De Angelis, R., & Feola, R. (2020). Circular business models in biological cycles: The case of an Italian spin-off. *Journal of Cleaner Production*, 247, 119603.

De Jesus, A., Antunes, P., Santos, R., & Mendonça, S. (2018). Eco-innovation in the transition to a circular economy: An analytical literature review. *Journal of Cleaner Production*, 172, 2999–3018.

De Sousa Jabbour, A. B. L., Jabbour, C. J. C., Godinho Filho, M., & Roubaud, D. (2018). Industry 4.0 and the circular economy: A proposed research agenda and original roadmap for sustainable operations. *Annals of Operations Research*, 270(1–2), 273–286.

Ekbia, H. R. (2009). Digital artifacts as quasi-objects: Qualification, mediation, and materiality. *Journal of the American Society for Information Science and Technology*, 60(12), 2554–2566.

European Commission (2015). *Digital Transformation of European Industry and Enterprises*. Report of the Strategic Policy Forum on Digital Entrepreneurship. http://ec.europa.eu/DocsRoom/documents/9462/attachments/1 /translations/en/renditions/native.

Fini, R., Rasmussen, E., Siegel, D., & Wiklund, J. (2018). Rethinking the commercialization of public science: From entrepreneurial outcomes to societal impacts. *Academy of Management Perspectives*, 32(1), 4–20.

Geels, F. W. (2004). From sectoral systems of innovation to socio-technical systems: Insights about dynamics and change from sociology and institutional theory. *Research Policy*, 33(6–7), 897–920.

Geissdoerfer, M., Savaget, P., Bocken, N. M., & Hultink, E. J. (2017). The circular economy: A new sustainability paradigm? *Journal of Cleaner Production*, 143, 757–768.

George, G., Merrill, R. K., & Schillebeeckx, S. J. (2020). Digital sustainability and entrepreneurship: How digital innovations are helping tackle climate change and sustainable development. *Entrepreneurship Theory and Practice*. https://doi.org/10.1177/1042258719899425.

Ghisellini, P., Cialani, C., & Ulgiati, S. (2016). A review on circular economy: The expected transition to a balanced interplay of environmental and economic systems. *Journal of Cleaner Production*, 114, 11–32.

Giones, F., & Brem, A. (2017). Digital technology entrepreneurship: A definition and research agenda. *Technology Innovation Management Review*, 7(5).

Henry, M., Bauwens, T., Hekkert, M., & Kirchherr, J. (2020). A typology of circular start-ups: Analysis of 128 circular business models. *Journal of Cleaner Production*, 245, 118528.

Hockerts, K., & Wüstenhagen, R. (2010). Greening Goliaths versus emerging Davids: Theorizing about the role of incumbents and new entrants in sustainable entrepreneurship. *Journal of Business Venturing*, 25(5), 481–492.

Hofmann, F. (2019). Circular business models: Business approach as driver or obstructer of sustainability transitions? *Journal of Cleaner Production*, 224, 361–374.

Hojnik, J., & Ruzzier, M. (2016). What drives eco-innovation? A review of an emerging literature. *Environmental Innovation and Societal Transitions*, 19, 31–41.

Homfeldt, F., Rese, A., & Simon, F. (2019). Suppliers versus start-ups: Where do better innovation ideas come from? *Research Policy*, 48(7), 1738–1757.

Kopp, R., Dhondt, S., Hirsch-Kreinsen, H., Kohlgrüber, M., & Preenen, P. (2019). Sociotechnical perspectives on digitalisation and Industry 4.0. *International Journal of Technology Transfer and Commercialisation*, 16(3), 290–309.

Korhonen, J., Nuur, C., Feldmann, A., & Birkie, S. E. (2018). Circular economy as an essentially contested concept. *Journal of Cleaner Production*, 175, 544–552.

Kraus, S., Palmer, C., Kailer, N., Kallinger, F. L., & Spitzer, J. (2018). Digital entrepreneurship: A research agenda on new business models for the twenty-first century. *International Journal of Entrepreneurial Behavior & Research*, 25(2), 353–375.

Krippendorff, K. (2018). *Content Analysis: An Introduction to its Methodology* (4th ed.). Thousand Oaks, CA: Sage Publications.

Li, A. Q., Rich, N., Found, P., Kumar, M., & Brown, S. (2020). Exploring product–service systems in the digital era: A socio-technical systems perspective. *The TQM Journal*, 32(4), 897–913.

Lieder, M., & Rashid, A. (2016). Towards circular economy implementation: A comprehensive review in context of manufacturing industry. *Journal of Cleaner Production*, 115, 36–51.

Mathisen, M. T., & Rasmussen, E. (2019). The development, growth, and performance of university spin-offs: A critical review. *Journal of Technology Transfer*, 44(6), 1891–1938.

Merli, R., Preziosi, M., & Acampora, A. (2018). How do scholars approach the circular economy? A systematic literature review. *Journal of Cleaner Production*, 178, 703–722.

Nambisan, S. (2017). Digital entrepreneurship: Toward a digital technology perspective of entrepreneurship. *Entrepreneurship Theory and Practice*, 41(6), 1029–1055.

Nambisan, S., Wright, M., & Feldman, M. (2019). The digital transformation of innovation and entrepreneurship: Progress, challenges and key themes. *Research Policy*, 48(8), 103773.

Novotny, A., Rasmussen, E., Clausen, T. H., & Wiklund, J. (eds.) (2020). *Research Handbook on Start-Up Incubation Ecosystems*. Cheltenham, UK and Northampton, MA, USA: Edward Elgar Publishing.

Pagoropoulos, A., Pigosso, D. C., & McAloone, T. C. (2017). The emergent role of digital technologies in the circular economy: A review. *Procedia CIRP*, 64, 19–24.

Prieto-Sandoval, V., Jaca, C., & Ormazabal, M. (2018). Towards a consensus on the circular economy. *Journal of Cleaner Production*, 179, 605–615.

Ranta, V., Aarikka-Stenroos, L., & Väisänen, J.-M. (2021). Digital technologies catalyzing business model innovation for circular economy: Multiple case study. *Resources, Conservation and Recycling*, 164, 105155.

Ranta, V., Keränen, J., & Aarikka-Stenroos, L. (2020). How B2B suppliers articulate customer value propositions in the circular economy: Four innovation-driven value creation logics. *Industrial Marketing Management*, 87, 291–305.

Rasmussen, E. (2011). Understanding academic entrepreneurship: Exploring the emergence of university spin-off ventures using process theories. *International Small Business Journal*, 29(5), 448–471.

Ries, E. (2011). *The Lean Startup: How Today's Entrepreneurs Use Continuous Innovation to Create Radically Successful Businesses*. London: Penguin Books.

Rippa, P., & Secundo, G. (2019). Digital academic entrepreneurship: The potential of digital technologies on academic entrepreneurship. *Technological Forecasting and Social Change*, 146, 900–911.

Sahut, J.-M., Iandoli, L., & Teulon, F. (2021). The age of digital entrepreneurship. *Small Business Economics*, 56, 1159–1169.

Schaltegger, S., Lüdeke-Freund, F., & Hansen, E. G. (2016). Business models for sustainability: A co-evolutionary analysis of sustainable entrepreneurship, innovation, and transformation. *Organization & Environment*, 29(3), 264–289.

Secundo, G., Rippa, P., & Cerchione, R. (2020). Digital academic entrepreneurship: A structured literature review and avenue for a research agenda. *Technological Forecasting and Social Change*, 157, 120118.

Shane, S. A. (2004). *Academic Entrepreneurship: University Spinoffs and Wealth Creation*. Cheltenham, UK and Northampton, MA, USA: Edward Elgar Publishing.

Tukker, A. (2015). Product services for a resource-efficient and circular economy: A review. *Journal of Cleaner Production*, 97, 76–91.

Zaheer, H., Breyer, Y., & Dumay, J. (2019). Digital entrepreneurship: An interdisciplinary structured literature review and research agenda. *Technological Forecasting and Social Change*, 148, 119735.

Zink, T., & Geyer, R. (2017). Circular economy rebound. *Journal of Industrial Ecology*, 21(3), 593–602.

22. Towards measuring innovation for circular economy using patent data

Dolores Modic, Alan Johnson and Miha Vučkovič

INTRODUCTION

The circular economy (CE) describes an economic system that operates with closed material loops (Stahel 2016) replacing the 'end-of-life' concept of the linear economy. Specifically, keywords like: 'Recycle', 'Recover', 'Reuse', 'Reduce', 'Remanufacture', 'Refurbish', 'Repurpose', and 'Remine' are applied to all materials in production, distribution, and consumption processes, with the overarching objective of achieving sustainable development (Kirchherr et al. 2017). CE policies and practices are increasingly being adopted across countries, from China, an early adopter, to Europe, a recent front runner (Kalmykova et al. 2018; Su et al. 2013).

Applied technical innovation efforts underpin many aspects of CE, e.g., 'Remanufacture'. While business model innovation and public policy rewards and penalties are important preconditions for CE adoption and diffusion, realizing CE through technical innovation is the driver that we focus on. The European Union (EU) pointed out the importance of both sustainable development and technical innovation in its grand strategy Europe 2020 (EC 2010) and continues to acknowledge innovation as a major driver for CE (EC 2015, 2020).

Our starting point are the methodological concerns about measuring and analysing data about CE activity (Eurostat 2020a). To achieve a broad-spectrum CE related technical innovation indicator, we focus on patent data – a well-established source of information on innovation (Griliches 1990; Harhoff et al. 2003). If it were coded appropriately, patent data could capture information on technical innovation for the circular economy and address research questions about innovation activity related to the circular economy (Popp 2005; Oltra et al. 2010).

Extensive prior efforts have been dedicated by organizations such as the European Patent Office (EPO) to identifying (technical) innovation in particular fields, including climate change-mitigation, by developing a Y-tagging system (Veefkind et al. 2012; Angelucci et al. 2018). Circular economy and climate change-mitigation may be related concepts in public consciousness, but their enabling innovations cannot be measured using the same instruments for scientific research purposes. The EPO on the other hand cannot be expected to indulge every 'next big thing' and implement their complex, and resource intensive process to identify relevant innovation. Furthermore, the Eurostat's (2020a) CE related technical innovation patent stock (PS) indicator – now used as part of the CE indicators by the European Commission – is restricted insofar as it includes only innovations tagged with specific Y-tags, i.e., those related to 'Recycle' and 'Recover' of secondary raw materials. We argue this is too narrow a spectrum for CE related innovation.

Our main contribution to the CE literature is to outline a general measurement approach to technical innovation, which we developed to address the data requirements for technology management and public policy research questions about CE (technical) innovation. To facilitate replication and continuous updating over time, we follow previous work on Y-tags and build our procedure on the existing patent taxonomy (Veefkind et al. 2012). Due to the current metrics' deficiencies in identifying and analysing CE related technical innovation, a 'budget' method is required for researchers to develop custom Y-tags, say 'Y*-tags', that can provide similar measurement quality at a fraction of the cost.

Providing new protocols to identify and analyse patent data will allow us to get a better overview of the bulk, scope and direction of innovation for CE. A 'budget' method could also facilitate postdictive technology lifecycle studies, e.g., biotechnology or digital technology, to address research questions about effective management decisions and public policy interventions (Cartwright and Hardie 2012). We could also answer questions such as: What is the impact of public policies interventions and how do they compare across countries? Where are the technological competencies and research activity: clusters of inventors, commercial organizations, or research institutions? For emerging technologies, how does the innovation and diffusion process unfold over time and is it any different to established technologies?

The first section showcases the usability of patent data to study the scope and direction of the CE-related innovation. The main emphasis of the second section is on investigating and critically evaluating approaches to identifying CE-related innovations. The third section provides the details of our 'budget' Y*-tag method. The final section concludes.

INNOVATION, CIRCULAR ECONOMY AND PATENT DATA

Circular Economy Innovations

There are several connected and even overlapping concepts of (technical) innovations related to supporting sustainability; from green, clean, environmental, low-carbon, to climate change-mitigation (CCMT) and eco-innovation (Lanjouw and Mody 1996; Johnstone et al. 2010; Dechezleprêtre et al. 2011, 2017; Veefkind et al. 2012; Dussaux et al. 2017; Brunel 2019; Eurostat 2020a). The innovation for CE (CE innovation) is however sufficiently distinct from all of them to warrant separate examination. Certain technologies that would typically not be included in green or climate change-mitigation innovation, would however be enveloped in CE innovation. For example: a recycling chloride battery is a CE innovation, but it would not be included in green innovation; a reusable food container is in line with advancing solutions for reuse, but falls out of scope of the climate change-mitigation (see Table 22.1).

Table 22.1   2-by-2 matrix on CE innovations

	Green economy		Climate change – mitigation	
	Brown	Green	Yes	No
Circular economy	Recycling chloride batteries	Fuel cell	Recovery of heavy metal oxidation catalyst	Reusable casing for sausages

We define innovations for circular economy (CE innovations) as those that are new or novel combinations to help achieve circular economy 'Rs' to transition to a more circular economy. There have been several attempts at defining these Rs; some are related to smarter product use and manufacture: e.g., refusing, rethinking, reducing, reservitizing; some to supporting the extended lifespan of products and its parts, e.g., reusing, repairing, refurbishing, remanufacturing, repurposing; and others to supporting useful (re-)applications of materials, such as recycle, remine and recover (Reike et al. 2018; Potting et al. 2017; Morseletto 2020).

Patent Data: What Does It Say about CE Innovation?

Figure 22.1 confirms the conclusions of the Eurostat's Circular Economy (Eurostat 2020a, 2020b) patent stock indicator (PS indicator) – now commonly seen as a proxy of available CE-related innovation. According to Figure 22.1 China's early steering towards CE innovation seemingly paid off, both in terms of recycling, as well as other 'Rs'. The European patent landscape depicts a much lower CE inventive activity.

The PS indicator however focuses especially on recycling and secondary raw materials. Criticism in the EU focuses on the public policy excessively rewarding 'Recycle' (Perella 2014; Blomsma and Brennan 2017), which steers CE related activity and innovation away from other 'Rs', e.g., 'Reuse' or disassembly. This is problematic since CE theorists argue that 'Recycle' activity has *low* value retention compared to the other 'Rs', such as 'Remanufacture'

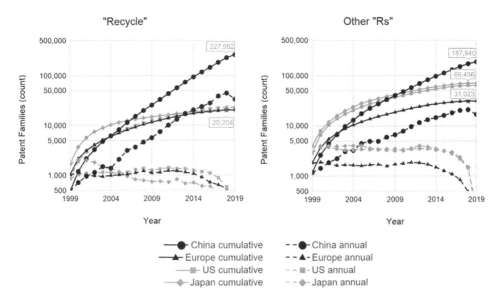

Note: Figure 22.1 illustrates that the cumulative 'Recycle' patent stock is ten-times higher and growing in China compared to Europe where it is static. In addition, the cumulative other 'Rs' patent stock is five-times higher in China compared to Europe. Other 'Rs' include Recover, Remanufacture, Refurbish, Repurpose, Remine. Data extracted from Espacenet. (Espacenet's language query tool is used. In all keyword searches, keywords variants are included in searches inside the following patent document fields: Title, Abstract, and Claims.)

Figure 22.1   Annual and cumulative counts for patent family (1999–2019) comparing 'Recycle' (left panel) and other 'Rs' (right panel)

(Reike et al. 2018; Potting et al. 2017). But Figure 22.1 shows that the innovative activity is also high in other more 'high-value retention' 'Rs', e.g., repurpose.

The information on CE-related innovation, actors, innovation trends, and CE emerging technologies can also be derived from additional information included in patents. Using the Espacenet database, the applicant data for China reveals that European applicants account for less than 60 per cent of all patents in Europe, with the US applicants contributing a whopping 20 per cent. Next, we can utilize data on forward patent citations to reveal key innovations in a particular field that have influenced further innovations which can indicate relevant emerging technologies within the circular economy. Based on the IPLOD dataset[1] we consider the three most influential patents in electronics, i.e., patents with highest citation counts. They are indicative of the current trends in CE. The most cited patent is representative of the trend related to stimulating the markets for used goods (EC 2020). The highly cited patents dealing with dismantling and recovering parts are indicative of innovation directed at finding new ways of increasing the circularity of goods in electronics (Awasthi et al. 2019). We came to similar conclusions using the text mining RAKE algorithm approach (Rose et al. 2010; Modic et al. 2020), since its application confirms that disposal, dismantling and recycling are three of the most important CE innovation areas in electronics.

Patent data can thus reveal many facets of innovation activity within CE. In general patent data provides information about a patent as an exclusive right to exploit an invention. Patent data has the reliability of public archived panel data sources, including inventor names and their collaborators, applicant affiliations, geographic location, invention content, and forward and backward citations, and rich potentially available complementary data sources (Modic et al. 2020). But current metrics have serious deficiencies. To illustrate, if we perform a keyword search in Espacenet for 'refurbish', we can find e.g., a patent on refurbishing of a golf ball (KR101735542) with no CPC code or Y-tag, or a rail valve seat refurbishing tool (US2015314414) which does include a CPC code, but no Y-tag. Consequently, neither of these patents would be included in the Y-tag searches nor be a part of the PS indicator.

To cite Kerr (1975) in another context, there is an element of the 'folly of [measuring] A, while hoping for B', which can be detected in the previous work on measuring innovation related to CE, which is also touched upon by both Haas and his colleagues (2015) and the Circularity Gap Report (Haigh et al. 2021). Caution is also dictated due to the fact that poor quality measurement attenuates the relations between variables in subsequent analyses (Cook and Campbell 1979) and patent data is no different (Raffo and Lhuillery 2009).

INDICATORS IN USE

Identification is the first step in analysing relevant patents related to supporting sustainability. We identify five strategies: Strategy 1: relying solely on keywords; Strategy 2: relying solely on patent classifications, i.e., the International Patent Classification (IPC) or Cooperative Patent Classification (CPC), codes; Strategy 3: starting with keywords and using CPC; Strategy 4: starting with CPC and using keywords; and Strategy 5: using Y tags. Figure 22.2 presents these strategies together with some typical studies and their main objectives.

Search strategies using exact string match keywords are a popular approach when analysing both patents and publications, including some using the 'Rs' (Morseletto 2020). The keywords strategy can generate significant noise; when e.g., relying solely on exact matches there can be

Note: The works are divided according to the strategy used to identify patents. In dotted boxes are works dedicated to identifying narrow technologies, for example those relating to printed circuit board recycling. In dashed there are those related to different types of innovations supporting sustainability, e.g., low-carbon or green innovations. In solid-line boxes are works that deal with CE innovations. The brackets bring information on the (main) objectives of the papers: IPol = measuring the impact of policies; ITrend = understanding the direction of innovation and/or trends; DTK = diffusion of technology and knowledge; CCPC = cross-country performance comparison; Mthd = advancement of methodology.

Figure 22.2   Strategies to identify innovations related to supporting sustainability

Table 22.2   Results for number of patent families from 'R' keyword searches by document parts

	Title only	Abstract only	Title or abstract	Claims only	*Title, abstract, or claims*	Description only	All fields
Recycle	**70,898**	**249,529**	**259,268**	**214,198**	**400,719**	**1,136,276**	**1,251,828**
Recover	48,876	206,172	220,637	384,790	518,495	1,501,029	1,652,486
Reuse	9,835	77,701	80,435	65,305	131,911	745,482	791,897
Remanufacture	847	1,694	1,805	2,126	3,083	14,376	15,269
Refurbish	395	646	796	2,211	2,704	11,537	12,304
Repurpose	120	229	284	472	641	5,375	5,505
Remine	36	90	103	154	242	920	1,073
Reduce	162,077	2,991,500	3,035,378	1,729,561	4,290,619	18,407,723	19,328,313

a variety of false negatives (observations we are not able to pick up, simply due to alternative spelling). On the other hand, due to search terms being too broad, the results can be riddled with significant false positives (observations falsely identified as CE innovations). Our selection of keywords can thus significantly influence the results. If we observe the extraction of some of the common 'Rs' within patent documents by using Espacenet data from 1960–2019, the exact word matching can be done from various parts of the patent document, with very different results (see Table 22.2). For example, searching for 'recycling' in titles produces approximately one third of observations than if we search in titles and abstracts (70,898 as opposed to 259,268). Furthermore, common permutations of the words also cause similar disparities in patent counts. Searching through descriptions produces the highest number of patent documents, yet they are often riddled with false positives, and thus less reliable.

Patent classifications, i.e., CPC or IPC, were used, for example, to identify green patents (Lindman and Söderholm 2016; Dechezleprêtre et al. 2017; Brunel 2019). Both are generated with the help of machine learning algorithms (Venugopalan and Rai 2015). CPC/IPCs in essence represent inventive concepts and can envelop CE innovations in a number of very diverse classes. CPC/IPC searches are more independent of terminology and jargon changes over time. As an example, there have been several names for what was later officially named as COVID-19; yet, all would be encompassed in the same CPC/IPC, or same set of CPC/IPCs.

Next, using Y-tags is one of the strategies often used in identifying relevant environmental innovations; e.g., Dussaux et al. (2017) used them to identify low-carbon technology innovations or Dechezleprêtre et al. (2017) to identify clean technology innovations. The Y-tags represent general tagging of new technological developments and cross-sectional technologies (USPTO 2021). The tags were originally developed for the field of information technology (IT), i.e., nanotechnology (Scheu et al. 2006) and environment, i.e., the climate change-mitigation technologies, CCMT (Veefkind et al. 2012).

Inside the CE indicators package, the PS indicator of the Eurostat (Eurostat 2020a) is based on the Y-tags for CCMT. The PS indicator supposedly tracks CE patent families. The indicator is narrow, which Eurostat (2020b) acknowledges, and includes only recycling and secondary raw materials patents. The indicator only uses so-called Y02W Y-tags. Examining 1,500 patent documents, which include recycling and other 'R' keywords (but exclude reduce), extracted from the IPLOD data (Modic et al. 2020), we see that the Y02W codes are able to identify a mere 3.9 per cent of the keyword-generated patents. Instead of Y02W codes or tags, some other Y-tags, especially those connected to climate change-mitigation technologies (CCMT), are connected to a higher percentages of CE patents. The most promising among them is Y02P (CCMT in the production or processing of goods), which includes 14.5 per cent of all tagged documents, with Y02E also including 3.6 per cent – comparable to Y02W. Manual check confirms that the degree of false positives remains low. Nonetheless, several works reuse this, too narrow, approach to draw conclusions about the state of the CE (e.g., Marino and Pariso 2020; Sverko Grdic et al. 2020).

THREE PASS 'BUDGET Y*-TAG' METHOD

Existing Y-tags were designed and built to provide 'gold standard' measures of innovation in nanotechnology (Y01) and climate change-mitigation technology (Y02). These research efforts were led by the EPO and used extensive internal and external resources of people, time, and money (Scheu et al. 2006; Veefkind et al. 2012). Furthermore, albeit the examiners have abundant knowledge on the technologies themselves, they have limited knowledge in CE. But the measurement problem for technical innovation from emerging technologies is that content taxonomies for patent documents, e.g., CPC and IPC, are organized mainly along traditional scientific disciplines and are less suited to new streams of innovation that cross disciplines (Scheu et al. 2006).

Ideally, the 'budget' method is based on the existing patent taxonomies to facilitate replication and continuous updating over time, where appropriate. Our three pass procedure thus builds on previous work to introduce Y-tags to measure innovations coming from emerging technologies. The objective for our 'budget' Y*-tags, using an analogous low-cost version of the EPO methodology, is to achieve a below 5 per cent type I error rate (false positives) and a below 20 per cent type II error rate (false negatives), which is in line with social science measurement principles (Cook and Campbell 1979). Obviously, a manual coding procedure is not appropriate to classify the tens of millions of patent documents in the EPO databases. Any custom Y*-tag classification procedure must be designed and built using a considerable amount of automation. Nevertheless, we do not propose a 'black box' machine learning solution, but include several manual and statistical tests of validity along the way. We draw on previous work on name disambiguation for bibliographic data sources (Modic et al. 2020) to help produce Y*-tag innovation measures within our precision and recall objectives (Raffo and Lhuillery 2009).

First Pass

The first pass is made up of extensive and iterative CE related keyword searches in the Title, Abstract, and Claims fields of patent documents, i.e., the 'R' words. These come from previous CE theory and research. Keyword searches for 'circular economy' and related 'buzzwords' are less useful for preliminary analyses because they produce a fraction of the hits and are likely to be biased downward before CE became a 'thing' in the 1990s. Some keywords, e.g., Reduce, Reuse, tend to be quite 'noisy' because they appear in many non-CE innovations, e.g., reduce speed, and consequently, they allow too many false-positive patent documents to enter the training sample. Most 'R' keywords are used regularly in ordinary language. Manual checks of search results using different keyword combinations and parsing techniques can reveal anomalies and help achieve a balance between false positives and false negatives through several iterations. Additional CE related keywords can help differentiate CE patent documents from other patent documents, beyond the 'Rs' and CE 'buzzwords'. They can be generated from these initial search results using tools from the data science toolbox, e.g., the rapid automatic keyword extraction, RAKE (Rose et al. 2010), or some neural attention model for sentence summarization (Rush et al. 2015).

Patent examiners with experience in prior art searches suggest that keyword searches alone, without their detailed knowledge, deliver noisy results. To this end, EPO led Y-tag efforts use 'technical experts' for manual checks of a sample of the search results produced in the first pass (Scheu et al. 2006) but there is no funding for 'technical experts' in our 'budget' method. Nevertheless, our experience suggests that researchers familiar with CE can typically grasp whether a patent document contains some CE related innovation, with conventional reliability, by reading the Title and Abstract. In addition to manual checks, we also recommend automated checks to validate the keyword searches to refine and extend the keywords and other 'buzzwords' that can be used to build-out the training sample. Some keywords and 'buzzwords' can be problematic, e.g., 'Using discarded material', but most can be refined in the second pass using qualifiers to the search. For example, with 'Recover' we qualified the search to exclude CPCs connected to medical preparations, e.g., A61K, to reduce the number of false positives. Conversely, keywords like 'Refurbish' can identify CE innovations with remarkable precision, e.g., an 'invention' that "prolongs the lifetime of the valve by delaying the moment when a refurbishing of the seating surfaces becomes necessary" (EP-80302900). In addition, EP-80302900 patent has CPC code F01L designating it as a valve for an engine or machine, but no Y-tags. Thus, keyword searches in the first pass allow CE related innovations, which would have been excluded using Y02-tags alone, back into the training sample.

Second Pass

The second pass establishes connections between the best fitting CE related keywords from the first pass and the existing CPC taxonomy. As before, the first step is to manually identify potentially relevant CPC subclasses that are correlated with patent documents related to CE.

As Scheu and his co-authors (2006) found for nanotechnology, it may be that EPO examiners, who are continuously creating new CPC categories, are already coding them systematically but without 'circular economy' or 'R' words in the label. Thus, the next step is to differentiate between three types:

1. CPC subclasses where *most* patent documents fall within scope for CE,
2. CPC subclasses where *some* patent documents fall within scope for CE, and
3. CPC subclasses where *some* patents documents are extensively cited as prior art but do not obviously fall within scope for CE themselves, according to either CE theory and research or funding agencies.

Scheu and co-authors rely heavily on testimony from EPO examiners, but previous work in scientific bibliographic data suggests that other rule-governed procedures could also refine the nascent Y*-tags from the first pass using one or more forward or backward citations from *valid* CE related patents.

Strategically, identifying CPC subclasses that contain 'valid' CE related patent documents is the main task for the second pass. Other Y*-tags will follow from there. In addition to forward or backward citations, these nascent Y*-tags can be validated using inventor name, collaboration, affiliation, location, and content (Modic et al. 2020), based on the assumption that the innovation process for CE does not happen in a vacuum, but needs support from people and institutions in its environment. However, our experience suggests that this is an iterative process where CPC subclasses that might appear to contain *mostly* CE related patents in early iterations will turn out to be *less* so in later iterations as more patent documents are checked manually. *Tactically*, we have found it easier to make sense of results if we focus on segments of the EPO database, e.g., automotive, packaging, or focus on several small European countries: Norway, Slovenia, and Ireland.

Third Pass

The third pass establishes connections between the nascent Y*-tags for CE related innovations and major value chains of economic activity that are of concern to CE stakeholders, e.g., Eurostat, European Commission. Previous Y-tag efforts have attempted to reach out to the stakeholder community before assigning subclasses to the nascent measure of emerging technology (Scheu et al. 2006). The European Commission (EC 2018) has developed a typology for CE that encompasses stages in the lifecycle of resources, products, and services, which is a worthy contender for adoption as a model for at least some of our innovation subclasses. The EC 'monitoring framework for CE', albeit relatively confined to the topics of recycling, does point out some major potential interest areas; e.g., in terms of waste, the supporting innovation could be related to solutions for municipal waste, major mineral waste, overall packaging, plastic packaging, e-waste, or construction and demolition waste.

Similar to Y01-tags and Y02-tags, one can imagine how the foregoing classes might be mapped onto CPC codes, which are promising for CE related innovations identified in the second pass. As before, a patent document can be tagged with more than one class. Patent documents can be classified with Y*CE-tags in three ways:

1. Automatically for patent documents in one of the CPC categories where *most* records fall within scope for CE (identified in the second pass).

2. Manually by the researcher to fall within scope for CE (EPO uses 'senior examiners').
3. Automatically for patent documents that are:
   (a) classified with Y*CE-tags in one of the previous steps 1 or 2, and
   (b) is also validated with at least one piece of additional information about forward or backward citation, inventor name, inventor collaboration, affiliation, location, or content (Modic et al. 2020).

In our experience, iterative use of systematic data harmonization procedures, similar to those outlined above, and reviewed in greater detail in Modic et al. (2020) can produce high resolution name results, which in principle work just as well for Y*CE-tags to reflect CE related innovation streams as they do for disambiguating person names. Obviously, the patents that are classified inside the Y02W for the most part bring no additional value above the already developed and used CE innovation indicator (PS indicator) by Eurostat. The rest are a valuable add-on to identifying relevant CE patents, and to increasing our knowledge on the CE-related innovation activity and the directions of CE.

CONCLUSION

While contributions on environmental innovation captured and measured by patent statistics are increasing, as also suggested by our literature review, the state-of-the art for measuring circular economy innovation remains underdeveloped. Consequently, some important insights go unnoticed, e.g., who is responsible for the Chinese CE innovation stock. Furthermore, we also show that the current circular economy indicator used by Eurostat, does not capture 'Rs' beyond 'Recycle' and remains too narrow. Our literature review suggests the lack of reasonable alternatives to measure CE related innovation leads to the use of deficient metrics. But the existing 'gold-standard' protocol to develop Y-tag indicators that capture innovations from emerging technologies, e.g., CE, are costly, take considerable time to develop and relay on patent examiners which are not CE domain experts. Hence, we argue for a more 'budget' protocol to develop Y*-tags that allow capture of a reasonable amount of CE related innovation, which would be an improvement on the Eurostat indicator currently in use.

Our work facilitates evidence-based policymaking in relation to CE and especially in supporting innovation for circular economy. The derived data based on the proposed method on circular economy innovation can also support strategic decision making for (public and private) investors or funding agencies that wish to facilitate the transition to more innovation for circular economy. Furthermore, our proposed approach can simplify the search for circular economy patents, thus supporting companies' CE decisions regarding investments in circular innovations. The chapter is also a specific *aide-mémoire* for researchers, allowing them to go beyond simply utilizing previously developed strategies, which were optimized to discover and analyse similar innovation, e.g., green, but which do not cover the whole spectrum of circular economy; or strategies that are extremely costly, e.g., designing a new Y-tag for innovation for circular economy following existing protocols.

Nonetheless, using patent data is not without its limitations. It is an indirect output measurement. A more direct output measure alternative would be e.g., announcements in trade or professional journals on innovation, specific area product databases or product-patent databases. The first however contain highly unstructured and unconsolidated data. In terms of the second the data coming from reputable sources is usually very limited; and in terms of the third, the most promising one, the iproduct.com, has only limited data. That said, patent data is still among the most viable sources of data on (technical) innovation, including for identifying CE innovation.

NOTE

1. The basic data is derived from the IPLODB database, which is combining patent and publication data, and capitalizing on the linked open data approach, to allow for more linkability between data (Modic et al. 2020). The values for the indicator of forward citations are generated from EPO's Patstat database. The sample includes 306 patents with Y02W and does not include some technologies that could be included here (e.g., belonging to Y02D not included in PS indicator); but which are cited above average – e.g., those prolonging the lifetime of batteries (EP-97307660).

REFERENCES

Angelucci, S., Hurtado-Albir, F. J., & Volpe, A. (2018). Supporting global initiatives on climate change: The EPO's 'Y02-Y04S' tagging scheme. *World Patent Information*, 54, 85–92.

Awasthi, A. K., Li, J., Koh, L., & Ogunseitan, O. A. (2019). Circular economy and electronic waste. *Nature Electronics*, 2(3), 86–89.

Blomsma, F., & Brennan, G. (2017). The emergence of circular economy: A new framing around prolonging resource productivity. *Journal of Industrial Ecology*, 21(3), 603–614.

Brunel, C. (2019). Green innovation and green imports: Links between environmental policies, innovation, and production. *Journal of Environmental Management*, 248, 109290.

Cartwright, N., & Hardie, J. (2012). *Evidence-Based Policy: A Practical Guide to Doing It Better*. Oxford: Oxford University Press.

Cook, T. D., & Campbell, D. T. (1979). *Quasi-Experimentation: Design & Analysis Issues for Field Settings*. Boston: Houghton Mifflin.

De Vries, F. P. & Withagen, C. A. M. (2005). *Innovation and Environmental Stringency: The Case of Sulfur Dioxide Abatement*. CentER Discussion Paper Series No. 2005-18. https://ssrn.com/abstract=670158.

Dechezleprêtre, A., Glachant, M., Haščič, I., Johnstone, N., & Ménière, Y. (2011). Invention and transfer of climate change-mitigation technologies: A global analysis. *Review of Environmental Economics and Policy*, 5(1), 109–130.

Dechezleprêtre, A., Ralf, M., & Mahnen, M. (2017). *Knowledge Spillovers from Clean and Dirty Technologies*. Centre for Climate Change and Economics Working Paper No. 151.

Dussaux, D., Dechezleprêtre, A., & Glachant, M. (2017). *Intellectual Property Rights Protection and the International Transfer of Low-Carbon Technologies*. Centre for Climate Change and Economics Working Paper No. 323. https://hal.archives-ouvertes.fr/hal-01693539/document.

EC (2010). *EUROPE 2020: A Strategy for Smart, Sustainable and Inclusive Growth*. Brussels: European Commission.

EC (2015). *Closing the Loop – An EU Action Plan for the Circular Economy* (COM(2015) 614 final). Brussels: European Commission.

EC (2018). *On a Monitoring Framework for the Circular Economy* (COM(2018) 29 final). Brussels: European Commission.

EC (2020). *A New Circular Economy Action Plan: For a Cleaner and More Competitive Europe*. Brussels: European Commission.

Eurostat (2020a). *Patents related to recycling and secondary raw materials* (cei_cie020). https://ec.europa.eu/eurostat/cache/metadata/en/cei_cie020_esmsip2.htm.

Eurostat (2020b). *ANNEX – List of CPC codes used for indicator calculation*. https://ec.europa.eu/eurostat/documents/8105938/8465062/cei_cie020_esmsip_CPC-codes.pdf.

Griliches, Z. (1990). *Patent Statistics as Economic Indicators: A Survey.* Part 1-2 (No. 3301). National Bureau of Economic Research.

Haas, W., Krausmann, F., Wiedenhofer, D., & Heinz, M. (2015). How circular is the global economy? An assessment of material flows, waste production, and recycling in the European Union and the world in 2005. *Journal of Industrial Ecology,* 19(5), 765–777.

Haigh, L., de Wit, M., von Daniels, C., Colloricchio, A., Hoogzaad, J., et al. (2021). *The Circularity Gap Report 2021.* Amsterdam: Ruparo.

Harhoff, D., Scherer, F. M., & Vopel, K. (2003). Citations, family size, opposition and the value of patent rights. *Research Policy,* 32(8), 1343–1363.

Johnstone, N., Haščič, I., & Kalamova, M. (2010). Environmental policy characteristics and technological innovation. *Economia Politica,* 27(2), 277–302.

Kalmykova, Y., Sadagopan, M., & Rosado, L. (2018). Circular economy: From review of theories and practices to development of implementation tools. *Resources, Conservation and Recycling,* 135, 190–201.

Kerr, S. (1975). On the folly of rewarding A, while hoping for B. *Academy of Management Journal,* 18(4), 15.

Kirchherr, J., Reike, D., & Hekkert, M. (2017). Conceptualizing the circular economy: An analysis of 114 definitions. *Resources, Conservation and Recycling,* 127, 221–232.

Lanjouw, J. O., & Mody, A. (1996). Innovation and the international diffusion of environmentally responsive technology. *Research Policy,* 25, 549–571.

Lindman, Å., & Söderholm, P. (2016). Wind energy and green economy in Europe: Measuring policy-induced innovation using patent data. *Applied Energy,* 179, 1351–1359.

Marino, A., & Pariso, P. (2020). Comparing European countries' performances in the transition towards the circular economy. *Science of the Total Environment,* 729, 138142.

Marinova, D., & McAleer, M. (2006). Anti-pollution technology strengths indicators: International rankings. *Environmental Modelling & Software,* 21(9), 1257–1263.

Modic, D., Johnson, A. R., Lužar, B., Hafner, A., Rožac, B., Vučkovič, M., & Rasmussen, E. A. (2020). *Intellectual Property Linked Open Data Building Bridges (IP LodB) Project: Final Report* [EPO Academic Research Programme Project Final Report]. http://documents.epo.org/projects/babylon/eponet.nsf/0/FD9B4950FFA72013C125867D0059FFAD/$File/ARP2018_Modic_en.pdf.

Morseletto, P. (2020). Targets for a circular economy. *Resources, Conservation and Recycling,* 153, 104553.

Oltra, V., Kemp, R., & De Vries, F. P. (2010). Patents as a measure for eco-innovation. *International Journal of Environmental Technology and Management,* 13(2), 130–148.

Perella, M. (2014). EU circular economy framework proposals lack teeth, critics say. *Edie.net,* 11 June. https://www.edie.net/news/5/EU-circular-economy-framework-proposals-lack-teeth--critics-say/.

Popp, D. (2005). Lessons from patents: Using patents to measure technological change in environmental models. *Ecological Economics,* 54(2–3), 209–226.

Popp, D., Haščič, I., & Medhi, N. (2011). Technology and the diffusion of renewable energy. *Energy Economics,* 33(4), 648–662.

Potting, J., Hekkert, M. P., Worrell, E. & Hanemaaijer, A. (2017). *Circular Economy: Measuring Innovation in the Product Chain.* The Hague: PBL Publishers.

Raffo, J., & Lhuillery, S. (2009). How to play the 'Names Game': Patent retrieval comparing different heuristics. *Research Policy,* 38(10), 1617–1627.

Reike, D., Vermeulen, W. J., & Witjes, S. (2018). The circular economy: New or refurbished as CE 3.0? Exploring controversies in the conceptualization of the circular economy through a focus on history and resource value retention options. *Resources, Conservation and Recycling,* 135, 246–264.

Rocchetti, L., Amato, A., & Beolchini, F. (2018). Printed circuit board recycling: A patent review. *Journal of Cleaner Production,* 178, 814–832.

Rose, S., Engel, D., Cramer, N., & Cowley, W. (2010). Automatic keyword extraction from individual documents. In M. W. Berry & J. Kogan (eds.), *Text Mining: Applications and Theory.* Chichester: Wiley, 3–20.

Rush, A. M., Chopra, S., & Weston, J. (2015). A neural attention model for abstractive sentence summarization. *Proceedings of the 2015 Conference on Empirical Methods in Natural Language Processing,* 379–389. https://doi.org/10.18653/v1/D15-1044.

Scheu, M., Veefkind, V., Verbandt, Y., Galan, E. M., Absalom, R., & Förster, W. (2006). Mapping nanotechnology patents: The EPO approach. *World Patent Information*, 28(3), 204–211.

Stahel, W. R. (2016). The circular economy. *Nature*, 531(7595), 435–438.

Su, B. W., Heshmati, A., Geng, Y, & Yu, X. M. (2013). A review of the circular economy in China: Moving from rhetoric to implementation, *Journal of Cleaner Production*, 42, 215–227.

Sverko Grdic, Z., Krstinic Nizic, M., & Rudan, E. (2020). Circular economy concept in the context of economic development in EU countries. *Sustainability*, 12(7), 3060.

USPTO (2021). *Classification Resources: CPC Section Y*. https://www.uspto.gov/web/patents/classification/cpc/html/cpc-Y.html.

Veefkind, V., Hurtado-Albir, J., Angelucci, S., Karachalios, K., & Thumm, N. (2012). A new EPO classification scheme for climate change mitigation technologies. *World Patent Information*, 34(2), 106–111.

Venugopalan, S., & Rai, V. (2015). Topic based classification and pattern identification in patents. *Technological Forecasting and Social Change*, 94, 236–250.

23. The geography of circular economy technologies in Europe: evolutionary patterns and technological convergence

Fabrizio Fusillo, Francesco Quatraro and Cristina Santhià

INTRODUCTION

The last decades have witnessed an increasing awareness of the long-run unsustainable strains of economic activities on the environment. In order to address such societal challenges, supranational institutions have prominently spent effort in supporting and influencing policy agendas, providing inspirational frameworks and incentives. Circular economy, because of its closed-loop and regenerative economy approach, is more and more put forward as a strategy to give substance to the sustainable development concept. Reducing the exploitation of non-renewable resources, employing wastes or by-products as raw materials, increasing product lifespan, delivering solutions and functionality rather than products and ownership, are all strategies which might optimize resource supply and waste assimilation (namely, improve the 'circularity' of materials) and ease the environmental burden of production and consumption (Kirchherr et al. 2017; Ghisellini et al. 2016).

The European Commission is undoubtedly one of the most committed institutions to including circular economy (CE) principles in the political agenda. In the recent Circular Economy Action Plan, adopted by the Commission in March 2020, the transition to the circular economy is described as a "systemic, deep and transformative" process to underline the depth of transformation that the circular approach can bring in the entire economic system (European Commission 2020). The European strategy encompasses initiatives in terms of commodities' design, production process and by-products and waste recovery with the final aim of facilitating the exploitation and trade in secondary use materials in the market.

Alongside the definition of the objectives, the Commission has also developed a whole system of indicators covering different fields of actions to monitor progress and supply policymakers, economic actors, and citizens with evidence of improvements. The monitoring framework consists of ten indicators broken down into four thematic sections. The first one is related to production and consumption, the second is focused on waste management, the third covers the topic of secondary raw materials and the last one is dedicated to competitiveness and innovation. The latter encompasses two indicators, one of which is entitled "Patents related to recycling and secondary raw materials as a proxy for innovation", which aims to measure the innovation activity taking place in recycling and materials reuse domains within the European borders. The inclusion of such an indicator denotes the European Commission's acknowledgement that regulatory interventions need to be coupled with incentives for the private sector and civil society in order to stimulate CE adoption and technological advancements and accelerate the transition toward a more sustainable growth.

Conceiving the CE transition as a transition towards sustainability implies a systemic view. Transitions are complex dynamic processes involving multiple actors and institutions that entail a co-evolution of technology and society (Markard et al. 2012). Moving from an established system to a different one leads to a transformation of products and services, organizational structures and value chains, regulations and accepted behaviours. CE has been already presented as a pattern leading to a new model of socio-technical organization (Ghisellini et al. 2016). Bearing in mind that transitions imply technological and non-technological innovations, in our work we draw attention to the former one.

Since the CE concepts have already been translated into political targets and measures, with the European institutions at the forefront, and given the role played by innovation and technological development for a profitable and effective CE system, the primary aim of this chapter is to provide a mapping of the new technological system behind CE innovation in European regions, tracking its evolution over time and space. By exploiting patenting activity in European regions, from 1980 to 2015, the chapter contributes existing literature in two ways. First, we focus on the whole set of CE related technologies in order to provide a description of the CE innovative efforts, the main actors involved and the key technologies. Secondly, we employed network analysis techniques and ranking analysis to map the technological and geographical evolution of the CE knowledge base, identifying and tracing technological trajectories over time and regional specialization patterns.

THEORETICAL BACKGROUND

Until now, the topic of innovation related to environmental issues has been dominated by research on eco-innovations (EI), i.e. innovations conceived to improve the environmental impact of economic activities, and green technologies (Barbieri et al. 2016). Only recently has the role of EI been investigated specifically within a CE framework (Cainelli et al. 2020; De Jesus et al. 2018). Indeed, the introduction of CE practices in economic activities requires some degree of innovation, and, in this sense, the concept of eco-innovation (Kemp 2000, 2010) is crucial to investigate this dynamic. CE encompasses multidimensional and integrative transformations at societal, institutional and organizational level striving for a sustainable economic development; eco-innovations entail socio-technical solutions that may serve as strategic enablers for the transition towards circular economy (De Jesus et al. 2018). The availability of technical knowledge is a prerequisite to trigger production reorganization and let new consumption habits spread (EEA 2016). Yet, research effort has provided an insight into the evolution of single technologies applied in specific domains closed to the circular economy; for instance, a quantitative approach based on patent data is employed by Barragán-Ocaña et al. (2021) who sought to identify the technological trajectory of wastewater reuse technologies. However, a study with a similar approach but targeting a broader sample of CE technologies is still missing.

Even the role of geography remains largely unexplored. Technological change is a complex and evolutionary process, shaped by the knowledge capabilities embedded in inventors, institutions and organizations (Freeman 1987). The set of these actors' behaviours, together with institutional forces and their relations, differ from place to place and characterize the knowledge stocks of regions. According to the recombinant knowledge theory (Kauffman 1993; Weitzman 1998; Arthur 2009), a large fraction of discoveries and innovations can be created by the recombination of existing ideas, information or technological components. Limited access to resources, risk aversion, and other organizational impediments may reduce the search process through existing know-how and narrow the possibility to develop new technological knowledge (Fleming 2001). Moreover, following a smart specialization strategy approach, the strategic identification of growth opportunities, and their effective implementation, is strictly linked to the evaluation of territorial uniqueness of regions and their relative comparative advantages (Boschma et al. 2015; Boschma and Giannelle 2014; Foray 2009; McCann and Ortega-Argilés 2015; Montresor and Quatraro 2017). In turn, technological evolution results from the joint effect of, on the one hand, the persistence of different knowledge stocks pushing the spatial evolutions toward distinct patterns; on the other hand, of the cumulative nature of knowledge and ideas, shaping the technological development toward a trajectory convergence (Essletzbichler 2015; Kogler et al. 2017; Quatraro 2010; Rigby and Essletzbichler 1999). In other words, knowledge development in a given place shapes the geographic evolution of technology, and in turn, technological trajectories are shaped by the knowledge embedded in places. Therefore, a detailed investigation of how some technologies develop and persist in some places and how these characterize the technological trajectories may yield precious insight on the strategic development and policy implementation, particularly in new technological systems such as circular economy. Silvestri et al. (2020) made a first attempt to map CE application and improvements at the European regional level through a systemic perspective. The authors built composite indicators providing a static and a dynamic picture of CE diffusion, where the technological dimension is one among others. On the contrary, we draw our attention to the technological evolution within the same geographic context.

To the best of our knowledge, this is the first study examining the technological trajectory and the geographic evolution of CE technologies as a whole. In particular, we move a step forward in the understanding of CE technological developments by investigating the evolutionary patterns within the CE technological change and how its knowledge base evolved over space, referring to the broader sample of CE related technologies instead of targeting a limited knowledge area.

DATASET AND METHODOLOGICAL APPROACH

In this section of the chapter, we first present the selection process of patents related to the circular economy and their geographical allocation. We then discuss the measures employed to derive the network of technological proximities in order to map the CE knowledge base. Third, we focus on the methodology behind the identification of technological communities and present how these communities are, in turn, employed to trace over time the evolution of the trajectories in the CE technological field.

Identifying Circular Economy Related Technologies

Our main source of data is represented by the information contained in patent documents. Patent data are widely accepted as a means of assessing technological progress, though their use may present some drawbacks (Griliches 1990). Bearing in mind that not all relevant innovations are or can be patented, this remains the most valid alternative to explore knowledge development and track technological evolution (Jaffe and Trajtenberg 2002; Strumsky et al. 2012).

We employ data from the Organisation for Economic Co-operation and Development (OECD) REGPAT database, January 2020, relative to patents' applications at the European Patent Office (EPO) published between 1980 and 2015. Given the time required to complete the patent application process, it is reasonable to limit the period under consideration to the year 2015. Patents' geographic origin is identified according to the inventor's address, provided at Territorial Level 2 (TL2). A patent with inventors from different regions is proportionally allocated to each one of these. Technological classes of patent applications are used to select patents related to the circular economy. With respect to the selection criteria, we rely on the Cooperative Patent Classification (CPC) codes detected by the European Commission and falling within the monitoring indicator of innovation activity provided by Eurostat named "Patents related to recycling and secondary raw materials".[1] All the technological fields comprised in the indicator belong to the technological subclass Y02W, namely "Climate change mitigation technologies related to wastewater treatment or waste management" and are related to waste treatment and reduction. In turn, we classify as "Circular economy patent" each patent covering at least one of these technology fields. The selection process has resulted in 10,724 patents over the period 1980–2015, 6,407 of which include at least one European country among their contributors.

Social Network Analysis and Map Equation Algorithm

In order to derive the circular economy knowledge base, we rely on data contained in patent documents about technological classes. By exploiting the technological classification, a large stream of literature on geography and innovation provided several empirical measures of the proximity between technologies (Colombelli et al. 2014; Jaffe 1989; Neffke and Henning 2008; Yan and Luo 2016). Recently, such measures have also been used to develop global maps of the knowledge space, which can provide valuable information about promising areas and the positioning of specific entities (Kogler et al. 2013; Leydesdorff et al. 2014; Rigby 2015). In turn, these fields/communities are traced over time in the form of trajectories in order to provide some evidence on the evolutionary patterns of the structure of the CE knowledge base and the relationship between knowledge and geographical spaces.

In this chapter, to measure technological proximity, we make use of the co-occurrence of technology classes in CE patents. Co-occurrence (often referred to as co-classification measure) is a measure of proximity between technologies based on how similar their artefacts are. We obtained our CE related co-occurrence proximity measure by counting the number of times two technology classes, at the CPC 4-digit level, appear together in the CE patents from 1980 to 2015. Therefore, our proximity measure is based on the concept that if two classes are often classified together in patent documents it means that they possess some degree of relatedness. The resulting symmetric matrix of proximities between technologies can be seen as a network adjacency matrix where technologies represent the nodes and their proximities measure the strength of their links. In this way, the matrix can be plotted using network analysis techniques, providing a visual representation of a knowledge space.

To identify coherent technological communities, showing strong connections within and sparse connections between them, we follow the methodological approach described in Haller and Rigby (2020) and employ the map equation community detection algorithm (Rosvall and Bergstrom 2008). The map equation is built on a flow-based and information-theoretic foundation taking advantage of the duality between finding community structure in networks and minimizing the description length of a random walker's movements on a network. In other words, the algorithm takes a random walk through the network, a community is identified as a set of nodes in which the random 'walker' takes a long time before moving to other nodes (or set of nodes). By applying the map equation to our 5-year proximity matrices we are able to trace the evolution of trajectories in the CE technological field and capture their dynamics. In this way, we can trace the flow of technological communities and explore, visually, how they merge, decline or expand, from one period to the other.

RESULTS

Development and Technological Composition of Circular Economy Related Patents

Our first set of results focuses on the description of the innovative efforts in the CE fields and the identification of the main actors and the key technologies. Figure 23.1 illustrates the growth rate of the number of patents related to the circular economy with respect to the year 1980. A steep and fast rise in the growth rate is visible during the 1980s. In the following decades, the rate has fluctuated experiencing cyclical periods of steady increase. And still, the rate of change has always been more than 150 per cent compared to the base year.

In the global ranking of top contributors in patents involving circular economy technologies the predominant role of European regions can easily be detected (Table 23.1). Despite Southern-Kanto (JP) and Kansai (JP) regions confirming their leading role in patent inventions also in the area concerning the circular economy, several American regions do not reflect their global tendency to innovate also in this specific field. France and Germany are the European countries where the highest number of patents is developed.

Within the European Union, Germany demonstrates the most impressive ability to innovate in technological fields closed to the circular economy. France stands out with Île-de-France as the territorial area which obtained the highest number of CE patents (namely, 270), and Rhône-Alpes in the sixth position of this ranking. Among the top 10 regions, we also find Lombardy and Upper Austria with 142 and 131 patents respectively, at seventh and tenth position.

Very heterogeneous industrial sectors are at the origin of circular economy related patents, contrary to what happens for non-specific ones where the electronic industry guides technological evolution. Best performing companies mostly belong to the chemical and engineering sectors, but they are highly diversified.

As reported in earlier to illustrate the selection process of patents, these can be classified as circular if they include specific technological classes belonging to the three CPC groups identified by the European Commission to monitor the innovation process in CE and described below. The most dynamic field of innovation is the one related to materials' recovery (that is, CPC group Y02W 30/00) counting 5,303 patents. However, further examining the more detailed breakdown of this technological group it emerges that this category mainly deals with recycling and recovery, as well as technologies designed to improve the collection and transfer of wastes, dismantling and pre-treatment processes. Plastic recycling and recovery of other polymers appear among the four most recurring technologies. This sheds light on the actual

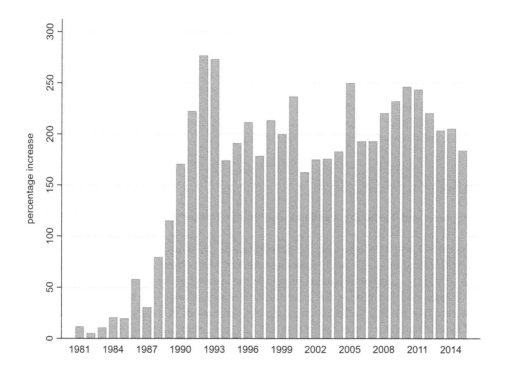

Figure 23.1　Growth rate of the number of patents related to the circular economy, base year 1980

spread and burden of these materials, but also on the efforts to improve their recyclability and foster their second use minimizing the overall production of wastes.

Of no lesser importance are the technologies developed for wastewater treatment (Y02W 10/00) with a total of 2,224 patents. Indeed, the technological breakdown reveals that breakthroughs involving the aerobic processes within the biological treatment of water are the most frequently occurring. The third circular technological group identified concerns enabling technologies projected for greenhouse gas emissions mitigation (Y02W 90/00). They are currently limited in number (21 patents) and their expansion dates back to the last decade.

Considering the technologies not classified as 'circular' that most often are embedded in CE patents, the role of those developed to perform operations and transports (letter B) emerges. These technologies are designed for storage and transport, separation, mixing and, generally, disposal of solid waste, in agreement with the relevance that solid waste treatment experience among the circular technologies themselves. Particularly noteworthy is the repeated presence of technologies related to the working of plastics, identified with B29, in line with what we have suggested above. The most prevalent technologies in CE patents are listed and defined in Table 23.2.

Table 23.1   *Top 10 contributors to patents and patents related to the circular economy by region (TL2) at global and European level, from 1980 to 2015*

	Patents		Circular economy patents	
Region	Number	Region	Number	
Worldwide				
Southern-Kanto (Japan)	295334.88	Southern-Kanto (Japan)	519.02	
California (USA)	193365.07	Kansai region (Japan)	275.11	
Kansai region (Japan)	110076.16	Île-de-France (France)	270.04	
Île-de-France (France)	91742.36	Düsseldorf (Germany)	237.79	
Toukai (Japan)	68682.51	Oberbayern (Germany)	203.50	
Oberbayern (Germany)	67702.36	California (USA)	168.83	
Capital Region (Korea)	65122.76	Köln (Germany)	166.30	
New York (USA)	64426.09	Darmstadt (Germany)	156.79	
Stuttgart (Germany)	62072.09	Rhône-Alpes (France)	144.54	
New Jersey (USA)	53996.84	Lombardy (Italy)	142.67	
Europe				
Île-de-France (France)	91742.36	Île-de-France (France)	270.04	
Oberbayern (Germany)	67702.11	Düsseldorf (Germany)	237.79	
Stuttgart (Germany)	62072.09	Oberbayern (Germany)	203.50	
Darmstadt (Germany)	43699.78	Köln (Germany)	166.30	
Düsseldorf (Germany)	43622.44	Darmstadt (Germany)	156.79	
North Brabant (Netherlands)	41959.87	Rhône-Alpes (France)	144.54	
Rhône-Alpes (France)	40685.60	Lombardy (Italy)	142.67	
Köln (Germany)	38245.66	Germany – not regionalized	132.95	
Lombardy (Italy)	37253.35	Tübingen (Germany)	132.45	
Karlsruhe (Germany)	34282.58	Upper Austria (Austria)	131.42	

Table 23.2   *Top 10 technological classes included in patents related to the circular economy, from 1980 to 2015*

CPC classes	No. of patents
Y02W 'Circular'	10,724
C02F – Treatment of water, wastewater, sewage, or sludge	3,729
Y02P – Climate change mitigation technologies in the production or processing of goods	2,066
B29B – Preparation or pre-treatment of the material to be shaped; making granules or preforms; recovery of plastics or other constituents of waste material containing plastics	1,890
B29K – Indexing scheme associated with subclasses B29B, B29C OR B29D, relating to moulding materials or to materials for {moulds}, reinforcements, fillers or preformed parts (e.g. inserts)	1,371
C05F – Organic fertilizers not covered by subclasses C05B, C05C (e.g. fertilizers from waste or refuse)	1,207
C08J – Working-up; general processes of compounding; after-treatment not covered by subclasses C08B, C08C, C08F, C08G	1,205
B29L – Indexing scheme associated with subclass B29C, relating to particular articles	1,065
Y02E – Reduction of greenhouse gas [ghg] emissions, related to energy generation, transmission or distribution	920
B01D – Separation	888

Geographic Evolution of Circular Economy Technologies

We now turn to the investigation of the spatial distribution of CE innovative effort and its evolution across European countries and regions. First, Figure 23.2 (top) shows the spatial dis-

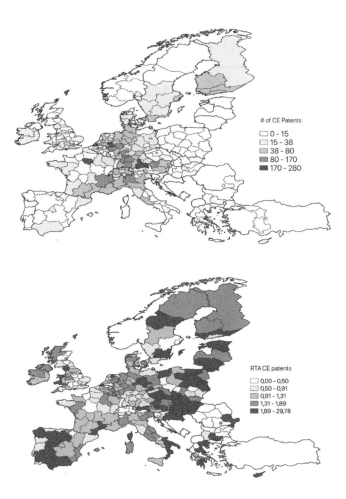

Figure 23.2   Geographic distribution of the total number of patents (top) and relative specialization (RTA index) (bottom) in CE related technologies of European NUTS2 regions, from 1980 to 2015

tribution of the overall inventive activity in CE related technologies across European NUTS2 regions, in terms of number of patents from 1980 to 2015. Darker areas are associated with the highest patenting levels. As already highlighted in the previous section, patenting activity in CE related technologies is highly concentrated in central Europe regions, in particular in German, northern Italy, Austria and southern France regions (except for the Île-de-France region, centred around Paris). Medium levels of CE patenting can be observed in Ireland, Sweden and Finland regions.

The absolute level of patents gives us a first snapshot of the geographic concentration of CE inventive activity in Europe. To dig into the relevance of CE related technologies in the regional innovative portfolios, we build a simple measure of a region's relative specialization in CE technologies. The measure is based on the Revealed Technological Advantage (RTA) index (often referred to as location quotient or Balassa index) and provides an indication of the relative importance of a selected technology field in the country/region technology base compared to the relative importance of this field in the overall economy. In our case, the relative specialization of European regions in CE related technologies is calculated as the ratio between the share of CE patents in a given region and the share of CE patents in the European patent portfolio. By construction, the RTA index ranges between 0 and positive infinite, where the higher the RTA index the higher the relative specialization in CE of a given region. The geographic distribution of CE regional specialization is presented in Figure 23.2 (bottom). Interestingly, while the central European regions of Germany, France and Italy still present medium-high levels of relative specialization in CE technologies, more peripheric regions, in particular of Eastern Europe and Spain are characterized by the highest specialization rates. This suggests that, notwithstanding the lower number of patents in absolute terms (with respect to both overall and CE related technologies), the relative weight of CE related patents in these regions is surprisingly high compared to the most performing regions.

The analysis of Figure 23.2 suggests that absolute inventive efforts do not necessarily reflect the relative importance and intensity of specific technology fields in the overall regional knowledge base. In order to explore the evolution of the spatial distribution of CE related technologies, we split the total sample into consecutive five-year time periods and perform a ranking analysis by comparing countries and regional relative positioning over time. Ranking evolution is performed both at the country and regional level and compares rankings in absolute patenting activities and relative specialization (RTA) in CE related technologies.[2]

Figure 23.3 (top) presents the ranking evolution of European countries in terms of CE number of patents. As expected, Germany and France rank first and second, having the highest level of CE patents throughout the whole period. Austria, United Kingdom and Italy follow, ranked respectively third, fourth and fifth in 1985 and after some fluctuations, fifth, third and fourth in 2015. Some countries present in 2015 entered the ranking after 1990, as in the case of Denmark, Ireland and Finland. Spain and the Czech Republic filed their first patents in CE technologies after 1995 and, eventually Poland only in 2005. The ranking evolution of countries CE specialization, in Figure 23.3 (bottom), shows that, other than Austria, the first ranked countries in 1985 do not correspond to the most prolific countries. This mismatch seems quite persistent throughout the whole period, though with much less stable ranking patterns, culminating in 2015 where the most CE specialized country is Hungary, followed by Poland, Czech Republic and Finland. Leading countries such as France, UK and Germany rank among the last position in 2015, experiencing big drops in their CE specialization mainly from 1995/2000 onwards.

The analysis of ranking evolution of European regions in terms of CE patents, presented in Figure 23.4 (top), is largely in line with the countries' evidence.[3] German regions dominate the ranking in 1985, maintaining, partially, a prominent position until 2015. Interestingly, in the first two positions in 2015, we find two France regions, Île-de-France (FR10) and Rhône-Alpes (FR71), which rapidly scaled up since the 2000s. Among the first 10 positions in 2015, we find the Upper Austria, AT (AT31) and Lombardy, IT (ITC4) regions, which ranked only 8th and 13th in 1985. Figure 23.4 (bottom) shows instead the ranking evolution based on regional relative specialization in CE related technologies. If, on the one hand, rankings in CE patents and CE specialization are still quite different at the regional level, on the other hand, they also provide surprising evidence on the evolution of regional CE specialization. The upsurge of Eastern Europe regions and (partially) of some Spanish regions is not confirmed when looking at the temporal evolution of CE specialization. This discrepancy can be explained by the

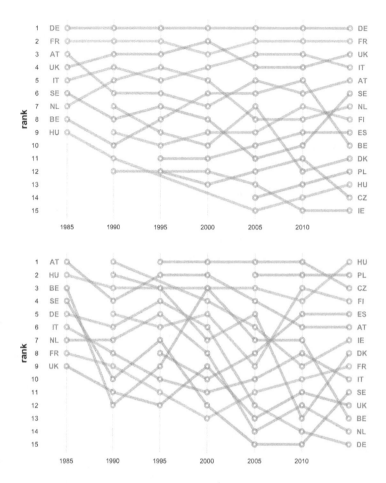

Figure 23.3   *Ranking evolution of European countries in terms of total number of*
CE patents (top) and relative CE specialization (RTA index) (bottom) in
consecutive 5-year sub-periods from 1980 to 2015

fact that the CE patenting efforts of those regions cumulates at the country and overall level, allowing them to show higher scores. However, this cumulative effect seems to disappear when regional specialization is disentangled across the geographic and temporal dimensions.

Technology Trajectory and Evolutionary Patterns in Circular Economy Technologies

The analysis carried out in the previous section provides evidence on the rate of technological change in the circular economy technological field. However, we have not yet said anything about the direction of technological change. This aspect can be grasped by looking at the evolutionary patterns of the field's knowledge base over the period under scrutiny (Krafft et al. 2011, 2014).

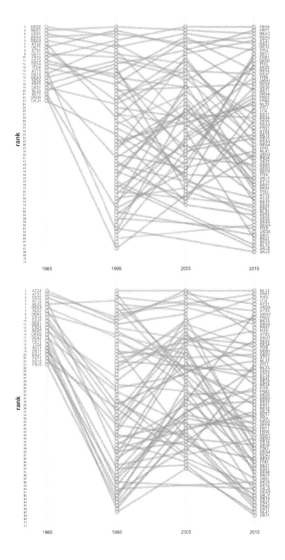

Figure 23.4   Ranking evolution of European NUTS2 regions in terms of total number of CE patents (top) and relative CE specialization (RTA index) (bottom) in consecutive 5-year sub-periods from 1980 to 2015

As discussed earlier, we exploit technological class information on CE patents to build a co-occurrence network of CE related technology. The network is then employed to derive our co-occurrence based proximity measure from which we obtain the global map of the knowledge base behind CE related technologies, shown in Figure 23.5. The size of the nodes is proportional to the overall number of patents by the technology class. The central and most relevant technology is, indeed, the 'pure' circular economy technologies (corresponding to those technology classes identified by the European Commission as "CE technologies" at the CPC 4-digit level). This cluster mainly comprises also technologies related to the sustainable

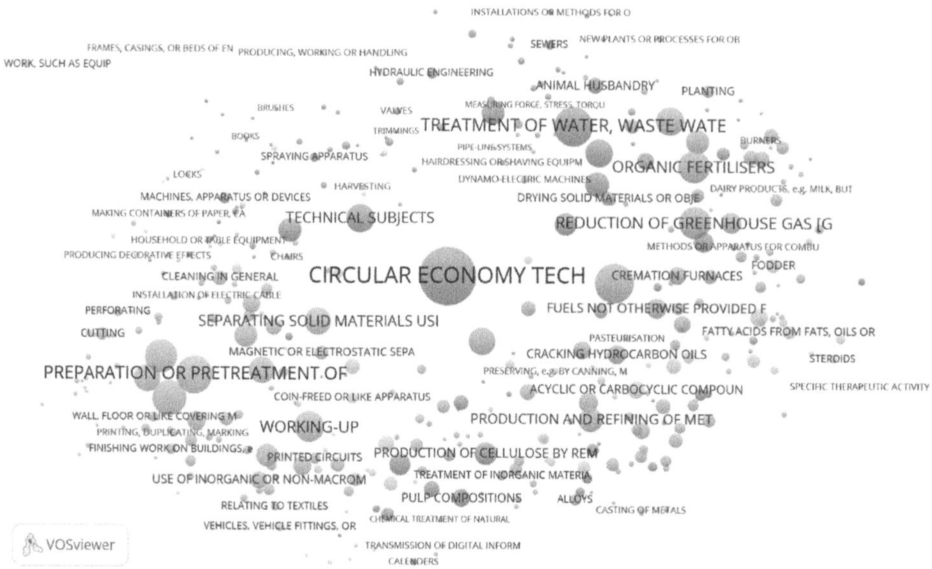

Figure 23.5   Global map of CE knowledge space, from 1980 to 2015

treatment of water and wastewater, suggesting that the CE knowledge base in Europe has predominantly concerned the handling and purification of water, developing instruments and processes for its reuse. The other two most prominent clusters are related to the other two main technology areas covered by the CE field: on the one hand, we find technologies aimed at reducing the greenhouse gases, from fertilizers to fuels; on the other hand, there are technologies related to the management of solid waste, in particular concerning the treatment of plastic materials and the separation of material (i.e. plastic recycling).

The grouping of technologies into categories (technological communities) can be also performed at shorter interval times, in the form of trajectories, that can be traced and compared over time.

Figure 23.6 shows the evolution of the European CE technology space from 1980 to 2015. Notwithstanding the highly fragmented evolution of trajectories, distinct patterns can be traced over time. Some CE communities were present in 1980 and remain prevalent throughout the whole period. This is the case, for example, of CE technologies related to wastewater treatment and the treatment of plastics, which constitute the foundation of CE technologies. Though the two trajectories had a turbulent history, indeed, some of their components, in particular those related to CE water treatment technologies, were combined with the other trajectories, before eventually splitting into several new specialized categories, after the 2000s. In this way emerged the new categories of paper recycling, metals treatment or climate change mitigation technologies related to transportation and energy. The components that made up the chemical processes category in 1985 were split among several trajectories, joining and transforming some of them (e.g. from plastic treatments to plastic recycling or material for food packaging together with components coming from the plastic trajectory), or becoming completely new categories over time (e.g. chemical compounds). The evolution of CE trajectories suggests that actors actively involved in the generation of CE related technology, though based on founda-

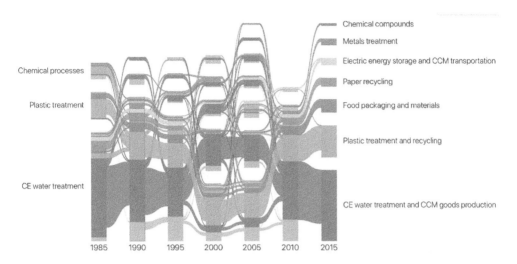

Chemical compounds

Metals treatment

Electric energy storage and CCM transportation

Paper recycling

Food packaging and materials

Plastic treatment and recycling

CE water treatment and CCM goods production

Figure 23.6   Evolution of CE technological trajectories, from 1980 to 2015

tional technologies, have continuously re-combined the highly interdependent components from different CE technology areas.

The technological grouping and communities' detection can also be re-scaled at a finer geographical level, allowing, therefore, the analysis of trajectories evolution at the regional level. To do so, we, firstly, identify all CE patents and their technological classification on a regional base. Then, we construct regional technology proximity matrix and apply the map equation algorithm to visualize the evolution of CE technologies. The analysis is performed on three selected NUTS2 regions, among the top 10 most prolific regions in CE patenting: Düsseldorf (DE), Île-de-France (FR) and Lombardy (IT). The CE trajectory evolution for our three focus regions is presented in Figure 23.7. The figure reveals some interesting patterns. While until 1985 the major communities that made up the CE knowledge space are also predominant in the regional profiles (e.g. CE related to water treatment or treatment of plastic), these took different evolutionary trajectories in the three regions. Their specialization varied greatly over time, with several technologies disappearing from the 2000s, as in the case of Düsseldorf and Île-de-France, and entirely new clusters arising in recent years, as in the case of Lombardy. Interestingly, in 2015 the composition of local CE knowledge spaces in our example highlight that, if on the one hand, regional CE inventive effort influences the CE technological trajectories, on the other hand, they developed quite different specializations that characterize (and are shaped by) the local existing capabilities.

DISCUSSION AND CONCLUSIONS

This chapter moves an important step forward in the understanding of the innovative efforts and technological evolution in the circular economy system. The analysis is carried at the European level, from 1980 to 2015, with a focus on European NUTS2 regions. We exploited EPO patent data and their technological classification to identify CE related technologies and provide a description of the CE patenting activity, the main actors involved and the key

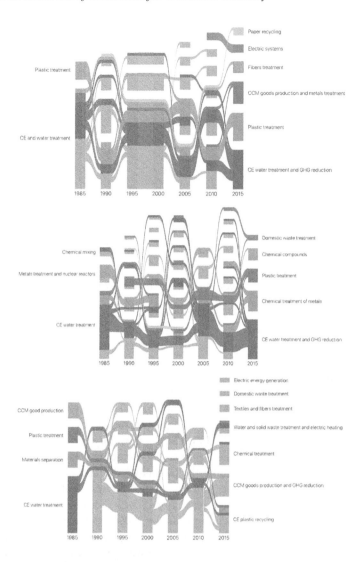

Figure 23.7   Evolution of CE technological trajectories by selected regions, from 1980 to 2015: Düsseldorf (DE) (top); Île-de-France (FR) (middle); and Lombardy (IT) (bottom)

technologies. Then, using patent inventor location information, we employed network analysis techniques and ranking analysis to map the geographical and technological evolution of the CE knowledge base in European regions. The emergence, growth and decline of techno-logical trajectories are examined over time and across regions, together with countries and regional CE innovative efforts and their relative specialization. The results suggest that the CE innovative space is a dynamic technological field, though still in its development stage. The evolutionary trajectory of CE related technologies is continually changing and adapting to new recombination opportunities and regional specific trajectories. In particular, we find that the three main trajectories constituting the foundation of CE technologies until the early 1980s – i.e. CE technologies related to wastewater treatment, treatment of plastics and chemical processes – experienced a turbulent period of growth, decline and recombination from the 2000s onwards. On the one hand, this paved the way to the emergence of new independent promising trajectories such as paper recycling, food packaging and climate change mitigation technologies related to transportation and energy. On the other hand, the evolution led to the consolidation of CE water treatment related technologies as the dominant trajectory, thanks to the contribution of climate change mitigation technologies related to goods production, together with the transformation of the plastic treatment trajectory that merged with recycling related technologies. The geographic distribution reveals that CE innovative efforts tend to be concentrated in the higher-performing regions of central Europe, while CE relative specialization is highly fragmented and seems to be stronger in more peripheral regions. In addition, the temporal geographical evolution of CE suggests that the specialization patterns are still largely heterogeneous not only between regions of different countries but also within countries, with countries concentrating huge CE innovative efforts in very few regions (e.g. Germany) and others distributing their CE competences among several regions (e.g. Hungary).

Our findings lead to important policy implications. The heterogeneous and evolutionary trajectories of regional CE innovation systems and specializations resonate with the key role of regional capabilities in the Smart Specialization Strategies (S3) approach. The efficacy of huge investment efforts for a sustainable transition pass through the deployment of 'smart strategies' that prioritize new growth opportunities in CE related technological domains. These smart strategies should be designed with the aim of aligning growth opportunities with existing competencies. Also, while recognizing the benefits of heterogeneous place-specific technological characteristics and dynamism, strategic wider coordination toward a common goal should not be neglected. Indeed, regions play a crucial role in improving the institutional framework and their innovation ecosystems for stimulating the development and adoption of CE. Detailed knowledge of region-specific CE technological competencies and specialization can guide regions to increase communication and awareness, improving business and research local actors' knowledge of CE potentials. This may, in turn, attract and create incentives toward directed investments and funding, also supporting the creation of stakeholders' networks and clusters for stimulating and coordinating collaborative learning potential.

NOTES

1.   The Eurostat indicator is available at https://ec.europa.eu/eurostat/cache/metadata/en/cei_cie020_esmsip2.htm.
2.   It is worth highlighting that only countries and regions with more than five CE patents in each sub-period covered are included.
3.   As in Figure 23.3 the regional ranking evolution is performed at 5-year consecutive intervals. However, to allow a better and clearer visualization only 10-year intervals are plotted.

REFERENCES

Arthur, B. (2009). *The Nature of Technology. What It Is and How it Evolves*. New York: Free Press.
Barbieri, N., Ghisetti, C., Gilli, M., Marin, G., & Nicolli, F. (2016). A survey of the literature on environmental innovation based on main path analysis. *Journal of Economic Surveys*, 30(3), 596–623.

Barragán-Ocaña, A., Silva-Borjas, P., & Olmos-Peña, S. (2021). Scientific and technological trajectory in the recovery of value-added products from wastewater: A general approach. *Journal of Water Process Engineering*, 39, 101692.

Boschma, R., Balland, P., & Kogler, D. F. (2015). Relatedness and technological change in cities: The rise and fall of technological knowledge in US metropolitan areas from 1981 to 2010. *Industrial and Corporate Change*, 24(1), 223–250.

Boschma, R., & Giannelle, C. (2014). *Regional Branching and Smart Specialisation Policy*. S3 Policy Brief Series 06/2014. Seville: European Commission.

Cainelli, G., D'Amato, A., & Mazzanti, M. (2020). Resource efficient eco-innovations for a circular economy: Evidence from EU firms. *Research Policy*, 49(1), 103827.

Colombelli, A., Krafft, J., & Quatraro, F. (2014). The emergence of new technology-based sectors in European regions: A proximity-based analysis of nanotechnology. *Research Policy*, 43(10), 1681–1696.

De Jesus, A., Antunes, P., Santos, R., & Mendonça, S. (2018). Eco-innovation in the transition to a circular economy: An analytical literature review. *Journal of Cleaner Production*, 172, 2999–3018.

Essletzbichler, J. (2015). Relatedness, industrial branching and technological cohesion in US metropolitan areas. *Regional Studies*, 49, 752–766.

European Commission (2020). Communication from the Commission. *A New Circular Economy Action Plan. For a Cleaner and More Competitive Europe*. https://eur-lex.europa.eu/legal-content/EN/TXT/?qid=1583933814386&uri=COM:2020:98:FIN.

European Environment Agency (2016). *Circular Economy in Europe: Developing the Knowledge Base*. https://www.eea.europa.eu/publications/circular-economy-in-europe.

Fleming, L. (2001). Recombinant uncertainty in technological search. *Management Science*, 47(1), 117–132.

Foray, D. (2009). Understanding 'smart specialisation'. In D. Pontikakis, D. Kyriakou, & R. Van Bavel (eds.), *The Question of R&D Specialisation: Perspectives and Policy Implications JRC-IPTS*. Seville: European Commission, 14–27.

Freeman, C. (1987). *Technology Policy and Economic Performance: Lessons from Japan*. London: Pinter.

Ghisellini, P., Cialani, C., & Ulgiati, S., (2016). A review on circular economy: The expected transition to a balanced interplay of environmental and economic systems. *Journal of Cleaner Production*, 114, 11–32.

Griliches, Z. (1990). *Patent Statistics as Economic Indicators: A Survey*. NBER Working Paper no. 3301.

Haller, M., & Rigby, D. L. (2020). The geographic evolution of optics technologies in the United States, 1976–2010. *Papers in Regional Science*, 99, 1539–1559.

Jaffe, A. B. (1989). Characterizing the 'technological position' of firms, with application to quantifying technological opportunity and research spillovers. *Research Policy*, 18(2), 87–97.

Jaffe, A. B., & Trajtenberg, M. (2002). *Patents, Citations, and Innovations: A Window on the Knowledge Economy*. Cambridge, MA: MIT Press.

Kauffman, S. A. (1993). *The Origins of Order: Self-Organization and Selection in Evolution*. New York: Oxford University Press.

Kemp, R. (2000). Technology and environmental policy: Innovation effects of past policies and suggestions for improvement. *OECD Proceedings Innovation and the Environment*. Paris: OECD, 35–61.

Kemp, R. (2010). Eco-innovation: Definition, measurement and open research issues. *Economia Politica*, 27(3), 397–420.

Kirchherr, J., Reike, D., & Hekkert, M. (2017). Conceptualizing the circular economy: An analysis of 114 definitions. *Resources, Conservation and Recycling*, 127, 221–232.

Kogler, D., Essletzbichler, J., & Rigby, D. (2017). The evolution of specialization in the EU knowledge space. *Journal of Economic Geography*, 17(2), 345–373.

Kogler, D. F., Rigby, D. L., & Tucker, I. (2013). Mapping knowledge space and technological relatedness in US cities. *European Planning Studies*, 21(9), 1374–1391.

Krafft, J., Quatraro, F., & Saviotti, P. P. (2011). The knowledge-base evolution in biotechnology: A social network analysis. *Economics of Innovation and New Technology*, 20(5), 445–475.

Krafft, J., Quatraro, F., & Saviotti, P. P. (2014). The dynamics of knowledge-intensive sectors' knowledge base: Evidence from biotechnology and telecommunications. *Industry and Innovation*, 21(3), 215–242.

Leydesdorff, L., Kushnir, D., & Rafols, I. (2014). Interactive overlay maps for US patent (USPTO) data based on International Patent Classification (IPC). *Scientometrics*, 98(3), 1583–1599.

Markard, J., Raven, R., & Truffer, B. (2012). Sustainability transitions: An emerging field of research and its prospects. *Research Policy*, 41(6), 955–967.

McCann, P., & Ortega-Argilés, R. (2015). Smart specialization, regional growth and applications to European Union cohesion policy. *Regional Studies*, 49(8), 1291–1302.

Montresor, S., & Quatraro, F. (2017). Regional branching and key enabling technologies: Evidence from European patent data. *Economic Geography*, 93(4), 367–396.

Neffke, F., & Henning, M. S. (2008). Revealed relatedness: Mapping industry space. *Papers in Evolutionary Economic Geography*, 0819.

Quatraro, F. (2010). Knowledge coherence, variety and economic growth: Manufacturing evidence from Italian regions. *Research Policy*, 39, 1289–1302.

Rigby, D. (2015). Technological relatedness and knowledge space: Entry and exit of US cities from patent classes. *Regional Studies*, 49(11), 1922–1937.

Rigby, D., & Essletzbichler, J. (1999). Evolution, process variety, and regional trajectories of technological change. *Economic Geography*, 73, 269–284.

Rosvall, M., & Bergstrom, C. T. (2008). Maps of random walks on complex networks reveal community structure. *Proceedings of the National Academy of Sciences*, 105(4), 1118–1123.

Silvestri, F., Spigarelli, F., & Tassinari, M. (2020). Regional development of circular economy in the European Union: A multidimensional analysis. *Journal of Cleaner Production*, 255, 120218.

Strumsky, D., Lobo, J., & Van der Leeuw, S. (2012). Using patent technology codes to study technological change. *Economics of Innovation and New Technology*, 21, 267–286.

Weitzman, M. L. (1998). Recombinant growth. *Quarterly Journal of Economics*, 113, 331–360.

Yan, B., & Luo, J. (2016). Measuring technological distance for patent mapping. *Journal of the Association for Information Science and Technology*, 68, 423–437.

PART VI

INFRASTRUCTURE ENABLING
A CIRCULAR ECONOMY

24. Fund model innovations for circular economy investing

Puck D. Hegeman

INTRODUCTION

Financial capital is a key resource that must be mobilized to drive system transformation (Perez 2011). The circular economy (CE) is a new system of economic organization "based on the principles of designing out waste and pollution, keeping products and materials in use, and regenerating natural systems" (Ellen MacArthur Foundation 2020). This system represents a shift from a linear material and energy throughput flow (Korhonen et al. 2018) to a circular flow by focusing on the slowing, closing, and narrowing of resource loops (Geissdoerfer et al. 2017; Bocken et al. 2016). The CE concept is far-reaching, as it concerns a fundamental transition to a new socioeconomic system. A lack of investment is identified as one of the main barriers to the CE transition by Ellen MacArthur Foundation and Systemic Ltd. (2017), and they estimate the CE investment opportunity to be vast; for Europe, it is projected to total €320 billion by 2025.

While the CE literature currently focuses on businesses and consumers as actors in the CE system transformation, there is limited knowledge concerning the providers of financial capital (Dewick et al. 2020; Hall et al. 2017). Private equity funds (PEFs) and venture capital funds (VCFs) represent a major class of financial assets (Preqin 2020) and are notable contributors to economic development and innovation (Lerner and Nanda 2020). However, the fund model is designed based on a neoclassical economic logic rooted in profit maximization and economic rationality (Metrick and Yasuda 2011). Based on the same neoclassical economic logic, the market for CE investing is conceived as inefficient, thin, and unproven, making it a challenging investment proposition for PEFs and VCFs. This chapter therefore questions how funds innovate in order to invest in the CE market and it examines the barriers they encounter. It uses three pioneering fund managers operating different models for investing in CE ventures as illustrative cases. It reveals how funds can play an advantageous role in the transition to the CE by adjusting their strategy and organization.

This chapter widens the scope of CE research by placing fund managers in the landscape of the CE transformation. It also contributes to literature on PEFs and VCFs. While extant research has shown how fund investments have contributed to economic development, research on funds' potential to create broader societal impacts remains nascent (Lerner and Nanda 2020). Furthermore, uncovering barriers is considered most instructive for practitioners aiming to stimulate the CE (Kirchherr et al. 2017), and hence, this chapter presents recommendations for practitioners.

THE FUND INVESTMENT MODEL

This section starts with a description of the traditional fund model. Thereafter, the problems that arise when the traditional fund model is used for investing in the CE market are described.

The Traditional Fund Model

Fund investments are a major class of financial assets (Phalippou and Gottschalg 2008). VCFs focus on investing in the very early stages of start-ups. In the later stages or infrastructure projects, PEFs become involved. By 2019, PEFs and VCFs were estimated to have over $4 trillion in assets under management around the world (Preqin 2020).

Virtually all funds are structured in a similar fashion (Metrick and Yasuda 2010), and this structure has been deployed since the industry took off in the late 1970s (Gompers and Lerner 2001). Figure 24.1 depicts an outline of the structure. A fund management team serves as the general partner or fund manager. The team initiates the fund and determines its strategy. It also approaches potential investors to raise the capital that will be invested. The providers of capital to the fund are its limited partners. Typically, institutional investors, such as pension funds, insurance companies, and sovereign wealth funds or family offices, enter the fund structure as limited partners. After the fund has been established, the fund manager is responsible for the investment cycle. It selects portfolio companies, manages the investments, and works toward exits of the portfolio companies. Exit routes include the sale of a venture to another corporation or listing it on a stock exchange. The typical life of a limited partnership structure is ten years. In the first five, investments can be made, while the latter five are solely focused

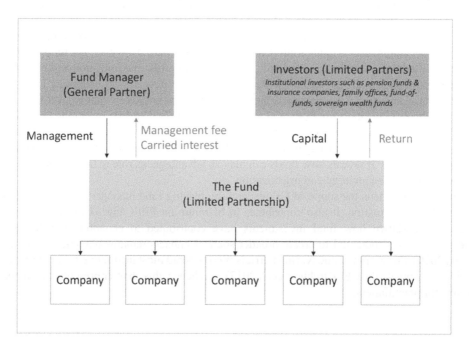

Figure 24.1   The traditional fund model

on adding value to portfolio companies and realizing exits. The structure clearly defines payments to the fund manager. The manager receives an annual management fee to carry out its activities. In addition, there is a variable component called 'carried interest'. This interest is awarded to the management team after the limited partners have received their money back including a previously agreed upon return.

Limited partners choose to channel their equity investments via the fund model, as this allows them to diversify their investments in an efficient manner. They make one investment, which, through the intermediation of the fund manager, is invested in multiple ventures. Investing via a fund also allows the limited partners to become acquainted with unfamiliar sectors, industries, and markets. When even more diversification is warranted, for instance when very new territory is entered, investors can choose to invest in a fund-of-funds structure (Brown et al. 2004). In this structure, the management team of the fund-of-funds pools capital from limited partners to be invested in funds, thereby adding a layer to the fund model.

The Traditional Fund Model and Investing in the CE

The fund management industry is guided by a neoclassical economic logic (Schoenmaker and Schramade 2019). This logic is eminent in the central theory of the efficient market hypothesis (EMH) (Fama 1970). It is based on the premise that investors are rational actors and markets are efficient and transparent (Louche et al. 2019). Rational actors will always invest in the sole financial interests of their own funds (Lydenberg 2014). Markets are efficient and transparent when prices of securities fully reflect all available information (Fama 1970). Following the EMH, investment decisions are based on the net present value of investment propositions using the financial returns of future cash flows that are discounted based on their risk characteristics (Shleifer 2000).

However, in the CE investment market, returns are broader than the financial profit of one's own funds (Ghisellini et al. 2016). The value created through the more appropriate and environmentally sound use of resources is an important aspect of the total value creation (Lüdeke-Freund et al. 2019). Additionally, in order to value CE investment opportunities, the risks accounted for when discounting the investment opportunity should reflect the lower sustainability and eco-efficiency risk caused (Derwall et al. 2005). Neoclassical economic thinking fails to account for the broader value proposition that characterizes CE investment opportunities (Dumas and Louche 2016), which results in the CE market being inefficient and presenting several problems to the fund model.

For CE investments to be appropriately appraised, both fund managers and limited partners need to move away from linear mindsets that suffer from the "bigger-better-faster-safer syndrome" (Stahel 2016, p. 436) and, accordingly, let go of the EMH's dominant logic (Ameli et al. 2020). Institutional investors are known to be conservative, and attracting them to an innovative investment proposition can be challenging (Schoenmaker and Schramade 2019). Another problem for fund managers caused by market inefficiency is that impact measurement is not standardized and not applied industry wide (Ameli et al. 2020). Only when all fund managers include the positive and negative impacts their investments create when calculating risk-adjusted returns, can investment propositions be compared (Reeder and Colantonio 2013). Finally, following the EMH logic, the fund model is organized to maximize profit. To do that, the traditional fund model favours investments in technologies with high potential growth while having low capital intensity and low complexity and uncertainty (Mazzucato

2013). Similarly, the traditional fund model favours short-term investments over longer-term ones, as these also boost financial returns (Ghosh and Nanda 2010). CE ventures, however, often need longer lead times to prosper (Gaddy et al. 2017), and due to a combination of technological and business model innovations, these investments are often complex (Bocken et al. 2016; Lüdeke-Freund et al. 2019).

Moreover, the market for CE investing can be described as thin, meaning that there is a limited number of investors and investment opportunities (Gans and Stern 2010; Bertoni et al. 2019). While some technologies are more investor ready, such as those in recycling and waste management (Malinauskaite et al. 2017), many are emerging, and further innovation is necessary overall (Lau et al. 2020). A thin market results in high transaction costs and limited investor confidence. Traditionally, thin markets have been the targets of government policies aimed at increasing both the supply of and the demand for investing in entrepreneurial ventures to spur innovation (Grilli and Murtinu 2014; Cumming et al. 2017). Governments play an especially significant role in the transition to the CE, as it concerns a purposive and intended transition (Markard et al. 2012; Hekkert et al. 2020). As a result, governments assume various roles in an effort to stimulate CE investment, including that of underwriter, co-investor, offtaker, and contractor (Dewick et al. 2020; Wood et al. 2013). Fund managers are reluctant to depend on governments and be exposed to changing regulations; governments' actions are largely outside of their control, though they can greatly affect the value of their investments.

A final issue affecting CE investments is that they lack performance data compared to traditional investments (Adams et al. 2017). Although Park et al. (2010) identified several dimensions that positively impact the business value of CE ventures, including cost reduction, revenue generation, and resiliency, these dimensions are unproven. The uncertainty this creates leads to an increased risk profile (Sanders and Boivie 2004).

It is clear that investing in the CE market is challenging when using the traditional fund investment model. Therefore, pioneering fund managers who want to commit to the CE must innovate to overcome these challenges.

METHOD

For this chapter, three pioneering fund managers were interviewed to examine how they overcame the issues that the traditional fund model creates when investing in the CE market. The managers were selected based on the distinctive pro-CE adaptations they made in their organization. The interviews were conducted via Zoom with a senior member of each fund management team in the summer of 2020. They lasted an average of 80 minutes. The three fund managers are introduced below.

Case A: Closed Loop Partners

Closed Loop Partners (CLP) is a New York-based fund management firm. It was established in 2014, and as of 2020, it had over $255 million committed to its various funds. In addition to its VCF, it manages a project-based finance, growth equity, and private equity fund, thereby covering the whole spectrum of risk capital provision to CE ventures. Its investment philosophy is based on the premise that transformation to a CE leads to sustained and profitable investment opportunities. CLP's VCF invests early-stage capital in companies commercializing breakthrough solutions in sectors that include fashion, technology, food and agriculture, and plastics and packaging. Project-based finance concentrates on modernizing, enhancing, and improving recycling systems and infrastructure in the United States, while its PEF acquires CE companies and scales them. Its growth equity fund provides capital to advance CE transformation in the fashion industry. Its limited partners include family offices, multinational corporations, and, increasingly, institutional investors.

The fund management team comprises 24 people with operational experience as former industry leaders, and it also includes experienced investors and former heads of government agencies in the CE sphere.

In addition to managing its funds, CLP runs an innovation centre called the Center for the Circular Economy, which works on the toughest bottlenecks that do not yet have investment-grade solutions. It supports the identification, testing, and commercialization of circular technologies, products, and services, leading collaborations between different actors including industry experts and leading brands.

Case B: Climate Fund Managers

Climate Fund Managers (CFM) is a fund manager with offices in The Hague, Singapore, and Cape Town. It commenced operations in 2015, and since then, its limited partners have committed over $850 million. CFM employs a blended finance approach through which commercial investments are combined with public co-finance from governments and donors who accept higher risks. CFM's aims are twofold. First, it wants to enable commercial investors to move into sectors generating high environmental impacts in markets that lack private capital flows. Second, CFM expedites project implementations, thereby building more projects faster to create positive impacts.

In order to do so, CFM has adapted the fund model and constructed a facility: an entity that overarches the traditional fund structure. This facility consists of a combination of funds with distinctive risk and return profiles, targeting different investors at different stages of a project. CFM currently manages two such facilities. The first, Climate Investor One (CI1), focuses on renewable energy projects in emerging markets. Climate Investor Two (CI2) emphasizes water, sanitation, and ocean infrastructure in emerging markets, including water and waste treatment projects. Each facility consists of a Development Fund, a Construction Equity Fund, and a Refinancing Fund. CI1's Development Fund consists of approximately $50 million and finances all activities prior to construction, including feasibility studies, permits, and environmental and social assessments. It is funded by donors and does not seek a commercial return but does seek a replenishment of its capital. CI1's Construction Equity Fund amounts to approximately $800 million and is divided into three tranches. The junior tranche takes the highest risk position in the structure, and its capital is also provided by donors. Development finance institutions and commercial investors fund the ordinary equity tranche. The senior equity tranche has the lowest risk profile and has a full export credit agency. Capital for this tranche is provided by institutional investors. The Refinancing Fund, which is still under conceptual design and has yet to be raised, will introduce debt to the balance sheets of investee projects. CI2 is in the process of being raised. For both facilities, the lifetime of funds is twenty years, allowing capital to be recycled.

The CFM team consists of nearly 60 people and comprises development finance specialists, technical engineers, and environmental and social professionals. Beyond the core funding for the development and construction of the CI1- and CI2-supported projects, the CFM team has initiated a series of community development programmes to support vulnerable groups either directly affected by or within the vicinity of its core infrastructure projects.

Case C: Wire Private Markets Fund

Wire Private Markets Fund (WPMF) was found in 2019 and had over €49 million in assets under management in 2020. It uses a fund-of-funds approach in which families and high net worth individuals (HNWIs) are the limited partners. Wire Group, an initiative commenced in 2010, is the manager of the fund-of-funds. WPMF's investment philosophy is based on the regeneration of human and natural capital, as the team argues that both have been depleted in the linear economic system. The fund-of-funds is seen as a tool for transforming the mindsets of families and HNWIs from one of investing to create financial wealth to one of investing based on broader notions of value creation. WPMF aptly describes this new approach as "conscious wealth management".

Before starting its fund-of-funds, Wire Group focused on achieving this transformation through education, research, strategy development, and building and managing the portfolios of families and HNWIs. Experiencing the challenges their clients faced when trying to identify suitable investment opportunities led to the establishment of WPMF.

The fund-of-funds structure overcomes a number of hurdles: it allows for individuals and families to commit to funds that are generally closed to smaller investors, and it provides ample diversification, allowing investors to become acquainted with unfamiliar investment propositions. In line with Wire Group's investment philosophy, being based on regeneration of both human and natural capital, it invests in typical CE industries, such as agriculture, oceans, and renewable energy, but it also invests in funds that focus on social impacts, such as health-care propositions in underserved areas.

The team managing WPMF consists of seven professionals with backgrounds in development finance, consultancy, and impact measurement development. In addition to its investment activities, Wire Group continues to contribute to the development and diffusion of conscious wealth management through education, research and preparing investment strategy advice.

FINDINGS[1]

The three fund managers in this chapter employed a multitude of innovations but still experienced barriers. First, this chapter will present the changes that they implemented related to their investment strategies, fund terms, reporting, and team compositions. Then their efforts to attract investors to CE investing will be described. While all three funds made such efforts, they used distinct approaches. Finally, the barriers will be presented.

Investment Strategy

All fund managers' innovations are cemented in a fundamental shift in mindset from traditional fund management. Their investment philosophies break away from EMH logic and are instead based on a broader values system. Investment strategies are as a result not directed toward the potential for maximum exit proceeds, but the creation of ventures with positive financial, environmental, and social outcomes. CLP, for example, does not aim its venture capital investments toward the creation of unicorns (start-ups worth over $1 billion). Instead, its VCF is designed to build companies that "are going to be cashflow-generating businesses, have long term viability, and have impact". The fund managers do not only invest in and manage opportunities developed in the market; rather, part of their strategy is to proactively develop opportunities for CE investing.

Fund Terms

The general partners adapt the terms of their fund to align with the characteristics of CE investing. Where traditionally carried interest is a performance fee incentivizing the management team to achieve financial returns, in WPMF's case carried interest is for 50 per cent based on financial return and 50 per cent on impact created by the fund's investments. WPMF recounted how challenging it was for lawyers to write this amended structure down in the agreements, as it was seldom seen before. This change in carried interest attests to the assertion that impact represents at least half of the fund's value proposition and ensures that the management team actively pursues it. On another note, CFM has structured its facilities to have 20-year tenors, doubling that of a traditional fund, allowing for longer investment horizons and enabling the recirculation of capital to maximize impact potential.

Teams

The professional backgrounds of the general partners of all three funds are extremely diverse and included environmental, social, and governance experience, senior governmental experience in the CE sphere, and experience developing impact-measurement frameworks. Additionally, the teams are considerably larger than traditional funds managing similar amounts of capital. The management style of all fund managers is markedly active. Interactions with limited partners, investees, and government are intensive. This active stance is made possible by having larger teams in place.

Reporting

All three fund managers extensively measure and report the impacts associated with CE investment's reduced environmental damage and improved social advancement. WPMF stated that it believes "societal value and financial value are equal, but we have to make societal value tangible to be able to use it". WPMF monetizes the net impact it creates on the basis of the best available academic evidence, using methodologies from health economics and environmental economics. CLP and CFM, on the other hand, report key metrics to describe their realized impacts. The transparency provided by these fund managers is therefore infinitely beyond what is generally provided by and expected from traditional fund managers.

Opening Up the CE Space to Traditional Investors

The three fund managers take different approaches to attracting traditional investors to the CE investment proposition. Before structuring their facilities, the founders of CFM thought that "there needs to be more intelligent ways to unlock the commercial sector ... to give them

[a] track record and to expose them to the market so that their perception of the risk is more commensurate to the actual risk rather than what they currently believe to be the case." CFM then created its blended finance structure with the aim of opening up unfamiliar sectors and markets to institutional investors: "we help investors make that leap and make that journey."

WPMF uses the fund-of-funds model in its general effort to educate HNWIs and guide them in the transition to conscious wealth management. It actively engages with its limited partners through discussion and by preparing position papers. Indicating how central market building is to its aim, WPMF said, "We would be interested in raising a second fund, but it is to be hoped that a third fund will not be necessary, as the market by then has evolved sufficiently."

While the CE investment opportunity was evident to the CLP team, institutional investors did not share their view when CLP started fundraising in 2014. Therefore, their fundraising instead focused on large corporations. CLP said, "I would have a situation where I would talk to an asset allocator about the transition to a circular economy and they would be thinking that I was too idealistic. I would walk into a global consumer goods company [and] they would tell me that they are already working on the circular economy and decide to invest." By building a track record with corporates as limited partners, CLP became able to attract institutional investors.

Challenges and Barriers

The main challenge for all fund managers lies in attracting institutional investors. The asset allocation industry is conservative and remains dominated by neoclassical economic thinking. Interest is growing due to, for instance, climate change's effects on vulnerable assets and the increasing acceptance of a broader concept of value creation, but attracting institutional investors to CE investing remains a challenge. CFM stated that "whether the motivation is from a social consciousness perspective or a risk perception perspective, we're seeing real movements in the industry, but there's still a long way to go."

To accommodate investors who are used to the traditional fund structure, pioneering fund managers must walk a fine line between being recognizable as fund managers and pushing boundaries. This results in trade-offs among innovations deployed by the fund managers. WPMF stated that "we have opted for a traditional structure, as we're innovative and different on so many levels already." As a result, their fund-of-funds is excluded from investing in certain innovative fund structures, such as those with a focus on regenerative agriculture or clean technologies, as the time horizon for such investments may be too long.

Another hurdle for fund managers is scale. Scale is needed to attract institutional investors who aim to make substantial investments. CLP stated that "a lot of the capital is sucked up by the large asset managers" who can accommodate such ticket sizes. For donors and governments, exactly the opposite is true: these parties commit smaller buckets for small individual projects. There is thus a mismatch between what governments offer and institutional investors require.

All three fund managers agree that for this paradigm shift to happen, greater transparency in the market is imperative. A lack of impact reporting in the fund management industry has led to difficulties comparing fund investment propositions. It is rather paradoxical that the funds that make positive impacts are those that report their impacts, while traditional fund managers are able to ignore the negative externalities their investments create.

Finally, working with governments both as investors and through investee companies can be challenging. While governments are seen as market shapers, interacting with them can nevertheless be bureaucratic and time consuming. CFM stated how they have had to adapt their working style to become more versatile, "As a team you have to appreciate the different lens in which government approaches investing and whilst processes can take longer and require effort from both sides to make it a success, the challenges are not prohibitive." Additionally, unstable regulation makes CE investment propositions less attractive.

DISCUSSION

The three pioneering fund managers in this chapter show the need and ability for wide-ranging innovation to overcome the issues created by the CE market's inefficiency, thinness, and unproven nature. Regarding its inefficiency, the main innovation applied by the fund managers is a distinct investment philosophy that include a broader concept of value creation in the understandings of both risks and returns. The fund managers are thus able to break with the traditional neoclassical economic logic and the EMH that dominates financial thought (Louche et al. 2019). While the CE concept has been criticized for largely neglecting social equity (Murray et al. 2017; Sauvé et al. 2016), the fund managers include social impacts in their investment propositions. Their ability to break away from the dominant finance logic seems to be enabled by the fund management teams' untraditional backgrounds. In order to attract limited partners to their fund proposition, the three fund managers emphasize knowledge creation and diffusion to help investors move away from the traditional logic guiding their investment decisions. Reinforcing the findings of Schoenmaker and Schramade (2019) and Ameli et al. (2020), institutional investors continue to adhere to the traditional investment logic implied by the EMH, They are therefore hardest to attract to innovative fund propositions. Given the magnitude of institutional investors in terms of capital under management (Clark and Hebb 2005), this investor type is indispensable, as it drives the fund industry (Metrick and Yasuda 2011).

This study examines how three fund managers move in at relatively early stages while the market is thin and unproven. In sectors like biotech, the internet, and nanotechnology, the VCF market came 15–20 years after public sector funds made significant investments and developed the market (Mazzucato 2013). However, this chapter's pioneering fund managers are not merely building on the value created by public investments. Instead, they are actively developing the CE market by creating investment opportunities. They are also able to move in early because they work actively with government. Governments are market shapers in the sense that they co-finance innovative structures and support the development of portfolio companies, but for a fund manager to benefit from this requires an active stance, versatility and informed team members.

Overall, investing in the CE market means that the managers must analyse investment opportunities for broader value creation, align multiple actors, actively build the market and closely cooperate with governments. This is more time consuming and complex than traditional investing, and it requires a broader skill set. Fund managers must therefore employ considerably larger teams with more diversified skill sets than what is conventional in traditional funds (Zarutskie 2010; Dimov and Shepherd 2005).

Implications and Limitations

The findings of this study have implications for universities, governments, and CE entrepreneurs. First, actions should be targeted on expediting the paradigmatic shift needed in the thinking of both fund managers and institutional investors. Educators can play a role here. Today's university finance educations have not changed much from those of the early 2000s (Schoenmaker and Schramade 2019). A focus on the broader value proposition in finance courses and MBAs will ensure future asset allocators enter the industry with knowledge of the opportunities and urgency of moving away from a linear economic model. Furthermore, research has a role to play in studying and presenting the value created and returns made when investing in the CE. As proposed by Agrawal and Hockerts (2021), context-specific studies can provide practical recommendations regarding impact measurement. Finally, example cases throughout the system should be highlighted and celebrated. The current VCF literature has mostly focused on the issues sustainable investing raises for fund managers (Hegeman and Sørheim 2021). Investors can be inspired and encouraged if they are made aware of the innovations introduced and the returns made by fund managers investing in the CE.

Second, governments are indispensable and omnipresent in the CE investment sphere. Further policy support can therefore accelerate the investment opportunity. Governments can increase the transparency of the economy by imposing reporting requirements on all actors in the system. This would allow for meaningful comparisons among fund managers. Furthermore, the call for stable regulations and support for innovations and entrepreneurs in the CE sphere remains. In addition to policy changes, fund managers would benefit from more flexibility from donors and governments when setting up innovative fund models, including public–private partnerships.

Third, this study has implications for CE entrepreneurs. When approaching investors, it may be worthwhile to approach funds with an investment philosophy that aligns with the CE concept. These funds may have adapted their terms and organization to support the characteristics of such a venture. In addition, they can provide the knowledge and networks needed to provide essential nonfinancial value to prosper in the developing CE market.

As all studies do, this study has limitations. By purposely focusing on pioneering fund managers, it zeros in on a niche in the fund management industry. The contribution lies in the rich and contextualized description of how fund managers can organize to position themselves for CE financing. However, the findings are therefore not generalizable to the whole fund management industry. Further research could look at, for example, whether and how traditional VCFs and PEFs are adapting to finance for sustainability. Another fruitful research avenue would be to establish how CE investing relates to the broader impact-investing universe in both scale and organization. Overall, this chapter demonstrates that fund managers are willing and able to extensively reorganize, enabling them to play a valuable role in the transition to a CE.

NOTE

1.   All quotes in the findings section stem from the interviews with the senior members of the three fund manager teams. In the text, the fund manager name is used to refer to them.

REFERENCES

Adams, K. T., Osmani, M., Thorpe, T., & Thornback, J. (2017). Circular economy in construction: Current awareness, challenges and enablers. *Proceedings of the Institution of Civil Engineers-Waste and Resource Management*. London: Thomas Telford, 15–24.

Agrawal, A., & Hockerts, K. (2021). Impact investing: Review and research agenda. *Journal of Small Business & Entrepreneurship*, 33(2), 153–181.

Ameli, N., Drummond, P., Bisaro, A., Grubb, M., & Chenet, H. (2020). Climate finance and disclosure for institutional investors: Why transparency is not enough. *Climatic Change*, 160, 565–589.

Bertoni, F., D'Adda, D., & Grilli, L. (2019). Self-selection of entrepreneurial firms in thin venture capital markets: Theory and empirical evidence. *Strategic Entrepreneurship Journal*, 13, 47–74.

Bocken, N. M. P., De Pauw, I., Bakker, C., & Van Der Grinten, B. (2016). Product design and business model strategies for a circular economy. *Journal of Industrial and Production Engineering*, 33, 308–320.

Brown, S. J., Goetzmann, W. N., & Liang, B. (2004). Fees on fees in funds of funds. *Journal of Investment Management*, 2, 39–56.

Clark, G. L., & Hebb, T. (2005). Why should they care? The role of institutional investors in the market for corporate global responsibility. *Environment and Planning A: Economy and Space*, 37, 2015–2031.

Cumming, D. J., Grilli, L., & Murtinu, S. (2017). Governmental and independent venture capital investments in Europe: A firm-level performance analysis. *Journal of Corporate Finance*, 42, 439–459.

Derwall, J., Guenster, N., Bauer, R., & Koedijk, K. (2005). The eco-efficiency premium puzzle. *Financial Analysts Journal*, 61, 51–63.

Dewick, P., Bengtsson, M., Cohen, M. J., Sarkis, J., & Schröder, P. (2020). Circular economy finance: Clear winner or risky proposition? *Journal of Industrial Ecology*, 24, 1192–1200.

Dimov, D. P., & Shepherd, D. A. (2005). Human capital theory and venture capital firms: Exploring "home runs" and "strike outs". *Journal of Business Venturing*, 20, 1–21.

Dumas, C., & Louche, C. (2016). Collective beliefs on responsible investment. *Business & Society*, 55, 427–457.

Ellen MacArthur Foundation (2020). *What is the Circular Economy?* https://www.ellenmacarthur foundation.org/circular-economy/what-is-the-circular-economy.

Ellen MacArthur Foundation & Systemic Ltd. (2017). Achieving 'growth within'. https://www.elle nmacarthurfoundation.org/publications.

Fama, E. F. (1970). Efficient capital markets: A review of theory and empirical work. *The Journal of Finance*, 25, 383–417.

Gaddy, B. E., Sivaram, V., Jones, T. B., & Wayman, L. (2017). Venture capital and cleantech: The wrong model for energy innovation. *Energy Policy*, 102, 385–395.

Gans, J. S., & Stern, S. (2010). Is there a market for ideas? *Industrial and Corporate Change*, 19, 805–837.

Geissdoerfer, M., Savaget, P., Bocken, N. M. P., & Hultink, E. J. (2017). The circular economy: A new sustainability paradigm? *Journal of Cleaner Production*, 143, 757–768.

Ghisellini, P., Cialani, C., & Ulgiati, S. (2016). A review on circular economy: The expected transition to a balanced interplay of environmental and economic systems. *Journal of Cleaner Production*, 114, 11–32.

Ghosh, S., & Nanda, R. (2010). Venture capital investment in the clean energy sector. *IDEAS Working Paper Series from RePEc*.

Gompers, P., & Lerner, J. (2001). The venture capital revolution. *The Journal of Economic Perspectives*, 15, 145–168.

Grilli, L., & Murtinu, S. (2014). Government, venture capital and the growth of European high-tech entrepreneurial firms. *Research Policy*, 43, 1523–1543.

Hall, S., Foxon, T. J., & Bolton, R. (2017). Investing in low-carbon transitions: Energy finance as an adaptive market. *Climate Policy*, 17, 280–298.

Hegeman, P. D., & Sørheim, R. (2021). Why do they do it? Corporate venture capital investments in cleantech start-ups. *Journal of Cleaner Production*, 294, 126315.

Hekkert, M. P., Janssen, M. J., Wesseling, J. H., & Negro, S. O. (2020). Mission-oriented innovation systems. *Environmental Innovation and Societal Transitions*, 34, 76–79.

Kirchherr, J., Reike, D., & Hekkert, M. (2017). Conceptualizing the circular economy: An analysis of 114 definitions. *Resources, Conservation and Recycling*, 127, 221–232.

Korhonen, J., Honkasalo, A., & Seppälä, J. (2018). Circular economy: The concept and its limitations. *Ecological Economics*, 143, 37–46.

Lau, W. W., Shiran, Y., Bailey, R. M., Cook, E., Stuchtey, M. R., Koskella, J., Velis, C. A., Godfrey, L., Boucher, J., & Murphy, M. B. (2020). Evaluating scenarios toward zero plastic pollution. *Science*, 369, 1455–1461.

Lerner, J., & Nanda, R. (2020). Venture capital's role in financing innovation: What we know and how much we still need to learn. *Journal of Economic Perspectives*, 34, 237–261.

Louche, C., Busch, T., Crifo, P., & Marcus, A. (2019). Financial markets and the transition to a low-carbon economy: Challenging the dominant logics. *Organization & Environment*, 32, 3–17.

Lüdeke-Freund, F., Gold, S., & Bocken, N. M. P. (2019). A review and typology of circular economy business model patterns. *Journal of Industrial Ecology*, 23, 36–61.

Lydenberg, S. (2014). Reason, rationality, and fiduciary duty. *Journal of Business Ethics*, 119, 365–380.

Malinauskaite, J., Jouhara, H., Czajczyńska, D., Stanchev, P., Katsou, E., Rostkowski, P., Thorne, R. J., Colón, J., Ponsá, S., Al-Mansour, F., Anguilano, L., Krzyżyńska, R., López, I. C., Vlasopoulos, A., & Spencer, N. (2017). Municipal solid waste management and waste-to-energy in the context of a circular economy and energy recycling in Europe. *Energy*, 141, 2013–2044.

Markard, J., Raven, R., & Truffer, B. (2012). Sustainability transitions: An emerging field of research and its prospects. *Research Policy*, 41, 955–967.

Mazzucato, M. (2013). *The Entrepreneurial State: Debunking Public vs. Private Sector Myths*. London: Anthem Press.

Metrick, A., & Yasuda, A. (2010). The economics of private equity funds. *The Review of Financial Studies*, 23, 2303–2341.

Metrick, A., & Yasuda, A. (2011). Venture capital and other private equity: A survey. *European Financial Management*, 17, 619–654.

Murray, A., Skene, K., & Haynes, K. (2017). The circular economy: An interdisciplinary exploration of the concept and application in a global context. *Journal of Business Ethics*, 140, 369–380.

Park, J., Sarkis, J., & Wu, Z. (2010). Creating integrated business and environmental value within the context of China's circular economy and ecological modernization. *Journal of Cleaner Production*, 18, 1494–1501.

Perez, C. (2011). Finance and technical change: A long-term view. *African Journal of Science, Technology, Innovation and Development*, 3, 10–35.

Phalippou, L., & Gottschalg, O. (2008). The performance of private equity funds. *The Review of Financial Studies*, 22, 1747–1776.

Preqin (2020). *2020 Preqin Global Private Equity & Venture Capital Report*. London.

Reeder, N., & Colantonio, A. (2013). *Measuring Impact and Non-Financial Returns in Impact Investing: A Critical Overview of Concepts and Practice*. The London School of Economics and the European Investment Bank Institute.

Sanders, W. G., & Boivie, S. (2004). Sorting things out: Valuation of new firms in uncertain markets. *Strategic Management Journal*, 25, 167–186.

Sauvé, S., Bernard, S., & Sloan, P. (2016). Environmental sciences, sustainable development and circular economy: Alternative concepts for trans-disciplinary research. *Environmental Development*, 17, 48–56.

Schoenmaker, D., & Schramade, W. (2019). Investing for long-term value creation. *Journal of Sustainable Finance & Investment*, 9, 356–377.

Shleifer, A. (2000). *Inefficient Markets: An Introduction to Behavioural Finance*. New York: Oxford University Press.

Stahel, W. R. (2016). The circular economy. *Nature*, 531, 435–438.

Wood, D., Thornley, B., & Grace, K. (2013). Institutional impact investing: Practice and policy. *Journal of Sustainable Finance & Investment*, 3, 75–94.

Zarutskie, R. (2010). The role of top management team human capital in venture capital markets: Evidence from first-time funds. *Journal of Business Venturing*, 25, 155–172.

25. The circular economy, openness, and dispersed access to research results

Haakon Thue Lie, Knut Jørgen Egelie, Christoph Grimpe and Roger Sørheim

INTRODUCTION

A circular economy aims at eliminating waste by using resources continually (Esposito et al. 2018). As a consequence, participants in a circular economy need to engage in transactions aimed at exchanging knowledge, resources and other materials. These transactions are all regulated by contracts and intellectual property rights. Our concern is the very formation of these circular chains of transactions: how access and openness to new knowledge from publicly sponsored research affect the circular economy. We define openness as a continuum from no openness at all, that is, the research results are trade secrets,[1] to full openness as published and indexed knowledge. Openness can be measured in terms of publication restrictions and secrecy provisions.[2] Research results may be published and free for all to read, but without the possibility for using the results, due to, for example, patents or database rights. Access to those results would remain limited. Thus, if the access is restricted, and not dispersed, the benefit for the public of the publicly sponsored research is reduced to spillover effects only. If the research results are secret, then there are no spillover effects. These issues are often overlooked in discussions on the public value of science and discussions on research policy (David et al. 2000; Rothaermel and Thursby 2005).

Understanding where an innovation project is heading, in terms of openness and access, is crucial for the circular economy. If the intellectual property rights and the contractual arrangements for the research results are open, then search is facilitated (Grimpe and Sofka 2016). Others can find the results, and further research is encouraged. If the results are also dispersed in terms of ownership and contractual regulations, then collaboration, competition and diversity in innovation can be enhanced (Rosenkranz and Schmitz 2003). Then, in addition, there is the standardization that in circular economies serves both as a framework for implementing and measuring life cycle costs,[3] but more importantly, as a means for ensuring that the physical reuse of goods is possible. Benachio et al. (2020) review the literature on the circular economy in the construction industry and point to standardization as a research gap. In construction, reuse of materials can be impossible if safety standards are not met or if, for example, a door to be reused does not fit the opening in the new building. Standards can emerge as consensus on the best way to produce goods or services, such as indicated in the concept 'dominant design' (Srinivasan et al. 2006). However, many standards are actively formed. When the parties that wish to ensure future standardization come together to agree, a prerequisite is that the knowledge is open and that ownership is dispersed (Ho and O'Sullivan 2019; Papachristos and Kaa 2021; Podszun 2019; Teece 2018). Recently, Chakrabarti et al. (2020) discuss the term 'open sustainability' where standards have a crucial role.

In the early phase of innovation, the terms of agreements in research consortia can be so complicated and entangled that they hinder collaboration and reuse of the research results. Nor can such complicated terms inform policymaking and management that seek to foster sustainability (Jarvenpaa and Välikangas 2014, pp. 72, 73). Policymakers may lack the tools for spotting emerging knowledge monopolies if research results are kept secret and inaccessible. They then provide public sponsorship to research without governing future openness and access to the knowledge flow. Research managers in both industry and universities may engage in collaborative research without a clear understanding of the agreed access to, or the openness of, the research results. We discuss how collaborative research projects between universities and industry agree on the openness and access to their results. We then outline how this understanding may profoundly impact the governance of collaborative research aiming to be a part of the circular economy. Such governance includes both how managers see the scope of the research projects and how a public funding body or an organization view their portfolio of collaborative research projects.

We conceptualize such reconsideration and apply a novel method for managing access and openness, as we spot possible knowledge monopolies ex-ante and ask what characteristics promote openness and dispersed access (Egelie et al. 2019). As an illustrative example, we demonstrate how we applied the method to an institute-led Horizon 2020 project comprising universities and industry. In that sense, our research question asks how openness and access in collaborative research can be governed in order to contribute to the transition towards circular economy solutions.

BACKGROUND: OPENNESS VERSUS ACCESS

The term 'openness' has been used in many connotations. 'Open innovation', 'open science', 'open business models', 'open source', and lately 'open access' are some of the concepts that claim openness. Bogers et al. (2017) review the open innovation concept and point to how it has evolved from a firm centric distributed innovation process managed across organizations to become a term for a wide range of related concepts that include public governance, ecosystems and human behaviour. Still, a managed and distributed flow of knowledge is the core of open innovation. However, the knowledge that flows in open innovation needs not to be open. It could, for example, be licensing that includes trade secrets. Bogers (2011) describes the tension field between collaborators in open innovation as a balancing act between knowledge sharing and protection. Laursen and Salter (2014) point to the same paradox of openness. They connect the firms' openness to the appropriability mechanisms managers use and how that use orients the firm towards external innovation process actors.

In legal terms, more specifically, the terms used in contractual regulations, one vital distinction between openness and access is how patents and copyright may provide control of access to open knowledge. Even if the knowledge can be found, read and understood, it may not be accessible for commercial use[4] (Long 2001; Walsh and Huang 2014). An often-used clause in university and public research funding organization agreements concerns further freedom to research and disseminate the research. Public open access is essential and for universities, even trumps commercial use and possible commercial profits. The term 'open access' coins this differentiation in that an open access publication can be found and read and the copyright licence is open, so it allows royalty-free reproduction. The unrestricted right to reproduce the verbatim text and figures is a sort of access to the research results. However, if the research results are technical, there might be patents or other intellectual property to stop the research results' commercial utilization. Thus, an open-access publication implies openness, but not necessarily access.

Egelie et al. (2019) address openness in research results and propose a typology based on a study of contracts in publicly funded life science research projects. They score the contractual provisions in terms of openness and access opportunities. Openness refers to whether the results are unrestricted, that is published, or restricted and thus confidential. Access is either concentrated or dispersed. Dispersed is typically non-exclusive licensing; concentration could be a patented technology that is not shared. Both openness and access can be combined cross-tabulated, leading to four typical situations that we will outline. This method builds on collaborative research projects, but it could be applied to any set of research or development projects.

Behind this model is the debate on the transformative technology CRISPR. The clustered, regularly interspaced, short palindromic repeats (CRISPR) and the associated protein (Cas9) system is a powerful new technology platform for genome editing. One possible use is for improving fungal biotechnology that enables the production of biofuels and food. Access to and utilization of the technology depend on the intellectual property management and contractual terms devised by the technology owners. Thus, the agreement terms for research collaborations between universities and industry are essential for academic knowledge to be used in the circular economy. Industry benefits from accessing scientific knowledge that they can use to anticipate future research problems in new technological areas. The technology owners' identity, the technology coverage of their appropriation mechanisms, such as patents that have been filed for different components, and the geographical distribution of those appropriation mechanisms all influence future access to the technology. Patents and unknown future licensing models are issues with the CRISPR platform that affect the research results' public utility. There is an ongoing patent dispute involving exclusive licensing creating uncertainty about the eventual licence terms and how they can fit into a circular economy. They no longer license fundamental technologies that were developed by universities. Instead, they offer surrogate licences through intermediate commercial licensing companies (Egelie et al. 2018; Graff and Sherkow 2020; Meyer et al. 2020; Sherkow 2017).

There are differences between industries in how openness is managed. In the information and communication technology (ICT) industry, the 5G technology platform (the fifth-generation mobile network, the basis for the 'Internet of Things', IoT) uses a model from the previous collaborative efforts of developing networks. Technology ownership is handled through extensive cross-licensing through patent pools. The regime has invented new mechanisms such as the definition of 'Standard Essential Patents' (SEPs)[5] and licences under 'Fair, Reasonable and Non-Discriminatory' terms (FRAND).[6] The system regulates openness and access, but not without tensions (Heiden 2017; NGMN Alliance 2015; Teece 2018).

Another example is in the energy sector. There is an evolution where the network market effects that guide the ICT sector now become more prominent.[7] The Smart Grid, where energy production is a system involving products and services from many actors, is a technology platform that relies on standardization. Both public and private actors are engaged (Ho and O'Sullivan 2019). The effect of standards is not only present in high-tech industries but also in, for example, agriculture. Manning and Reinecke (2016) show how private standard-setters such as the Rainforest Alliance and Fairtrade affect agriculture and the coffee sector.

Standardization allows for regulations on soil conservation practices and the abolition of child labour. Other industries have yet to introduce sustainability in their standardization processes. Future standards on mobile networks could address sustainability. If universities hold SEPs, they could require adherence to sustainability terms for a licence. A prominent example could be to follow the coffee industry and deny a licence if a manufacturer depends on the use of child labour.[8]

Thus, industries differ in how to develop platforms and control these in terms of intellectual property. For some platform technologies in, for example, biotechnology companies, trade secrets are potentially their most powerful form of innovation appropriation (Sherkow 2016). For other industries, platform innovation interaction is critical, and intellectual property control requires other mechanisms (Gawer 2014).

APPLYING THE MODEL TO CIRCULAR ECONOMIES

Developing a Conceptual Framework

During a collaborative research project, the parties assemble knowledge controlled by intellectual property rights through contractual agreements and provisions. The results are likely to be used in the next phase of an innovation process or become part of a platform that can spawn many new products and services. The intellectual property rights will then be reassembled in another form. However, before that can occur, the initial project must disassemble the rights and make them available for the next phase of innovation (Granstrand and Holgersson 2014). That is, there must be access to the research results in a form that allows a circular economy. In the model by Egelie et al. (2019), 'access' is seen as either concentrated or dispersed. Access is controlled by ownership and specific use rights to the research results, such as the right to use a part of it or use it for a given purpose, often education or further research. A technology platform usable in the circular economy must then have dispersed access. However, one actor could keep a technology exclusive and create a sustainable service or product. An obvious question for the managers of public sponsorship is then if such innovation should be financed by the public.

To determine the conditions that are conducive for a circular economy, we need to focus on those projects that are both open and have dispersed access to research results. Projects where the results are kept secret and access is only for the participants, can be knowledge monopolies that may not be part of a circular economy. The study by Egelie et al. (2019) provides us with a conceptual framework to study the provisions of collaborative projects. In this regard, access is defined as dispersed ownership or dispersed use rights (that is, the commercial rights to use of the foreground, the research results). Concentrated ownership and use rights on the side of industry or university lead in that sense to inaccessible results. Openness is defined as publication opportunities and the absence of confidentiality rules. Figure 25.1 shows the results of the conceptual model when access and openness dimensions are combined. Egelie et al. (2019) demonstrated how this model could be used on a portfolio of projects sponsored by the public. Policymakers and research managers can analyse the portfolio in terms of the number of projects where the agreements on openness and access could lead to the formation of knowledge monopolies. They could then, for example, investigate further whether a knowledge monopoly is needed to commercialize the research results and to what extent that should be sponsored.

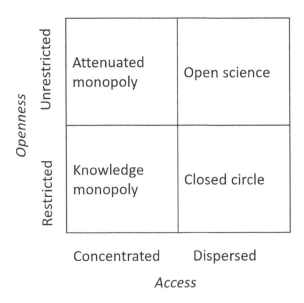

Figure 25.1   Conceptual model

Analysing the Agreements for a Single Research Consortium

The framework we developed is also of value for the governance and management of a single collaborative research project, as we illustrate in the case of an EU-funded project. AlSiCal is a research and innovation project aiming at making the mineral and metal industry more sustainable and environmentally sound. The consortium will research and develop a new technology platform. Two of the consortium partners have, as the starting point, patented a novel process. This process gives no CO_2 emissions and no problematic by-products as compared to the current process. There are 16 partners from nine countries in the consortium. Four of the partners are universities, three research institutes, two industry associations, and seven commercial firms. The EU's Horizon 2020 programme funds 100 per cent of the AlSiCal project with 5.8 million euro over four years, beginning in 2019 (Aranda 2019).

We scored the consortium agreement that uses the DESCA template (DESCA 2017). The ownership and use rights to the results are dispersed. The openness is restricted, as there are confidentiality clauses that could limit the flow of knowledge out of the project. However, within the project, there are non-disclosure clauses that ensure a free flow of knowledge between the parties. Using the two-by-two matrix of Figure 25.1, we placed the project within the 'Closed circle' quadrant. However, we drew an arrow towards the 'Open science' quadrant. The arrow indicates that the project steering group may, within the consortium agreement's scope, decide to make the project results available to the public without restrictions. If the patents that are part of the background information in the project, together with the research results, are licensed out on FRAND-like terms, and no results are kept a secret, then the research results would qualify as 'Open science'.

As the project started in late 2019, they do not know how the coming research results may be of best use to society. It could be that a closed circle is a preferred way of launching a new platform technology, creating a technology platform and then eventually launch standards that enable a circular economy. The technology that AlSiCal develops is disruptive in that it seeks to replace the current dominant process that goes back to an invention by the chemical company Bayer in 1888 (Habashi 1995). If the AlSiCal project succeeds, they may form an ecosystem that gives a greener mineral and metal industry. The parties to the project may benefit from understanding the project as being a closed circle with the option of moving towards open science. Policymakers and public sponsors may use this insight to orchestrate further efforts to develop a new ecosystem, with the needed standards for technology and sustainability.

DISCUSSION AND CONCLUSION

When considering a portfolio of research projects regarding the public benefit from the research results, then openness could matter more than access. If the research results are secrets, such as trade secrets, then they are not accessible to others other than those who belong to the project consortium, simply because the secrets cannot be found by search. If the access is restricted, but the knowledge is available to the public, such as for patented technology in an attenuated monopoly, then the government can introduce measures to make the technology available. One example is through financial incentives, where a public body rewards licensing, for example, through standards. Another example is that most jurisdictions have laws on compulsory licences for copyright or patents. Thus the government could interfere if a needed technology is unavailable for a critical circular economy. However, Henry and Stiglitz (2010) point to how the implementation of trade agreements, such as TRIPS, have hindered developing countries in using compulsory licences. A question is then how trade agreements will support sustainability and circular economies. A similar broad question is asked by Ballardini et al. (2021): In private law in the EU that concerns both tangible and intellectual property, "issues related to environmental sustainability have largely been ignored". An example is how intellectual property rights can limit the possibilities to repair goods – or, as we discuss here, to use research results.

In the AlSiCal case, ownership of the results is dispersed, and the consortium agreement allows for trade secrets. Thus, the research results fall into the closed circle category. A critical modifier is that this possibility for trade secrets is not a secret by itself. The consortium is open vis-à-vis the public sponsors. The agreements allow that they choose trade secret licensing if this for a period is the optimal way of transferring the knowledge and initiating the change to a greener industry. In that way, the research results' openness is already high and in line with the EU Commission's objectives when they sponsor a project 100 per cent. Keeping the option for trade secrecy ensures the possibility of a meaningful renegotiation between the parties.

In the AlSiCal case, we showed how analysis of the consortium agreements using the discussed two-by-two matrix might assist the project manager and the steering group in creating an open technology platform for a circular economy. Similarly, the model from Egelie et al. (2019) allows for the analysis of a portfolio of projects in a firm, research institution or sponsoring organization. The case example illustrates essential issues related to the stimulation of innovation for a circular economy: (1) there will often be a need for a consortium to establish a closed circle of knowledge in order to facilitate situations where the innovations can be developed among the partners and (2) after a 'grace' period, the agreements must open for more sharing of the knowledge and solutions created in the consortium. The two-by-two typology in Figure 25.1, as applied in our illustrative case, shows how consortia ex-ante could guide the development of innovations to be beneficial for partners and society in the search for circular innovations. Further research could see if such ex-ante and ex-post typologies can be aligned, improving the evaluation of research results and the resulting technologies' contribution to sustainability.

ACKNOWLEDGEMENTS

The authors thank NORSI – the Nordic Research School in Innovation and Entrepreneurship, CIP Center for Intellectual Property with Ulf Petrusson and Bowman Heiden at Gothenburg University, Wolfgang Sofka at Copenhagen Business School and Asunción Aranda at the Institute for Energy Technology (IFE, Norway) for valuable discussions. The following organizations have contributed as funding and supporting partners: NTNU Technology Transfer AS, Dehns and The Research Council of Norway as part of Industrial PhD grants 247566 and 238770; the AlSiCal consortium under the EU's Horizon 2020 programme grant No 820911.

NOTES

1. Trade secrets imply secrecy for commercial reasons. Other reasons, that we do not discuss, could be privacy or national security.
2. We use secrecy and confidentiality as synonyms. In a contract the heading of the clause that defines the parties' right to require information being secret is often 'Confidentiality'.
3. An example is a European standard that specifies how to calculate Life Cycle Assessment (LCA) of a building, 'Sustainability of construction works. Assessment of environmental performance of buildings. Calculation method', EN 15978:2011.
4. Firms may take their chances and not bother with others' intellectual property rights. It can make make sense startegically to infringe, and prepare for a possible infringment lawsuit that may never come.
5. SEPs are patents that in important markets cover one or more essential function of a standardized technology. The patent claims will read on one or more specified and mandatory parts of the standard.
6. A FRAND declaration is a voluntary commitment from the SEP owner to a standardization body that licence terms will follow common rules on non-exclusive non-discriminatory licensing. In the case of disagreement for example on the value of the patented technology in a mobile phone, a court of law may consider this commitment and for example refuse a preliminary injunction to stop the sales of the phones.
7. The systemic value of the network increases with a squared function of the number of users, as for communication networks. Metcalfe's Law states that the value of a network grows as the square of the number of users. The growth of, for example, the value of Facebook has followed this law (Metcalfe 2013).
8. Cobalt is vital in the lithium-ion batteries in mobile phones. Most cobalt is mined in the Democratic Republic of Congo. Amnesty International reports that the government there will eliminate child labour in the mining industry by 2025. The phone manufacturers now list the sources of their cobalt (Amnesty International 2017).

REFERENCES

Amnesty International (2017). Democratic Republic of Congo: Government must deliver on pledge to end child mining labour by 2025. https://www.amnesty.org/en/latest/news/2017/09/democratic-republic-of-congo-government-must-deliver-on-pledge-to-end-child-mining-labour-by-2025/.

Aranda, A. (2019). *Towards Sustainable Mineral and Metal Industry: ZERO Bauxite Residue and Zero CO2 from Co-production of Alumina, Silica and Precipitated Calcium Carbonate by the Aranda-Mastin Technology*. Brussels: European Commission.

Ballardini, R. M., Kaisto, J., & Similä, J. (2021). Developing novel property concepts in private law to foster the circular economy. *Journal of Cleaner Production*, 279, 123747.

Benachio, G. L. F., Freitas, M. de C. D., & Tavares, S. F. (2020). Circular economy in the construction industry: A systematic literature review. *Journal of Cleaner Production*, 260, 121046.

Bogers, M. (2011). The open innovation paradox: Knowledge sharing and protection in R&D collaborations. *European Journal of Innovation Management*, 14(1), 93–117.

Bogers, M., Zobel, A.-K., Afuah, A., Almirall, E., Brunswicker, S., Dahlander, L., … Ter Wal, A. L. J. (2017). The open innovation research landscape: Established perspectives and emerging themes across different levels of analysis. *Industry and Innovation*, 24(1), 8–40.

Chakrabarti, R., Henneberg, S. C., & Ivens, B. S. (2020). Open sustainability: Conceptualization and considerations. *Industrial Marketing Management*, 89, 528–534.

David, P. A., Hall, B. H., & Toole, A. A. (2000). Is public R&D a complement or substitute for private R&D? A review of the econometric evidence. *Research Policy*, 29(4), 497–529.

DESCA (2017). *DESCA 2020 Model Consortium Agreement*. http://www.desca-2020.eu/.

Egelie, K. J., Lie, H. T., Grimpe, C., & Sørheim, R. (2019). Access and openness in biotechnology research collaborations between universities and industry. *Nature Biotechnology*, 37(12), 1413–1419.

Egelie, K. J., Strand, S. P., Johansen, B., & Myskja, B. K. (2018). The ethics of access to patented biotech research tools from universities and other research institutions. *Nature Biotechnology*, 36, 495.

Esposito, M., Tse, T., & Soufani, K. (2018). Introducing a circular economy: New thinking with new managerial and policy implications. *California Management Review*, 60(3), 5–19.

Gawer, A. (2014). Bridging differing perspectives on technological platforms: Toward an integrative framework. *Research Policy*, 43(7), 1239–1249.

Graff, G. D., & Sherkow, J. S. (2020). Models of technology transfer for genome-editing technologies. *Annual Review of Genomics and Human Genetics*, 21(1), 509–534.

Granstrand, O., & Holgersson, M. (2014). The challenge of closing open innovation: The intellectual property disassembly problem. *Research Technology Management*, 57(5), 19–25.

Grimpe, C., & Sofka, W. (2016). Complementarities in the search for innovation: Managing markets and relationships. *Research Policy*, 45(10), 2036–2053.

Habashi, F. (1995). Bayer's process for alumina production: A historical perspective. *Bulletin for the History of Chemistry*, 17(18), 15.

Heiden, B. J. (2017). The battle to define the meaning of FRAND. PhD thesis, Chalmers University of Technology.

Henry, C., & Stiglitz, J. E. (2010). Intellectual property, dissemination of innovation and sustainable development. *Global Policy*, 1(3), 237–251.

Ho, J.-Y., & O'Sullivan, E. (2019). Addressing the evolving standardisation challenges of 'smart systems' innovation: Emerging roles for government? *Science and Public Policy*, 46(4), 552–569.

Jarvenpaa, S. L., & Välikangas, L. (2014). Opportunity creation in innovation networks: Interactive revealing practices. *California Management Review*, 57(1), 67–87.

Laursen, K., & Salter, A. J. (2014). The paradox of openness: Appropriability, external search and collaboration. *Research Policy*, 43(5), 867–878.

Long, P. O. (2001). *Openness, Secrecy, Authorship: Technical Arts and the Culture of Knowledge from Antiquity to the Renaissance*. Baltimore, MD: Johns Hopkins University Press.

Manning, S., & Reinecke, J. (2016). A modular governance architecture in-the-making: How transnational standard-setters govern sustainability transitions. *Research Policy*, 45(3), 618–633.

Metcalfe, B. (2013). Metcalfe's law after 40 years of ethernet. *Computer*, 46(12), 26–31.

Meyer, V., Basenko, E. Y., Benz, J. P., Braus, G. H., Caddick, M. X., Csukai, M., ... Gunde-Cimerman, N. (2020). Growing a circular economy with fungal biotechnology: A white paper. *Fungal Biology and Biotechnology*, 7, 1–23.

NGMN Alliance (2015). 5G white paper. *Next Generation Mobile Networks, White Paper, 1*.

Papachristos, G., & Kaa, G. van de (2021). A system dynamics model of standards competition. *IEEE Transactions on Engineering Management*, 68(1), 18–32.

Podszun, R. (2019). Standard essential patents and antitrust law in the age of standardisation and the internet of things: Shifting paradigms. *IIC – International Review of Intellectual Property and Competition Law*, 50(6), 720–745.

Rosenkranz, S., & Schmitz, P. W. (2003). Optimal allocation of ownership rights in dynamic R&D alliances. *Games and Economic Behavior*, 43(1), 153–173.

Rothaermel, F. T., & Thursby, M. (2005). University–incubator firm knowledge flows: Assessing their impact on incubator firm performance. *Research Policy*, 34(3), 305–320.

Sherkow, J. S. (2016). Protecting products versus platforms. *Nature Biotechnology*, 34(5), 462–465.

Sherkow, J. S. (2017). Patent protection for CRISPR: An ELSI review. *Journal of Law and the Biosciences*, 4(3), 565–576.

Srinivasan, R., Lilien, G. L., & Rangaswamy, A. (2006). The emergence of dominant designs. *Journal of Marketing*, 70(2), 1–17.

Teece, D. J. (2018). Profiting from innovation in the digital economy: Enabling technologies, standards, and licensing models in the wireless world. *Research Policy*, 47(8), 1367–1387.

Walsh, J. P., & Huang, H. (2014). Local context, academic entrepreneurship and open science: Publication secrecy and commercial activity among Japanese and US scientists. *Research Policy*, 43(2), 245–260.

26. Opportunity domains for new entrants in the circular economy: a keyword-in-context analysis of Norwegian R&D tax incentive projects

Roberto Rivas Hermann, Are Jensen and Peter Gianiodis

INTRODUCTION: STATE OF THE ART AND CONTEXT

With the conceptual development of the circular economy (CE) and its growing influence on the global economy, academics and policy makers require greater clarity when analysing CE discourse (Friant et al. 2020). Specifically, there is a need for scholars to clarify the CE's implications across multiple societal stakeholders, especially its macro effects (Ortega Alvarado et al. 2021). Recent research has revealed issues related to the construction of public policy aimed to support the transition to CE practices (Simoens and Leipold 2020), including tensions emerging from public policies (Friant et al. 2021). Several studies employing discourse analysis frameworks have considered the primary points of tension between macro-level policies supporting the CE and the CE-related activities of societal actors (Humalisto et al. 2021; Johansson and Henriksson 2020).

Further, while several recent studies have examined CE policy packages and industrial-oriented CE promotion policies (Fitch-Roy et al. 2020; Humalisto et al. 2021), two gaps remain in the literature: first, there is a lack of knowledge regarding the specific types of CE innovation that have most benefited from policy programmes supporting the CE; and second, it remains to be understood how these innovations address the concerns of various stakeholders (example: government agencies, upstream supply-chain beneficiaries of the innovations, or citizens). Closing these gaps is necessary in order to design better CE policies (Humalisto et al. 2021). One area in particular need of greater research attention is the question of how national research and development (R&D) support programmes promote firms' transition towards CE, and how to map the variety of firms' participating in these programmes and the reach of CE promotion packages to new ventures and types of stakeholders (Humalisto et al. 2021).

National R&D policies increasingly support technological innovation through a range of public subsidy schemes, which often require companies to complete very detailed application forms (Bodas Freitas et al. 2017). Archived applications for these subsidies provide valuable data on companies' motivations and strategies for investing scarce R&D resources in CE transition. Previous research has started to connect CE with entrepreneurship (Zucchella and Urban 2019). The notion that start-ups are more innovative compared to incumbents, and thus better able to recognize opportunities linked to market externalities, is a traditional argument for focusing on start-ups. (Dean and McMullen 2007). Echoing the call to better understand the CE's social impact and how stakeholders navigating governmental support systems employ CE-oriented language, this chapter advances our understanding of: (1) the importance of 'language games' related to CE participation, and (2) CE policy's alignment to emerging innovations. Specifically, we explore how firms frame CE opportunities, and how public policies support entrepreneurial ventures in exploiting these opportunities. Our research question is thus framed as: *How has venturing within the circular economy – related to R&D, innovation, commercialization, etc. – emerged in response to incentive-based public policies?*

This chapter makes two key contributions to the literature. The first concerns methodology; we demonstrate the potential of text mining methodologies to enhance the discourse analysis methods applied in a number of previous CE-related studies. This approach has allowed us to make full use of the rich dataset provided by the Research Council of Norway. By enabling the robust analysis of large datasets such as this, our approach contributes to the overall methodological rigour of CE research. It is this methodological approach which has enabled us to make the second key contribution of this chapter: identification and analysis of the semantic communities in which entrepreneurial firms develop innovations aligned with CE discourses and public policy initiatives. We expect that our methodological innovations can help managers and public policy stakeholders identify and quantify CE innovations, while the CE dictionary we have developed in this study may contribute useful data to guide policy recommendations.

ANALYTICAL FRAMEWORK

Discourse Analysis and Circular Economy

Academic scholarship has provided comprehensive definitions of the CE (Friant et al. 2020; Korhonen et al. 2018; Schöggl et al. 2020). For example, Chapter 1 in this handbook offers a well-documented summary of these various definitions. The literature emphasizes the socially constructed nature of CE discourse, which allows it to represent the socio-technological imaginaries of all stakeholders, even when their interests vis-à-vis environmental problems appear contradictory (Friant et al. 2020; Genovese and Pansera 2021). Discourses are competing concepts and ideas which are translated into everyday practices, and have a concrete meaning in the world (Richardson 2002). The prevalence of discourse analysis in the study of environmental policy emerges from the 'argumentative turn' in the study of public policy (1990s); thus, rather than searching for objective truths, it focuses on deliberation in the framing of environmental problems and potential solutions (Leipold et al. 2019). This deliberative character is present in the current state of CE policymaking because CE is open to multiple policies aiming to support national research and development systems. One by-product of this 'openness' is a limited understanding of how generic CE policies align with business initiatives (Humalisto et al. 2021).

Opportunities for New Entrants in the Circular Economy

There is a relative lack of research in the existing literature on how CE packages promote R&D and innovation (cf. Chapter 1 for exemplar exceptions), and especially how actors respond to project calls and funding options. One important evolution is the change in perception in the early 2000s which saw assumptions that the locus of CE resides in large industrial parks occupied by multinational enterprises (Ghisellini et al. 2016) give way to the current prevailing view emphasizing 'micro-level' considerations of how organizations incorporate CE into their core strategies and activities. This change in discourse clarifies the need to incorporate CE principles (see Chapter 1) into core business strategies such as business models (Geissdoerfer et al. 2020), supply chain management (Genovese et al. 2017) product design (den Hollander et al. 2017) or stakeholder management (Kazancoglu et al. 2021).

Context of Study

Norway, although not an European Union (EU) member state, is influenced by EU institutions through its European Economic Area (EEA) and European Free Trade Association (EFTA) memberships – a key example of the latter being the EU's Action Plan on CE (Ortega Alvarado et al. 2021). A white paper entitled "Waste as a resource – waste policy and circular economy" was the first official document to clearly indicate the Norwegian government's position on CE (Klima- og miljødepartementet 2015). This paper is seen as a Norwegian adoption of the EU's Action Plan on CE. In this paper, the Norwegian government establishes four key aspects of CE implementation: ecological modernization, product-oriented policies, upgrading the national system of innovation, and waste policy. It also outlines key science funding pro- grammes to facilitate the implementation of CE (Klima- og miljødepartementet 2015).

What makes it empirically interesting to answer the research question of the present study, is that 10 years before the adoption of the CE principles, Norway started the SkatteFUNN programme: subsidies on corporate taxes for firms performing R&D activities. It is designed to have a low barrier to entry; any company can apply for the programme, and it has a 72 per cent acceptance rate as of 2020 (SkatteFUNN 2020). The purpose of the SkatteFUNN programme is to encourage R&D with a focus on all innovation activities (SkatteFUNN 2020). Since application to the SkatteFUNN programme requires applicants to (1) perform targeted R&D activities and (2) provide detailed information about these activities, the applications can be seen as clear representations of applicants' strategic R&D choices. The analysis of a longitudi- nal sample of SkatteFUNN projects can thus provide a better insight into how firms embraced circular opportunities, up to the year when CE became official public policy though Klima- og miljødepartementet (2015).

METHODS

The Keyword-in-Context Framework

We adopt the keyword-in-context (KWIC) method of archival text analysis (Bernard et al. 2010), an approach based on identifying the extent to which certain stakeholders use specific keywords. The definition of 'extent' incorporates both frequency of use and the type of con- nections a given keyword has to the stakeholder's overall corpus. By 'corpus', we mean a large and structured body of text, here the project descriptions submitted to the Research Council of Norway, SkatteFUNN programme. As a result, we adapt and expand the KWIC methodology for large corpuses in innovation studies (Jurowetzki 2015). The adaptation requires the inclu- sion of one additional phase (dictionary development), and the use of alternative software with user-friendly interface (RapidMiner).

Dictionary Development

Phase 1 of this study was the development of a CE 'dictionary'. In line with previous studies, we employed Leximancer, a web-based tool that analyses a text corpus (e.g., scientific paper abstracts and titles) and identifies a set of high-level concepts. These concepts are reported in a graph and an exportable spreadsheet (Leximancer Pty Ltd. 2017). Leximancer's analysis relies on co-occurrence matrices and the adaptation of latent semantic analysis (LSA) (Deerwester et al. 1990). We used Leximancer to produce a dictionary of the key concepts associated with CE in the scientific literature using abstracts and titles of papers in the Scopus database published between 2000 and 2017. Some of these concepts identified reflected literature trends related to planning and policy in the context of CE, including regulations, development models, systemic change, and sustainability. A second stream of concepts related to the technological aspects of the CE; we focused on these to identify start-ups developing new products and services through tax incentives. The literature indicates that CE technologies can be grouped around the concepts of waste, production, resources, and treatment. Each of these concepts contains numerous tokens (sequence of characters grouped together and separated by a space) that statistically build on the concepts generated by the Leximancer software. We focused on tokens with high scores (above 1.0) for each of these concepts. The authors independently read through the list of tokens and highlighted those that referred directly to a technology (i.e., a product, service, or process) or a component of a technology. After comparing their curated lists, the researchers agreed on 420 key terms, which were subsequently translated into the Norwegian language (Appendix 1).

Corpus from the SkatteFUNN Programme

To generate the corpus for our analysis, we obtained access to all SkatteFUNN applications between 2004 and 2015 through a collaboration with the Research Council of Norway. Our dataset contained 4,072 such applications submitted by new established firms that had been operating for less than four years at the time of the applications. We then assembled our text corpus from the project descriptions included in firms' responses to two questions on the application: *What is the project's main goal?* and *Describe the project background* (in earlier applications, this was instead termed *Summary of the project background*). Using NVivo 11 software, we automatically coded these two variables and created a text file for each application. We refer to each application as a 'document'; the corpus is the collection of these documents, each containing approximately 500 words in response to these two questions.

Corpus Processing

The SkatteFUNN corpus was subsequently processed to enable comparison between each individual document and the dictionary, in order to identify the documents with the highest similarity to the dictionary. The first step in processing the corpus was to transform the text into data, which was accomplished through the use of natural language processing (NLP) (Joshi 1991). The objective of the NLP treatment is to generate a simplified form of each document, i.e., a so-called bag-of-words representation, which removes repetitive words such as pronouns and adverbs (Manning and Schütze 2000).

The NLP procedure adapted from Jurowetzki (2015) included three steps: parsing (analysing a sentence into its synthetic parts), tokenizing (creating instances of a type, like unigrams or bigrams), and stemming (removing suffixes). We relied on the NLP package RapidMiner Studio 9.0 (Ertek et al. 2014), which enables workflows with specific NLP functions. After the NLP process, each document was reduced to a bag-of-words representation containing nouns for comparison with the CE dictionary in the next step.

Identification of CE Entrepreneurs through Vector Space Modelling

The next step in our analysis was converting each individual document into a numerical representation. In NLP processing, vector representation is a common approach based on principles of information retrieval and text mining (Manning and Schütze 2000). The vector space model establishes a high-dimensional space in which each dimension is associated with a particular token, and each value is defined by a given term's occurrence within a document. Each document has a unique position in this space, corresponding to the unique combination of tokens specific to that document (Manning and Schütze 2000). A cosine similarity matrix was produced for all documents and the CE dictionary using Manning and Schütze's (2000) methodology. We selected documents whose similarity to the CE dictionary fell above a threshold of significance and retained this sample for further processing.

Social Network Analysis/Clustering/Community Detection

From the reduced sample described in the previous paragraph a subset of CE projects (N = 329) was used as an input for the social network analysis. Following Jurowetzki (2015), we generated a second similarity matrix based on this smaller sample, with the goal of identifying how closely their vocabularies resembled one another, thereby creating 'clusters' of conceptually connected CE entrepreneurs. Using RapidMiner, we generated a similarity matrix that functioned as the input for the social network analysis. The documents represented the nodes in the social network graph, while the cosine similarity values represented the edges. We imported the matrix into the Gephi software (Bastian et al. 2009), which calculates so-called communities of documents that cluster together in their use of similar terms. A randomized Louvain algorithm analysis (Blondel et al. 2008) with a resolution of 1.02 was selected as most appropriate. The number of resulting communities was six (Appendix 2).

Community Analysis and Results

As an output of the Gephi software, we obtained a community number for each project application in a database format (.csv). We linked these numbers to their respective project IDs for a follow-up analysis, and used term frequency to analyse the results and identify the discourses within each community and year of application. For each community, we analysed the documents and summarized the most frequent keywords using the IBM Watson software (IBM 2020).

RESULTS

We identified six semantic communities representing CE technologies and start-ups within the entrepreneurial ecosystem (Table 26.1). The community size, represented by the number of projects, ranged from 28 to 120; larger communities represent a wider range of industries, while smaller communities are those focused on the development of emerging niche industries, e.g., bio-based products. The mean project size was similar across communities, although the community linked to the oil and gas industry had particularly large projects. This reflects the capital-intensive nature of this sector. Since the sample consisted mostly of start-up companies, the typical firm size across communities was comparable. The distribution of the projects' starting years was also similar across communities, indicating that there was no period in which any given type of project was particularly popular. In the next section, we analyse in more detail the characteristics of each community, with a particular focus on the relationship between the technologies, external collaboration, and the impact of the project.

Table 26.2 summarizes a few representative examples of the projects within each community. This qualitative representation of the project types within each community highlights the underlying connections between technological innovation and the principles of CE. We next discuss the findings from this analysis and their implications for theory and practice.

DISCUSSION AND CONCLUSION

Theoretical and Practical Implications

Our discourse analysis of CE in the Norwegian context identified six semantic communities where start-ups developed solutions aligned with CE discourses in academic debates. The findings show that when start-ups have not achieved legitimacy – due to limited resources and market experience – they develop R&D projects to exploit opportunities created by the 'buzz' around CE. For example, CE buzz influenced the emergence of the 'oil and gas' community in the results. It is unsurprising that start-ups often develop innovations to supply the oil and gas sector as this is the primary economic driver in Norway. The other communities reflect other important sectors of the Norwegian economy, such as energy and aquaculture.

These findings support the broad finding in the extant literature that traditional R&D funding mechanisms such as tax-deduction schemes have value for promoting CE transitions. This value has, surprisingly, not yet been highlighted in most of the recent studies whose focus has been CE packages and policies (Fitch-Roy et al. 2020; Friant et al. 2021; Johansson and Henriksson 2020). Our findings also highlight the gap in the literature related to the alignment of generic, top-down policy tools with stakeholder interests. For example, these tools can reach and connect with a large variety of industry actors and stakeholders to avoid path dependencies (Humalisto et al. 2021). In addition, the success of our discourse mapping method shows that using archival data analysis with existing project applications can help government agencies map different CE-related domains of opportunity. By using a similar approach, governments can develop more targeted policy programmes by considering the number of projects and complementarity over the years, thus highlighting areas to align with stakeholders interests.

This finding has practical implications, especially for start-ups and small and medium-sized enterprises (SMEs). These scarce-resourced firms often struggle to prioritize R&D efforts,

Table 26.1   *CE communities based on KWIC analysis – R&D and innovation projects SkatteFUNN programme 2004–2015*

Community	Size (number of projects)	Mean firm size (number of employees)	Project mean value (x 1000 Norwegian Krone)	External collaboration (% projects with at least one external partner)	Mean project start year	Most frequent keywords
Biofuels	28	15.6	5045	35.3	2008	Biofuels, solar cell, solar power, photovoltaics, petroleum, diesel fuel, paper, crystalline silicon, paper and solar energy
Waste and emissions	30	11.2	4040	53.3	2010	Waste, waste management, recycling, hazardous waste, composting, biodegradable waste, waste collection and pollution
Oil and gas	33	5.2	7795	44	2009	Petroleum, oil well, water purification, water, drinking water, drilling rig, petroleum industry, drilling
Production / general	120	19	3701	48	2008	Testing, companies, process, information, production, materials, systems and reuse
Energy and biogas	59	8.8	4475	41	2008	Methane, biogas, natural gas, waste, energy, turbine, waste management and anaerobic
Aquaculture / food	59	14.3	4753	53	2009	Industry, freeze-drying, fish, material, manufacturing, process management, project management

creating uncertainty and forcing them to align their R&D to existing ecosystems or investments in novel offerings not found in existing value chains (Garcia et al. 2003). We suggest that entrepreneurial founders and managers of SMEs adapt analysis of project applications as a methodology in a manner analogous to patent analysis. These firms can integrate the identification of market failures (Dean and McMullen 2007) into their organizational CE strategy, which can improve the organizational transition towards the CE. This can be achieved, for example, by accessing public databases (media, patent registers, or public funding agencies)

Table 26.2 Examples of projects within each community

Community	Examples
Biofuels	The project will contribute to increased knowledge of alternative measures and strategies that can be implemented to streamline and further develop production of biodiesel based on used cooking oil, along with the potential for biodiesel production through the utilization of animal fat in Norway.
Waste and emissions	The system is suitable for converting wet organic waste into a component that can be included in fertilizers or soil additives. A full-scale treatment plant for the production of fertilizer and soil improvement products intended for agriculture, horticulture and public activities is planned.
Oil and gas	Example 1: Utilize the patent-pending pump for particulate materials for research, development and commercialization of biomass fuel feed. Understand and describe processes in the pump for particulate materials/design patent application. Installation and testing of the vertical pump on a large pellet silo.
	Example 2: The R&D objective in the project is to develop an environmentally friendly particle-based system that can be injected into an oil or gas well to selectively control and reduce water production without reducing, and preferably while increasing, oil and gas production.
Production / general	Example 1: Develop a new environmentally friendly wood coating agent.
	Example 2: To develop a method for the biological treatment of cuttings and other oil-contaminated waste from the oil and gas industry.
Energy and biogas	Development of substrate biogas treatment plants. The plant will clean wet organic waste from households, slaughterhouses, fish processing, returned consumer products, etc. to produce clean biogas substrates for use in biogas plants.
Aquaculture / food	The main objective of the project is to increase the utilization of certain kinds of raw material for food or other industrial production so that the waste we currently pay to dispose of instead contributes to value creation in the company through profitable products that we can sell.

and identifying what type of CE technology discussions are trending at any given time, or by analysing changes in contextual dynamics such as competition and customer demand.

Agenda for Future Research

The automatic content analysis methodology is not without risks, some of which emerge from the multiple controls we applied along the process. As our methodology did not involve reading all the SkatteFUNN applications in full, we were only able to account for the frequency in which key CE terms occurred in the corpus. This could have led to omissions in how they were used in context. However, a random reading of the applications in each community gives the impression that the understanding of circularity is not central to any of these communities. Rather, the CE aspects are often associated with incremental improvement in firms' processes and/or product offerings. Thus, the occurrence of CE-related terminology in applications may not translate to transformative integration of circularity into firms' R&D strategies.

The CE is usually understood as a complex restructuring of existing economic activity (e.g., supply chains). This complex idea is impossible to translate into computer language, as the current NLP packages are based on the analysis of tokens and short phrases rather than complex concepts. Our method, therefore, is dependent on the analysis of word frequencies (KWIC) which requires significant scrubbing of the database. Similarly, a certain degree of subjectivity is present in the vector space model values' benchmark definition. This indicates that we can choose whether or not to include in our sample those projects which might not entirely adopt the concept of CE. Future research should strive to improve on this method, and to limit some of the relevant risks associated with its use.

As with other demonstrations of modelling techniques, our results are meant to be illustrative to inform the potential of our approach for future use. The method is not meant to predict with statistical accuracy whether a classification of a document 100 per cent aligns with CE. As a result, we encourage the adoption of machine learning techniques (neural networks, Bayesian algorithms) to enhance our methodology for future research. Specifically, to provide an automatic classification of documents, to enhance its predictive power, for public funding agencies. From the more theoretical discussion about CE, we suggest further work in the analysis of the evolution of CE discourse and the interaction between public discourse and the funding of science and R&D projects.

ACKNOWLEDGEMENTS

This project benefited from data access to SkatteFUNN through Professor Tommy H. Clausen. Early versions of this chapter benefited from critical comments by Professor Rosanna Garcia (University of Denver) and Dr Mario Pansera (Universitat Autònoma de Barcelona). No conflict of interest is reported by the authors.

REFERENCES

Bastian, M., Heymann, S., & Jacomy, M. (2009). Gephi: An open source software for exploring and manipulating networks. *Third International AAAI Conference on Weblogs and Social Media*. https://doi.org/10.1136/qshc.2004.010033.

Bernard, H. R., Wutich, A., & Ryan, G. W. (2010). *Analyzing Qualitative Data; Systematic Approaches*. Thousand Oaks, CA: Sage Publications.

Blondel, V. D., Guillaume, J.-L., Lambiotte, R., & Lefebvre, E. (2008). Fast unfolding of communities in large networks. *Journal of Statistical Mechanics: Theory and Experiment*, 2008(10), P10008.

Bodas Freitas, I., Castellacci, F., Fontana, R., Malerba, F., & Vezzulli, A. (2017). Sectors and the additionality effects of R&D tax credits: A cross-country microeconometric analysis. *Research Policy*, 46(1), 57–72.

Dean, T. J., & McMullen, J. S. (2007). Toward a theory of sustainable entrepreneurship: Reducing environmental degradation through entrepreneurial action. *Journal of Business Venturing*, 22(1), 50–76.

Deerwester, S., Dumais, S. T., Furnas, G. W., Landauer, T. K., & Harshman, R. (1990). Indexing by latent semantic analysis. *Journal of the American Society for Information Science*, 41(6), 391–407.

den Hollander, M. C., Bakker, C. A., & Hultink, E. J. (2017). Product design in a circular economy: Development of a typology of key concepts and terms. *Journal of Industrial Ecology*, 21(3), 517–525.

Ertek, G., Tapucu, D., & Arin, I. (2014). Text mining with RapidMiner. In M. Hofmann & R. Klinkenberg (eds.), *RapidMiner: Data Mining Use Cases and Business Analytics Applications*. Boca Raton, FL: CRC Press, 241–261.

Fitch-Roy, O., Benson, D., & Monciardini, D. (2020). Going around in circles? Conceptual recycling, patching and policy layering in the EU circular economy package. *Environmental Politics*, 29(6), 983–1003.

Friant, M. C., Vermeulen, W. J., & Salomone, R. (2020). A typology of circular economy discourses: Navigating the diverse visions of a contested paradigm. *Resources, Conservation and Recycling*, 161, 104917.

Friant, M. C., Vermeulen, W. J., & Salomone, R. (2021). Analysing European Union circular economy policies: Words versus actions. *Sustainable Production and Consumption*, 27, 337–353.

Garcia, R., Calantone, R., & Levine, R. (2003). The role of knowledge in resource allocation to exploration versus exploitation in technologically oriented organizations. *Decision Sciences*, 34(2), 323–349.

Geissdoerfer, M., Pieroni, M. P. P., Pigosso, D. C. A., & Soufani, K. (2020). Circular business models: A review. *Journal of Cleaner Production*, 277, 123741.

Genovese, A., Acquaye, A. A., Figueroa, A., & Koh, S. C. L. (2017). Sustainable supply chain management and the transition towards a circular economy: Evidence and some applications. *Omega*, 66, 344–357.

Genovese, A., & Pansera, M. (2021). The circular economy at a crossroads: Technocratic eco-modernism or convivial technology for social revolution? *Capitalism Nature Socialism*, 32(2), 95–113.

Ghisellini, P., Cialani, C., & Ulgiati, S. (2016). A review on circular economy: The expected transition to a balanced interplay of environmental and economic systems. *Journal of Cleaner Production*, 114, 11–32.

Humalisto, N., Åkerman, M., & Valve, H. (2021). Making the circular economy online: A hyperlink analysis of the articulation of nutrient recycling in Finland. *Environmental Politics*, 30(5), 833–853.

IBM (2020). *What is Watson? Enterprise-ready AI*. https://www.ibm.com/watson/about.

Johansson, N., & Henriksson, M. (2020). Circular economy running in circles ? A discourse analysis of shifts in ideas of circularity in Swedish environmental policy. *Sustainable Production and Consumption*, 23, 148–156.

Joshi, A. K. (1991). Natural language processing. *Science*, 253(5025), 1242–1249.

Jurowetzki, R. (2015). *Unpacking Big Systems – Natural Language Processing Meets Network Analysis. A Study of Smart Grid Development in Denmark* (No. 2015-15; SPRU Working Paper Series). https://papers.ssrn.com/sol3/papers.cfm?abstract_id=2744519.

Kazancoglu, I., Sagnak, M., Kumar Mangla, S., & Kazancoglu, Y. (2021). Circular economy and the policy: A framework for improving the corporate environmental management in supply chains. *Business Strategy and the Environment*, 30(1), 590–608.

Klima- og miljødepartementet (2015). *Meld. St. 45 (2016–2017) Avfall som ressurs – avfallspolitikk og sirkulær økonomi* [Waste as a resource – waste policy and circular economy]. https://www.regjeringen.no/no/dokumenter/meld.-st.-45-20162017/id2558274/.

Korhonen, J., Nuur, C., Feldmann, A., & Birkie, S. E. (2018). Circular economy as an essentially contested concept. *Journal of Cleaner Production*, 175, 544–552.

Leipold, S., Feindt, P. H., Winkel, G., & Keller, R. (2019). Discourse analysis of environmental policy revisited: Traditions, trends, perspectives. *Journal of Environmental Policy & Planning*, 21(5), 445–463.

Leximancer Pty Ltd. (2017). *Leximancer: Product Manual*. Leximancer User Guide. Release 4.5. https://doc.leximancer.com/doc/LeximancerManual.pdf.

Manning, C. D., & Schütze, H. (2000). *Foundations of Statistical Natural Language Processing*. Cambridge, MA: MIT Press.

Ortega Alvarado, I. A., Sutcliffe, T. E., & Berker, T. (2021). Emerging circular economies: Discourse coalitions in a Norwegian case. *Sustainable Production and Consumption*, 26, 360–372.

Richardson, T. (2002). Freedom and control in planning: Using discourse in the pursuit of reflexive practice. *Planning Theory & Practice*, 3(3), 353–361.

Schöggl, J.-P., Stumpf, L., & Baumgartner, R. J. (2020). The narrative of sustainability and circular economy: A longitudinal analysis of two decades of research. *Resources, Conservation and Recycling*, 163, 105073.

Simoens, M., & Leipold, S. (2020). *Trading Radical for Incremental Change: The Politics of a Circular Economy Transition in the German Packaging Sector*. University of Freiburg, Chair in Circular Economy and Sustainable Transitions Working Paper. https://doi.org/doi.org/10.31235/osf.io/mvx5q.

SkatteFUNN (2020). *About SkatteFUNN*. https://www.skattefunn.no/en/about-skattefunn/.

Zucchella, A., & Urban, S. (2019). *Circular Entrepreneurship: Creating Responsible Enterprise*. Cham: Palgrave Macmillan.

APPENDIX 26.1

Replication dataset

For the replication dataset, see Rivas-Hermann, R. (2019). *Circular Economy Technologies Dictionary – Norwegian Language*. Mendeley Datasets. https://doi.org/10.17632/wkj5cg3btm.2

APPENDIX 26.2

CE discursive communities following the social network analysis step

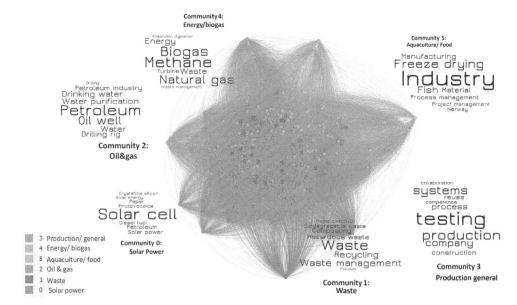

Figure A26.1   CE discursive communities following the social network analysis step

27. Circular public procurement: innovation tool for municipalities?

Elena Dybtsyna, Dolores Modic, Kristina Nikolajeva and Raymond Sørgård Hansen

INTRODUCTION

The public sector is a key actor in addressing a number of issues of transitioning to a more sustainable and more circular economy (Murray et al. 2017; Witjes and Lozano 2016; Neto 2020; Sönnichsen and Clement 2020; Yu et al. 2020; Lăzăroiu et al. 2020). By using the public sector's purchasing power to choose goods and services with lower environmental impacts, public actors can make important contributions to sustainable consumption and production, in particular in the transition to a more circular economy. One way to achieve this is through public procurement.

Public procurements account for considerable proportions of GDP and are also one of the 'policy enablers' unlocking value for the circular economy (WEF 2020). In the European Union (EU) public procurement on average accounts for 14 per cent of gross domestic product (GDP) (European Commission 2017). In Norway it accounted for more than 16 per cent of GDP in 2017 (Ministry of Trade, Industry and Fisheries 2019) with green requirements becoming increasingly dominant in both the EU and Norway (Liu et al. 2019). Initial evidence speaks in favour of changes in public procurement and unveils the potential to change other actors' behaviours (De Giacomo et al. 2019). The primary purpose of public procurement is to fulfil the needs and demands of the public administration. However, there is an increasing interest in utilizing public procurement as a multi-level innovative policy tool (Obwegeser and Müller 2018; Uyarra and Flanagan 2010; Uyarra et al. 2014; Ghisetti 2017). This view is in line with the notion of public procurement as a mechanism through which the policies of circular economy aiming to change patterns in order to tackle current sustainability challenges and facilitating can be supported and enable the shift away from the linear 'take-make-use-dispose' model of production and consumption (Klein et al. 2020).

We aim to contribute to the circular economy literature by shedding light how circular economy is currently practised (see e.g., Klein et al. 2020) at the organizational level in public sector organizations. The circular economy practices and their implementation at the organizational level have received a lot of attention when focusing on the corporate sector and private companies (see e.g., Bocken et al. 2017). However, there has been limited focus on the role and practices of local, i.e., municipal, levels (Alhola et al. 2017; Liu et al. 2019), although several important international organizations, such as the European Commission and the World Economic Forum point out that the municipalities can play an important role (WEF 2020; European Commission 2017). We in turn investigate how circular public procurement practices are carried out in a Norwegian municipality by scrutinizing the existing practices of how environmental impact is considered in preparation ahead of tenders and reflected inside the tenders. We focus on the building and construction sector, because it is considered one of the priorities by the Norwegian government when it comes to promoting green growth, including initiatives on circular economy (Ministry of Climate and Environment 2017). This chapter provides other municipalities with new insights about engagement in circular public procurement practices.

We also aim to add to the existing innovation literature (see e.g., Obwegeser and Müller 2018) by bringing in a more nuanced picture of public procurement as an innovation policy tool. The research on innovation in public procurement still represents an emergent, inherently practice-oriented field (Obwegeser and Müller 2018). Consequently, we use the selected case as the backdrop to discuss how municipalities can and should push innovative efforts towards circularity through the procurement process. Consequently, we offer a more comprehensive understanding of how circular economy innovations can be supported by utilizing public procurement as a multi-level innovative policy tool and especially deliberating on missed opportunities. Our results indicate that the environmental criteria are a part of public procurement in the construction sector in Bodø municipality. However, we demonstrate that there is a gap between the strategic initiatives of the municipality and insufficient practical implementation of circular public procurement and also unrealized potential in terms of using public procurement innovatively to support the transition to more circularity.

The chapter is organized as follows: in the following section we define and differentiate between environmentally focused public procurement practices. The next section deals with public procurement as an innovation policy tool. The empirical context as well as our method and data collection are presented after that. Then we present the results of our study. In the fifth and last part we further discuss the results of our study, and present our conclusions and some implications for public authorities, suppliers and policy-makers to enable the transition to circular public procurement.

CONCEPTS OF PUBLIC PROCUREMENT: SUSTAINABLE, GREEN AND CIRCULAR

The public sector plays an important role in achieving sustainable development goals, in particular SDG 12 (ensuring sustainable consumption and production patterns), by addressing the specific target of promoting sustainable procurement practices (UN 2015). Studies on public procurement practices show that green and sustainable public procurement gained prominence for addressing societal, environmental and social challenges (Sönnichsen and Clement 2020). However, the literature on circular public procurement remains scarce. For the purposes of this chapter, we choose to define the concepts of sustainable, green and circular public procurement and show how they are interlinked. *Sustainable, green and circular* public procurement are very similar and share the same features, yet there are important distinctions.

Sustainable Public Procurement

Sustainable public procurement has recently attracted more attention, reflecting a more widespread political concern about achieving sustainable development. The European Commission (2019) defines it as "a process by which public authorities seek to achieve the appropriate balance between the three pillars of sustainable development – economic, social and environmental – when procuring goods, services or works at all stages of the project". To procure in a sustainable way means looking beyond short-term needs and taking into consideration the longer-term impacts of each purchase. Sustainable procurement is used by both public and private sector organizations to ensure that their purchasing reflects broader goals linked to resource efficiency, climate change, social responsibility and economic resilience (Clement et al. 2016).

Green Public Procurement

Green public procurement and sustainable procurement are often used interchangeably – however, green public procurement considers only the environmental impacts of purchasing decisions, whereas sustainable procurement considers all aspects of sustainability (Clement et al. 2016). Green public procurement is defined as "a process where public authorities seek to purchase goods, services and works with a reduced environmental impact throughout their life-cycle compared to goods, services and works with the same primary function which would otherwise be procured" (European Commission 2019). Nissinen et al. (2009, p. 1839) state that environmental criteria in green public procurement can be referred to as "obligatory technical specifications for the product or service, e.g., material selection, chemical content and characteristics of products, or that can be used as award criteria".

Circular Public Procurement

There is an ongoing discussion about the standard definition in the literature on circular public procurement (see e.g., Alhola et al. 2017, 2018). The European Commission defines circular public procurement as "the process by which public authorities purchase works, goods or services that seek to contribute to closed energy and material loops within supply chains, whilst minimising, and in the best case avoiding, negative environmental impacts and waste creation across their whole life-cycle" (European Commission 2017, p. 5). Circular and sustainable public procurement differ from each other in that while sustainable procurement covers economic, social and environmental aspects under purchases, circular procurement has environmental impact as an additional consideration. Circular and green public procurement have several similarities, and circular procurement is considered to be an approach to the greening of procurement. However, in contrast to the concepts of green and sustainable public procurement, circular procurement focuses on closed material loops and value retention, i.e., remanufacturing and reusing products and materials several times in a circular manner without causing additional harmful impacts (Alhola et al. 2017).

The academic literature agrees that these three types of procurement raise the level of complexity in public procurement (Sönnichsen and Clement 2020). Furthermore, the field of public procurement is very practitioner oriented (Obwegeser and Müller 2018), which is also true when using public procurement as an innovation policy tool to support the transition to circular economy. Nonetheless, there still seems to be a gap between the innovation research output and the output that could be used by practitioners (Rolfstam 2012) to understand how they can innovatively use public procurement to support the transition to more circularity.

PUBLIC PROCUREMENT AS AN INNOVATION POLICY TOOL

The role of public authorities through available financial mechanisms, such as public procurement, is key to engaging in the activities needed to bring about systemic transformation, since it allows for a financial premium for more sustainable business operations and also gives transparency to companies' practices. Thus, it is a corrective to the fact that the market still does not unequivocally support sustainable businesses (Durand et al. 2019). Within public procurement this incorporates the promotion of the Rs in the public tendering – such as reducing, refusing, reusing, repairing, refurbishing, remanufacturing, repurposing, recycling, recovering, re-mining or re-servitization (Reike et al. 2018) – and the procuring process to go beyond purchases at the lowest up-front price.

There is a growing awareness of public procurement as an innovation policy tool (Obwegeser and Müller 2018; Uyarra and Flanagan 2010; Uyarra et al. 2014; Ghisetti 2017). Utilizing public procurement as an innovation policy tool has also sparked the interest of policy-makers in connection with the transition to the circular society (European Commission 2017, 2019; WEF 2020). According to the OECD (2015) more than 90 per cent of OECD member states have already initiated mission-oriented policies or strategies pursuing green and sustainable initiatives, and according to its 2019 report (OECD 2019), all OECD states have developed these. However, progress so far regarding circular initiatives implementation is limited (Kirchherr et al. 2018), likewise its potential to influence new innovative solutions.

The framework proposed by Obwegeser and Müller (2018) differentiates three different innovation related levels in terms of public procurement: firstly, innovations in the public procurement process; secondly, innovation of public services by means of procurement; and thirdly, the use of public procurement as a tool for demand-side innovation policy-making. In line with the first of these, the question is whether public procurement can drive circular economy-oriented innovation (including e.g. innovating companies' business models to become more circular) and support innovative circular practices. The second focuses on if and how public services themselves can be innovated to support transition to a more circular society. The third level begs the question as to how public institutions can procure innovatively, i.e. what are some new relationships and value realizations that can lead to more circular procurement strategies?

All these levels require a structured approach to public procurement, since policy instruments like public procurement are often used without attention to overall goals (Borrás and Edquist 2013). There is a distinguishable need to change the behaviour of public procurers from pure cost-efficiency to investing in innovative, but riskier, solutions, which would shift the focus of procurement decisions onto long-term perspectives (Yeow and Edler 2012; Eadie et al. 2013), such as those connected to circularity.

EMPIRICAL SETTING

The Norwegian laws and regulations, and in the wake of its first Circular Economy Strategy, have been moulded to better support sustainable, green and circular goals. The revised Norwegian law on public procurement states "Public procurement shall contribute to reduce environmental impact and to promote environmental-friendly solutions wherever it is possible. This shall be done, among other things, by contracting authorities taking into consideration life-cycle costs" (Procurement law 2016). In 2017, the Ministry of Climate and Environment published its White Paper (Meld. St. 45) "Waste as resource – waste policy and circular economy", where it points out that "green public procurement is the tool to promote green growth, including initiative on circular economy" (Ministry of Climate and Environment 2017, p. 14). This was followed by the White Paper (St. Meld. 22) issued by the Ministry of Trade, Industry and Fisheries on "Smarter purchase – effective and professional public procurement", where circular public procurement is one of the priorities when "public authorities should, in particular, review their procurement practices" (Ministry of Trade, Industry and Fisheries 2019, p. 82).

Bodø is a municipality in northern Norway with a population of around 50,000 and committed to being a "smart and sustainable city" (Bodø municipality 2018). Their commitment to green and circular economy is apparent in several municipal documents and the municipality also engages in innovative procurement practices. Bodø is moreover involved in one of the largest construction projects in Norway, the re-allocation of its airport and repurposing of the space – both offering considerable potential to introduce innovative circular solutions.

METHOD AND DATA COLLECTION

This chapter builds on the single case study approach (see e.g., Yin 2018). The empirical case of Bodø municipality enables us to study circular public procurement practices at organizational level in depth and to ascertain how these existing practices can push innovation throughout the procurement process. In this manner, it becomes the setting for learning about public sector engagement in circular economy practices and their potential to use public procurement innovatively to support the transition to more circularity. We build on data collected through documentary analysis and observations. The first allows us to shed light on the current circular public procurement process, while the second enables us to gain additional insight into ongoing discussions related to the implementation of circular economy practices by the municipality.

The document analysis was based on tender documents in the construction sector by Bodø municipality. Tender documents were collected from Doffin[1] – the Norwegian national notification database for public procurement. Our search yielded seven tenders in the period 2019 to 2020. Each tender consists of 2 to 17 documents of different types, hence the total number of documents was 92. We analysed all documents related to the tenders. For the purpose of this chapter, we chose to focus on the preparation ahead of tender, i.e. tender specifications as presented in tenders, and assessed the content of tenders, instead of dealing with types of tenders. We dealt specifically with parts devoted to the definition of products and/or services, criteria specifications and the selection of suppliers to identify environmental aspects of tendering as a key issue in the transition to circular economy (European Commission 2020).

The observations were conducted within the framework of the CityLoops project,[2] when in February 2020 Bodø municipality organized two workshops with practitioners involved in public procurement.

CIRCULAR PUBLIC PROCUREMENT IN BODØ MUNICIPALITY

Bodø has published various documents that reflect their commitment to green and circular public procurement as well as to innovative procurement. In *Climate and Energy Plan* (2019–2021), Bodø declares that "Bodø municipality shall be the leading municipality within climate and energy-related solutions – smart, green, future-oriented and sustainable" (Bodø municipality 2018, p. 3). To ensure green and circular public procurement Bodø municipality elaborates in the action part (p. 29) of the *Climate and Energy Plan*, that in terms of public procurement the local authorities are to follow the methodology offered by "Innovative Procurement",[3] where Bodø is a partner (Bodø municipality 2018). The methodology of "Innovative Procurement" points to the importance of dialogue with the market before the procurement, communication of the users' needs and leaving the solution to the suppliers (Innovative Procurement n.d.). Further actions in the *Climate and Energy Plan* stipulate that public procurement practices shall include environmental and climate specifications. The environmental impact should be documented in all purchases and be weighted as at least 30 per cent of the total score.

Against the backdrop of an existing legal framework underlying the potential for circular public procurement, the municipality also engaged in organizing relevant workshops, in order to support the transition to the circular society. These workshops were dedicated to discussing sustainable and circular requirements, while the public authorities select the suppliers of goods and services. This demonstrates that the criteria and tendering processes are, at least up to a point, the focus of general debates among the relevant actors. However, these discussions cannot really be seen as connected to concrete public procurement tenders.

To understand the municipality's public procurement practices, we then examined all seven tenders we could identify and the environmental specifications therein. Table 27.1 presents these tenders, their relevant specifications and the award criteria.

All tenders (Ts) included environmental specifications. Five of them (T2, T3, T4, T6 and T7) included requirements that the bidder should have an approved environmental management system, scheme or certificate, e.g., Eco-lighthouse (in Norwegian *Miljøfyrtårn*). This specification in the tender documents shows that the bidders should have relevant environmental labels or certifications, thereby demonstrating that Bodø municipality relies on those mechanisms to identify companies implementing more environmentally friendly practices.

The next most used specification was environmental plan or follow-up, which appeared in T3, T6 and T7. In T3 and T6, the bidder was required to present its own environmental plan to meet the environmental targets in the projects. In tender T7 the environmental plan was prepared by Bodø municipality, meaning that the supplier would be required to implement it. The inclusion of the environmental plan exemplifies the tailoring of the procurement processes towards more circularity in the format of environmental activities after the tender procedure.

Tender T7 included a requirement that all reinforcing steel plating was to be based on 100 per cent recycled metal and that vehicles used for transportation should meet the European standard (e.g. Euro 5) on acceptable limits for exhaust emissions. Requirements regarding health and environmentally hazardous substances were included in two tenders: T1 required documentation on the absence of floor glue, and T3 that none of the materials should contain any environmentally hazardous elements. Both T2 and T6 specified that contaminated masses should be delivered to an authorized waste management facility. In T1 and T6, 60 per cent

Table 27.1   *Tenders in the construction sector in Bodø municipality with award criteria*

Tenders (Ts)	Environmental specifications				Award criteria used
	Environmental certificate	Environmental follow up/plan	Recycled or environmentally friendly materials	Waste management	
Restoration of three floors in assisted living housing (T1)			✓	✓	Lowest price
Renovation of existing kindergarten premises (T2)	✓			✓	Price: 90% Quality: 10%
New school and kindergarten (T3)	✓	✓	✓		Price: 70% Implementation: 20% Quality: 10%
New road construction (T4)	✓		✓	✓	Price/costs: 100%
Road maintenance (T5)			✓	✓	Price: 70% Quality/implementation: 20% Execution time: 10%
Skating park (T6)	✓	✓		✓	Price: 25% Suggested solution: 40% Risk management: 15% Implementation: 10% Progress: 10%
Green park construction (T7)	✓	✓	✓		Price: 70% Quality: 15% Implementation and organization: 15%

of the waste was to be sorted by the source. Requirements regarding waste management and health and environmentally hazardous substances were mentioned in T4 and T5.

Although all tenders contain green or circular specifications, as innovative practices in circularity, none of the tenders used these specifications as award criteria. The price was weighted between 70 and 100 per cent of the total award score and was the main award criterion in all tenders.

DISCUSSION: FROM PUBLIC PROCUREMENT REALITY TO MISSED OPPORTUNITIES FOR INNOVATIVE AND EFFICIENT CIRCULAR PROCUREMENT

Our empirical findings show that at the organizational level of the municipality in the context of Norway, a circularity conscious country, a gap exists between the strategic initiatives of the municipal administration and insufficient practical implementation of circular economy practices. There is also untapped potential to use public procurement innovatively to support the transition to more circularity.

Environmental impact is included in the focal municipality's tender specifications, showing that public procurement is in line with a transition towards circular economy. However, it is not reaching the threshold for making a difference in terms of the selected bidder and their bid. Descriptions of products or services fails to prioritize the environmental impact – which is something highly recommended by the EU (European Commission 2016). Tender documents in Bodø municipality included an environmental aspect in the specification requirements for the construction sector, but in none of them did this appear among the award criteria.

In terms of different levels of innovation, our empirical findings show that the municipality followed the second innovation-related level (Obwegeser and Müller 2018). The municipality does so when itself investing in innovative efforts to support a transition to circular economy by including the environmental impact requirements in the preparation ahead of the tenders and arranging workshops to discuss sustainable and circular requirements with relevant actors from the public and private sectors. However, it still lacks in its practices the implementation of the recommended steps of circular public procurement, including market engagement (see e.g., European Commission 2017).

The dialogue with the market or market engagement is important when it comes to greening purchases as well as innovation push (e.g., Witjes and Lozano 2016; Alhola et al. 2017; Sönnichsen and Clement 2020). None of our findings indicate that Bodø municipality engaged in cultivating the proper dialogue with suppliers to identify the potential and feasibility of circular solutions. Not involving market actors in needs assessment (see e.g., Uyarra et al. 2014), shows that Bodø relies on bidders' existing environmental certificates and their alleged ability to fulfil the environmental plan as the main element of greening the purchases. Here, the more elaborated market dialogue via e.g. Public Private Innovation (PPI) (see e.g., European Commission 2017) can push for more circularity, making it possible to improve the quality of tenders and adding substantial requirements to the tender rather than price.

Bodø municipality has shown a willingness to learn and practise more circular public procurements with emphasis on environmental aspects. This is evidenced by the workshops, taking part in the different projects, as well as introducing the underlying innovative policies at the local level (see e.g., *Climate and Energy Plan*). But in spite of political goodwill in terms of circularity, the operationalization on the municipal level is still lacking. Designing and including more circular-conscious tender specifications (e.g., using more 'non-traditional' aspects of circular economy, like reuse and/or extended life-cycles) and being more receptive towards innovative solutions (e.g., buying services instead of products or innovating with product design, using phase and end of life) can bring Bodø municipality beyond the already known practices and approaches and represent an advance towards comprehensive circularity. Eventually, the cycle between innovative and circular public procurement practices can be closed, and they can be mutually reinforcing.

CONCLUSION

In our study we focused on circular public procurement practices being carried out at the organizational level in one Norwegian municipality. We shed the light on how municipalities can push innovation towards circularity through the procurement process. Our analysis indicated that environmental criteria are a part of public procurement, but that these criteria were not wholly implemented in concrete tendering processes. We showed that environmental impacts do play a role as specification requirements, but that their role in the awarding of contracts was not decisive. Our results confirm earlier research showing that a large obstacle to achieving national public procurement outcomes related to innovation, environment and sustainability is the predominance of the lowest price as the ultimate award criterion (OECD 2019).

Municipalities in their efforts to implement circular public procurement need more specifically designed tender specifications and greater willingness to embrace innovative solutions. Municipalities can play an important role in implementing competitive public tenders promoting a product-to-services shift. Consequently, the dialogue with the market and market engagement is of the utmost importance in exploiting and promoting new and innovative circular solutions and aim at further circularity. This will enable to explore potential innovations to raise the quality of tendering and adding substantial requirements to the tender rather than focusing on price. Suppliers should be able to recognize from the tender specifications and the award criteria that the products, services or work manifesting good recognition of environmental impacts will be prioritized. Best practices reports from the EU and Norway dealing with reduced environmental impact can help to prepare tailor-made requirements in terms of specifications and award criteria and also in deciding how to evaluate the circularity aspects of tenders and downplay the significance of price in the contract.

NOTES

1.   Doffin – database for public procurement: https://www.doffin.no/en.
2.   In 2019 Bodø municipality and partners received the EU-financed research and innovation project "CityLoops: Closing the loop for urban material flows". The project aims at closing the loops of urban material flows and increasing their regenerative capacity to drive the transition to a circular economy.
3.   Innovative procurement is a national programme for innovations in the public sector through public procurement. See Innovative anskaffelser: https://innovativeanskaffelser.no/om-oss/.

REFERENCES

Alhola, K., Ryding, S.-O., Salmenperä, H., & Busch, N. J. (2018). Exploiting the potential of public procurement: Opportunities for circular economy. *Journal of Industrial Ecology*, 23(1), 96–109.
Alhola, K., Salmenperä, H., Ryding, S.-O., & Busch, N. J. (2017). Circular public procurement in the Nordic countries. https://norden.diva-portal.org/smash/get/diva2:1092366/FULLTEXT01.pdf.
Bocken, N. M. P., Ritala, P., & Huotari, P. (2017). The circular economy: Exploring the introduction of the concept among S&P 500 firms. *Journal of Industrial Ecology*, 21, 487–490.
Bodø municipality (2018). *Climate and Energy Plan (Klima- og energiplan)* (2019–2031). https://bodo.kommune.no/getfile.php/1313122-1562053022/Natur%2C%20miljø%20og%20landbruk/Bodø%20kommunes%20klima-%20og%20energiplan%202019-2031%281%29.pdf.
Borrás, S., & Edquist, C. (2013). The choice of innovation policy instruments. *Technological Forecasting and Social Change*, 80(8), 1513–1522.
Clement, S., Watt, J., & Semple, A. (2016). *The Procura+ Manual: A Guide to Implementing Sustainable Procurement* (3rd ed.). https://procuraplus.org/fileadmin/user_upload/Manual/Procuraplus_Manual_Third_Edition.pdf.
De Giacomo, M. R., Testa, F., Iraldo, F., & Formentini, M. (2019). Does green public procurement lead to life cycle costing (LCC) adoption? *Journal of Purchasing and Supply Management*, 25(3), 100500.

Durand, R., Paugam, L., & Stolowy, H. (2019). Do investors actually value sustainability indices? Replication, development, and new evidence on CSR visibility. *Strategic Management Journal*, 40(9), 1471–1490.

Eadie, R., McKeown, C., & Anderson, K. (2013). The impact of recession on construction procurement routes. *International Journal of Procurement Management*, 6(1), 24–38.

European Commission (2016). *Buying Green! A Handbook on Green Public Procurement*. https://ec .europa.eu/environment/gpp/pdf/Buying-Green-Handbook-3rd-Edition.pdf.

European Commission (2017). *Public Procurement for a Circular Economy: Good Practice and Guidance*. https://ec.europa.eu/environment/gpp/pdf/CP_European_Commission_Brochure_webversion_small.pdf.

European Commission (2019). *Green and Sustainable Public Procurement*. https://ec.europa.eu/ environment/gpp/versus_en.htm.

European Commission (2020). *A New Circular Economy Action Plan. For a Cleaner and More Competitive Europe*. COM(2020) 98final. https://eur-lex.europa.eu/legal-content/EN/TXT/?qid= 1583933814386&uri=COM:2020:98:FIN.

Ghisetti, C. (2017). Demand-pull and environmental innovations: Estimating the effects of innovative public procurement. *Technological Forecasting and Social Change*, 125, 178–187.

Innovative Procurement (n.d.). *Procedure and tools (Metode og verktøy)*. https://innovativeanskaffelser .no/metode/.

Kirchherr, J., Piscicelli, L., Bour, R., Kostense-Smit, E., Muller, J., Huibrechtse-Truijebs, A., & Hekkert, M. (2018). Barriers to the circular economy: Evidence from the European Union (EU). *Ecological Economics*, 150, 264–272.

Klein, N., Ramos, T., & Deutz, P. (2020). Circular economy practices and strategies in public sector organizations: An integrative review. *Sustainability*, 12, 4181.

Lăzăroiu, G., Ionescu, L., Uță, C., Hurloiu, I., Andronie, M., & Dijmărescu, I. (2020). Environmentally responsible behavior and sustainability policy adoption in green public procurement. *Sustainability*, 12(5), 2110.

Liu, J., Xue, J., Yang, L., & Shi, B. (2019). Enhancing green public procurement practices in local governments: Chinese evidence based on a new research framework. *Journal of Cleaner Production*, 211, 842–854.

Ministry of Climate and Environment (2017). White Paper (Melding til Stortinget 45) (2016–2017). Waste as resource – waste policy and circular economy (Avfall som resurs – avfallpolitikk og sirkulær økonomi). https://www.regjeringen.no/contentassets/4c45f38bddee47a7b7847af108894c0c/no/pdfs/ stm201620170045000dddpdfs.pdf.

Ministry of Trade, Industry and Fisheries (2019). White Paper (Melding til Stortinget 22) (2018–2019) Smarter purchase – effective and professional public procurement (Smartere innkjøp – effektive og profesjonelle offentlige anskaffelser). https://www.regjeringen.no/no/dokumenter/meld.-st.-22 -20182019/id2641507/.

Murray, A., Skene, K., & Haynes, K. (2017). The circular economy: An interdisciplinary exploration of the concept and application in a global context. *Journal of Business Ethics*, 140(3), 369–380.

Neto, B. (2020). Analysis of sustainability criteria from European public procurement schemes for food-services. *Science of the Total Environment*, 704, 135300.

Nissinen, A., Parikka-Alhola, K., & Rita, H. (2009). Environmental criteria in the public purchases above the EU threshold values by three Nordic countries: 2003 and 2005. *Ecological Economics*, 68(6), 1838–1849.

Obwegeser, N., & Müller, S. D. (2018). Innovation and public procurement: Terminology, concepts, and applications. *Technovation*, 74, 1–17.

OECD (2015). Government at a glance. https://www.oecd-ilibrary.org/governance/government-at-a -glance-2015_gov_glance-2015-en.

OECD (2019). Government at a glance. https://www.oecd-ilibrary.org/governance/government-at-a -glance-2019_8ccf5c38-en.

Procurement law (Anskaffelsesloven) (2016). Law on public procurement (Lov om offentlige anskaffel-ser) (LOV-2016-06-17-73). https://lovdata.no/lov/2016-06-17-73.

Reike, D., Vermeulen, W. J., & Witjes, S. (2018). The circular economy: New or refurbished as CE 3.0? Exploring controversies in the conceptualization of the circular economy through a focus on history and resource value retention options. *Resources, Conservation and Recycling*, 135, 246–264.

Rolfstam, M. (2012). An institutional approach to research on public procurement of innovation. *Innovation: The European Journal of Social Science Research*, 25(3), 303–321.

Sönnichsen, S. D., & Clement, J. (2020). Review of green and sustainable public procurement: Towards circular public procurement. *Journal of Cleaner Production*, 245, 118901.

United Nations (2015). *Transforming Our World: The 2030 Agenda for Sustainable Development.* https://sdgs.un.org/2030agenda.

Uyarra, E., Edler, J., Garcia-Estevez, J., Georghiou, L., & Yeow, J. (2014). Barriers to innovation through public procurement: A supplier perspective. *Technovation*, 34(10), 631–645.

Uyarra, E., & Flanagan, K. (2010). Understanding the innovation impacts of public procurement. *European Planning Studies*, 18(1), 123–143.

Witjes, S., & Lozano, R. (2016). Towards a more circular economy: Proposing a framework linking sustainable public procurement and sustainable business models. *Resources, Conservation and Recycling*, 112, 37–44.

World Economic Forum (WEF) (2020). *Recommendations for Policy-Makers to Reset towards a New Nature Economy.* http://www3.weforum.org/docs/WEF_NNER_II_The_Future_of_Business _and_Nature_Policy_Companion_2020.pdf?fbclid=IwAR1ypAqesjvoGZa12iVtBpbRwvocQToQO _yr7w4FHxpAZ0G87mHboOmwF8o.

Yeow, J., & Edler, J. (2012). Innovation procurement as projects. *Journal of Public Procurement*, 12(4), 472.

Yin, R. (2018). *Case Study Research: Design and Methods* (5th ed.). Thousand Oaks, CA: Sage Publications.

Yu, A. T. W., Yevu, S. K., & Nani, G. (2020). Towards an integration framework for promoting electronic procurement and sustainable procurement in the construction industry: A systematic literature review. *Journal of Cleaner Production*, 250, 119493.

Index

3D printing 3, 239, 242, 252–3
3Rs 47–50, 52–3, 55, 75
    see also recycling; reducing; reusing;
      R-models
5G technology 309

academic spin-offs *see* digital academic spin-offs
Adaptive city mobility 226, 230
additive manufacturing 239, 242, 251
Agrawal, A. 304
Airbnb 253
algorithms 268–9, 280–81, 289, 320, 324
AlSiCal 311–12
Altia 201, 204
Ameli, N. 303
anthropogenic world 12–15, 21
Antikainen, M. 176
Apaydin, M. 207
aquaculture 146, 165, 168, 215, 321–3
    see also fish farming
Arctic Cluster Team 154–5
argumentative turn 317
Artificial Intelligence 16, 20
artificial intelligence 242, 245, 247, 251–6
Ataseven, C. 119
Australian Fashion Council 226, 231
automation 242, 246, 251, 255

Badger Explorer 255, 259
Ballardini, R. M. 312
Bamomas 202, 205
Barragán-Ocaña, A. 278
barriers *see* drivers and barriers
batteries 201–2, 204–5, 226, 230, 266
Baumgartner, R. J. 32
Bayer 312
Benachio, G. L. F. 307
Bergans 38–45
Bestseller 51
Betolar 201
big data 16, 239, 242, 252, 256, 260
biochar 198, 200
bio-cycles 12–14, 21
biodegradability 17, 41–2, 52, 196, 199–200, 229, 322
biofuels 66, 200, 309, 322–3
biogas 135–6, 141, 167, 216, 322–3
Bio-PU 18

biotechnology 266, 303, 309–10
Black Friday 41
blockchains 252–4
Blue Origin 15
Bocken, N. M. P. 217, 226
Bogers. M. 308
Bönte, W. 94
Boomerang 51
Boska Holland 226, 228
bottle return system 206
Boulding, K. E. 185
Bowen, G. A. 39
Brewed Protein 51–2
Brown, P. 69
Bugaboo 226
business activism 76–81
business case 41, 50–52, 55, 77–8, 118, 160, 189, 228, 233
business experimentation 8, 223–6
business model innovation 8, 36, 38, 40–41, 43–4, 48, 63, 65, 67, 70, 163, 174–9, 195–7, 205–8, 210, 236, 248, 265, 298
business models 7–8, 19–21, 26, 41, 43, 54, 56, 75, 85, 107, 111–12, 114, 123, 129–31, 166, 168, 195–6, 203, 207, 236–8, 240, 247–8, 318, 331
    see also business model innovation
    circular 3, 8, 72, 93, 98–9, 111–12, 161, 171, 183–92, 197, 222–7, 229, 233, 254, 261, 331
    'fast fashion' 48, 54
    new 8, 10, 21, 38, 163, 170, 198, 222–33, 253–4
    open 308
    sustainable 8, 123, 131, 183, 222, 225
business parks *see* industrial parks
business strategies 28, 31, 64–6, 70, 174, 177, 192, 318
business to business 75, 103, 106, 134, 136, 140
by-products 112, 122–3, 131, 144–5, 148–50, 152, 155–6, 163–4, 166–8, 190, 200–201, 205, 211, 217, 277, 311, 317

Cai, Biao 17
Calefa 202, 205
Çalışkan, K. 124
Callon, M. 124
carbon credits 124, 127
carbon emissions *see* greenhouse gas emissions

carbon footprint 50, 115
Carbons/Carbofex 200
case studies 7, 41, 50–52, 55, 60–61, 76, 99, 107,
    113, 115, 119–20, 123–5, 133–4, 139–41,
    144, 146, 164, 169, 171, 198, 213, 237,
    240, 254, 332
Celsa Armeringsstål 147–9
Chakrabarti, R. 307
circular business models 3, 8, 72, 93, 98–9, 112,
    161, 163, 171, 183–92, 197, 222–7, 229,
    233, 254, 261, 331
circular chemistry 18–19
Circular Collaboration Canvas 223–5, 232
circular economy
    access to research results 307–13
    adoption of environmental process
        innovations 85–95
    business model innovation for *see* business
        model innovation
    business models *see* business models
    challenge for rapid growth of 160–72
    characteristics of innovations for 4–6
    circular water economy 133–41
    conceptual framework 47–8
    definition of 48, 72, 144, 161, 184, 317
    drivers and barriers for industrial symbiosis
        7, 133–6, 139, 144–56, 190, 317
    fashion industry solutions 47–56
    food banks 7, 110, 112–13, 118, 120
    full innovation process 59–70
    fund model innovations for 295–304
    geography of CE technologies in Europe
        277–91
    how digital technologies boost value 236–48
    impact of digital academic spin-offs 251–62
    in industrial parks 7, 133–6, 139, 144–56,
        190, 317
    map of intervention types 195–208
    material to immaterial 'world' 12–21
    measuring innovation using patent data
        265–74
        see also patents
    and the need for innovation 3–4
    opportunity domains for new entrants
        316–24
    and public procurement 6, 9, 15, 328–36
    and resource circularity 210–18
    in SMEs 7, 14, 54, 72–81, 133, 135, 138–9,
        226–7, 232, 254, 321–3
    and surplus heat exchange 7, 122–31, 205
    urgent need for 2–3
    value retention in 36–45, 167, 222, 267–8,
        330
Circular Fashion Games 226, 231
circular industry 7, 156, 215, 218

circular innovations 7–8, 10, 26, 28–33, 59–70,
    72, 152, 160–72, 210, 212–13, 217–18,
    225, 273, 313
circular metallurgy 19–20
circular sciences 16–21
circular transitions 160–61, 163–4
circularity 3, 7–10, 12, 25, 33, 36–9, 43–4, 59, 76,
    78–9, 85–6, 99, 105–7, 110, 129, 135–7,
    140–41, 149, 155–6, 163, 167, 174–5,
    183–4, 189, 207, 210–18, 223–5, 227–33,
    236–8, 248, 268, 277, 323, 329–36
Circularity Deck 223–5, 227
CityLoops 332
climate challenge 25–7, 30–31, 33, 162
climate change 12, 14, 25, 184, 207, 210, 265–6,
    283, 288, 302, 330
climate change mitigation technology 266, 270,
    280, 291
climate innovation initiatives 25–33
closed loop processes 3, 38, 51, 56, 72, 161, 163,
    277, 298, 330
clothing utilization 47, 52–3
    see also fast fashion
cloud technologies 242–3, 245–7
Club of Rome 184
co-creation workshops 222, 227–31, 233
Collaboration Canvas 227
Comex 256, 258
commercialization 59–70, 251, 253, 255–6, 260,
    298–9, 317, 323
composting 2, 18, 41–2, 44, 196, 322
consumer behaviour 10, 81, 176
consumer-to-consumer 204
Cookson Group 15
Cooperative Patent Classification 268–70, 272,
    280
coordination problem 161–2
corporate social responsibility 39, 47
cost leadership 30–31
cost reductions 27–8, 30–32, 244, 260, 298
COVID-19 20–21, 79, 174, 270
creativity 12, 61, 81
CRISPR 309
Crossan, M. M. 207
CSR 39, 47
customer engagement 36, 38, 43–4, 89, 248
Cyberlab 256
cyber-physical systems 239, 242

damage prevention 189
data analytics 16, 256
data science 271
Davis, G. F. 73–4
De Angelis, R. 119, 254
De Brito, M. P. 107

De Jesus, A. 187–8, 260
De Jong, J. P. 89
Dechezleprêtre, A. 270
decoupling 184, 186
deforestation 2
Dekker, R. 107
Delgado-Ceballos, J. 25
design thinking 223, 227, 232–3
Dienes, C. 94
digital academic spin-offs 8–9, 251–62
digital artefacts 252, 255–7, 260–61
digital entrepreneurship 251–62
digital infrastructure 8, 252, 255–6, 258–61
digital innovation 8, 251, 253–6, 260–61
digital platform 252, 256–7, 260–61
digital technology 8, 16, 177–8, 236–48, 251–9, 266
digitalization 8, 184, 202, 240
disassembly 50, 52, 100–107, 196, 267, 310
district heating networks 123, 125, 127–9, 205
Doh, J. P. 188
DolphiScan 255
'double externality' problem 6
Dow Chemical 16
Dowell, G. 188
downcycling 49
DrillScience 256
Drilltronic 258
drivers and barriers 7, 21, 32, 47, 76, 78–9, 81, 119, 123, 131, 144–56, 175–6, 188, 190–92, 260, 265, 321
Durat 198–200
Dussaux, D. 270

Earth Overshoot Day 160
Ebner, D. 32
eco-innovation 4–6, 36–40, 42–3, 48, 187, 195, 206–7, 260, 266, 278
economic growth 47, 99, 110, 174, 186, 190–91
EcoSairila 133–4, 136
ecosystems 2–3, 6–7, 47–8, 59–70, 73, 111–13, 133–41, 161, 163, 174, 176, 184, 191–2, 198, 224–5, 231–2, 237, 242, 248, 252, 254, 260–61, 291, 308, 312, 321–2
    sustainable entrepreneurial ecosystems 7, 133–4, 139, 141
effectuation 223, 227, 233
efficient market hypothesis 297, 300, 303
Egelie, K. J. 309–10, 312
Eide, A. E. 32, 187
Eisenhardt, K. M. 76, 81
e-learning 255–7, 260
Elhacham, E. 12–13
Elkem Rana 147–8, 155
Ellen MacArthur Foundation 3, 53, 72, 184

emerging technologies 266, 268, 270, 272–3
emission trading 149
end-of-life management 26, 101, 103, 205, 214, 239, 265, 335
end-of-pipe solutions 27–8
energy efficiency 14, 19, 22, 26, 85, 89, 122, 125, 128, 131, 154, 202
Enevo 202, 205
enterprise resource planning systems 242, 244
entification 123–4
entrepreneurs 14, 21, 74, 77, 79–81, 131, 133–6, 138–41, 171, 175, 179, 187–9, 191–2, 223, 226–7, 232, 253, 255, 304, 320
entrepreneurship 81, 133–5, 137–41, 179, 183, 186–9, 251–3, 316, 322
entropy law 185, 191
environmental criteria 329–30, 335
environmental process innovation 7, 85–95
environmental process technologies 85
European Free Trade Association 318
European Commission 160–61, 265, 272, 277, 280–81, 287, 328–30
European Economic Area 318
European Green Deal 183–4
European Manufacturing Survey 89, 94
European Patent Office 265, 270–72, 280
European Regional Development Fund 74
European Union 99, 183–4, 265, 267, 281, 311–12, 318, 328, 335–6
    Renewable Energy Directive 61, 122
Eurostat 265, 267, 270, 272
Evides 226–9
exergy 185–6, 190–91
Extended Product Responsibility 99

Facebook 41, 228–9
Fagerberg, J. 4
Fair, Reasonable and Non-Discriminatory 309, 311
Fairtrade 309
fashion industry 6–7, 15, 41, 47–56, 226, 251, 299
fast fashion 48, 54
feedstocks 61–5, 67–8, 241, 245
Feola, R. 254
Ferroglobe 147–8
fertilizer 136, 141, 198, 200–201, 204–5, 216, 241, 246–7, 283, 288, 323
Fesil Rana Metall 147–9, 152–3
Filippa K 51
financial capital 295
Finnish Innovation Fund 198
first movers 169–70, 260
fish farming 7–8, 122, 126, 161, 164–8, 170–71, 210–17, 258

see also aquaculture
Fjällräven 38–45
focus groups 62, 125, 223, 228, 233
Fontaine, A. 123, 130, 132
food banks 7, 110, 112–13, 118, 120
food systems 7, 110–20
food waste 75, 110, 115–17, 119, 202, 204–5
Foss, N. J. 176
fossil fuels 26, 61–2, 64, 201, 203, 215, 239
Franatech 259
Fresh-R 226, 228
full employment 186
full innovation process 59–70
fund management 295–304
fund model innovations 295–304
fund-of-funds model 297, 300, 302
furniture industry 7, 79, 99–107

game theory 7, 161–4, 169, 171
gazelles 179
GDP 186, 328
Geiger, S. 74
gene editing 13
genome editing 309
Georgescu-Roegen, N. 185
Gina Tricot 51
Global Sustainable Development Report 160
global warming *see* climate change
Gold & Green 199–200
Grassrooted 226, 231
green innovation 32, 136, 187, 266, 269
green technologies 5, 278
greenhouse gas emissions 2, 6, 12, 14, 17, 25–6,
    32, 52, 61, 103, 105, 114, 119, 124, 128,
    148, 153–4, 199–204, 207, 282–3, 288,
    311
gross domestic product *see* GDP
growth imperative 184, 186, 189–91
    see also economic growth

H&M 48, 51
Haglöfs 38–45
Haller, M. 280
Hart, S. L. 188
Hawkey, D. 124, 130–31
Henry, C. 312
Henry, M. 254
high net worth individuals 300
Hobson, K. 124, 130
Hockerts, K. 304
Hofmann, F. 261
Hojnik, J. 260
Honkajoki 198, 200
Horizon 2020 308
Houdini 38–45

hydropower 215
hydrotreated vegetable oil 204

IBM Services 20
Icebug 38–45
I:CO 47, 51–3, 56
ICT 100, 102, 105, 146, 309
IFIXIT 50, 52, 56
immaterial world 6, 12–16, 21
impact investing 304
Indiska 51
industrial parks 7, 133–6, 139, 144–56, 190, 317
industrial symbiosis 7, 123, 130–31, 133, 140,
    144–56, 260–61
Ingulfsvann, A. S. 37
innovation, definition of 4
innovation indicator 265, 273
innovation management 59–60, 69, 163, 195–6,
    207
innovation process 4, 7, 25, 36, 59–66, 69–70, 80,
    122, 125–6, 130–31, 134, 137, 167, 208,
    213, 252, 272, 281, 308, 310
innovation strategy 7, 59–60, 62, 70
Instagram 44
intellectual property 86, 89, 307, 309–10, 312
internal activism 7, 72–81
International Patent Classification 268–70
International Resource Panel 160
International Sustainability & Carbon
    Certification 61–2
Internet of Things 16, 20, 239, 242–5, 247–8,
    251–2, 254, 256, 260, 309
intrapreneurs 74, 77, 80
Iron and Steel Society 19
IV-infra 226, 231

Jakobsen, S. 131
Jiménez-Parra, B. 107
job creation 99, 174
Jurowetzki, R. 320

KappAhl 51
keyword-in-context 318, 322–3
Kirchherr, J. 36, 48, 183
knowledge transfer 81, 188, 260
Kognita 255, 257
Kokkola LCC 199–200
Konecranes 202, 205
Kraaijenhagen, C. 226
Kramer, M. R. 112–13, 118–20
Kvarøy Smolt 147–8

LafrageHolcim 20
landfill 37, 51, 53, 115, 241

land-use change 2
Lau, J. 17
Laursen, K. 308
lawsuits 14
lean start-up 177, 223, 227, 233
Lewandowski, M. 188
Leximancer 319
licensing 86–7, 308–9, 312
Life Cycle Inventory Analysis 14
Lindex 51
Lindström 203, 206
Linear Industrial Economy 184, 186, 190–91
linear model 2, 4, 47–8, 53, 60, 144, 161, 163,
    174, 187–8, 192, 207, 218, 233, 251, 253,
    260, 304, 328
    see also take-make-dispose
literature review 4, 7, 62, 86–9, 99–100, 106, 113,
    177, 252–4, 273
living conditions 2, 110
longitudinal case study 62, 113, 144, 146
loops *see* resource loops
Lynch, N. 124, 130

machine learning 19–20, 269–70, 324
MacKenzie, D. 124
make-use-dispose *see* take-make-dispose
Manning, S. 309–10, 320
manufacturing sector 6, 12, 14, 16, 25–33, 80,
    85–6, 90, 93, 104, 106, 206
marine pollution 2, 80, 168, 170, 212
market innovation 36, 38, 40–41, 43–5
market learning 60–61
marketing 38, 42, 59, 62, 64, 67–8, 100, 147, 179,
    229
Marsili, O. 89
Mauss, M. 124
Mendonça, S. 187–8
Merli, R. 4, 187
Metrics cards 223–5
Mikkeli Blue Economy Water Hub *see* EcoSairila
MIKSEI 137–8
Miljøhugging 168
Millette, S. 188
Minamata Convention on Mercury 15
Miniloop 226, 230
MIP AS 146–8, 154–6
Mo Fjernvarme 147–9
Mo Industrial Park 144–56
Montiel, I. 25
motivations 14, 28–32, 72, 74, 76–7, 79, 81, 111,
    127–8, 152, 154, 161–2, 164, 169–70, 189,
    218, 302, 316
Mud Jeans 226, 228
Müller, S. D. 331
multinational enterprises 299, 317

multiple-case studies 7–8, 74, 107, 125, 198, 213,
    237, 240, 254
municipalities 9, 111, 114, 116, 118–19, 125–6,
    128–9, 131, 147, 152, 154, 189, 228–9,
    244, 328–36

Nambisan, S. 252
nanotechnology 21, 270, 272, 303
NAPS 203, 206
NASA 15–16
natural language processing 319–20
neoclassical economics 297
Neste Oyj 60–65, 201, 204
network innovation 36, 38, 40, 42–5, 56
new business models 8, 10, 21, 38, 163, 170, 198,
    222–33, 253–4
NGOs 14, 62, 64–5, 67–70, 78, 112, 160, 188
Nissinen, A. 330
non-governmental organizations *see* NGOs
Norsk Jernverk 146
North Face 51
Norwegian Food Safety Authority 168
nutrient recycling 200, 202, 205

Obwegeser, N. 331
Octaga 257
open access 308–9
open business models 308
open innovation 6–7, 85–95, 103, 156, 167, 308
open science 308, 311–12
openness 307–13
optimize value logic 238
Ord, T. 162
Organisation for Economic Co-operation and
    Development 280, 331
organizational boundaries 6–7, 72–81, 126
organizational structure 36, 38, 44, 122, 260, 278
Ormazabal, M. 38–9
Osterwalder, A. 175–6
outdoor brands 36–45, 50–51
overproduction 52–3, 253
ownership-based business models 177–8

Päivärinne, S. 123
Palpa 203, 206
paradox of scarcity in abundance 110
Paris Agreement 162
Park, J. 298
Patagonia 47, 50–53, 56
patent classification 268–9, 280
patents 9, 265–74, 277–90, 307–9, 311–12, 322–3
Patzelt, H. 187
Peerby 226, 228
Penrose, E. T. 210, 213, 217
performance economy 4, 15–16, 20

Pfitzer, M. W. 113, 119–20
pharmacogenomics 14
Philips 226–7, 229
physics of economic value 184–6, 189
Pieroni, M. P. 73
Pigneur, Y. 175–6
piloting 134, 138, 141
pollution 2, 5, 47–8, 72, 78, 212, 251
    marine pollution 2, 80, 168, 170, 212
polychlorinated biphenyls 217
Ponsse 203, 205
population growth 160, 186
Porter, M. E. 32, 112, 118
poverty 114, 116, 118–19
PrediChem 257
Prieto-Sandoval, V. 36, 38, 43
privacy 147
private equity 9, 295–6, 298–9
process innovation 8, 26, 36, 38, 42–4, 56, 73,
    80, 85–6, 163, 197, 204, 207, 211, 255–6,
    258–60
    see also environmental process innovation
product design 102, 144, 177, 196–7, 210, 318,
    335
product innovation 4, 8, 26, 36, 38, 40–44, 56, 80,
    85, 104, 107, 196–8, 211, 255–8, 260
product-service systems 239
Product-Service Systems 256
profitability 10, 27, 101, 103, 111, 161, 227, 261
Pronavis 257
prototyping 138, 223, 227, 230
Public Private Innovation 335
public procurement 6, 9, 15, 328–36

R&D *see* research and development
radical innovation 6–7, 10, 16–18, 60–61, 65,
    187, 192, 253, 255, 260
Rainforest Alliance 309
Ranfjord Fiskprodukter 147–9
Ranta, V. 238, 260
reassembly 196, 310
recombinant-knowledge approach 5, 278–9
recycling 2–3, 7–10, 17–18, 26–7, 33, 36–7,
    41–5, 47–56, 75–6, 78, 80, 98–100, 102,
    104–5, 133, 137, 151, 160, 166, 168,
    184–5, 190, 196–207, 216, 225, 237–9,
    246, 253–4, 261, 265–70, 272–3, 277,
    280–82, 288, 291, 298–9, 322, 331, 333–4
reducing 36–7, 40, 44, 48–9, 52–4, 261, 271
refurbishing 2, 36–7, 102, 104–5, 204, 254, 265,
    267–9, 271, 331
refusing 36, 40
regenerative agriculture 13
regenerative medicine 13
regional development 135, 137

Reike, D. 36–7, 43
Reinecke, J. 309–10
remanufacturing 36–7, 102, 206, 239, 330
remining 36–7, 42–4, 177, 265, 267, 269
Renault 49
renewable energy 3, 60–61, 122, 149, 215, 226,
    230, 299–300
Renewable Energy Directive 61, 122
Rennings, K. 6
RePack 201
repairing 2–3, 14, 16, 20, 36–8, 40–45, 50, 52,
    54, 100, 102, 105, 190, 196, 199, 203, 205,
    238, 253, 256, 261, 267, 312, 331
replace value logic 238–9
repurposing 36–7, 41–4, 206, 265, 267–9, 331–2
research and development 9, 18, 27, 60, 62,
    64–70, 81, 85–90, 92–5, 100, 134–5,
    152–6, 168, 188, 239, 248, 257, 311,
    316–24
Research Council of Norway 167, 317, 319
research results, dispersed access to 307–13
reselling 37, 41–5, 50–52, 55, 203, 205
ReSOLVE framework 3, 184, 261
resource challenge 25–6, 30–31, 160, 162, 171
resource efficiency 8, 16, 32, 115, 160, 174, 187,
    195, 207, 241, 254–5, 260–61, 330
resource loops 8, 164, 166, 170–71, 196, 199,
    204, 207, 210–18, 239, 295
    closed 3, 38, 51, 56, 72, 161, 163, 277, 298,
        330
    closing 122, 144, 164, 187, 196–7, 205, 207,
        217, 261, 295
    narrowing 9, 217, 239–40, 246, 261, 295
    slowing 187, 191, 196, 225, 239–40, 246,
        261, 295
Resource Quantity Surveying 14
resource scarcity 72, 145, 210
resource utilization 51–2, 54, 114–15, 118
ResQ Club 202, 204–5
resurrect value logic 238
retention *see* value retention
reusing 14, 16–17, 36–7, 41–2, 44, 47–50, 53–5,
    75–6, 102, 110, 190, 196, 207, 239, 254,
    261, 265, 267, 269, 271, 277, 330
reverse logistics 7, 48, 51, 98–107, 177–8, 201,
    204
Ries, E. 223
Rigby, D. L. 280
Rinki 201, 204
Rippa, P. 253
R-models 184, 190, 261, 266–72, 331
    see also 3Rs; *individual elements*
robotics 255–6, 259–60
Rocher, L. 123, 130, 132
Rose, P. 242

Rousseau, J.-J. 162
Royal Institute of Technology 19
Rubio, S. 107
Ruukki Profiler 147–9, 153, 155
Ruzzier, M. 260

Saebi, T. 176
Safe-Chem 16
salmon farming firms 8, 165, 210–18
    see also fish farming
Salter, A. J. 308
Santos, F. M. 76, 81
Scheu, M. 272
Schoenmaker, D. 303
Schramade, W. 303
Schuit, C. 226
Schumpeter, J. 5
Schütze, H. 320
Secundo. G. 253
Seeger, P. 2
sensors 167, 205, 239, 242, 252, 255–6, 259–60
service innovation 8, 36, 38, 40, 43–4, 196–7, 204, 207
Seven C's 134–41
share value logic 238
shared value creation 7, 77, 110–20, 128, 130, 136, 178
sharing economy 238, 253
Shepherd, D. A. 187
Silvestri, F. 279
simulation 239, 242
simultaneous adoption 7, 160–72
SkatteFUNN 318–19, 323
small/medium-sized enterprises *see* SMEs
Smart Energy 256–7
Smart Grid 309
Smart Specialization Strategies 291
SMEs 7, 14, 54, 72–81, 133, 135, 138–9, 226–7, 232, 254, 321–3
social intrapreneurs 74, 77, 80
social network analysis 280–81, 320, 327
social responsibility 47, 56, 330
    see also CSR
software 3, 62, 167, 170, 230, 240–42, 252, 255–8, 261, 318–20
Soilfood 202, 205
sources of information 89, 91–4, 265
Space X 15
spare parts 41, 44, 105, 202–3, 205, 241, 244
specialization 133, 278–9, 284–7, 289–91
Spiber 47, 51–3, 56
spillover effects 253, 307
Spinnova 201
spin-offs 8–9, 74, 89, 251–62
Stag Hunt 162–3, 169–71

Stahel, W. R. 184
Standard Essential Patents 309–10
start-ups 133, 135, 137–9, 168, 175, 177, 179, 223, 226–7, 233, 253–4, 260, 296, 301, 316, 319, 321
Steinmo, M. 131
Stiglitz, J. E. 312
stormwater management 198
Sulapec 199–200
supply chains 3, 7, 48, 55, 63, 77, 79–80, 86, 93, 98–107, 110–18, 120, 166–7, 170–71, 174, 210, 236, 238, 242, 245, 247, 316, 318, 323, 330
surplus heat 7, 122–31, 205
Sustainability Development Goals 26, 117, 329
sustainability innovations 25–33, 165–6, 169–70
Sustainable and Circular Business Model Pilot Canvas 223–5, 227
sustainable business models 8, 123, 131, 183, 222, 225
sustainable development goals 114
sustainable entrepreneurial ecosystems 7, 133–4, 139, 141

take-back processes 51, 98, 178, 201, 204, 206, 238
take-make-dispose 2–3, 47, 49, 161, 184, 210, 222, 251, 253, 328
    see also linear model
Tata Steel 20
tax incentives 145, 155, 319
Taylor, C. 39
technological trajectories 253, 260, 278–9, 289–90
technology innovation 65–6, 248, 270
tempered radicals 74, 77–9
tenders 9, 105, 107, 272, 328, 331–6
Tevi 74–6, 81
text mining 268, 317, 320
Thelma 256, 258
top managers 32, 54, 62, 64, 66–8, 74, 100, 145, 231
Top Shop 48
Tori.fi 202, 204
Toxic Release Inventories 16
Tracegrow 201
tragedy of the commons 162
transmission electron microscopes 17
transparency 62, 128, 254, 297, 301–2, 304
transport 3, 14, 16, 19, 21, 62, 64, 100–101, 103–5, 116, 122, 135, 145–6, 167, 206, 253, 282, 288, 291, 333
triple bottom line 111
TRIPS 312
Trump, D. 162

Uber 253
unicorns 179
UNIDO 16
Uniqlo 48
United Nations 26
      Environment Programme 160–61
      International Resource Panel 160
      Sustainability Development Goals 26, 117,
            329
Unwaste 226, 231
upcycling 49–52, 54, 78
UPM 203, 205
Urgenda Climate Case 14

Vale Manganese Norway 147–9, 152, 154
Valkokari, K. 176
Valtra 203, 206
valuation 7, 122–31
value capture 174–5, 197, 222, 229–30, 236, 238
value chains 3, 5–6, 10, 32–3, 36, 38, 48, 55, 60,
            161, 163, 165–6, 168–72, 177, 184–5, 187,
            192, 197, 254, 260–61, 272, 278, 322
value creation 7–8, 25–6, 28, 30–32, 40, 49, 98,
            110, 163, 167, 174–8, 184–6, 189–91, 197,
            210, 214, 216–17, 222, 229–30, 236–42,
            247–8, 261, 297, 300, 302–4, 323
      shared value creation 7, 77, 110–20, 128,
            130, 136, 178
value potential 116–17, 236–48
value proposition 8, 61, 63, 65, 68–9, 80, 167,
            174–6, 178, 186, 191, 197, 207, 222–3,
            225, 228–31, 236–7, 260, 297, 301, 304
value realization 236–48, 331

value recovery 99, 111
value retention 36–45, 167, 222, 267–8, 330
Van de Vrande, V. 89, 94
Van der Linde, C. 32
Van Tulder, R. 54
venture capital 9, 295–6, 298–9, 301, 303–4
venturing 86, 317
Vereijken Hooijer 226, 228
versatility of resources 210–11, 303
Vlajic, J. 111
Voi/Tier 203, 206
volunteers 111, 114, 116–19
von der Leyen, U. 21

Waste and Resources Action Programme 50
waste management 75, 115, 202, 205, 231, 241,
            244, 247, 277, 280, 298, 322, 333–4
wastewater 7, 19, 133, 135, 139, 145, 278, 280,
            282–3, 288, 291
Webb, J. 124, 130–31
Welcome to the Village 226–7, 229–30
Wong, S. K. S. 27
workshops 75, 78, 100, 125, 141, 222, 225, 228,
            257, 332–3, 335
World Economic Forum 328

Xie, X. 27

Yuima Nakazato 51

Zaheer, H. 253
Zara 48

Printed and bound by CPI Group (UK) Ltd, Croydon, CR0 4YY

16/04/2025

14658393-0002